Modelling Financial
Time Series

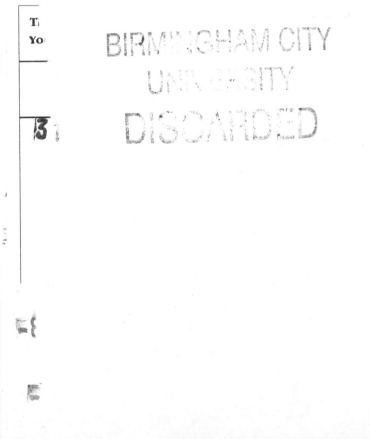

Modelling Financial Time Series

Stephen Taylor
School of Management and Organisational Sciences
University of Lancaster

JOHN WILEY & SONS
Chichester · New York · Brisbane · Toronto · Singapore

Library of Congress Cataloging in Publication Data:

Taylor, Stephen (Stephen J.)
  Modelling financial time series.
  Bibliography: p.
  Includes indexes.
  1. Stocks—Prices—Mathematical models.
2. Commodity exchanges—Mathematical models.
3. Financial futures—Mathematical models.   4. Time
series analysis.   I. Title.
HG4636.T35   1986   332.63'222'0724   85-31498

ISBN 0 471 90993 9

British Library Cataloguing in Publication Data:

Taylor, Stephen
  Modelling financial time series.
1. Investment analysis   2. Time-series analysis
I. Title
332.6   HG4529

ISBN 0 471 90993 9

Printed and bound in Great Britain at The Bath Press, Avon

To my priceless wife
Sally

_____ *Contents*___

		Page
Preface		xv

1 INTRODUCTION — 1
  1.1 Financial time series — 1
  1.2 About this study — 2
  1.3 The world's major financial markets — 3
  1.4 Examples of daily price series — 4
  1.5 A selective review of previous research — 8
      Important questions — 8
      The random walk hypothesis — 8
      The efficient market hypothesis — 10
  1.6 Daily returns — 12
  1.7 Models — 13
  1.8 Models in this book — 15
  1.9 Stochastic processes — 16
      General remarks — 16
      Stationary processes — 16
      Autocorrelation — 17
      Spectral density — 18
      White noise — 19
      ARMA processes — 20
      Gaussian processes — 23
  1.10 Linear stochastic processes — 23
      Their definition — 23
      Autocorrelation tests — 24

2 FEATURES OF FINANCIAL RETURNS — 26
  2.1 Constructing financial time series — 26
      Sources — 26
      Time scales — 27
      Additional information — 27
      Using futures contracts — 28

2.2   Prices studied   28
        Spot prices   28
        Futures prices   30
        Commodity futures   30
        Financial futures   31
        Extended series   32
2.3   Average returns and risk premia   32
        Annual expected returns   33
        Common stocks and ordinary shares   35
        Spot commodities   36
        Spot currencies   36
        Commodity futures   36
2.4   Standard deviations   38
        Risks compared   39
        Futures and contract age   40
2.5   Calendar effects   41
        Day-of-the-week   41
        Stocks   41
        Currencies   41
        Agricultural futures   42
        Standard deviations   42
        Month-of-the-year effects for stocks   43
2.6   Skewness   44
2.7   Kurtosis   44
2.8   Plausible distributions   45
2.9   Autocorrelation   48
        First-lag   49
        Lags 1 to 30   50
        Tests   50
2.10 Non-linear structure   52
        Not strict white noise   52
        A characteristic of returns   52
        Not linear   56
        Consequences of non-linear structure   57
2.11 Summary   58
Appendix 2(A) Autocorrelation caused by day-of-the-week effects   58
Appendix 2(B) Autocorrelations of a squared linear process   60

3   MODELLING PRICE VOLATILITY   62
3.1   Introduction   62
3.2   Elementary variance models   63
        Step change, discrete distributions   63
        Markov variances, discrete distributions   64

	Step variances, continuous distributions	65
	Markov variances, continuous distributions	66
3.3	A general variance model	67
	Notation	69
3.4	Modelling variance jumps	69
3.5	Modelling frequent variance changes not caused by prices	70
	General models	70
	Stationary models	72
	The lognormal, autoregressive model	73
3.6	Modelling frequent variance changes caused by past prices	75
	General concepts	75
	Caused by past squared returns	76
	Caused by past absolute returns	78
	ARMACH models	78
3.7	Modelling autocorrelation and variance changes	79
	Variances not caused by returns	81
	Variances caused by returns	82
3.8	Parameter estimation for variance models	83
3.9	Parameter estimates for product processes	84
	Lognormal AR(1)	86
	Results	88
3.10	Parameter estimates for ARMACH processes	90
	Results	92
3.11	Summary	93
Appendix 3(A) Results for ARCH processes		95
4	**FORECASTING STANDARD DEVIATIONS**	**97**
4.1	Introduction	97
4.2	Key theoretical results	98
	Uncorrelated returns	98
	Correlated returns	100
	Relative mean square errors	100
	Stationary processes	100
4.3	Forecasts: methodology and methods	101
	Benchmark forecast	101
	Parametric forecasts	101
	Product process forecasts	102
	ARMACH forecasts	103
	EWMA forecasts	103
	Futures forecasts	104
	Empirical RMSE	105
4.4	Forecasting results	106
	Absolute returns	106

Conditional standard deviations 107
Two leading forecasts 108
More distant forecasts 108
Conclusions about stationarity 110
Another approach 110
4.5 Recommended forecasts for the next day 110
Examples 113
4.6 Summary 114

5 THE ACCURACY OF AUTOCORRELATION ESTIMATES 116
5.1 Introduction 116
5.2 Extreme examples 117
5.3 A special null hypothesis 118
5.4 Estimates of the variances of sample autocorrelations 119
5.5 Some asymptotic results 120
Linear processes 121
Non-linear processes 122
5.6 Interpreting the estimates 123
5.7 The estimates for returns 124
5.8 Accurate autocorrelation estimates 126
Rescaled returns 127
Variance estimates for recommended coefficients 128
Exceptional series 130
5.9 Simulation results 130
5.10 Autocorrelations of rescaled processes 131
5.11 Summary 132

6 TESTING THE RANDOM WALK HYPOTHESIS 133
6.1 Introduction 133
6.2 Test methodology 134
6.3 Distributions of sample autocorrelations 135
Asymptotic limits 136
Finite samples 136
6.4 A selection of test statistics 137
Autocorrelation tests 137
Spectral tests 138
The runs test 140
6.5 The price-trend hypothesis 141
Price-trend autocorrelations 141
An example 142
Price-trend spectral density 143
6.6 Tests for random walks versus price-trends 143
6.7 Consequences of data errors 145

6.8   Results of random walk tests   146
         Stocks   150
         Commodities and currencies   152
         About the rest of this chapter   156
6.9   Some test results for returns   157
6.10 Power comparisons   159
6.11 Testing equilibrium models   161
         Stocks   161
         Simulation results   163
         Tests   165
         Other equilibrium models   166
         Conclusion   166
6.12 Institutional effects   167
         Limit rules   167
         Bid–ask spreads   169
6.13 Results for subdivided series   169
6.14 Conclusions   170
6.15 Summary   172
      Appendix 6(A) Correlation between test values for two related
      series   172

7 FORECASTING TRENDS IN PRICES   174
7.1   Introduction   174
7.2   Price-trend models   174
         A non-linear trend model   176
         A linear trend model   176
7.3   Estimating the trend parameters   178
         Methods   178
         Futures   179
         Spots   181
         Accuracy   183
7.4   Some results from simulations   183
         Estimates   183
         A puzzle solved   185
7.5   Forecasting returns: theoretical results   185
         The next return   186
         More distant returns   187
         Sums of future returns   187
7.6   Empirical forecasting results   188
         Benchmark forecasts   188
         Price-trend forecasts   189
         Summary statistics   189
         Futures   190
         Spots   192

7.7   Further forecasting theory   193
      Expected changes in prices   193
      Forecasting the direction of the trend   194
      Forecasting prices   194
7.8   Summary   194

8 EVIDENCE AGAINST THE EFFICIENCY OF FUTURES MARKETS   196
   8.1   Introduction   196
   8.2   The efficient market hypothesis   197
   8.3   Problems raised by previous studies   199
         Filter rules   199
         Benchmarks   200
         Significance   201
         Optimization   201
   8.4   Problems measuring risk and return   201
         Returns   201
         Risk   202
         Necessary assumptions   203
   8.5   Trading conditions   203
   8.6   Theoretical analysis   204
         Trading strategies   204
         Assumptions   205
         Conditions for trading profits   206
         Inefficient regions   207
         Some implications   209
   8.7   Realistic strategies and assumptions   210
         Strategies   211
         Assumptions   212
         Notes on objectives   213
   8.8   Trading simulated contracts   213
         Commodities   214
         Currencies   215
   8.9   Trading results for futures   216
         Calibration contracts   216
         Test contracts   217
         Portfolio results   222
   8.10 Towards conclusions   223
   8.11 Summary   224

9 VALUING OPTIONS   225
   9.1   Introduction   225
   9.2   Black–Scholes option pricing formulae   226
   9.3   Evaluating standard formulae   227

9.4 Call values when conditional variances change   228
     Formulae for a stationary process   228
     Examples   230
     Non-stationary processes   233
     Conclusions   233
9.5 Price trends and call values   234
     A formula for trend models   234
     Examples   235
9.6 Summary   237

10 CONCLUDING REMARKS   238
10.1 Price behaviour   238
10.2 Advice to traders   239
10.3 Further research   240
10.4 Stationary models   241
      Random walks   241
      Price trends   242

APPENDIX: A COMPUTER PROGRAM FOR MODELLING FINANCIAL
TIME SERIES   243
     Output produced   243
     Computer time required   244
     User-defined parameters   244
     Optional parameters   245
     Input requirements   245
     About the subroutines   247
     FORTRAN program   248

References   256

Author index   262
Subject index   264

Preface

The prices of stocks, commodities and currencies are for ever changing. Anyone interested in financial prices soon discovers that changes in prices are frequently substantial and are always difficult to forecast. This book describes the behaviour of prices from a statistical perspective. Prices recorded at regular intervals of time define a time series from which much can be learnt. In particular, past prices can be used to give insights into future price behaviour. Forecasts of future prices and of the volatility of future prices are especially interesting.

Forty time series are investigated in this text. They include prices for stocks in New York and London, agricultural futures in Chicago, London, and Sydney, spot bullion and metal contracts in London, and currency futures in Chicago. These prices are used to construct statistical models and to explore the benefits from relevant forecasts.

Although several books cover time series in general, following the methods established by Box and Jenkins, and a few books focus on economic time series, particularly the text by Granger and Newbold, this is the first book about financial time series since the pioneering works by Granger, Morgenstern, and Labys fifteen years ago.

It will be shown that new models are needed because standard models incorporate assumptions which are not fulfilled by financial time series. Unfortunately researchers often assume or investigate unsatisfactory models. I hope this book will help researchers to use and develop better models.

Readers will need to be familiar with statistical concepts and some prior study of time series methods is desirable, although not essential. Investment analysts should find this book instructive even if they find the statistical material demanding.

Chapters 1 and 2 provide an introduction to financial markets, properties of day-to-day returns on investments in financial assets, previous research, and also time series definitions and models. Chapters 3 to 7 cover the construction of accurate models for daily returns. These models include changes in variance corresponding to changes in price volatility. Certain models also include weak dependence between price changes as the familiar random walk hypothesis is shown to be false. Forecasts are discussed in some detail. Chapters 8 and 9 explore interesting implications of the models for traders of futures and options. An appendix gives a computer program for readers wanting to model their own series.

I am very grateful to the many people who have made this research possible. Special thanks are due to those who generously gave me price data or collected it for me, especially Lakshman Balasuriya, Carmelo Giaccotto, Rui Guimaraes, Brian Kingsman, Lester Madden, Ash Patel, Peter Praetz, and Harry Shaw. Monash University, Australia, provided excellent resources for me to write this book whilst on sabbatical leave from the University of Lancaster. Barry Goss and Peter Praetz kindly arranged my visit down-under. The manuscript was typed with remarkable fortitude by Anne Welsby at Lancaster and by Kathy Fullard and Julie Harder at Monash. Various tables and figures are reproduced here by kind permission of Basil Blackwell Ltd, Chapman and Hall Ltd, the Operational Research Society, the Royal Statistical Society, and the Western Finance Association.

University of Lancaster   Stephen Taylor
Lancaster LA1 4YX
England
September 1985

_Chapter 1___

Introduction

1.1 FINANCIAL TIME SERIES

Financial prices are continually brought to our attention. Daily news reports on television and radio inform us, for example, of the latest stock market index values, currency exchange rates, and gold prices. The reports often highlight substantial changes in prices. Over a period of a few months prices can move up or down by several per cent from their original levels. The Dow Jones index was 777 during August 1982 and rose by over 50 per cent to 1174 exactly one year later. The number of US dollars sold for one pound sterling increased from 1.11 in January 1985 to 1.44 in September 1985 whilst the price of certain coffee futures fell from £2410 to £1674 during the same period. Many more examples of large price movements could be given.

It is often desirable to monitor price behaviour frequently and to try to understand the probable development of prices in the future. Suppose you have planned a holiday abroad and will need to buy foreign currency. This purchase could be made months in advance or left until you arrive at your destination. You may well look up the latest exchange rates from time to time and try to forecast them. We call the series of prices thus obtained a _financial time series_. This title will be used for any series of numbers based upon financial prices and we will especially consider stock, currency and commodity prices. A clearer picture emerges when prices are recorded at regular intervals. We consider series for which the price is recorded once for every day that an appropriate market is open.

The first objective of price studies is to understand how prices behave. This is such a complex subject that we cannot rely solely on theoretical explanations but must instead look in depth at actual prices. Statistical methods are the natural way to investigate prices and as computer technology advances we can learn more from longer price series using less computing time. Tomorrow's price is uncertain and it must therefore be described by a probability distribution. Many researchers have concen-

1

trated upon the problem of using past prices to estimate the average values of future distributions. This has usually produced the simple forecast that the best estimate of tomorrow's price is today's price. It is better to try to describe the entire probability distribution and this will be done in Chapters 2 to 7. The variance of the distribution is particularly relevant and we need to understand something about how it changes through time.

A second objective of investigations into financial time series is to use our knowledge of price behaviour to take better decisions. Chapters 7 to 9 explore practical applications of our price models. Improving on the simple price forecasts described above is difficult, but not always impossible. Decisions based upon better forecasts are profitable for trading currencies and commodities. The size of price-changes, ignoring their direction, can be predicted to some degree. This provides a way to anticipate and perhaps avoid the risk of a large adverse change in prices. Forecasts of the variances of future price-changes are very helpful for assessing prices at the relatively new option markets.

1.2   ABOUT THIS STUDY

Many studies of financial time series have been published. My study differs from previous work in four ways. Firstly, it covers a very broad selection of financial markets, listed later in Section 2.2. These markets are situated in New York, Chicago, London, and Sydney. They include several of the most important stock, currency, and commodity markets. Both spot and futures markets are considered in detail. Consequently, general results can be established without having to rely on UK markets, say, being like US markets or spot markets like futures markets.

Financial time series do not conform with the usual requirements for orthodox time series analysis. The second innovation in this study is the development of suitable methods for analysing financial series. These methods have to overcome statistical problems caused by apparent changes in the variance of day-to-day price changes. Variance changes are rather elusive and the third feature of this book is a systematic investigation of variance models.

There have been many arguments about the existence of price-trends but little conclusive evidence for them. This is partly because the trend idea is vague. My fourth contribution is a model-based approach to trends. This allows rigorous tests and uncovers quite a lot of evidence for trends in currency and commodity prices, albeit small ones.

The remainder of this introductory chapter covers elementary information about financial markets and some models for time series. Major markets are described in Section 1.3 and a few examples of their price series are discussed in Section 1.4. A brief review of previous research into financial time series follows as Section 1.5; many further studies are referred to in later chapters.

Statistical methods are used throughout this text to describe prices and numbers obtained from prices. We will model day-to-day changes in the logarithms of prices. These changes are called returns and the reasons for analysing them are given in Section 1.6. Relevant criteria for model building are described in Section 1.7, followed in Section 1.8 by a summary of how models are used in the later chapters. Our models are stochastic processes, which specify the multivariate distributions of returns in varying degrees of detail. An introduction to simple processes, including ARMA models, is presented in Section 1.9. Most time series methods assume that the relevant stochastic process is linear, explained in Section 1.10. However, we will later see that good models for financial returns must be non-linear.

A short overview of the contents of Chapters 2 to 9 is given in Section 1.8 after describing some necessary definitions and concepts in Sections 1.3 to 1.7.

1.3   THE WORLD'S MAJOR FINANCIAL MARKETS

Stocks, commodities, currencies, and other goods are traded at financial markets and exchanges. There are many motives for trading. Some examples are the reduction of business risks, purchases and sales of raw materials, and the investment of personal or corporate wealth. We consider those markets where prices change frequently and thus an investment will produce an uncertain return.

Market size can be measured by the value of the goods traded. Using this criterion, the largest markets are in New York, Chicago, and London. There are also important markets in Amsterdam, Frankfurt, Paris, Tokyo, Hong Kong, Sydney, Montreal, and many other cities.

Various types of goods and investments are traded at financial markets. For example, suppose it is believed that gold prices will rise. Then action can be taken by trading spot bullion, futures contracts, or options. Spot, futures, and options markets offer a variety of trading possibilities.

Spot markets are used for a straightforward and quick exchange of goods. The most interesting spot markets for investors are probably stock and share markets where all sorts of listed and unlisted securities are traded. Almost all the industrialized nations in North America, Western Europe, the Far East, and Australasia have active stock exchanges. Producers of primary commodities use spot markets to sell directly to consumers and manufacturers.

Futures markets allow people to agree a price for exchanging goods at some later date, perhaps several months into the future. The buyer of a futures contract may sell it before the delivery date and thus avoid a physical exchange of the goods bought. Likewise a seller can cancel an obligation to deliver goods by subsequently buying a contract. Many business risks can be reduced substantially by trading futures, an activity called hedging. Investors can back their predictions by trading futures, often called speculation, without having to own, transport or store physical goods.

The Chicago Board of Trade and the Chicago Mercantile Exchange run very large futures markets and there are substanial markets in New York and London. Agricultural and mineral futures have been traded for several decades. These include markets for crops, animals, and metals, and very recently petroleum products. Some important examples are corn, cattle, gold, copper, and heating oil. Financial futures have been traded at Chicago since the early 1970s, and now have a dominant position in the futures industry. Transactions in Sterling, Deutschmarks, Swiss francs, Yen, Treasury bills and bonds have particularly high trading volume. In 1982, futures for stock indices commenced trading in the US and a financial futures market was opened in London.

An option gives its owner the right to engage in a particular spot or futures transaction at a formerly agreed price. The right does not have to be exercised; it is optional. Options can be traded on stocks, stock index futures, currency and gold futures, and other goods, at markets in Chicago, London, and Amsterdam.

Spot and futures prices are analysed in great detail in this book. Option pricing is discussed but prices are not examined empirically. An understanding of the behaviour of the associated spot or futures prices is essential for valuing an option. The empirical results for spot and futures prices have several implications for effective option trading.

We will consider prices and only occasionally discuss institutional arrangements. Further information about the organization of financial markets and procedures for trading can be found in the short yet comprehensive text by Geisst (1982), in Sharpe (1981), and in the books on stocks by Stonham (1982), on commodity futures by Teweles *et al*. (1974) and Granger (1979), and on options by Bookstaber (1981) and Cox and Rubinstein (1985).

1.4   EXAMPLES OF DAILY PRICE SERIES

Figure 1.1 shows nearly 2000 consecutive daily gold prices, covering the seven and a half years from April 1975 to December 1982. In the first half of this series, the spot price begins at about $180, falls to just over $100 during the following 18 months and then increases steadily to about $200. The second half of the series shows the price of gold rising sharply from $200 to

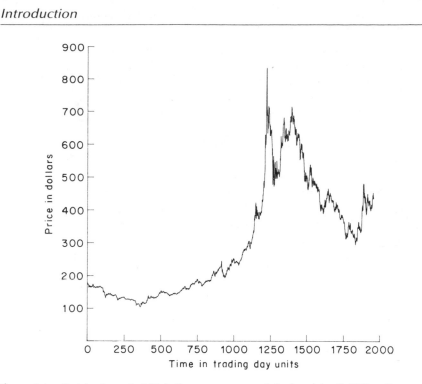

Figure 1.1 Gold prices, in US dollars per ounce, daily from April 1975 to December 1982

a peak of $835 in just one dramatic year, followed by various fluctuations between $500 and $750 for the next year and a half, then a sustained fall to $300 and finally a recovery to $450. The highest price is more than eight times the lowest price, not an untypical range for a series of 2000 commodity prices.

Figure 1.2 illustrates the result of investing $1 in the stock of General Motors at the New York Stock Exchange. This series covers the 11 year period from January 1966 to December 1976. Dividends have been reinvested and trading costs have been ignored. The investment shows a loss for the first four years and recovers to a breakeven position after seven years. Half the investment is then lost in the next two years. Fortunately the remaining 50 cents grow to more than $1.40 in the final two years. The highest value is nearly three times the lowest.

Currency prices are relatively stable compared with stock and commodity prices. Figure 1.3 shows 2000 values of the dollar–sterling exchange rate between November 1974 and September 1982. The highest rate is just over one and a half times the lowest rate. The long decline at the beginning of

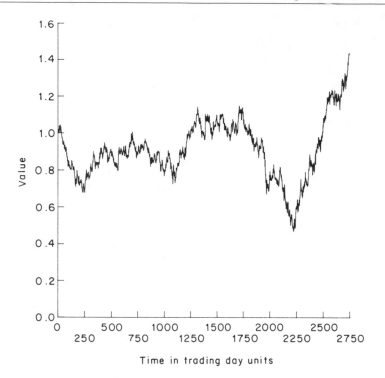

Time in trading day units

Figure 1.2   Value of $1 invested in General Motors stock on 1 January 1966, daily to
December 1976

the series from $2.40 to $1.60 lasts for two years. Then the rate climbs back
to $2.40 during the following four years, although there are several tempor-
ary reversals. After regaining $2.40 there is a sudden collapse to $1.80, a
slight recovery and then a final fall to $1.70.

These first three figures show long-term substantial changes in prices.
There are also major price movements within shorter periods of time.
Figure 1.4 shows this for two sugar futures contracts. A year of prices are
plotted for both the December 1963 and December 1966 contracts, traded
at London in sterling units. Within 1963, the sugar price went from £33 to
£97, fell to £40 and then surpassed its earlier high and went on to reach £102.

All the figures demonstrate that there are frequent large and important
changes in financial prices. Figure 1.4 also shows that there are large
changes in the volatility of prices—prices changed very quickly in 1963 but
changed much slower in 1966. Much of this book is about improving
forecasts of future prices and the size of future price-changes. Satisfactory
forecasts of these quantities are clearly very important.

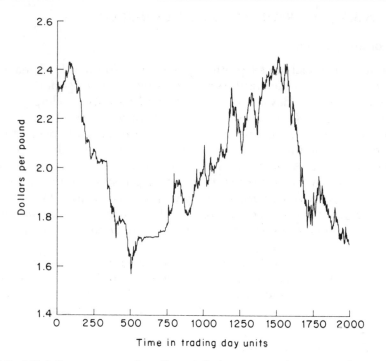

Figure 1.3 US dollars per pound sterling, daily from November 1974 to September 1982

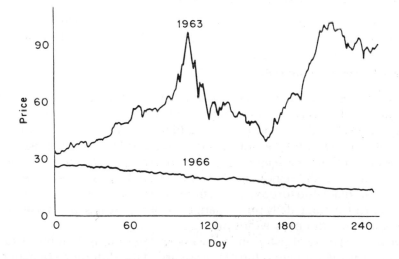

Figure 1.4 Prices in pounds per tonne for two December sugar futures. *Reproduced from Taylor and Kingsman (1978) by permission of the Operational Research Society Ltd*

1.5   A SELECTIVE REVIEW OF PREVIOUS RESEARCH

Important questions

Graphs of financial prices, plotted against time, frequently appear to show trends in prices. An upward trend occurs when prices generally continue to rise for several days. A downward trend describes falling prices. The preceding figures certainly appear to display trends. Throughout this century, brokers, investment managers and individual speculators have plotted price pictures, tried to predict trends and then traded or persuaded others to do so. A moment's reflection shows us that for everyone who gains money by trading someone must have lost it. Therefore predicting prices cannot be easy. Further thought may cause us to believe that if one person can deduce a good trading system then other people will eventually discover it. Then the system will be used so much that eventually its profit potential will disappear.

Accurate price forecasts and easy trading gains cannot and should not be expected. Research into price forecasting and trading methods has been very extensive and usually based on detailed empirical analysis of prices and further information. Much of this research has attempted to answer two questions:

(1) Is the most accurate forecast of tomorrow's price simply today's price plus an estimate of the long-run average daily price change?
(2) Can profits be made by frequently changing a market position, buying and selling the same goods many times?

These questions define two of the most important hypotheses for price research, which are now reviewed briefly and later assessed empirically.

The random walk hypothesis

All forecasts are based upon information. If we want to forecast tomorrow's price for a stock, say, then we might look at today's price, the prices on several previous days, and perhaps additional information. A plausible forecast is today's price because many traders will be (at least) reasonably up-to-date in their assessment of information about the stock. Over a long period of time it will be noticed that stock prices have a long-run tendency to rise. Our plausible forecast could then be revised to be today's price plus the long-run average daily price change. Other forecasts might use today's price and a number of previous prices.

The usual statistical criterion for assessing forecasts is their mean square error. This is the average value of the square of the difference between the forecast made and the actual value observed. The *random walk hypothesis* is a statement that price changes are in some way random and so prices wander ('walk') in an entirely unpredictable way. Consequently, forecasts based on today's price cannot be improved by also using the information in previous prices. Alternatively, the mean square error cannot be reduced by using previous prices.

There are many ways to phrase the random walk hypothesis in statistical terms. A number of definitions have been published. In every case the best forecast of tomorrow's price requires today's price but not previous prices. Bachelier (1900) in a most remarkable thesis implied that price changes have independent and identical normal distributions. Fama (1965) removed the assumption of normal distributions. The hypothesis is then that price changes are independent and have identical distributions. Granger and Morgenstern (1970, pp. 71–3) do not require the price changes to be identically distributed. We follow their convention in this book. The random walk hypothesis is defined by constant expected price changes and zero correlation between the price changes for any pair of different days. Zero correlation will be sufficient, for practical purposes, to ensure that out-of-date prices are irrelevant when forecasting.

Empirical tests of the random walk hypothesis have been published for nearly all the world's major financial markets. The earliest studies include important investigations by Working (1934), Kendall (1953), and Fama (1965). Working showed that several series of commodity futures prices strongly resembled an artificial series obtained by simulating a random walk. Kendall, after analysing wheat prices, cotton prices, and share indices, concluded that investors ought to assume that prices followed random walks. Fama studied the prices of all 30 stocks in the Dow Jones Industrial Average index in considerable detail. His results show that US stock prices either follow random walks or something very similar.

Fama's paper rightly had a significant impact on academic research. After 1965, many researchers assumed that prices followed random walks and then sought answers to other questions about optimal investment decisions. Tests of the random walk hypothesis continued to be done with conclusions that tended to agree with Fama's. Prices at large stock markets appeared to be random walks. However, at smaller stock markets and at commodity futures markets slight deviations from random behaviour were often claimed.

There have been so many random walk investigations that it is impractical to mention all the important ones. The following lists certainly contain many of the most interesting books and articles.

(a) Stocks
    in the USA: Fama (1965) and Granger and Morgenstern (1970)
    in the UK: Dryden (1970a) and Cunningham (1973)

in Scandinavia: Jennergren and Korsvold (1974) and Jennergren
                         and Toft-Nielsen (1977)
  in Australia: Praetz (1969)
  and in many countries: Cooper (1982).
(b) Commodity futures
  in the USA: Labys and Granger (1970), Dusak (1973), and
                         Cargill and Rausser (1975)
  in the UK: Taylor (1980)
  and in Australia: Praetz (1975).
(c) Currency exchange rates: Cornell and Dietrich (1978) and Levich (1979).

As will become clear in Chapters 2 to 5 inclusive, the statistical methodology used for random walk tests has often been inappropriate and some reported conclusions are questionable. New methods are presented and the random walk hypothesis is tested for several US and UK markets.

The efficient market hypothesis

When prices follow a random walk the only relevant information in the series of present and past prices, for traders, is the most recent price. Thus the people involved in the market have already made perfect use of the information in past prices. Suppose prices are available very frequently. Then if only the latest price is relevant it follows that prices very quickly reflect the information in the historical record of prices. A market will be called *perfectly efficient* if the prices fully reflect available information, so that prices adjust fully and instantaneously when new information becomes available (Fama, 1976, p. 140).

In many economists' conception of an ideal world, financial markets would be perfectly efficient. Real markets do not use information perfectly. This statement will be justified later. However, many markets are so good at processing information that traders certainly ought not to be using the information to run trading systems. A trading system is simply some systematic method for repeatedly buying and selling the same goods. Information which is useless for trading systems can still be helpful. For example, it can be used to optimally design a diversified portfolio for long-term investment.

A market for some asset will be called *efficient* if the results obtained by using certain information to trade are not better than the results obtained by using the information to help decide the optimal quantity (if any) of the asset in a static portfolio (cf. Jensen, 1978, p. 96). Results are measured by the risk-adjusted return net of all costs; costs include commission, taxes and any payments for acquiring information. Risk adjustments are essential to ensure that trading strategies are compared with equally risky alternative investments. In this book we will only consider the information available in the present price and past prices. If the market is efficient with respect to this information we say that the *efficient market hypothesis* is true, otherwise the hypothesis is false.

To be more precise, these statements refer to the so-called weak form of the hypothesis. This is the only version of the hypothesis investigated in the text. Expanding the set of information to include all relevant publicly available information about the asset leads to a semi-strong form of the hypothesis. Including private information gives the strong form. Further details and reviews of relevant research appear in Fama (1970, 1976) and Jensen (1978). Grossman and Stiglitz (1980) present persuasive theoretical arguments against perfect efficiency. Their model is approximately compatible with semi-strong efficiency in the manner discussed here: informed traders must be compensated for acquiring costly information by prices revealing such information slowly. We discuss definitions of an efficient market again in Section 8.2.

Many people have used trading systems to investigate the (weak form) efficient market hypothesis. Some researchers have rejected the random walk hypothesis and have then wanted to know if the departures from random behaviour can be exploited. Other people have not trusted statistical tests to find evidence for price patterns and have preferred to look at trading systems instead.

The most popular trading rule in academic research is the filter rule of Alexander (1961). This rule assumes there are trends in prices. The intention is to buy when it is believed an upward trend has already begun and then to sell as soon as there is sufficient evidence that a downward trend has commenced. Alexander's rule can begin by supposing an asset is bought on day number i. It is then sold on the first day j for which the price is x percent less than the highest price between days i and $j - 1$ inclusive. The trader also goes short if possible on day j. When the price is x percent more than the least price on or after day j then the asset is once again bought. The parameter x is usually assessed within the range 0.5 to 25.

Filter trading results depend on the type of market in much the same way as the results of random walk tests. Gross trading profits are generally less than the costs of trading for stock markets. The opposite conclusion has, however, been claimed for certain commodity futures markets. Some of the more interesting studies are the following.

(a) Stocks

in the USA:	Fama and Blume (1966)
in the UK:	Dryden (1970b)
and in Sweden:	Jennergren (1975).

(b) Commodity futures
   in the USA: Stevenson and Bear (1970) and Leuthold (1972)
   and in Australia: Praetz (1975).
(c) Metals
   in the UK: Bird (1985).
(d) Currency exchange rates: Cornell and Dietrich (1978).

Praetz (1976a, b) and others have shown that the methodology frequently used to assess trading rules is inadequate. Appropriate methodology and a critical review of previous results are presented in Chapter 8. New trading rules and empirical results are also presented for commodity and currency futures markets.

1.6   DAILY RETURNS

Direct statistical analysis of financial prices is difficult, because consecutive prices are highly correlated and the variances of prices increase with time. Prices are not 'stationary', a concept introduced in Section 1.9. Consequently, it is more convenient to analyse changes in prices. Results for changes, for example a forecast, can easily be used to give appropriate results for prices.

Suppose the price is recorded once on each trading day, always at the same time of day. Closing prices are usually recorded. Let z_t be the price on trading day t and let d_t be the dividend (if any) paid during day t; d_t will only be non-zero for stocks and then only on a few days every year. Three types of price changes have been used in previous research:

$$x_t^* = z_t + d_t - z_{t-1},$$
$$x_t = \log(z_t + d_t) - \log(z_{t-1}), \text{ and}$$
$$x_t' = (z_t + d_t - z_{t-1})/z_{t-1}.$$

The first differences x_t^* depend on the price units, so comparisons between series are difficult. They have the further disadvantage that their variances are proportional to the price level. For these reasons, either the x_t or the x_t' are nearly always studied in modern research.

One unit of money, invested in $1/z_{t-1}$ items at the price z_{t-1}, is worth

$$(z_t + d_t)/z_{t-1} = 1 + x_t' = e^{x_t} = 1 + x_t + \tfrac{1}{2}x_t^2 + \cdots. \tag{1.6.1}$$

when the price z_t is recorded on day t. Thus x_t' is the one day rate of return obtained on the investment, whilst x_t is the rate of return with continuous compounding; for $\exp(x_t)$ is the limit of $(1 + x_t/n)^n$ as $n \to \infty$.

We see from (1.6.1) that x_t and x_t' are almost equal, since they are nearly always within the range -0.1 to 0.1.

Some researchers prefer to study the compound return x_t, others the simple return x_t', and those who have studied both find that the important conclusions are the same for each type of return. In this book we investigate compound returns. The adjective 'compound' will only be used when it is particularly helpful, so generally x_t is called the *return* on day t.

There are two major reasons for preferring the compound definition. Firstly, continuous time generalizations of discrete time results are then easier and secondly returns over more than one day are simple functions of single day returns. For example, at the end of day $t + 1$ the original unit of money is worth

$$e^{x_t + x_{t+1}} = (1 + x_t')(1 + x_{t+1}').$$

Ignoring dividends, the two-day returns are

$$x_{t+1,2} = \log(z_{t+1}) - \log(z_{t-1}) = x_t + x_{t+1} \qquad (1.6.2)$$

and

$$x_{t+1,2}' = (z_{t+1} - z_{t-1})/z_{t-1} = x_t' + x_{t+1}' + x_t' x_{t+1}'. \qquad (1.6.3)$$

The former equation, (1.6.2), is the easiest one to work with when considering the total return over two days; likewise the x_t provide straightforward results for total returns over more than two days.

All our definitions of return give nominal results, that is they ignore inflation. So-called real returns, which take inflation into account, cannot be calculated sensibly for daily series so we follow the accepted convention of looking at nominal returns. Nevertheless, the consequences of inflation for random walk and efficient market tests are considered later on.

The returns definitions also ignore trading on margin. This is considered unimportant. If a unit of money can be used to finance a purchase of g/z_{t-1} items, with gearing $g > 1$, one day later the investment will be worth

$$1 + g(z_t + d_t - z_{t-1})/z_{t-1} = 1 + gx_t' = 1 + g(e^{x_t} - 1). \qquad (1.6.4)$$

The return on the geared investment is thus g times the ungeared return, exactly for simple returns and approximately so for compound returns. It can be argued that no capital is needed to finance trades at US futures markets in which case returns definitions like (1.6.1) and (1.6.4) have no clear economic interpretation. In these circumstances x_t remains an important number for modelling prices and testing hypotheses.

Finally, note that interest paid on currencies bought at a spot market and deposited in the banking system does not appear in the definition of x_t. Adjustments for interest rates are given later, in Section 6.11.

1.7 MODELS

Financial prices and hence returns are determined by many political, corporate, and individual decisions. A *model* for prices (or returns) is a detailed description of how successive prices (or returns) are determined. We will say that the description contains enough detail to be called a model if it can be used to simulate prices. A good model will be capable of providing simulated prices which look just like real prices. For such a model, if we gave someone a long series of real prices (from an un-named market) and an equally long series of simulated prices then the person could only guess which of the two series was real. Thus a good model must describe all the known properties of recorded prices.

Models have been constructed using concepts from statistics, economics, and other sciences, such as psychology. The random walk hypothesis can be stated as a statistical model of price behaviour. However, the efficient market hypothesis is too general a statement about prices to be a model. It does not give enough detail for simulations. Instead, the hypothesis asserts that only a certain class of models should be considered.

Models can be conjectured from data or can be suggested by economic theory. Our models will be constructed by studying time series of price data, to obtain a probabilistic description of price behaviour. The models obtained are stochastic processes and a review of some relevant definitions follows in Section 1.9.

Any model will only be an approximation to the rules which convert relevant information and numerous beliefs and actions into market prices. Some approximations will be more accurate and helpful than others. We will seek models satisfying five criteria.

Firstly, models should be consistent with past prices. Secondly, hypotheses implied by a model ought to be amenable to rigorous testing so that, in principle, the model is falsifiable. A potentially falsifiable model may be called a scientific model. These first two criteria cause models for returns to be quite complicated if there are plenty of past prices for tests, as will be shown from Chapter 2 onwards. A third criterion is that models should nevertheless be as simple as possible. Few parameters are preferable to many, the so-called principle of parsimony.

The preceding criteria aim for model accuracy. For a model to be helpful in practice the following further criteria are essential. Fourthly, a model should provide forecasts of future returns and prices, which are statistically optimal assuming the model is correct. It is even better if probability distributions for future prices can be calculated. Fifthly, it is obviously beneficial if a model can be used to aid rational decision making. A satisfactory model will have implications for trading the asset considered and for pricing options to trade it at a later date. Simulation of the model may well indicate the best ways to take trading decisions.

To illustrate the application of the various criteria, consider a very simple model, the Wiener process. This model states that the return during T time units follows a normal distribution with mean and variance each proportional to T; also, that returns during any two non-overlapping time intervals are independent. The model was used by Black and Scholes (1973) to derive their famous and often used option pricing formula. A Wiener model is most scientific as it implies, *inter alia*, normal distributions, constant daily variance and independent returns and all these hypotheses can be tested. Indeed, some of the hypotheses are always rejected if a few years of prices are available. The Wiener model has two parameters and only the variance of daily returns needs to be estimated for option pricing, thus the model is certainly parsimonious. And, finally, probability distributions are easy to obtain for future dates, leading to rational option values.

1.8   MODELS IN THIS BOOK

Stochastic processes will be used to model daily returns. General defi-nitions and some important examples are given in the remainder of this introductory chapter, see Sections 1.9 and 1.10.

Chapter 2 reviews many statistical characteristics of returns for a com-prehensive selection of financial goods. Afterwards, we seek models able to match the most important characteristics. It is shown that the search for adequate models must take place outside the familiar framework of linear processes. The reason for this is changes in either the unconditional or conditional variance of returns.

Chapter 3 presents various models for the time-dependent variance of returns. Chapter 4 compares the accuracy of these models by assessing appropriate forecasts linked with optimal forecasts of future standard deviations. Chapter 5 evaluates the consequences of variance changes for random walk tests. It is suggested that returns are rescaled before tests are performed.

Chapter 6 tests the random walk model and special models derived from the idea of perfect markets. Several test statistics are considered. In particular, statistics are deduced from an alternative class of models containing trends in prices. Random behaviour is rejected for all the long series tested. Trend models are preferred for commodities and currencies but not stocks. Stocks reflect relevant information quickly if not perfectly.

Chapter 7 describes price-trend models in detail and shows how to estimate the model parameters. This completes the modelling of returns and the rest of the book covers applications. The chapter continues with a description of optimal forecasts for trend models and compares their empirical accuracy with random walk forecasts.

Chapter 8 considers the efficiency of futures markets by examining some theoretical and practical implications of trading rules constructed from price-trend models. These rules are good enough to create doubts about the applicability of the efficient market hypothesis to futures.

Chapter 9 discusses the implications of both variance and trend models for calculating the values of options. Option values are particularly sensitive to the variances of returns. Theoretical results demonstrate the importance of good variance models and satisfactory variance estimates.

Chapter 10 concludes the main text. It is followed by an appendix describing a computer program which readers may use to help model their own financial time series.

1.9 STOCHASTIC PROCESSES

General remarks

Let us now suppose that $\{x_1, x_2, x_3, \ldots, x_n\}$ is any observed univariate, *time series*, so that x_t is a single number recorded at time t and observations are available for n consecutive times. In our examples, t will count the number of days a market has been open after the first price is recorded for some investigation. Before a particular time t, the value of x_t will almost certainly not be known. Thus we may consider x_t to be the realized value of some random variable X_t. A sequence $\{\ldots X_1, X_2, X_3, \ldots, X_n \ldots\}$ of random variables is a *stochastic process* and we may wish to include variables for all times on an infinite scale. Stochastic processes will often be denoted by a typical variable in curly brackets, e.g. $\{X_t\}$. Sometimes they are called the process generating particular data or they are simply called a process or model.

Time series analysis is primarily the art of specifying the most likely stochastic process that could have generated an observed time series. We now review the definitions and properties of various stochastic processes. These have provided successful models for many physical and economic series. The first four chapters of Granger and Newbold (1977) provide a more detailed and mathematical description of useful stochastic processes. We will here highlight relevant information for empirical research involving *financial* time series.

Stationary processes

Any stochastic process will have parameters, such as the means of the X_t. Realistic estimation of the parameters will not be possible if they change at all frequently as time progresses. The most practical models will be those whose parameter values all remain constant. This will happen if any multivariate distribution of the X_t does not depend on the choice of times.

A stochastic process $\{X_t\}$ is said to be *strictly stationary* if for all integers i, j and all positive integers k the multivariate distribution function of $(X_i, X_{i+1}, \ldots, X_{i+k-1})$ is identical to that of $(X_j, X_{j+1}, \ldots, X_{j+k-1})$. In practice it is only possible to test some of the consequences of the assumption that a process is strictly stationary. Two consequences are particular important.

First, as X_i and X_j have identical distributions their means are identical, thus $E[X_t]$ equals some constant μ. Second, because the pairs $(X_i, X_{i+\tau})$ and $(X_j, X_{j+\tau})$ have identical bivariate distributions it follows that the auto-covariances

$$\text{cov}\,(X_t, X_{t+\tau}) = E[(X_t - \mu)(X_{t+\tau} - \mu)] = \lambda_\tau \qquad (1.9.1)$$

depend on the time lag τ alone. This will be true for all τ. In particular the X_t have constant variance λ_0. Note that in this chapter we assume the X_t have finite means and variances. We comment on infinite variance models for returns in Section 2.8.

A stochastic process whose first and second order moments (means, variances, and covariances) do not change with time is said to be second order stationary. We will abbreviate this to *stationary*.

Appropriate stochastic processes for financial prices are generally agreed to be not stationary. Inflation increases the expected values of most prices as time progresses. Thus the first moment changes. Deflating prices could give constant expected values. However, the variances of prices increase with time. This is obvious for a random walk. For if $\{Z_t\}$ is a model for prices or their logarithms and if $\eta_t = Z_t - Z_{t-1}$ is uncorrelated with Z_{t-1} and has positive variance, then

$$\text{var}\,(Z_t) = \text{var}\,(Z_{t-1} + \eta_t) = \text{var}\,(Z_{t-1}) + \text{var}\,(\eta_t) > \text{var}\,(Z_{t-1})$$

so the variances depend on the time t.

Although the price process is not stationary it is quite possible that returns can be modelled by stationary processes. We will provide evidence about the stationarity of the returns process on several occasions in later chapters.

Autocorrelation

The correlation between two random variables X_i and $X_{i+\tau}$ obtained from a stationary process is called the *autocorrelation* at *lag τ*. It will be denoted by ρ_τ. As X_i and $X_{i+\tau}$ both have variances equal to λ_0,

$$\rho_\tau = \text{cov}\,(X_i, X_{i+\tau})/\lambda_0 = \lambda_\tau/\lambda_0. \qquad (1.9.2)$$

Clearly $\rho_0 = 1$, also ρ_τ is defined for all integers τ and $\rho_\tau = \rho_{-\tau}$. As ρ_τ is a correlation coefficient, $-1 \leqslant \rho_\tau \leqslant 1$.

If we study a non-stationary process for which $\text{cor}\,(X_i, X_{i+\tau})$ depends on τ alone then we will still use the notation ρ_τ to denote the autocorrelation at lag τ. For example, the X_t could have time-dependent autocovariances yet possess autocorrelations determined by the time lag between variables.

Table 1.1   Definitions of certain types of stochastic processes

A process is...	If...
Strictly stationary	The multivariate distribution function for k consecutive variables does not depend on the time subscript attached to the first variable (any k).
Stationary	Means and variances do not depend on time subscripts, covariances depend only on the difference between the two subscripts. (Strictly stationary implies stationary.)
Uncorrelated	The correlation between variables having different subscripts is always zero.
Autocorrelated	It is not uncorrelated.
White noise	It is stationary and uncorrelated.
Strict white noise	The random variables are independent and have identical distributions.
Linear	It is a linear combination of the present and past terms from a strict white noise process.
Gaussian	All multivariate distributions are multivariate normal. Stationary and Gaussian implies linear.

In particular, we will say that the process generating prices is a random walk if the process generating returns has constant mean and zero autocorrelations at all positive lags, even if the variances of returns appear to be time dependent.

Any process, stationary or non-stationary, will be called *uncorrelated* if the correlation between X_i and $X_{i+\tau}$ is zero for all i and all $\tau > 0$. The adjective *autocorrelated* is used if a process is not uncorrelated. Table 1.1 summarizes the definitions of various types of processes.

An important property of the autocorrelations of a stationary process is that they are sufficient to obtain the optimal *linear forecasts* when optimal means least, mean squared error. For example, if

$$F_{t,1} = \mu + \delta + \sum_{i=0}^{\infty} a_i(X_{t-i} - \mu)$$

is a linear forecast of X_{t+1}, with δ and the a_i ($i \geqslant 0$) being constants, then it is easy to show that $E[(X_{t+1} - F_{t,1})^2]$ equals δ^2 plus a function of the numbers a_i and ρ_τ. Thus the optimal, linear forecast will be unbiased ($\delta = 0$) with the best a_i depending only on the sequence ρ_τ, $\tau > 0$.

Spectral density

The autocorrelations ρ_τ and the variance λ_0 conveniently summarize the second order moments of a stationary process. We will frequently use these quantities. Another representation of the second order moments is the *spectral density function*, which can be defined by

$$s(\omega) = \frac{\lambda_0}{2\pi} + \frac{1}{\pi} \sum_{\tau=1}^{\infty} \lambda_\tau \cos(\tau\omega) \qquad (0 \leqslant \omega \leqslant 2\pi). \qquad (1.9.3)$$

The integral of $s(\omega)$ over the interval from 0 to 2π is λ_0. High values of $s(\omega)$ might indicate cyclical behaviour at frequency ω with the period of one cycle equalling $2\pi/\omega$ time units. The frequency-domain function $s(\omega)$ is more difficult to estimate and comprehend than the time-domain sequence λ_τ. Consequently, we will concentrate on time-domain methods. Spectral tests of the random walk hypothesis can nevertheless be important. They will be discussed and compared with autocorrelation tests in Chapter 6.

White noise

The simplest possible autocorrelations occur when a stationary process consists of uncorrelated random variables so that

$$\rho_0 = 1 \quad \text{and} \quad \rho_\tau = 0 \qquad \text{for all } \tau > 0.$$

The optimal linear forecast of X_{t+1} will then be its mean μ, for any realization of the present and past variables $\{X_{t-j}, j \geqslant 0\}$. A stationary and uncorrelated process is called *white noise*, because its spectral density function equals a constant value for all frequencies ω. When, furthermore, the process has $E[X_t] = 0$ it is referred to by the name zero-mean white noise.

It is important when modelling financial returns to appreciate that if $\{X_t\}$ is white noise then X_i and X_j are not necessarily independent for $i \neq j$. Zero autocorrelation does not ensure that the distribution of X_j is independent of a realized value x_i, even when the X_t have identical, unconditional distributions. Examples are presented in Chapter 3. If, however, the X_t are independent and stationary then the stochastic process is called *strict white noise*.

The random walk hypothesis implies zero autocorrelation among returns. Various definitions of the hypothesis have been offered including:

(a) The returns process is strict white noise,
(b) The returns process is white noise,
(c) Returns are uncorrelated and their process is not necessarily stationary.

We will later see that it is easy to test and refute (a) but it is difficult to test (b) and (c).

ARMA processes

A zero-mean white noise process $\{\varepsilon_t\}$ can be used to construct new processes. We will describe three examples, used to model various returns or derived series in later chapters. Afterwards we present the general autoregressive-moving average (ARMA) model.

First, consider a process $\{X_t\}$ defined by

$$X_t - \mu = a(X_{t-1} - \mu) + \varepsilon_t, \tag{1.9.4}$$

so that X_t depends linearly on X_{t-1} and the *innovation* ε_t alone. The process $\{X_t\}$ is called an autoregressive process of order 1, abbreviated to AR(1). It is stationary if, as we will always assume, the autoregressive parameter a satisfies the inequality $|a| < 1$. Since $E[X_t] = E[X_{t-1}]$ for a stationary process and $E[\varepsilon_t] = 0$, it follows immediately that the mean parameter is simply $\mu = E[X_t]$. The remaining parameter of an AR(1) process is its variance, $\lambda_0 = \text{var}(X_t) = \text{var}(\varepsilon_t)/(1 - a^2)$.

Convenient results can often be obtained by using the *backshift operator* B, defined by $B\alpha_t = \alpha_{t-1}$ for any infinite sequence of variables or numbers $\{\alpha_t\}$. In particular, $B^k X_t = X_{t-k}$ and $B^k \mu = \mu$ for all positive integers k. Thus (1.9.4) can be rewritten as

$$(1 - aB)(X_t - \mu) = \varepsilon_t. \tag{1.9.5}$$

Since $|a| < 1$, we may correctly write

$$\frac{1}{1 - aB} = \sum_{i=0}^{\infty} (aB)^i$$

and therefore

$$X_t - \mu = \frac{1}{1 - aB} \varepsilon_t = \sum_{i=0}^{\infty} (aB)^i \varepsilon_t = \sum_{i=0}^{\infty} a^i \varepsilon_{t-i}. \tag{1.9.6}$$

Thus X_t is also an infinite-order weighted average of the present and past innovations.

We can now deduce the autocorrelations of the AR(1) process. Multiplying both sides of equation (1.9.4) by $X_{t-\tau} - \mu$ and taking expectations gives

$$\lambda_\tau = a\lambda_{\tau-1} + E[\varepsilon_t(X_{t-\tau} - \mu)]. \tag{1.9.7}$$

By (1.9.6), $\varepsilon_t(X_{t-\tau} - \mu) = \sum a^i \varepsilon_t \varepsilon_{t-\tau-i}$. As $\{\varepsilon_t\}$ is white noise any term $\varepsilon_t \varepsilon_{t-\tau-i}$ has zero expectation if $\tau + i > 0$. Thus (1.9.7) simplifies to

$$\lambda_\tau = a\lambda_{\tau-1} \quad \text{(all } \tau > 0)$$

and consequently $\lambda_\tau = a^\tau \lambda_0$. An AR(1) process therefore has autocorrelations $\rho_\tau = a^\tau$.

Second, consider the process $\{X_t\}$ defined by

$$X_t = \mu + \varepsilon_t + b\varepsilon_{t-1} \qquad (1.9.8)$$

so now X_t is a linear function of the present and immediately preceding innovations. This process is called a moving average process of order 1, summarized by MA(1). It will always be stationary with mean μ and if $|b| < 1$, as we will always assume, optimal forecasts can be calculated. The variances of X_t and ε_t, denoted by λ_0 and σ^2 respectively, are from (1.9.8) related to each other by $\lambda_0 = (1 + b^2)\sigma^2$. The autocovariances are simply

$$\lambda_\tau = \text{cov}(X_t, X_{t+\tau}) = E[(\varepsilon_t + b\varepsilon_{t-1})(\varepsilon_{t+\tau} + b\varepsilon_{t+\tau-1})]$$

which will be zero whenever $\tau > 1$, whilst $\lambda_1 = b\sigma^2$. Consequently the autocorrelations of an MA(1) process are

$$\rho_1 = \frac{b}{1 + b^2}, \qquad \rho_\tau = 0 \text{ for all } \tau \geqslant 2.$$

The jump to zero autocorrelation at lag 2 may be contrasted with the smooth, geometric, decay of AR(1) autocorrelations.

Third, consider the natural combination of the AR(1) and MA(1) models,

$$X_t - \mu = a(X_{t-1} - \mu) + \varepsilon_t + b\varepsilon_{t-1}. \qquad (1.9.9)$$

This mixed model is an autoregressive-moving average process, denoted ARMA(1,1). It will be used extensively to model various series derived from returns. We only consider the models for which $|a| < 1$ and thus $\{X_t\}$ is stationary and $|b| < 1$ so that, as soon shown, optimal linear forecasts can be obtained. Once more the mean is μ. Using the backshift operator, the model can be represented as

$$(1 - aB)(X_t - \mu) = (1 + bB)\varepsilon_t.$$

A pure moving-average model is given by

$$X_t - \mu = \frac{1 + bB}{1 - aB}\,\varepsilon_t = \left(\sum_{i=0}^{\infty} a^i B^i\right)(1 + bB)\varepsilon_t$$

$$= \varepsilon_t + (a + b)\sum_{i=1}^{\infty} a^{i-1}\varepsilon_{t-i}. \qquad (1.9.10)$$

Likewise, a pure autoregressive model can be obtained,

$$\frac{1 - aB}{1 + bB}(X_t - \mu) = (1 - aB)\left\{\sum_{i=0}^{\infty}(-bB)^i\right\}(X_t - \mu) = \varepsilon_t$$

and simplifying gives

$$X_t - \mu = (a + b)\sum_{i=1}^{\infty}(-b)^{i-1}(X_{t-i} - \mu) + \varepsilon_t. \qquad (1.9.11)$$

From (1.9.10) it is obvious that any product $(X_{t-\tau} - \mu)\varepsilon_{t-j}$ has zero expectation if $\tau > j$. This means that if we multiply both sides of (1.9.9) by $X_{t-\tau} - \mu$ and take expectations, $\lambda_\tau = a\lambda_{\tau-1}$ for $\tau \geqslant 2$ whilst $\tau = 1$ and $\tau = 0$ respectively give

$$\lambda_1 = a\lambda_0 + b\sigma^2 \quad \text{and} \tag{1.9.12}$$
$$\lambda_0 = a\lambda_1 + (1 + ab + b^2)\sigma^2,$$

yet again making use of (1.9.10) with $\sigma^2 = \text{var}(\varepsilon_t)$. Eliminating σ^2 from the preceding equations, the autocorrelations of an ARMA(1,1) process are found to be

$$\rho_\tau = \frac{(1 + ab)(a + b)}{1 + 2ab + b^2} a^{\tau-1} \qquad \tau \geqslant 1. \tag{1.9.13}$$

These autocorrelations decay at the rate $\rho_{\tau+1}/\rho_\tau = a\ (\tau \geqslant 1)$ like those of an AR(1) process, but unlike an AR(1) the ARMA(1,1) process has $\rho_1 \neq a$ if $b \neq 0$. We will only be interested in models for which a is positive, b is negative and $a > |b|$. Then ρ_1 can be much less than a if $a + b$ is a small number.

The optimal linear forecast of X_{t+1} as a function of random variables realized at time t or earlier can be deduced from equation (1.9.11). As ε_{t+1} is uncorrelated with every X_s and ε_s, $s \leqslant t$, the mean square error of a linear forecast must be at least the variance of ε_{t+1}. This minimum value is attainable by substituting zero for the innovation ε_{t+1} in an equation defining X_{t+1}. By replacing every t in equation (1.9.11) by $t + 1$, it is deduced that the optimal linear forecast of X_{t+1} is

$$F_{t,1} = \mu + (a + b) \sum_{i=1}^{\infty} (-b)^{i-1}(X_{t-i+1} - \mu). \tag{1.9.14}$$

It is then easy to obtain the more convenient formula

$$F_{t,1} = \mu + (a + b)(X_t - \mu) - b(F_{t-1,1} - \mu). \tag{1.9.15}$$

This formula will be used on a number of occasions with estimates $\hat{\mu}$, $\hat{a}$, and $\hat{b}$ replacing the parameters μ, a, and b, and a realized value x_t replacing X_t to give a realized forecast.

To forecast further into the future consider the following equation given by repeatedly using the definition (1.9.9):

$$X_{t+N} - \mu = a^{N-1}(X_{t+1} - \mu) + \sum_{i=1}^{N} c_i \varepsilon_{t+i}, \qquad N > 1,$$

with each c_i determined by a, b, and N. As the best linear forecast of ε_{t+i} $(i > 0)$ using variables X_{t-j} $(j \geqslant 0)$ is simply zero, it is possible to deduce the optimal linear forecast of X_{t+N} made at time t. Denoting this optimal forecast by $F_{t,N}$ it is

$$F_{t,N} = \mu + a^{N-1}(F_{t,1} - \mu). \tag{1.9.16}$$

The optimal linear forecasts for AR(1) and MA(1) processes can be deduced from (1.9.15) and (1.9.16) by substituting $b = 0$ and $a = 0$ respectively.

More general ARMA processes are defined by using p autoregressive and q moving-average parameters:

$$X_t - \mu = \sum_{i=1}^{p} a_i(X_{t-i} - \mu) + \sum_{j=0}^{q} b_j\varepsilon_{t-j} \tag{1.9.17}$$

with $b_0 = 1$, $a_p \neq 0$ and $b_q \neq 0$. This defines an ARMA(p,q) process. It will be stationary if all the solutions of $a_1z + a_2z^2 + \cdots + a_pz^p = 1$ are outside the unit circle, $|z| = 1$, z being a complex number. The process is said to be *invertible* if optimal linear forecasts can be obtained, which requires all solutions of $1 + b_1z + \cdots + b_qz^q = 0$ to be outside the unit circle.

Box and Jenkins (1976) describe an effective strategy for selecting an appropriate ARMA model, first published in 1970. Since then these models have been used to explain many economic and financial time series, see for example, Granger and Newbold (1977). Most models fitted to real series have $p + q \leqslant 2$ as in the three examples we have discussed.

Gaussian processes

The random variables X_t defining a stationary process can have any probability distribution. A stationary process is called Gaussian if the joint distribution of $(X_{t+1}, X_{t+2}, \ldots, X_{t+k})$ is multivariate normal for every positive integer k. A stationary Gaussian process will be strictly stationary because the first and second order moments completely specify the joint distributions. Also, Gaussian white noise is strict white noise since uncorrelated is equivalent to independent for bivariate normal distributions.

Although returns are certainly not generated by a stationary Gaussian process we will show in Chapter 3 that interesting models for returns can be constructed using Gaussian processes.

1.10   LINEAR STOCHASTIC PROCESSES

Their definition

Any stationary ARMA process is also a moving average of white noise innovations $\{\varepsilon_t\}$, perhaps of infinite order. Equation (1.9.6) gives an example and shows that an AR(1) process can be represented by an MA(∞) process. In general, a stationary process may have

$$X_t - \mu = \sum_{j=0}^{\infty} b_j \varepsilon_{t-j}, \tag{1.10.1}$$

for some zero-mean white noise process $\{\varepsilon_t\}$ and constants b_j. The innovations will be uncorrelated but may not be independent. There will be a representation (1.10.1) for a stationary process if it does not contain a deterministic component (Granger and Newbold, 1977, p. 36).

Equation (1.10.1) states that X_t is a linear function of the ε_{t-j}. A stationary process $\{X_t\}$ is said to be *linear* if it can be described by (1.10.1) with independent innovations, i.e. $\{\varepsilon_t\}$ is *strict* white noise. It is certainly possible that a stationary process is not linear and has no deterministic components. In fact, a white noise process need not be linear, as will be shown in Chapter 3. Stationary Gaussian processes are always linear.

The distinctions between white and strict white noise and between a linear and non-linear stationary process are extremely important, yet they have often been neglected in finance research. We will show in Section 2.10 that non-linear models are required for daily returns so their innovations cannot be strictly white although they might be white noise. Later on, in Chapter 5, we will quantify some consequences of using random walk tests upon non-linear processes when the tests are only valid for linear processes.

Autocorrelation tests

A time series of n observations, $\{x_1, x_2, \ldots, x_n\}$, can be used to estimate the autocorrelations ρ_τ of the process generating the observations, assuming that the process is stationary. Let $\bar{x}$ be the sample average, $\Sigma\, x_t/n$. Then we estimate the ρ_τ by the *sample autocorrelations*

$$r_\tau = \frac{\displaystyle\sum_{t=1}^{n-\tau} (x_t - \bar{x})(x_{t+\tau} - \bar{x})}{\displaystyle\sum_{t=1}^{n} (x_t - \bar{x})^2}, \qquad \tau \geq 1. \tag{1.10.2}$$

We can consider r_τ to be the realized value of a random variable $R_\tau = \Sigma\,(X_t - \bar{X})(X_{t+\tau} - \bar{X})/\Sigma\,(X_t - \bar{X})^2$, using the same summation limits as in (1.10.2). The estimates r_τ are often used to test hypotheses about the theoretical autocorrelations ρ_τ. Afterwards an appropriate stochastic model may be deduced. We need to know the distributions of the variables R_τ to perform hypothesis tests.

Detailed results about the distributions of the R_τ are available for large samples from *linear* processes. Comparable results are not known for non-linear processes. Anderson and Walker (1964) proved a very general theorem about the multivariate distribution of $(R_1, R_2, \ldots, R_k)$ for linear processes. It may be stated as follows. Consider a process $\{X_t\}$ defined by

$$X_t - \mu = \sum_{j=0}^{\infty} b_j \varepsilon_{t-j}$$

having innovations ε_t independently and identically distributed with finite variance and also $\Sigma |b_j|$ and Σjb_j^2 finite (summing over $j \geq 0$). Then the asymptotic distribution, as $n \to \infty$, of

$$\sqrt{n}(R_1 - \rho_1, R_2 - \rho_2, \ldots, R_k - \rho_k)$$

is multivariate normal with all means zero and covariance matrix W_k determined by the complete sequence ρ_τ, $\tau > 0$. All useful, finite variance, linear processes satisfy the conditions of the theorem.

Practical approximations can be obtained for long time series. In particular, for independent and identically distributed X_t (strict white noise), possessing finite variance, W_k is simply the $k \times k$ identity matrix. Therefore, for large n,

$$R_\tau \sim N(0, 1/n) \text{ approximately,} \tag{1.10.3}$$

and furthermore R_i and R_j are approximately independent for all $i \neq j$. The notation $N(\mu, \sigma^2)$ indicates the normal distribution whose mean and variance are μ and σ^2, respectively.

These conclusions are well known. However, the assumptions required to make these conclusions correct are often misquoted. Two misunderstandings are common. Firstly, the standard result (1.10.3) is generally false for a non-linear, uncorrelated process, even if it is finite variance, white noise. Such processes can have var (R_τ) far greater than $1/n$. Thus if sample autocorrelations are significantly different from zero, using (1.10.3), then we cannot correctly reject the hypothesis that the X_t are uncorrelated. All we could say is that the X_t are not independent and identically distributed. Secondly, the X_t do not need to have normal distributions for approximation (1.10.3) to be reasonable. The essential distributional requirement is merely finite variance.

_____Chapter   2___

Features of Financial Returns

The most important characteristics of daily returns are discussed in this chapter, before developing models and testing hypotheses in later chapters. Empirical results are gleaned from many sources and compared with results for forty time series filed at the University of Lancaster. These series are described in Section 2.2. Sources of prices and guidelines for constructing a financial time series are given in Section 2.1. From Section 2.3 onwards, the means, variances, distributions, and autocorrelations of daily returns are summarized. The chapter ends with a demonstration that non-linear stochastic processes are needed to model returns.

2.1   CONSTRUCTING FINANCIAL TIME SERIES

Sources

Prices can be obtained from university research centres, commercial organizations, some financial markets, newspapers, and other periodicals. The most comprehensive database of US stock prices and returns is maintained by the Center for Research in Security Prices, located within the University of Chicago. Daily returns on every common stock listed on the New York and American stock exchanges, beginning in 1962, can be bought for a few thousand dollars. There is no comparable source of daily European stock prices. Share price series available from commercial organizations are usually not long enough for intensive research. Futures prices are filed in another university database, supervised by the Center for the Study of Futures Markets at Columbia University, New York. Prices are kept for all important US, Canadian, and UK markets, in some cases recorded before 1970.

Collecting your own prices can be very time consuming. The annual handbooks published by the Chicago Board of Trade and the Chicago Mercantile Exchange are cheap and provide daily closing prices and other information. Several daily newspapers publish prices, for example the *Wall*

Street Journal, the *New York Times*, the *International Herald Tribune*, and the *Financial Times*.

Time scales

Price series have been studied for time scales ranging from every transaction, through daily, weekly, and monthly prices to annual prices. This book is exclusively about the analysis of daily prices, usually recorded at the close of a day's trading. One price per day is nearly always the most appropriate frequency in my opinion. The exceptions could be so-called thin markets where there are often no trades during a day; one price per week may then be suitable. Studying the prices at which every transaction was made produces vast amounts of data after a few months. A few examples of transaction price studies are Niederhoffer and Osborne (1966), Oldfield *et al.* (1977), and Martell and Helms (1979). A series of daily prices or returns contains useful information missing in a series of weekly or monthly prices. The extra information improves variance estimates, increases the power of random walk tests, and is essential for investigations of trading rules.

The duration of calendar time covered by a time series should be as long as possible. In my experience, at least four years of daily prices (i.e. 1000 observations) are required to obtain interesting results and if possible eight years of prices (2000 observations) or more should be investigated. The relationship between series size and the accuracy of test results is explored in Section 6.10. Over several years the best descriptive model may of course change. All the same it is better to have extra data and to seek solutions to any problems caused by changes in the process generating prices.

Additional information

As well as obtaining closing prices it can be helpful to collect daily opening, high and low prices, and daily trading volume. The additional prices can be used to improve variance estimates (Parkinson, 1980; Garman and Klass, 1980); however, this interesting idea will not be pursued here. Trading volume will indicate when a market is thin. Many instances of zero volume would suggest that published prices do not necessarily describe the prices at which transactions could have been agreed. Newspapers sometimes publish the closing bid and ask prices. When the bid–ask spread is large a thin market is again indicated. Actively traded goods have very small spreads and the average of the bid and ask prices can be used to define the closing price.

A low bid–ask spread does not ensure any trades could take place at or very near the closing price. A steady flow of transactions towards the end of the day is required to make the closing price a feasible transaction price. Thin trading is rarely a problem for the stocks of large companies and carefully selected futures contracts.

Prices recorded at different times must not be averaged as this creates correlation between consecutive changes in the averages. A week-long average of daily prices is no good (Working, 1960). Neither is the average of the day's high and low prices or the day's high acceptable: both possibilities lead to spurious correlation (Daniels, 1966, corrections in Rosenberg, 1970).

Using futures contracts

Long series of futures prices can only be constructed if several contracts are used. This causes few problems if the derived time series contain one return per trading day and each return is calculated using two prices for the same contract. A contract should contribute prices for a period when it is not thinly traded. Sellers of futures deliver goods to buyers on some or all days of the delivery month named in the contract. It is necessary for some futures and always advised to keep returns during the delivery month out of a constructed time series. Detailed examples follow in the next section.

2.2   PRICES STUDIED

To illustrate the statistical methods recommended later and to obtain new conclusions about price behaviour, we consider 23 spot series and 17 futures series. All of them provide series of daily returns. Prices and returns have been given to me by many generous people; their names can be found in the Preface. Some prices have been copied out of newspapers and commodity exchange handbooks.

Long series of prices can rarely be perfectly accurate. Series have been checked for errors, when possible, by comparing the prices causing the largest returns against alternative sources. The number of errors remaining is almost certainly so low that the major results are not affected.

Spot prices

Prices for 15 US stocks, the Financial Times 30-share index, 6 metals, and the dollar/sterling exchange rate are studied. Table 2.1 summarizes the series. The US stock series are the data previously analysed by Giaccotto (1978) and Ali and Giaccotto (1982). There are 2750 returns for each of the first fifteen stocks in the Dow Jones Industrial Average, covering the period

Table 2.1   Description of spot series

Series	Market	Dates From	To	Number of daily returns
Stocks				
Allied	New York	Jan. 1966	Dec. 1976	2750
Alcoa				
American Can				
AT and T				
American Brands				
Anaconda				
Bethlehem				
Chrysler				
Dupont				
Kodak				
General Electric				
General Foods				
General Motors				
General Telephone				
Harvester				
Stock index				
Financial Times 30	London	July 1975	Aug. 1982	1794
Metals				
Gold	London	Apr. 1975	Dec. 1982	1957
Silver		Jan. 1970	May 1974	1098
Copper		Apr. 1966	Dec. 1981	3970
Lead		Jan. 1970	Dec. 1981	3025
Tin		Jan. 1970	Dec. 1981	3025
Zinc		Jan. 1970	Dec. 1981	3025
Currency				
£/$	International	Nov. 1974	Sep. 1982	1997

from January 1966 to December 1976. These returns are based on prices in the *Daily Stock Record* published by Standard and Poor's Corporation.

The index series is the geometric average of the prices of thirty leading UK shares between 1975 and 1982. Dividends are ignored in the index. Price series for gold, silver, copper, lead, tin, and zinc at the London bullion market and metal exchange are defined in various ways, using closing (gold), fixing (silver), and settlement prices (metals). These series range in length from 1099 silver prices to 3971 copper prices between 1966 and 1981. The gold prices are always in dollar units whilst all the other UK data are in sterling units.

Currency prices are published by the International Monetary Fund in its monthly *International Financial Statistics*. The dollar/sterling rate has been looked at from November 1974 to September 1982.

Futures prices

Thirteen agricultural and four financial futures series are investigated, summarized by Table 2.2. Each of the goods is simultaneously traded for several delivery months. Thus there are several futures prices to choose from on any given day. I have selected certain months of the year and then used the first suitable price for the selected months.

For example, the currency prices are taken from June and December contracts. A June contract is used from December until the end of the following May, then a December contract from June until the end of November, as illustrated below.

Months	Contract used
December 1975 to May 1976	June 1976
June 1976 to November 1976	December 1976
December 1976 to May 1977	June 1977, etc.

Thus each of these contracts contributes six months of prices, ending with the final trading day of the month which precedes the delivery month. When the return on, say, the first day of June 1976 is calculated, the closing prices of December 1976 futures on that day and the last day of May 1976 are used. This method provides one return for each day of trading.

With the exception of the short Treasury Bond series, all the futures series are constructed from several blocks of prices as in the preceding example. Every block ends on the final day before the delivery month. The average amount of time covered by a particular contract is 3, 6, or 12 months, depending on the goods traded and the data available. Futures are generally traded very frequently during their final half-years but trading can be rather thin more than six months before delivery. Three months data per contract is not really enough for effective autocorrelation analysis. The ideal period for collecting prices from a contract is thus about six months for inclusion in a time series. It is helpful to have a further month or so of prices on a contract before its block begins. These additional prices can provide useful initial values (the first example appears in Section 3.10).

Commodity futures

Three series are studied for every one of corn traded at Chicago and cocoa, coffee, and sugar traded at London. The three series are given by taking either 3, 6, or 12 months of prices (on average) from various contracts, listed in Table 2.2. Each 12 month series uses a delivery month shortly after the main annual crop is harvested. Comparisons between the 3, 6, and 12 month series allow us to see how, if at all, the price generating process changes during the lifetime of a contract.

Table 2.2   Description of futures series

Series	Market	Months used	Dates From	To	Number of daily returns
Commodities					
Corn	Chicago (CBOT)	D	Jan. 1963	Dec. 1976	3195
	Chicago (CBOT)	Mr, S	Jan. 1963	Dec. 1976	3510
	Chicago (CBOT)	Mr, My, S, D	Jan. 1963	Dec. 1976	3510
Cocoa	London	S	Jan. 1971	Aug. 1981	2684
	London	Mr, S	Jan. 1971	Aug. 1980	2441
	London	Mr, My, S, D	Jan. 1971	Aug. 1980	2441
Coffee	London	N	Jan. 1971	Oct. 1981	2728
	London	My, N	Jan. 1971	Oct. 1980	2486
	London	Mr, My, S, N	Jan. 1971	Oct. 1980	2486
Sugar	London	D, Ja[a]	Jan. 1961	Dec. 1981	5302
	London	Mr, O	Jan. 1961	Sep. 1979	4741
	London	Mr, My, A, D	Jan. 1961	Nov. 1979	4786
Wool	Sydney	D	Nov. 1966	Nov. 1978	3270
Financial					
Sterling	Chicago (CME)	Jn, D	Jan. 1974	Nov. 1981	1990
Deutschmark	Chicago (CME)	Jn, D	Jan. 1974	Nov. 1981	1990
Swiss franc	Chicago (CME)	Jn, D	Jan. 1974	Nov. 1981	1990
T-Bond	Chicago (CBOT)	S[b]	July 1981	July 1983	518

Months: Ja = January, Mr = March, My = May, Jn = June, A = August, S = September, O = October, N = November, D = December.
[a] December contracts until 30 November 1979, then January contracts.
[b] All prices are for the September 1983 contract.

There are more than 3000 prices in the corn series, covering the period from 1963 to 1976. Previously, Guimaraes (1981) studied these prices from the perspective of a Portuguese corn importer. The sugar prices begin in 1961 and the 12 month series ends in 1981 to give 5303 prices, the longest series investigated here. Cocoa and coffee prices cover a decade beginning in 1971.

Wool futures have been traded in Sydney for a long time. Prices from 1966 to 1978 are studied and the first half of the series has been analysed by Praetz (1975).

Financial futures

Sterling, the deutschmark and the Swiss franc are the European currencies traded (at present) in large quantities by futures contracts at the International Monetary Market (IMM) in Chicago. These three currencies are studied. Daily settlement prices have been transcribed from IMM yearbooks for January 1974 to November 1981. As these prices are averages over the final minute of trading, they are effectively closing prices. There are almost 2000 prices in each series. The IMM publishes daily trading volumes by contract. Volumes are relatively low when the contract has more than six months to run, so six months per contract are used. It is possible to identify all the days when there was no trading in a contract. For sterling these occurred for 12 per cent of the market days before June 1976 and the percentages are smaller for the other series. After June 1976, the percentages decreased rapidly as the trading volume accelerated upwards. When the volume was zero and the IMM announced a settlement price it has been used; otherwise the preceding day's price has been used.

A short Treasury Bond series records the closing prices of the September 1983 contract (at the Chicago Board of Trade) for two years beginning in July 1981. There was some business in this future on every day and frequently thousands of contracts were traded in a day.

Extended series

Articles have been published about some of the prices studied here, since 1977. Over the years, prices have been added to many series to make them more up to date. Results are presented for the complete series throughout this book. Only very occasionally are the conclusions different to those published hitherto. Such differences are caused by the extra prices improving the power of tests to decide between rival hypotheses.

2.3 AVERAGE RETURNS AND RISK PREMIA

The distribution of observed returns $x_1, x_2, \ldots, x_n$ can be summarized by their average value ($\bar{x}$), standard deviation (s), skewness (b) and kurtosis (k). These statistics are defined by:

$$\bar{x} = \frac{1}{n} \sum_{t=1}^{n} x_t, \qquad s^2 = \frac{1}{n-1} \sum_{t=1}^{n} (x_t - \bar{x})^2,$$

$$b = \frac{1}{n-1} \sum_{t=1}^{n} (x_t - \bar{x})^3/s^3, \qquad k = \frac{1}{n-1} \sum_{t=1}^{n} (x_t - \bar{x})^4/s^4. \tag{2.3.1}$$

The statistics estimate the respective parameters of the process generating returns, if the process is strictly stationary. When the process is not stationary the statistics can still be interesting; for example, $\bar{x}$ then estimates the average expected return.

Tables 2.3 and 2.4 present the statistics for the time series recently described. We will discuss each statistic separately, commencing with the average return.

Table 2.3 Summary statistics for spot series

Series	Years	n	$10^4\bar{x}$	$10^2 s$	b	k	G%	A%
Stocks								
Allied	1966–76	2750	1.09	1.85	0.30	6.05	2.8	7.3
Alcoa			1.59	1.76	−0.30	7.40	4.1	8.2
Am. Can			1.00	1.29	0.15	5.70	2.6	4.7
AT and T			2.24	1.01	0.29	6.44	5.8	7.2
Am. Brands			2.87	1.34	0.34	6.17	7.5	10.0
Anaconda			0.45	2.35	0.71	11.25	1.2	8.4
Bethlehem			2.29	1.71	0.31	5.47	5.9	9.9
Chrysler			−2.09	2.44	0.40	6.96	−5.1	2.3
Dupont			−0.71	1.34	0.22	4.76	−1.8	0.5
Kodak			2.03	1.57	0.09	6.35	5.2	8.6
G. Electric			0.95	1.54	0.05	5.25	2.4	5.5
G. Foods			1.50	1.52	0.37	5.67	1.3	4.3
G. Motors			1.32	1.39	0.22	7.36	3.4	5.9
G. Telephone			1.47	1.70	0.13	4.97	3.8	7.6
Harvester			1.04	1.65	0.05	5.81	2.7	6.2
Stock index								
FT 30	1975–82	1794	3.26	1.29	0.01	3.51	8.6	10.9
Metals								
Gold	1975–82	1957	4.63	1.85	−0.14	11.42	12.4	17.3
Silver	1970–74	1098	10.05	1.89	−0.16	11.50	28.8	34.7
Copper	1966–81	3970	0.98	1.85	−0.06	10.09	2.5	7.0
Lead	1970–81	3025	3.22	2.02	−0.52	9.76	8.5	14.2
Tin	1970–81	3025	5.47	1.28	−0.18	10.13	14.0	17.2
Zinc	1970–81	3025	4.26	2.04	−0.43	15.15	11.3	17.3
Currency								
£/$	1974–82	1997	−1.61	0.59	−0.56	8.36	−4.0	−3.5

Notes
n is the number of returns.
$\bar{x}, s, b$, and k are defined by equation (2.3.1)
$G\% = 100 \{\exp (252\bar{x}) - 1\}$ and $A\% = 100 \{\exp (252\bar{x} + 126 s^2) - 1\}$.

Annual expected returns

Averages $\bar{x}$ are very small and they can be easier to interpret if we consider returns over one year. Suppose the relevant market trades for N days every year. Then $1 invested at time 0 would have been worth

$$\$z_n/z_0 = \$ \exp (x_1 + \cdots + x_n) = \$ \exp (n\bar{x})$$

n days or n/N years later, ignoring any transaction costs. The historic annual compound rate G giving the same return after n/N years is defined by

$$(1 + G)^{n/N} = e^{\bar{n}\bar{x}}, \quad \text{i.e.} \quad G = \exp (N\bar{x}) - 1.$$

Table 2.4   Summary statistics for futures series

Series (months)	Years	n	$10^4\bar{x}$	$10^2 s$	b	k	$G\%$	$A\%$
Corn (12)	1963–76	3195	2.12	1.30	0.01	8.29	5.5	7.8
Corn (6)	1963–76	3510	1.06	1.22	0.18	6.65	2.7	4.7
Corn (3)	1963–76	3510	1.00	1.22	0.17	6.57	2.6	4.5
Cocoa (12)	1971–81	2684	7.42	1.89	−0.15	10.09	20.6	26.1
Cocoa (6)	1971–80	2441	8.11	1.95	−0.28	9.09	22.7	28.7
Cocoa (3)	1971–80	2441	9.57	2.03	−0.30	9.19	27.3	34.1
Coffee (12)	1971–81	2728	5.52	2.26	1.42	26.99	14.9	22.6
Coffee (6)	1971–80	2486	4.83	2.13	0.62	17.90	12.9	19.6
Coffee (3)	1971–80	2486	4.79	2.18	0.77	22.02	12.8	19.8
Sugar (12)	1961–81	5302	2.43	2.34	0.00	8.34	6.3	13.9
Sugar (6)	1961–79	4741	1.86	2.24	0.02	8.61	4.8	11.6
Sugar (3)	1961–79	4786	2.10	2.29	−0.01	9.10	5.4	12.6
Wool (12)	1966–78	3270	1.17	1.32	0.27	23.25	3.0	5.3
Sterling (6)	1974–81	1990	0.53	0.60	−0.33	5.99	1.3	1.8
Deutschmark (6)	1974–81	1990	−0.21	0.60	0.01	5.03	−0.5	−0.1
Swiss franc (6)	1974–81	1990	1.16	0.73	0.04	4.38	3.0	3.7
T-bond	1981–83	518	1.76	1.01	0.30	3.96	4.5	5.9

Notes
Corn (12) is the corn series based on 12 months of prices per contract, corn (6) uses 6 months data per contract, etc.
For n returns, $\bar{x}$, s, b, and k are defined by equation (2.3.1) and G, A are defined by the formulae at the end of Table 2.3.

Values of G are presented in Tables 2.3 and 2.4, assuming there are $252 = N$ trading days per year.

Investors are often interested in the annual expected return during a future year, say from times n to $n + N$. The simple annual return is uncertain and equals

$$R = (Z_{n+N} - z_n)/z_n = \exp\left\{\sum_{h=1}^{N} X_{n+h}\right\} - 1.$$

Some researchers estimate $E[R]$ using historic simple annual returns. If $T = n/N$ is an integer then the obvious estimate of $E[R]$ is

$$\bar{r} = (1/T) \sum_{j=0}^{T-1} (z_{N(j+1)} - z_{Nj})/z_{Nj} = (1/T) \sum_{j} r_j \text{ say.} \tag{2.3.2}$$

The historic compound rate G is, however, a downwards biased estimate of $E[R]$. This can be seen for integral T by noting that $1 + G$ is the geometric mean of T terms $1 + r_j$, hence G is less than the arithmetic mean $\bar{r}$ which is unbiased.

Now, *if* the prices are a random walk and the returns process is stationary, with mean μ and variance σ^2, $\Sigma \, X_{n+h}$ is approximately normal with mean $N\mu$ and variance $N\sigma^2$ and so

$$E[R] \simeq \exp(N\mu + \tfrac{1}{2}N\sigma^2) - 1.$$

This suggests estimating $E[R]$ by $A = \exp(N\bar{x} + \tfrac{1}{2}Ns^2) - 1$. It must be noted that A could be seriously biased if the returns are autocorrelated, since then var $(\Sigma \, X_{n+h}) \neq N\sigma^2$. Values of A are given in Tables 2.3 and 2.4

Cheng (1984) discusses further ways to estimate the annual expected return $E[R]$. The methods are particularly relevant when there are only a few years of data.

Common stocks and ordinary shares

Financial theory states that investors in stock markets expect a return better than that offered on riskless investments like government debt. This is certainly observed over very long periods of time and we may safely assert that expected daily returns, $E[X_t]$, are positive.

Let $E[R]$ be the annual expected simple return for a particular stock, and let R_f be the known annual return from riskless investment. Then $E[R] - R_f$, the expected excess return, ought to depend on the risks investors accept. A very important model for expected returns, the capital–asset–pricing model, relates the risk premium for a particular stock $(E[R] - R_f)$ to that of the market portfolio (say $E[R_m] - R_f$), thus:

$$E[R] - R_f = \beta(E[R_m] - R_f).$$

The risk measure β equals cov $(R, R_m)/\text{var}(R_m)$ and, over all stocks in the market, has weighted average equal to one. This model is described in all respectable finance textbooks, for example Fama (1976) and Brealey and Myers (1984).

The market premium, $E[R_m] - R_f$, is usually estimated from historic annual or monthly returns. Ibbotson and Sinquefield have published a series of books and articles about various annual returns. These contain an estimate of the annual market premium for the New York Stock Exchange equal to 9 per cent, based on returns from 1926 to 1980 (Ibbotson *et al.*, 1982). The compound rates G were 9.4 per cent for common stocks and 2.8 per cent for US Treasury Bills so the premium in geometric terms was 6.6 per cent. Merton (1980) considers the relevant possibility that the premium may change as the level of market risk changes. His estimates of the New York Stock Exchange market premium range from 8 per cent to 12 per cent. Dimson and Brealey (1978) estimated the UK market premium for equities to be 9 per cent between 1919 and 1977. Thus US and UK premia appear to be similar.

Estimates of average returns are necessarily inaccurate because of the volatility of prices, a conclusion emphasized by Merton (1980). The standard errors of the annual premia for stocks are about 3 per cent despite having more than fifty years of data. To further illustrate the problem of inaccurate estimates, suppose daily returns are uncorrelated with $\mu = 6.17 \times 10^{-4}$ and $\sigma = 0.015$ giving an annual expected return $E[R] = 0.2$ over 250 days. Consider a ten year sample of daily returns. The 95 per cent probability interval for $250\bar{x}$ is then 0.154 ± 0.147, so the 95 per cent interval for the compound rate $G = \exp(250\bar{x}) - 1$ is from 1 to 35 per cent.

Our US stock series have low average returns and investors would have obtained better results from Treasury Bills. This observation further emphasizes the poor accuracy of estimated average returns.

Spot commodities

Raw materials prices increase over long periods of time because of inflation. Storing commodities is costly. Thus daily returns ought to have positive means and our sample means are indeed positive.

Spot currencies

Movements in spot exchange rates must reflect interest rates. If dollar interest rates stay higher than sterling interest rates for several months then the number of dollars required to buy one pound sterling will be expected to increase. Otherwise, UK investors could borrow sterling at the domestic rate, buy dollars and then invest them at a higher rate abroad. Levich (1979) has investigated similar strategies based on spot and forward exchange rates. He concluded that consistent profits cannot be obtained.

Commodity futures

The prices of futures reflect expectations about the spot price on a particular delivery day. This day does not change as time passes by. Thus futures prices are not affected systematically by inflation. Futures have no storage costs. It can thus be argued that the expected return from futures should be zero. Furthermore, brokers only require a small margin payment and the remaining capital invested in futures can be deposited in an account paying interest. And US exchanges will accept Treasury Bills as margin, so a speculator can sometimes keep the interest on the Bills.

But if the average return is zero why do speculators take risks by trading futures? Keynes and other economists have argued that producers of agricultural commodities are net sellers of futures, hence speculators are net buyers and should be rewarded for accepting risks by a positive premium. Against this, it has been argued that speculators are merely gamblers. Dusak (1973), Black (1976), and Chang (1985) summarize the theoretical arguments. The papers edited by Peck (1977) include contributions to the premium debate by Cootner, Gray, and Telser. Kamara (1984) surveys several studies of risk premia.

Like many authors we identify the premium with the expected return. We will say there is a positive risk premium if $E[X_t] > 0$. We do not subtract risk-free interest rates from expected returns when defining the premium—this is done for stocks because capital is invested whereas capital does not need to be invested in futures. Hedgers can be net buyers of futures making speculators net sellers. Thus our definition of the risk premium is rather casual. Chang (1985) considers returns to speculators allowing for both net buying and net selling. He asserts speculators have been rewarded for taking risks in the corn, wheat, and soybeans markets.

A statistical test for a premium could compare the t-statistic $t = \sqrt{n}\bar{x}/s$ with the standard normal distribution and reject the hypothesis $\mu = 0$ at the 5 per cent significance level only if $t > 1.65$. To attain a 50 per cent chance of detecting a positive premium then requires a sample of size $n = (1.65\sigma/\mu)^2$, which is a function of μ and σ. If, for example, the compound rate G is as high as the US stock estimate, i.e. 9 per cent, and σ is a relatively low 0.015, then supposing $\mu = \log(1.09)/250$ gives $n = 5147$. Even if we try to test $E[R] = 0$ by testing $\mu + \frac{1}{2}\sigma^2 = 0$, we need $n = (1.65\sigma/[\mu + \frac{1}{2}\sigma^2])^2 = 2946$ returns for a 50 per cent chance of rejecting the null hypothesis. It is quite clear that long series will not guarantee decisive results about the existence or otherwise of a risk premium.

As anticipated, empirical studies do not provide a clear conclusion. Dusak (1973) could find no premium for US corn, soybeans, and wheat futures between 1952 and 1967. However, Bodie and Rosansky (1980) estimated the average annual return from 23 US agricultural and mineral futures to be 14 per cent between 1950 and 1976. The 14 per cent figure is an average of (simple) annual returns from ungeared long positions. It includes interest on Treasury Bills worth about 4 per cent per annum. The implied premium is therefore 10 per cent, and its standard error is apparently 4 per cent. Thus the premium appears to be statistically significant. Nevertheless, the choice of years (1950 to 1976) may be fortuitous. There were high returns at both ends of the period. If 1950–1 and 1969–76 are discarded, the 14 per cent average falls to less than 5 per cent for 1952 to 1968 inclusive.

Table 2.4 gives the values of the annual compound returns G for my futures prices. The cocoa and coffee figures are high, 21 per cent and 15 per cent respectively for a year's prices per contract. Averages of simple annual returns are higher: 33 per cent for cocoa, 24 per cent for coffee, and 34 per cent for sugar, calculated using equation (2.3.2). The test for a premium using $t = \sqrt{n}\bar{x}/s$ only gives significant values for cocoa, at the 5 per cent significance level. There is no evidence for a premium on currency futures.

2.4   STANDARD DEVIATIONS

Returns often appear to have fluctuating standard deviations. Many references could be given, for example Merton (1980, p. 353) and Ali and Giaccotto (1982) for US stocks, and Labys and Thomas (1975) and Praetz (1975) for futures. Table 2.5 shows the considerable variation from year-to-year in the standard deviations of futures. Figure 1.4 (p. 7) emphasizes this variation by comparing the price histories of two sugar contracts.

Table 2.5   Contract standard deviations

12 months used per contract, standard deviation × 100 tabulated

Year	Corn	Cocoa	Coffee	Sugar	Wool
1961	—	—	—	0.91	—
1962	—	—	—	1.51	—
1963	0.82	—	—	3.43	—
1964	0.52	—	—	2.39	—
1965	0.42	—	—	1.56	—
1966	0.97	—	—	1.33	0.54
1967	0.82	—	—	2.75	0.56
1968	0.69	—	—	1.80	0.64
1969	0.77	—	—	1.66	0.41
1970	1.18	—	—	1.04	1.25
1971	1.42	1.17	0.49	1.02	1.00
1972	0.85	1.21	0.60	2.52	2.33
1973	2.44	2.01	0.88	1.49	3.08
1974	2.05	2.41	1.77	3.89	1.65
1975	1.72	2.11	2.37	4.35	0.77
1976	1.22	1.76	2.25	2.09	0.66
1977	—	3.05	3.91	1.47	0.54
1978	—	1.71	2.77	1.44	0.27
1979	—	1.38	1.98	1.56	—
1980	—	1.30	1.90	3.61	—
1981	—	1.32	3.07	2.48	—

6 months used per contract, s.d. × 100 tabulated

Year	Sterling		Deutschmark		Swiss Franc	
	June	Dec.	June	Dec.	June	Dec.
1974	0.76	0.38	0.77	0.62	0.87	0.68
1975	0.41	0.40	0.62	0.50	0.76	0.53
1976	0.51	0.71	0.36	0.29	0.40	0.39
1977	0.39	0.42	0.29	0.38	0.30	0.42
1978	0.57	0.64	0.62	0.77	0.80	1.04
1979	0.48	0.71	0.50	0.49	0.65	0.78
1980	0.67	0.52	0.68	0.51	0.92	0.65
1981	0.66	0.99	0.85	0.91	0.97	0.96

Reproduced from Taylor (1985) by permission of Chapman and Hall Ltd.

Tests for changes in standard deviation (or variance) usually specify normal distributions or strict white noise in the null hypothesis. Neither assumption is valid, as we shall soon see, hence tests are not straight-forward. Returns could come from a stationary process yet appear to have fluctuating standard deviations. We explore the reality or illusion of the fluctuations in Chapters 3 and 4. Until then, we concentrate on elementary comparisons.

Risks compared

Standard deviations measure the speed at which prices are changing. A low standard deviation will mean that the chance of a large price fall is relatively low. Thus the risks from two alternative investments can be contrasted by comparing their standard deviations. Investors ought to seek an expected return proportional to the risk accepted. When many investments can be combined into a portfolio then covariances with a market portfolio are a more important risk measure than individual variances. Calculating covariances is very difficult when stocks are not the only possible type of investment. Consequently, we will use the standard deviation (or variance) as a simple risk measure.

French (1980, p. 58) gave standard deviations for Standard and Poor's 500-share index from 1953 to 1977. Perry (1982, p. 863) and Kon (1984, p. 151) provide figures for the stocks of several large US companies whilst Brown and Warner (1985, p. 9) give an average standard deviation for a very large sample of randomly selected securities. Perry, Kon, Brown, and Walker all consider returns from 1962 until some date between 1977 and 1980. Using the US estimates and Tables 2.3 and 2.4 we can try to rank the riskiness of various investments, as follows. Obviously all figures are approximate.

Investment	Standard deviation of returns
Currencies	0.006
Standard and Poor's 500	0.007
Financial Times 30	0.013
US stocks (large)	0.015
Gold and metals	0.018
London agricultural futures	0.022
US stocks (random)	0.027

To see how these figures tell us something about risk, consider $1 invested for one year in a futures contract. Suppose the daily returns have zero mean, standard deviations as above and are uncorrelated. Also suppose there are 250 of them in a year and their total has a normal distribution. Then it can easily be shown that 95 per cent of the time a currency investment will be worth between $0.83 and $1.20 at the end of the year, compared with a range from $0.51 to $1.98 for a commodity like sugar.

Futures and contract age

It has been said that the standard deviation of futures returns depends on the age of the contract. As the delivery date comes closer, the standard deviation is believed to increase. Rutledge (1976) provided evidence in favour of this hypothesis but only studied one contract for each of four commodities.

The hypothesis can be assessed by comparing the standard deviations for subsets of a time series. Each contract is split in half and standard deviations calculated, say s_{i1} and s_{i2} for contract i. Thus if a series takes 12 months of prices from contract i, s_{i1} is the standard deviation over the period starting 13 months and finishing 7 months before the delivery date, with s_{i2} the standard deviation over times between 7 and 1 months before the contract terminates. Some contracts contribute less prices to a series than the standard number, usually because of the dates on which the series begins and ends. Such contracts have been excluded from the following calculations. The geometric mean g of the ratios $f_i = s_{i2}/s_{i1}$ estimates the increase, if any, in the standard deviation in the second period relative to the first. Now, for k contracts,

$$g^k = f_1 f_2 \ldots f_k \quad \text{and} \quad \log(g) = \sum_{i=1}^{k} \log(f_i)/k.$$

When s_{i1} and s_{i2} have identical distributions, random variables $\log(f_i)$ have zero expectations. A value of g is therefore significantly different from 1 if the k numbers $\log(f_i)$ have a sample mean significantly different from zero.

A standard, one-tailed Student's t test has been used with a 5 per cent significance level. The following table presents the geometric means for the 3, 6, and 12 months per contract series.

Futures	*Months used per contract*		
	3	*6*	*12*
Corn	0.84	1.04	1.43
Cocoa	0.98	1.01	1.46
Coffee	0.93	0.94	1.77
Sugar	1.02	1.09	1.02
Wool	—	—	0.98
Sterling	—	1.04	—
Deutschmark	—	1.03	—
Swiss franc	—	0.99	—

(Reproduced from Taylor (1985) by permission of Chapman and Hall Ltd.)

The values of g are only significant for the 12 month corn, cocoa, and coffee series. Indeed they would be significant at the 1 per cent level and each series has at most two years in which s_{i1} exceeded s_{i2}. All the other series have geometric means very close to 1. Therefore the standard deviation does not increase systematically during the final six trading months.

2.5 CALENDAR EFFECTS

Day-of-the-week

Most daily returns measure the return during 24 hours. Returns from Friday's close to Monday's close, however, represent the result of an investment for 72 hours. We might therefore expect returns calculated on Mondays to have a distribution differing from that of 24 hour returns. Stocks could be expected to have higher average returns on Mondays than on other days. Variances could be higher for Monday returns as more new information should appear in 72 hours than in 24. The empirical evidence is rather surprising.

Stocks

French (1980) calculated daily returns on the Standard and Poor's stock index between 1953 and 1977. The daily means and standard deviations are instructive.

	Monday	*Tuesday*	*Wednesday*	*Thursday*	*Friday*
Mean (×100)	−0.168	0.016	0.097	0.045	0.087
Standard deviation (×100)	0.843	0.727	0.748	0.686	0.660
Observations	1170	1193	1231	1221	1209

Monday's negative mean is very highly significant when a t-test for a zero population mean is performed. However, the assumptions for such a test (which include independent and identical distributions on all Mondays) will not be valid. French also shows that Monday's mean is negative for each of five sub-periods of five years and is negative for 20 of the 25 years. Gibbons and Hess (1981) looked at the 30 stocks in the Dow Jones index and discovered that every stock had a negative mean return on Mondays between 1962 and 1978. Articles by Keim and Stambaugh (1984) and Rogalski (1984) are also relevant. Beyond reasonable doubt, Monday prices have been determined in a strange way. No satisfactory explanation has yet been given for Monday's negative mean.

Currencies

MacFarland *et al.* (1982) investigated various spot and forward currency prices recorded between 1975 and 1979. Contracts denominated in dollars rose on Mondays and Wednesdays and fell on Thursdays and Fridays during the four-year period. It is not easy to determine the significance of these results because again the assumption of independent and identical distributions will not be valid. MacFarland *et al.* attribute the Wednesday rises and Thursday falls to the clearing system for these currency contracts (p. 695).

My currency futures give the following mean returns for the eight-year period from 1974 to 1981.

Mean × 100	Monday	Tuesday	Wednesday	Thursday	Friday
£/$	0.026	−0.012	0.115	−0.024	−0.058
DM/$	0.014	−0.021	0.105	−0.104	−0.009
SF/$	0.036	−0.035	0.155	−0.118	−0.000

A long position in all three currencies would have averaged a 0.12 per cent gain from the Tuesday close to the Wednesday close followed by an average loss of 0.08 per cent over the next 24 hours. Student *t*-tests reject the hypothesis of zero average returns on Wednesdays and Thursdays for five of the six possible tests, at the 1 per cent significance level; but again the test assumptions are dubious.

Agricultural futures

There is not strong evidence for daily effects in the mean returns from corn, cocoa, coffee, and sugar futures. The Friday averages for cocoa, coffee, and sugar are, however, all about 0.20 per cent. Roll (1984) reports daily averages for orange juice, only Monday's is negative.

Standard deviations

French's figures show clearly that the standard deviation for Monday's 72 hour return is more than that for 24 hour returns, at least for US stocks. The Monday standard deviation is about 1.2 times the standard deviation on other days. A far higher ratio of 1.73 ... = $\sqrt{3}$ is expected if prices follow a standard diffusion process in calendar time. Clearly they do not.

To compare standard deviations for specific days of the week, without having to model longer term changes in the standard deviation, I use the following method. Suppose $z_t, z_{t+1}, \ldots, z_{t+5}$ are prices from a Friday close to the next Friday close, let $x_{t+i} = \log (z_{t+i}/z_{t+i-1})$ as usual, and let $w_{t+i} = x_{t+i}^2/(x_{t+1}^2 + x_{t+2}^2 + \cdots + x_{t+5}^2)$. Then, for each day of the week, find the average value of w over all occasions when the market was open for six consecutive trading days commencing with a Friday. The five averages obtained, one for each day of the week, estimate the proportion of the total variance in a week due to each day. These estimated proportions are as follows for various futures series.

Percentage proportions of a week's variance

	Monday	Tuesday	Wednesday	Thursday	Friday
Corn	28.2	18.5	18.9	17.7	16.7
Cocoa	21.4	21.7	19.8	18.5	18.6
Coffee	22.8	18.7	19.9	18.7	19.9
Sugar	22.2	20.5	20.2	19.5	17.5
£/$	23.1	20.6	20.1	17.8	18.4
DM/$	26.0	19.9	19.6	18.6	16.0
SF/$	24.0	18.6	19.4	20.8	17.3
Average	24.0	19.7	19.7	18.8	17.8

Obviously Monday returns have higher standard deviations than other returns. The average variance proportion is 24 per cent for Mondays and about 19 per cent on the other four days. Thus the ratio of Monday's standard deviation to other days' standard deviation is about $\sqrt{(0.24/0.19)}$ or 1.12.

Month-of-the-year effects for stocks

Average returns from stocks are significantly higher in some months than others. Rozeff and Kinney (1976), Keim (1983), and Tinic and West (1984) have shown US returns are particularly high at the start of the new tax year in January. Praetz (1973) and Officer (1975) had previously shown Australian return distributions depend upon the month, whilst Gultekin and Gultekin (1983) have documented monthly means for 17 countries. Small firms earn higher returns on average than predicted by a market-factor model (Banz, 1981) and these anomalous excess returns tend to occur early in January (Keim, 1983). Schwert (1983) summarizes several papers about the firm size and January effects. Schultz (1985) provides empirical evidence that personal taxes are related to the January effect.

The magnitude of the January effect varies across companies. An average-risk US company appears to have returned 4 per cent per month on average in January between 1935 and 1982 but only 1 per cent on average in the other months (Tinic and West, 1984, p. 572). In daily terms the average difference between January and other returns is then 0.15 per cent, slightly less in magnitude than the estimated average difference between Monday and other returns.

Although calendar effects are puzzling from a theoretical viewpoint, fortunately they have negligible consequences for tests based upon autocorrelation coefficients calculated from daily returns. This is due to the high variability of returns. Theoretical arguments are summarized in an appendix to this chapter (Section 2(A)) and supported by simulations in Section 6.11.

2.6   SKEWNESS

Skewness statistics are used to assess the symmetry of distributions. Nearly all the estimates of b, defined by equation (2.3.1) and presented in Tables 2.3 and 2.4, are close to zero. This shows that the sample distributions are approximately symmetric. The standard error of an estimate b calculated from n returns depends on n and the population distribution. It is $\sqrt{(6/n)}$ for a random sample from a normal distribution. This formula is, however, of little value for returns, because their distributions have high kurtosis. One or two large observations, generally called outliers, can be responsible for an apparently large skewness estimate. This occurs for my coffee returns based on 12 months' data per contract. An outlier 13.8 standard deviations from the mean is mainly responsible for the estimate $b = 1.42$.

There is some evidence that US stock returns are positively skewed and that metals returns are negatively skewed. Considering US stocks, 14 of my 15 skewness estimates are positive. Perry (1982) has 33 out of 37 positive for longer series, all but one having about 3900 returns. The average value of Perry's skewness estimates is 0.13.

2.7   KURTOSIS

Normal distributions have kurtosis equal to 3. Sample estimates of the kurtosis (denoted by k) are nearly always far greater than 3; all my estimates exceed 3.5 and a majority of them have $k > 6$. The standard error of an estimate is $\sqrt{(24/n)}$ for Gaussian white noise. Every estimate given here exceeds 3 by more than four of these standard errors. It is very clear that the returns generating process is not even approximately Gaussian.

High values of k are caused by more observations several standard deviations from the mean than predicted by normal distributions. Only one observation in 15 800 is more than four standard deviations away from the mean of a normal distribution. The frequency of this event is 1 in 293 for my US stock returns, 1 in 138 for the metals, and 1 in 156 for the agricultural futures (12 months' data used per contract). It appears that metals and agricultural goods have more kurtosis and more extreme outliers than currencies and US stocks. Tables 2.6 and 2.7 describe the numbers and magnitudes of the outliers.

Table 2.6 Number of outliers, spot series

Frequency of event: $|x_t - \bar{x}| > ks^a$

Series	Returns	$k =$ 2	3	4	5	6	7	8	9
Stocks									
Allied	2750	145	45	10	2	1			
Alcoa	2750	144	34	10	5	3	2		
Am. Can	2750	151	35	4	3	1			
AT and T	2750	147	29	9	4	3			
Am. Brands	2750	146	35	14	2	1			
Anaconda	2750	137	42	17	6	5	4	1	
Bethlehem	2750	139	31	12	4				
Chrysler	2750	128	40	14	6	2			
Dupont	2750	158	29	7	1				
Kodak	2750	133	32	5	2	1	1	1	
G. Electric	2750	154	34	7	1				
G. Food	2750	140	30	7	3	1			
G. Motors	2750	150	33	9	4	3	2		
G. Telephone	2750	141	37	7	1				
Harvester	2750	147	33	9	3	1			
Stock index									
FT 30	1794	79	8	1					
Metals									
Gold	1957	110	27	9	7	2	1	1	1
Silver	1098	51	18	11	4	3	1		
Copper	3970	204	75	29	15	5	3	1	
Lead	3025	155	54	16	7	2	1	1	1
Tin	3025	151	61	27	8	4	1		
Zinc	3025	167	56	25	16	10	4	1	1
Currency									
£/$	1997	109	29	12	6	2	1		

$^a x_t$ = return on day t, $\bar{x}$ = average, s = standard deviation.
Only the non-zero frequencies are shown in the table.

2.8 PLAUSIBLE DISTRIBUTIONS

A satisfactory model for daily returns must have a probability distribution similar to the observed distribution. Symmetric distributions have usually been considered adequate and we will follow this convention. Thus we are interested in plausible, symmetric distributions having high or possibly infinite kurtosis. A literature review now follows; distributions are fitted to my data in the next chapter.

Normal distributions would be expected if the (log) price changes within a trading day are characterized by: (1) finite variance, (2) identical distribu-

Table 2.7   Number of outliers, futures series

Series		Frequency of event: $\|x_t - \bar{x}\| > ks^a$									
						$k =$					
(months[b])	Returns	2	3	4	5	6	7	8	9	10	11
Commodities											
Corn (12)	3195	238	55	6	2	2	1	1	1		
Cocoa (12)	2684	151	37	7	2	2	1	1	1	1	
Coffee (12)	2728	127	50	23	7	4	3	2	2	2	1[c]
Sugar (12)	5302	296	106	35	12	2	2				
Wool (12)	3270	162	74	41	20	10	5	4	2	2	
Financial											
£/$ (6)	1990	134	30	11	1						
DM/$ (6)	1990	128	24	2	1	1					
SF/$ (6)	1990	109	21	2	1						
T-bond (−)	518	20	4	1							

[a] x_t = return on day t, $\bar{x}$ = average, s = standard deviation.
[b] Months of returns used per futures contract.
[c] Represents return equal to $\bar{x} + 13.8s$.
Only the non-zero frequencies are shown in the table.

tions, (3) the same number of them each day, and (4) this number is large. These conditions ensure an asymptotic normal distribution for an infinite number of within-day changes. Normal distributions are not observed even when characteristic (4) occurs. Most derivations of plausible distributions either suppose (1) is false or at least one of (2) and (3) is false.

Mandelbrot (1963) and Fama (1965) supposed that any sum of (log) price changes belongs to the same parametric family of probability distributions. They do not assume finite variance. This leads to the stable or Pareto–Levy distribution, defined for a symmetric variable X_t by its characteristic function,

$$E[\exp (ikX_t)] = i\delta k - (\gamma|k|)^\alpha \tag{2.8.1}$$

with $i^2 = -1$ and k any real number. The parameters of this symmetric distribution are the characteristic exponent α, a dispersion parameter γ, and a location parameter δ. If a process $\{X_t\}$ is strict white noise then any total $X_t + X_{t+1} + \cdots + X_{t+j}$ will also have characteristic exponent α.

Fama and Roll (1968) describe a practical method for estimating α. Estimates are always between the special cases $\alpha = 1$ for Cauchy distributions and $\alpha = 2$ for normal distributions. Many researchers find the conclusion of infinite variance, when $\alpha < 2$, unacceptable. Detailed studies of stock returns have conclusively rejected the stable distributions (Blattberg and Gonedes, 1974; Hagerman, 1978; Perry, 1983). Hagerman, for example, shows that estimates of α steadily increase from about 1.5 for daily returns to about 1.9 for returns measured over 35 days. Returns over a month or more have distributions much closer to the normal shape than daily returns. A decade after his 1965 paper, Fama prefers to use normal distributions for monthly returns and so to discard stable distributions for daily returns (Fama, 1976, Ch. 1).

There is no reason to suppose that the number of price changes within each day is identical. Neither is it particularly reasonable to assume that every change in price has the same variance. Consequently, Praetz (1972), Clark (1973), and many others have argued that observed returns come from a mixture of normal distributions. The random variable X_t then has conditional distributions,

$$X_t | \omega_t \sim N(\mu, f(\omega_t))$$
(2.8.2)

for various possibilities ω_t; μ is supposed to be constant and $f(\omega_t)$ is the conditional variance. The quantity ω_t could be trading volume with $f(\omega_t) = A\omega_t^B$, $A, B > 0$ as in Clark (1973). Granger and Morgenstern (1970), Rogalski (1978), and Rutledge (1979) give further examples of the dependence of returns distributions upon trading volume. Or ω_t could measure the number of new pieces of relevant information arriving at the market on day t, with $f(\omega_t) = A + B\omega_t$, $A \geq 0$, $B > 0$ (e.g. Beckers, 1981a; Tauchen and Pitts, 1983). Tauchen and Pitts' paper is particularly novel and offers joint distributions for returns and volume conditional upon the amount of new information and the number of traders.

However we choose to interpret ω_t, the conditional variance $f(\omega_t)$ will have some distribution and hence X_t will have a particular unconditional distribution. Let V_t^2 denote the conditional variance on day t. Two distributions for V_t^2 can justify serious consideration.

First, Praetz (1972) suggested the inverted gamma, for which the density function of V_t^2 is a constant times

$$v^{-(k+2)} e^{-(1/2 k-1)\sigma^2/v^2},$$

σ^2 and $k > 2$ being the parameters of the distribution. The great advantage of the inverted gamma is a mathematically convenient density for returns. This is a Student's t density, with k degrees of freedom, defined by

$$h(x) = [(k - 2)^{1/2}\sigma B(\tfrac{1}{2}, \tfrac{1}{2}k)]^{-1}[1 + (x - \mu)^2/\{(k - 2)\sigma^2\}]^{-1/2(k+1)}.$$
(2.8.3)

The term $B(\tfrac{1}{2}, \tfrac{1}{2}k)$ is a Beta coefficient. The density $h(x)$ has mean μ and variance σ^2 with a shape determined by k. Values of $k \leq 4$ give infinite kurtosis, whilst for $k > 4$ the kurtosis is $3 + 6/(k - 4)$. As $k \to \infty$, $h(x)$ converges to a normal density. Blattberg and Gonedes (1974) use likelihood-ratio and other methods to show that Student distributions fit US stock returns far better than stable distributions. For 30 stocks, 8 maximum-likelihood estimates $\hat{k}$ were less than 4, and 16 estimates were between 4 and 6. Kon (1984) has all 33 estimates $\hat{k}$ between 3 and 6.

Second, Clark (1973) supposed that the conditional standard deviations and variances have lognormal distributions. If $\log (V_t) \sim N(\alpha, \beta^2)$ then V_t has density

$$[(2\pi)^{1/2}\beta v]^{-1} \exp \{-\tfrac{1}{2}(\log v - \alpha)^2/\beta^2\}. \tag{2.8.4}$$

All the moments of the returns distribution are then finite, however the density function must be expressed as an integral. Despite this difficulty, the lognormal permits the calculation of various relevant statistics. As $\log (V_t^r) = r \log (V_t) \sim N(r\alpha, r^2\beta^2)$ and $E[V_t^r] = \exp (r\alpha + \tfrac{1}{2}r^2\beta^2)$, it can be shown that the returns have variance $E[V_t^2] = \exp (2\alpha + 2\beta^2)$ and kurtosis $3E[V_t^4]/E[V_t^2]^2 = 3 \exp (4\beta^2)$. Further results for these distributions appear in the next chapter.

2.9   AUTOCORRELATION

The correlation between returns separated by a time-lag of τ days can be estimated from n observations by the sample autocorrelation coefficient:

$$r_{\tau,x} = \sum_{t=1}^{n-\tau} (x_t - \bar{x})(x_{t+\tau} - \bar{x}) \bigg/ \sum_{t=1}^{n} (x_t - \bar{x})^2, \qquad \tau > 0. \tag{2.9.1}$$

Alternative formulae have sometimes been used by other writers but the coefficients obtained are virtually identical for long series. There are a few more terms in the denominator of $r_{\tau,x}$ than in the numerator. This causes a slight bias. When we want to avoid it we use the adjusted coefficient $r'_{\tau,x} = nr_{\tau,x}/(n - \tau)$. The unadjusted coefficient always has variance less than $1/n$ for a strict white noise process but this is not true for the adjusted coefficient. Finite sample properties of the coefficients are discussed in Section 6.3.

Equation (2.9.1) should be altered for futures series. Suppose k contracts contribute returns to the series. Then $(k - 1)\tau$ of the products $(x_t - \bar{x})$ $(x_{t+\tau} - \bar{x})$ contain two returns calculated from different contracts, for sufficiently low τ. These $(k - 1)\tau$ mixed products cannot be expected to have the same distribution as the remaining $n - k\tau$ products. Consequently, for futures series, I omit the $(k - 1)\tau$ mixed products from the numerator of (2.9.1). Every remaining product is then calculated from two returns upon the same contract. The adjusted coefficient now becomes $r'_{\tau,x} = nr_{\tau,x}/(n - k\tau)$.

Autocorrelation formulae assume constant expected returns, $E(X_t)$, estimated by $\bar{x}$. Changes, if any, in expected returns are not large enough to make $r_{\tau,x}$ a seriously biased estimate of the population correlation, cor $(X_t, X_{t+\tau})$. This is shown in Appendix 2(A) for day-of-the-week effects, whilst inflation and other determinants of expected returns are covered in Section 6.11.

Autocorrelation coefficients $r_{\tau,x}$ have been calculated for all lags τ between 1 and 30 trading days inclusive. These coefficients are all close to zero. To summarize the signs and magnitudes of the coefficients each is assigned to one of six classes. These are:

(1) $r < -0.1$ (2) $-0.1 \leqslant r < -0.05$ (3) $-0.05 \leqslant r < 0$
(4) $0 \leqslant r \leqslant 0.05$ (5) $0.05 < r \leqslant 0.1$ (6) $0.1 < r$

Table 2.10 gives, by series, the coefficient at a lag of one day and the number of the 30 coefficients in each class. The information is here summarized for various sets of series using the six classes, firstly for $\tau = 1$ and secondly for $1 \leqslant \tau \leqslant 30$.

First-lag

All the first-lag coefficients are positive for the US stock returns between 1966 and 1976. The coefficients range from a minimum of 0.037 for Kodak to a maximum of 0.150 for Alcoa. Fama (1965) obtained 22 positive and 8 negative first-lag coefficients for US stocks between 1957 and 1962; Greene and Fielitz (1977) found 137 positive and 63 negative between 1963 and 1968; and Perry (1982) has all 37 first-lag coefficients positive for longer series, from 1962 to 1977. It therefore appears that US stock returns on consecutive days are positively correlated. Care is required, however, as all the returns depend on a common market factor and so the coefficients of different stocks are not independent of each other. More about this in the appendix to Chapter 6.

Stock indices can display more first-lag correlation than the individual stocks, because of the market factor and thin trading of smaller companies. Officer (1975), Scholes and Williams (1977), and Gibbons and Hess (1981) provide numerical evidence.

Seven of the eight long futures series used for Table 2.8 have a positive first-lag coefficient but the pattern is reversed for the metals; they only have one out of six positive.

Table 2.8   Frequencies of first-lag autocorrelations

Set of series	Class					
	1	2	3	4	5	6
15 US stocks	0	0	0	3	8	4
6 metals	0	4	1	1	0	0
8 futures [a]	0	0	1	6	1	0
31 various [b]	0	4	2	12	9	4

[a] Agriculturals, 12 months per contract, and currencies.
[b] 15 stocks, 6 metals, 8 futures, FT30, and £/$ spot.

Lags 1 to 30

Less than 10 per cent of the coefficients exceed 0.05 in absolute value and only about 1 per cent of the absolute values exceed 0.1. These low frequencies emphasize how small the sample autocorrelations are. Any dependence in the stochastic process generating returns must be small.

There is a notable preponderance of negative coefficients for the US stocks for lags of two days or more. Fifty-six per cent of the coefficients are negative for lags 2 to 30 inclusive. Fama (1965) notes the same negative tendency, for lags 2 to 10, using returns recorded for years preceding those studied here. The day-of-the-week effects, particularly negative Monday returns, might help to explain these results. Some calculations are given in Appendix 2(A).

A sharp contrast is provided by the futures coefficients. Consider the 240 coefficients for the eight series used in Table 2.9. For these coefficients, 57 per cent are positive at lags 2 to 30, and recall that 7 out of 8 are positive at lag 1. Of the 20 coefficients either above 0.05 or below -0.05, 17 are positive and only 3 are negative. Just 1 of the 17 largest positive coefficients is at a lag of one day. The reality and importance of small, positive autocorrelation at several lags will be looked at in depth throughout Chapters 6, 7, and 8.

Tests

The autocorrelation coefficients $r_{\tau,x}$ could be used to test whether the generating process $\{X_t\}$ is strict white noise. This will not be done as far more conclusive results can be obtained from transformed returns, as we will see in the next section.

Of course the really interesting hypothesis is not strict white noise but uncorrelated X_t. Tests for zero correlation cannot use the $r_{\tau,x}$ and a

Table 2.9 Frequencies of autocorrelations at lags 1 to 30

Set of series	Class					
	1	2	3	4	5	6
15 US stocks	0	9	234	191	12	4
	(0%)	(2%)	(52%)	(42%)	(3%)	(1%)
6 metals	1	13	63	86	14	3
	($\frac{1}{2}$%)	(7%)	(35%)	(48%)	(8%)	($1\frac{1}{2}$%)
8 futures	1	2	97	123	17	0
	($\frac{1}{2}$%)	(1%)	(40%)	(51%)	(7%)	
31 various	2	25	414	439	43	7
	(0.2%)	(2.7%)	(44.5%)	(47.2%)	(4.6%)	(0.8%)

Table 2.10   Autocorrelations $r_{\tau,x}$ for returns

Series	Lag 1 $r_{1,x}$	Lags 1–30, frequency by class [a]					
		1	2	3	4	5	6
Allied	0.086	0	1	14	13	2	0
Alcoa	0.150	0	1	16	12	0	1
Am. Can	0.144	0	0	18	11	0	1
AT and T	0.088	0	0	19	10	1	0
Am. Brands	0.093	0	2	18	9	1	0
Anaconda	0.057	0	0	18	11	1	0
Bethlehem	0.105	0	1	18	10	0	1
Chrysler	0.045	0	1	11	18	0	0
Dupont	0.114	0	0	11	18	0	1
Kodak	0.037	0	0	15	14	1	0
G. Electric	0.099	0	1	16	11	2	0
G. Food	0.089	0	0	15	14	1	0
G. Motors	0.050	0	1	13	15	1	0
G. Telephone	0.052	0	0	19	10	1	0
Harvester	0.086	0	1	13	15	1	0
FT 30	0.033	0	0	11	19	0	0
Gold	−0.052	0	2	10	14	4	0
Silver	−0.080	1	7	3	12	4	3
Copper	−0.052	0	1	10	19	0	0
Lead	−0.020	0	0	12	17	1	0
Tin	0.020	0	1	14	14	1	0
Zinc	−0.073	0	2	14	10	4	0
£/$, spot	0.038	0	1	9	20	0	0
Corn (12)	−0.026	0	2	14	10	4	0
Corn (6)	0.005	0	0	12	15	3	0
Corn (3)	0.013	0	0	13	15	2	0
Cocoa (12)	0.016	0	0	11	16	3	0
Cocoa (6)	0.035	0	0	11	15	4	0
Cocoa (3)	0.071	0	0	11	16	3	0
Coffee (12)	0.026	0	0	15	12	3	0
Coffee (6)	0.062	0	0	16	11	3	0
Coffee (3)	0.062	0	1	15	11	2	1
Sugar (12)	0.044	0	0	9	21	0	0
Sugar (6)	0.064	0	0	6	23	1	0
Sugar (3)	0.064	0	0	7	22	1	0
Wool (12)	0.075	1	0	15	11	3	0
£/$ (6)	0.034	0	0	8	22	0	0
DM/$ (6)	0.011	0	0	13	15	2	0
SF/$ (6)	0.049	0	0	11	17	2	0
T-bond	−0.093	0	4	15	7	4	0

[a] The six classes are (1) $r < -0.1$, (2) $-0.1 \leqslant r < -0.05$, (3) $-0.05 \leqslant r < 0$, (4) $0 \leqslant r \leqslant 0.05$, (5) $0.05 < r \leqslant 0.1$, (6) $r > 0.1$.

conventional standard error of $1/\sqrt{n}$ without risking dubious conclusions. This assertion will be justified in Chapter 5 and be strongly implied by the following results.

2.10   NON-LINEAR STRUCTURE

Not strict white noise

Recall that a process $\{X_t\}$ is strict white noise (SWN) if the X_t are independently and identically distributed. Also remember that the distribution of

$$R_{\tau,x} = \sum_{t=1}^{n-\tau} (X_t - \bar{X})(X_{t+\tau} - \bar{X}) \bigg/ \sum_{t=1}^{n} (X_t - \bar{X})^2$$

is approximately $N(0, 1/n)$ for finite-variance SWN (Section 1.10). Most of the first-lag coefficients listed in Table 2.10 have $\sqrt{n}|r_{1,x}| > 2$, suggesting that the returns series are not realizations of SWN.

    To establish this conclusion more decisively we introduce the idea of transforming returns and then finding autocorrelations, first suggested by Granger and Andersen (1978). For if $\{X_t\}$ is a SWN process so too are the processes $\{|X_t|\}$ and $\{X_t^2\}$. The first lag coefficients of observed absolute returns $|x_t|$ and squared returns x_t^2 are denoted by

$$r_{1,|x|} \quad \text{and} \quad r_{1,x^2}.$$

They are listed in Tables 2.11 and 2.12. Ignoring the short T-bond series, we can deduce that every other series has $r_{1,|x|} > 4.6/\sqrt{n}$ and $r_{1,x^2} > 3.5/\sqrt{n}$. The standard error of a coefficient calculated from absolute returns will be $1/\sqrt{n}$ if $\{X_t\}$ is finite-variance SWN; the same standard error is applicable for the coefficients of squared returns providing the X_t also have finite kurtosis. Finite variance is certainly a very reasonable conclusion. Thus the high correlation observed between $|x_t|$ and $|x_{t+1}|$ proves conclusively that the returns process is not SWN. Note that this tells us nothing about the correlation between returns.

A characteristic of returns

Coefficients $r_{\tau,|x|}$ and r_{τ,x^2} for lags τ up to 50 days are nearly always positive and larger than $r_{\tau,x}$, the autocorrelations of the returns. This can be seen by comparing Table 2.10 with Tables 2.11 and 2.12. Table 2.10 shows that less than 10 per cent of the returns coefficients are outside the range -0.05 to 0.05, for lags τ from 1 to 30. By contrast, most of the coefficients for data $|x_t|$ and x_t^2 are greater than 0.05; the proportions for squared returns are 58 per cent for US stocks, 85 per cent for the metals and 84 per cent for the futures

Table 2.11   Autocorrelations $r_{\tau,|x|}$ for absolute returns

Series	Lag 1 $r_{1,|x|}$	Lags 1–30, frequency by class					
		1	2	3	4	5	6
Allied	0.204	0	0	0	1	25	4
Alcoa	0.194	0	0	0	3	18	9
Am. Can	0.107	0	0	0	14	15	1
AT and T	0.168	0	0	5	17	6	2
Am. Brands	0.165	0	0	0	20	7	3
Anaconda	0.144	0	0	0	17	12	1
Bethlehem	0.130	0	0	3	19	7	1
Chrysler	0.127	0	0	0	9	18	3
Dupont	0.202	0	0	0	0	7	23
Kodak	0.146	0	0	0	0	16	14
G. Electric	0.195	0	0	0	0	0	30
G. Food	0.196	0	0	0	2	20	8
G. Motors	0.174	0	0	0	0	20	10
G. Telephone	0.154	0	0	0	1	24	5
Harvester	0.175	0	0	0	3	24	3
FT 30	0.109	0	0	0	3	19	8
Gold	0.294	0	0	0	0	0	30
Silver	0.284	0	0	0	0	0	30
Copper	0.280	0	0	0	0	0	30
Lead	0.336	0	0	0	0	0	30
Tin	0.321	0	0	0	0	0	30
Zinc	0.398	0	0	0	0	0	30
£/$, spot	0.271	0	0	0	0	1	29
Corn (12)	0.305	0	0	0	0	0	30
Corn (6)	0.407	0	0	0	0	0	30
Corn (3)	0.415	0	0	0	0	0	30
Cocoa (12)	0.281	0	0	0	0	1	29
Cocoa (6)	0.262	0	0	0	0	7	23
Cocoa (3)	0.247	0	0	0	7	7	16
Coffee (12)	0.374	0	0	0	0	0	30
Coffee (6)	0.394	0	0	0	0	0	30
Coffee (3)	0.449	0	0	0	0	0	30
Sugar (12)	0.311	0	0	0	0	0	30
Sugar (6)	0.298	0	0	0	0	0	30
Sugar (3)	0.273	0	0	0	0	8	22
Wool (12)	0.461	0	0	0	0	0	30
£/$ (6)	0.234	0	0	0	1	9	20
DM/$ (6)	0.241	0	0	0	0	7	23
SF/$ (6)	0.242	0	0	0	0	1	29
T-bond	0.050	0	0	2	10	12	6

Table 2.12   Autocorrelations r_{τ,x^2} for squared returns

Series	Lag 1 r_{1,x^2}	Lags 1–30, frequency by class					
		1	2	3	4	5	6
Allied	0.229	0	0	0	7	18	5
Alcoa	0.144	0	0	0	11	14	5
Am. Can	0.075	0	0	0	21	9	0
AT and T	0.131	0	0	11	16	2	1
Am. Brands	0.175	0	0	3	21	4	2
Anaconda	0.068	0	0	6	22	2	0
Bethlehem	0.107	0	0	3	21	4	2
Chrysler	0.113	0	0	1	15	13	1
Dupont	0.194	0	0	0	0	12	18
Kodak	0.178	0	0	0	3	16	11
G. Electric	0.191	0	0	0	0	1	29
G. Foods	0.189	0	0	0	9	15	6
G. Motors	0.168	0	0	0	7	19	4
G. Telephone	0.154	0	0	0	3	21	6
Harvester	0.170	0	0	1	10	17	2
FT 30	0.149	0	0	0	2	10	18
Gold	0.164	0	0	0	5	10	15
Silver	0.205	0	0	0	0	1	29
Copper	0.227	0	0	0	4	19	7
Lead	0.353	0	0	0	13	10	7
Tin	0.240	0	0	0	5	9	16
Zinc	0.291	0	0	0	0	1	29
£/$, spot	0.150	0	0	0	12	15	3
Corn (12)	0.342	0	0	0	0	0	30
Corn (6)	0.328	0	0	0	0	0	30
Corn (3)	0.336	0	0	0	0	0	30
Cocoa (12)	0.180	0	0	0	7	14	9
Cocoa (6)	0.189	0	0	0	10	15	5
Cocoa (3)	0.170	0	0	0	17	9	4
Coffee (12)	0.184	0	0	0	19	10	1
Coffee (6)	0.352	0	0	0	11	15	4
Coffee (3)	0.551	0	0	0	23	4	3
Sugar (12)	0.238	0	0	0	0	3	27
Sugar (6)	0.213	0	0	0	0	9	21
Sugar (3)	0.188	0	0	0	7	8	15
Wool (12)	0.289	0	0	0	0	0	30
£/$ (6)	0.178	0	0	0	9	17	4
DM/$ (6)	0.269	0	0	0	2	15	13
SF/$ (6)	0.284	0	0	0	1	9	20
T-bond	0.031	0	0	5	11	11	3

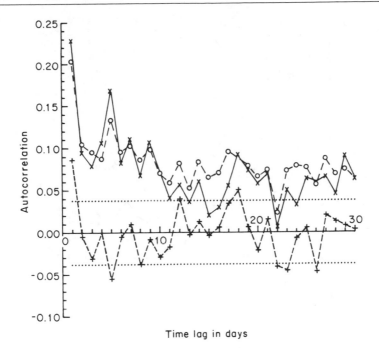

Figure 2.1 Autocorrelations for the first US stock series, for returns (+), absolute returns (○), and squared returns (×)

(excluding T-bonds). Figures 2.1 and 2.2 show the coefficients for returns, absolute returns and squared returns, for the first stock and the gold series. The dotted lines show $\pm 1.96/\sqrt{n}$.

The returns process is therefore characterized by *substantially more* correlation between absolute or squared returns than there is between the returns themselves. This means that large absolute returns are more likely than small absolute returns to be followed by a large absolute return, first noticed by Fama (1965). And, more generally, the distribution of the next absolute return can depend on several previous absolute returns.

One possible explanation of the autocorrelation found in absolute and squared returns is changes in the variances of returns. This and another explanation, involving changes in conditional variances, are both examined in the next chapter. Day-of-the-week effects cannot explain the autocorrelation, shown in the appendix, Section 2(A). Neither can a linear, correlated, process provide a satisfactory explanation. To show this we need some straightforward but lengthy mathematics. The conclusion is very certain and the next subsection need not be read if the reader believes Tables 2.11 and 2.12 suffice to reject all linear models.

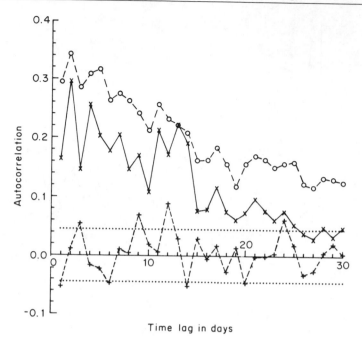

Time lag in days

Figure 2.2   Autocorrelations for the gold series, for returns (+), absolute returns (○), and squared returns (×)

Not linear

A process $\{X_t\}$ is linear if there are constants μ and b_j, $j \geq 0$, and a zero-mean SWN process $\{\varepsilon_t\}$ for which

$$X_t - \mu = \sum_{j=0}^{\infty} b_j \varepsilon_{t-j}, \qquad \text{with } b_0 = 1. \tag{2.10.1}$$

It will now be assumed that X_t has finite kurtosis, $\kappa = E(X_t - \mu)^4 / \{E(X_t - \mu)^2\}^2$. Let $S_t = (X_t - \mu)^2$.

Then, *if* $\{X_t\}$ is linear, and has autocorrelations $\rho_{\tau,X}$, it can be shown that $\{S_t\}$ has autocorrelations given by weighted averages

$$\rho_{\tau,S} = \frac{2}{\kappa - 1} \rho_{\tau,X}^2 + \frac{\kappa - 3}{\kappa - 1} \alpha_\tau \tag{2.10.2}$$

for certain constants α_τ determined by the b_j. This is proved in the appendix, Section 2(B). When $\{X_t\}$ is Gaussian, $\kappa = 3$ and $\rho_{\tau,S} = \rho_{\tau,X}^2$, proved by Granger and Newbold (1976). Let θ be the proportional reduction in mean square error obtained by optimal forecasts, so

$$\theta = \{\text{var}\,(X_t) - \text{var}\,(\varepsilon_t)\}/\text{var}\,(X_t).$$

Then the constants α_τ are constrained by

$$\alpha_\tau \geqslant 0 \text{ (all } \tau > 0\text{)}, \quad \sum_{\tau=1}^{\infty} \alpha_\tau \leqslant \theta/(1 - \theta)^2. \tag{2.10.3}$$

Consequently, for $\kappa \geqslant 3$,

$$0 \leqslant \sum_{\tau=1}^{\kappa} \rho_{\tau,s} \leqslant \text{maximum of } \sum_{\tau=1}^{\kappa} \rho_{\tau,x}^2 \quad \text{and} \quad \theta/(1 - \theta)^2. \tag{2.10.4}$$

For returns we may assume that $\theta \leqslant 0.05$ because no one has been able to find a forecast anywhere near 5 per cent more accurate than the random walk forecast. Also, Table 2.10 shows that we may assume $|\rho_{1,x}| \leqslant 0.15$ and $|\rho_{\tau,x}| \leqslant 0.1$ for $\tau > 1$. As $\kappa > 3$ for returns, a linear process will then have, by applying (2.10.4),

$$\rho_{1,s} < 0.06 \quad \text{and} \quad \sum_{\tau=1}^{30} \rho_{\tau,s} < 0.32. \tag{2.10.5}$$

For every series, $\rho_{\tau,s}$ has been estimated by the autocorrelations $r_{\tau,s}$ of the data $(x_t - \bar{x})^2$; these estimates are almost identical to the autocorrelations r_{τ,x^2}. The totals $r_{1,s} + \cdots + r_{30,s}$ estimate $\rho_{1,s} + \cdots + \rho_{30,s}$ and range from 0.48 to 4.91 for the stocks series and from 1.42 to 6.26 for the remaining series. All the totals $\Sigma r_{\tau,s}$ exceed the upper bound for $\Sigma \rho_{\tau,s}$ given by (2.10.5), frequently by a considerable margin. Therefore linear processes cannot generate observed returns. Any reasonable model for returns must be non-linear.

Consequences of non-linear structure

Many hitherto standard methods of financial research appear unreliable once we appreciate that long series of returns are not generated by either a strict white noise or a linear process. Tests for zero autocorrelation between returns must begin by realizing that the process will not be strict white noise even if it is uncorrelated. Therefore the standard errors of coefficients $r_{\tau,x}$ need not be $1/\sqrt{n}$. In fact the standard errors frequently exceed $3/\sqrt{n}$ (Chapter 5), so new test procedures are necessary. Popular option pricing models assume at least strict white noise. Option pricing formulae can therefore probably be improved by using a better model for returns (Chapter 9). The parameters of the returns distribution, e.g. k, μ and σ^2 for the Student's t distribution (Section 2.8), have been estimated by maximum-likelihood methods. However, the likelihood function can only be computed if, erroneously, strict white noise is assumed.

Mathematicians and statisticians have researched linear processes for many years. All we need for hypothesis testing, model building, and forecasting, within the linear framework, has been published. Methods of modelling non-linear systems are, however, at present (1985), few in number. Often these methods are not relevant for financial time series. New methods are still required and a number of innovations are suggested in the following chapters.

2.11   SUMMARY

Daily returns are characterized by firstly low autocorrelation, secondly approximately symmetric distributions having long tails and high kurtosis, and thirdly an unorthodox, non-linear, generating process. Stock returns have a positive mean but this cannot be proved for futures returns. Models consistent with the preceding major characteristics of returns will be investigated throughout the remainder of this book.

Monday returns have slightly higher variance than other returns and sometimes have a negative although small mean. Some returns may have marginally skewed distributions. These less important features of returns will usually be ignored when modelling the returns process.

APPENDIX 2(A)   AUTCORRELATION CAUSED BY DAY-OF-THE-WEEK EFFECTS

Suppose that the distribution of returns depends on the day of the week according to the simple model:

$$X_t = \mu_t + \sigma_t \varepsilon_t, \qquad \mu_t = \mu_{t+5}, \qquad \sigma_t = \sigma_{t+5},$$

with $\{\varepsilon_t\}$ a stationary, zero mean, unit variance process. Autocorrelations calculated from data $\{x_t, 1 \leqslant t \leqslant n\}$ will be influenced by the daily effects $\mu_i, \sigma_i, 1 \leqslant i \leqslant 5$. The numerical consequences, however, are very slight. Likewise, the consequences of month effects can be shown to be very small.

Returns

As $n \to \infty$, the autocorrelation estimators $R_{\tau, X, n}$ defined for n random variables X_t by $\Sigma (X_t - \bar{X})(X_{t+\tau} - \bar{X})/\Sigma (X_t - \bar{X})^2$ converge with probability one to a limit. Sample estimates $r_{\tau, x, n}$ will converge to the same limit. This limit will be denoted by $\pi_{\tau, X}$. It would equal $\rho_{\tau, X}$ if $\{X_t\}$ was stationary. As $n \to \infty$,

$$\bar{X} = \sum_{t=1}^{n} X_t / n \to \left(\sum_{i=1}^{5} \mu_i \right) \bigg/ 5 = \mu, \text{ say,}$$

and

$$\sum_{t=1}^{n-\tau} X_t X_{t+\tau}/n \rightarrow \left(\sum_{i=1}^{5} E[X_i X_{i+\tau}]\right)\Big/ 5.$$

Now *assume* $\{\varepsilon_t\}$ is white noise. Then it can easily be shown that the daily effects μ_i and σ_i cause the (asymptotic) estimated autocorrelations

$$\pi_{\tau,X} = \sum_{i=1}^{5} (\mu_i - \mu)(\mu_{i+\tau} - \mu)\Big/ \sum_{i=1}^{5} (\mu_i - \mu)^2 + \sigma_i^2. \qquad (2.A.1)$$

Clearly $\pi_{\tau,X} = \pi_{\tau+5,X}$ for all $\tau > 0$ and it can be deduced that $\pi_{1,X} = \pi_{4,X}$ and $\pi_{2,X} = \pi_{3,X}$.

To illustrate the small magnitudes of the $\pi_{\tau,X}$, suppose μ_i and σ_i are defined by French's estimates for the Standard and Poor's index, see Section 2.5. Then (2.A.1) gives these values of $\pi_{\tau,X}$:

τ	π
1,4	−0.003
2,3	−0.005
5	0.017

Squared returns

Let π_{τ,X^2} be the limit of estimators $R_{\tau,X^2,n}$. It is convenient to define $\gamma_i = E[X_i^2] = \mu_i^2 + \sigma_i^2$ and $\gamma = (\gamma_1 + \cdots + \gamma_5)/5$. Then, as $n \rightarrow \infty$,

$$\sum_{t=1}^{n} X_t^2/n \rightarrow \left(\sum_{i=1}^{5} E[X_i^2]\right)\Big/ 5 = \gamma$$

and

$$\sum_{t=1}^{n-\tau} X_t^2 X_{t+\tau}^2/n \rightarrow \left(\sum_{i=1}^{5} E[X_i^2 X_{i+\tau}^2]\right)\Big/ 5.$$

Now *assume* $\{\varepsilon_t\}$ is *strict* white noise with $E[\varepsilon_t^3] = 0$ and $E[\varepsilon_t^4] = \lambda$. Then, it is easy to show that

$$\pi_{\tau,X^2} = \sum_{i=1}^{5} (\gamma_i - \gamma)(\gamma_{i+\tau} - \gamma)\Big/ \sum_{i=1}^{5} (\gamma_i - \gamma)^2 + 4\mu_i^2\sigma_i^2 + (\lambda - 1)\sigma_i^4.$$

$$(2.A.2)$$

Again using French's estimates, (2.A.2) gives the following low auto-correlations firstly for the Gaussian case $\lambda = 3$ and secondly for $\lambda = 6$.

τ	$\lambda = 3$	$\lambda = 6$
1,4	−0.006	−0.002
2,3	−0.003	−0.001
5	0.017	0.007

A second example is based on the average variance proportions for futures, presented in Section 2.5, with all $\mu_i = 0$, as follows:

τ	$\lambda = 3$	$\lambda = 6$
1,4	−0.002	−0.001
2,3	−0.001	−0.000
5	0.005	0.002

APPENDIX 2(B) AUTOCORRELATIONS OF A SQUARED LINEAR PROCESS

Suppose $\{X_t\}$ is linear with mean μ and $\{\varepsilon_t\}$ is zero-mean, strict white noise, with

$$X_t - \mu = \sum_{i=0}^{\infty} b_i \varepsilon_{t-i}.$$

We assume $E[X_t^4]$ is finite. Then, without further loss of generality, we can assume $b_0 = 1$ and $E[\varepsilon_t^2] = 1$. Let $\lambda = E[\varepsilon_t^4]$ and define

$$S_t = (X_t - \mu)^2 = \sum_i b_i^2 \varepsilon_{t-i}^2 + 2 \sum_i \sum_{i<j} b_i b_j \varepsilon_{t-i} \varepsilon_{t-j},$$

and

$$S_{t+\tau} = \sum_k b_k^2 \varepsilon_{t+\tau-k}^2 + 2 \sum_k \sum_{k<l} b_k b_l \varepsilon_{t+\tau-k} \varepsilon_{t+\tau-l}.$$

Then $E[S_t] = \Sigma\, b_i^2$. To find the autocorrelations of $\{S_t\}$ we need $E[S_t S_{t+\tau}]$. To get this expectation consider the general product of four innovations and its expected value:

$$f(i, j, k, l) = E[\varepsilon_{t-i}\varepsilon_{t-j}\varepsilon_{t+\tau-k}\varepsilon_{t+\tau-l}].$$

The function f will be zero unless (a) $i = j = k - \tau = l - \tau$ or (b) there are two identical pairs of subscripts, e.g. $i = j \neq k - \tau = l - \tau$. Case (a) gives $f = \lambda$, case (b) gives $f = 1$, and otherwise $f = 0$. Also when $i < j$ and $k < l$, f can only be non-zero if $i = k - \tau$ and $j = l - \tau$.

It can now be shown, by straightforward algebra, that for all $\tau \geq 0$,

$$\text{cov}\,(S_t, S_{t+\tau}) = E[S_t S_{t+\tau}] - E[S_t]^2$$

$$= (\lambda - 3) \sum_{i=0}^{\infty} b_i^2 b_{i+\tau}^2 + 2 \left(\sum_{i=0}^{\infty} b_i b_{i+\tau} \right)^2.$$

Consequently,

$$\rho_{\tau,S} = \frac{(\lambda - 3) \Sigma\, b_i^2 b_{i+\tau}^2 + 2(\Sigma\, b_i b_{i+\tau})^2}{(\lambda - 3) \Sigma\, b_i^4 + 2(\Sigma\, b_i^2)^2}.$$

Now, firstly, X_t has kurtosis κ related to the kurtosis λ of ε_t by

$$(\kappa - 3)/(\lambda - 3) = \sum b_i^4 / (\sum b_i^2)^2$$

if $\lambda \neq 3$, and secondly the autocorrelations of $\{X_t\}$ are

$$\rho_{\tau,X} = \sum b_i b_{i+\tau} / \sum b_i^2$$

and, thirdly, the autocorrelations of the process

$$X_t^* = \sum b_i^2 \varepsilon_{t-i} \quad \text{are} \quad \alpha_\tau = \sum b_i^2 b_{i+\tau}^2 / \sum b_i^4.$$

Hence our previous equation for $\rho_{\tau,S}$ can be simplified into

$$\rho_{\tau,S} = \frac{(\kappa - 3)\alpha_\tau + 2\rho_{\tau,X}^2}{\kappa - 3 + 2}$$

This is equation (2.10.2). To establish bounds for the non-negative quantities α_τ, note that

$$\sum_{\tau=1}^{\infty} \sum_{i=0}^{\infty} b_i^2 b_{i+\tau}^2 = \frac{1}{2} \left\{ \left(\sum_{i=0}^{\infty} b_i^2 \right)^2 - \sum_{i=0}^{\infty} b_i^4 \right\}$$

and so

$$\sum_{\tau=1}^{\infty} \alpha_\tau = \frac{1}{2} \left\{ \left(\sum_i b_i^2 \right)^2 - \sum_i b_i^4 \right\} \Big/ \sum_i b_i^4.$$

Defining θ by $\{\text{var}(X_t) - \text{var}(\varepsilon_t)\}/\text{var}(X_t)$ and using

$$\sum_{i=0}^{\infty} b_i^2 = 1/(1 - \theta), \qquad \sum_{i=0}^{\infty} b_i^4 \geqslant 1,$$

it follows that (2.10.3) is true, i.e.

$$\sum_{\tau=1}^{\infty} \alpha_\tau \leqslant \frac{1}{2} \left\{ \frac{1}{(1 - \theta)^2} - 1 \right\} \leqslant \frac{\theta}{(1 - \theta)^2}.$$

Modelling Price Volatility

This chapter describes models for returns having either non-stationary variance or, conditional upon past observations, a variance dependent on such observations and additional variables. The models are non-linear, have high kurtosis for returns, and positive autocorrelation between squared returns. Thus they are consistent with the major characteristics of the returns process identified in Chapter 2.

3.1 INTRODUCTION

Variations in the level of activity at a market will cause changes in the variances of daily returns. Activity can be measured by many variables including trading volume and the amount of relevant new information. These variables change from day-to-day and so can the volatility of prices. Specific models have been described by Clark (1973), Tauchen and Pitts (1983), and others, summarized and extended in Section 3.5.

At first, in Sections 3.2 to 3.6, we consider variance models for which the returns process is uncorrelated. Later, Section 3.7 extends the models to include autocorrelation among the returns and Sections 3.8 to 3.10 present parameter estimates for stationary models.

A stationary model must have constant variance but certain conditional variances can change. For a non-linear stationary process $\{X_t\}$, var (X_t) is the same for all t but the conditional variance, var $(X_t | x_{t-1}, x_{t-2} \ldots)$, of X_t given observations x_{t-1}, x_{t-2}, etc. can depend on the observations. Simple examples clarify this in Section 3.2.

Section 3.3 describes a general method for modelling changes in variance or conditional variance based upon changes in market activity. Specific examples have a variety of variance structures: non-stationary variance (Section 3.4), changes in conditional variance caused by factors independent of prices (Section 3.5), and conditional variance changes caused explicitly by prices themselves (Section 3.6).

Much of this chapter is devoted to stationary models for returns. These models can be very useful especially when simulating price behaviour. It is not unreasonable to expect a stationary model to adequately approximate the true process for a relatively short period, say one year. Over longer periods, however, some non-stationarity might be expected. It is far from easy to determine the applicability of fitting stationary models to series covering several years. After fitting models in Sections 3.9 and 3.10 and assessing suitable forecasts in Chapter 4, it will be concluded in Section 4.4 that stationary models can be appropriate for some of our long series but not for all of them.

Some readers may prefer to skip substantial amounts of the mathematical material in this chapter. This can be achieved by skipping Sections 3.2, 3.6, 3.7, and 3.10.

3.2 ELEMENTARY VARIANCE MODELS

Changes in variance or a conditional variance can explain why there is far more autocorrelation between X_t^2 and $X_{t+\tau}^2$ than there is between X_t and $X_{t+\tau}$, for low τ, $\{X_t\}$ being the returns generating process. This is of course the non-linear characteristic of returns identified in Section 2.10. To motivate the conclusion about changes in variance, and to show why conditional variance can be relevant, we first consider very simple variance models. These models restrict the conditional variance of X_t to be one of two possibilities, either σ_1^2 or σ_2^2 with $\sigma_1 \neq \sigma_2$ and $\sigma_1, \sigma_2 > 0$. The models are too simple to describe returns adequately but they illustrate important features of non-linear fluctuating variance models. Realistic models permitting an infinite range of variances are introduced from Section 3.3 onwards.

Two ways that the variance can appear to change are now considered; $\{X_t\}$ is non-stationary for one way yet stationary for the other. Initially the X_t are given discrete distributions, subsequently continuous distributions are considered.

Step change, discrete distributions

Consider a variance change halfway through a series of n variables (n even), so that var $(X_t) = \sigma_1^2$ for $1 \leqslant t \leqslant \frac{1}{2}n$ and var $(X_t) = \sigma_2^2$ for $\frac{1}{2}n < t \leqslant n$. Suppose each X_t is either σ_1 or $-\sigma_1$ ($t \leqslant \frac{1}{2}n$) or is either one of σ_2 and $-\sigma_2$ ($t > \frac{1}{2}n$). Also suppose the X_t are independent random variables having $P(X_t > 0) = \frac{1}{2}$, all t; the notation $P(A)$ denotes the probability of the bracketed event A.

This process $\{X_t\}$ is non-stationary and hence non-linear because var (X_t) depends on the time t. It is uncorrelated because the X_t are independent of each other, so the sample autocorrelations of the x_t will be small. However, the series of squares x_t^2 is certain to consist of $\frac{1}{2}n$ consecutive observations

σ_1^2 followed by $\frac{1}{2}n$ observations σ_2^2. Easy algebra shows that if $\sigma^2 = \frac{1}{2}(\sigma_1^2 + \sigma_2^2)$ the sample autocorrelations of the squares are

$$r_{\tau,x^2} = \sum_{t=1}^{n-\tau} (x_t^2 - \sigma^2)(x_{t+\tau}^2 - \sigma^2) \bigg/ \sum_{t=1}^{n} (x_t^2 - \sigma^2)^2 = (n - 3\tau)/n$$

for $1 \leqslant \tau \leqslant \frac{1}{2}n$ and any variances σ_1^2 and σ_2^2. The variance change can cause a very high measured autocorrelation.

Markov variances, discrete distributions

Next consider a model in which the variance is stochastic, in a certain sense. It is necessary and important to distinguish between the variance of X_t and some conditional variances. A process of conditional variances, denoted $\{V_t^2\}$, follows a Markov chain in this model. Each V_t is either σ_1 or σ_2 with equal probabilities and $V_t = V_{t-1}$ with chance α, otherwise $V_t \neq V_{t-1}$. Assume $\alpha \neq \frac{1}{2}$ to avoid trivial results. As before, suppose each X_t is discrete and the only possible realized values for x_t are $\sigma_1, -\sigma_1$ (when $V_t = \sigma_1$) and $\sigma_2, -\sigma_2$ (if $V_t = \sigma_2$). This model can be described as follows:

$$X_t = V_t U_t, \tag{3.2.1}$$

$\{U_t\}$ is strict white noise,

$$P(U_t = 1) = P(U_t = -1) = \tfrac{1}{2}, \tag{3.2.2}$$
$$P(V_t = \sigma_1) = P(V_t = \sigma_2) = \tfrac{1}{2}, \quad \text{all } t, \tag{3.2.3}$$
$$P(V_t = v_t \mid V_{t-j} = v_{t-j}, \text{ all } j > 0) = \alpha \text{ if } v_t = v_{t-1} \tag{3.2.4}$$
$$= 1 - \alpha \text{ if } v_t \neq v_{t-1}$$

and $\{U_t\}$, $\{V_t\}$ are stochastically independent, i.e. the vectors $U = (U_1, U_2, \ldots, U_n)$ and $V = (V_1, V_2, \ldots, V_n)$ are independent for all integers n. Notation of the form $P(A \mid B)$ appears in (3.2.4) and denotes the probability of A conditional upon the event B being true.

As $\{U_t\}$ and $\{V_t\}$ are strictly stationary processes, and they are independent of each other, it follows that $\{X_t\}$ is strictly stationary. In particular, the X_t have constant variance,

$$\text{var}(X_t) = \tfrac{1}{2}(\sigma_1^2 + \sigma_2^2)$$

and they are clearly uncorrelated as

$$\begin{aligned} \text{cov}(X_t, X_{t+\tau}) &= E[X_t X_{t+\tau}] \\ &= E[V_t V_{t+\tau}] E[U_t] E[U_{t+\tau}] = 0 \end{aligned}$$

because the U_t are zero-mean strict white noise. Now if $x_{t-1} = \sigma_1$, v_{t-1} must be σ_1 and so

$$\begin{aligned} P(X_t = \sigma_1 \mid X_{t-1} = \sigma_1) &= \tfrac{1}{2} P(V_t = \sigma_1 \mid V_{t-1} = \sigma_1) = \tfrac{1}{2}\alpha \\ &\neq P(X_t = \sigma_1) = \tfrac{1}{4}, \text{ as } \alpha \neq \tfrac{1}{2}. \end{aligned}$$

Therefore X_{t-1} and X_t are not independent random variables. Consequently, when $\alpha \neq \frac{1}{2}$, the process $\{X_t\}$ *is white noise but it is not strict white noise*. And as the only linear white noise process is strict white noise, $\{X_t\}$ is not a linear process.

Although the X_t have constant variance, it is important to realize that the variance of X_t conditional upon the past observations $I_{t-1} = \{x_{t-1}, x_{t-2}, \ldots\}$ is not constant. As $x_{t-1}^2 = v_{t-1}^2$, given I_{t-1} the distribution of $X_t^2 = V_t^2$ becomes x_{t-1}^2 with chance α and $\sigma_1^2 + \sigma_2^2 - x_{t-1}^2$ with chance $1 - \alpha$. Thus,

$$\text{var}\,(X_t|I_{t-1}) = E[X_t^2|I_{t-1}] = \alpha x_{t-1}^2 + (1 - \alpha)(\sigma_1^2 + \sigma_2^2 - x_{t-1}^2).$$

This conditional variance depends on the previous observation x_{t-1}. The dependence of $\text{var}\,(X_t|I_{t-1})$ upon I_{t-1} contrasts with the result that any invertible linear process

$$X_t^* = \varepsilon_t + \sum_{i=1}^{\infty} \theta_i \varepsilon_{t-i}, \qquad \{\varepsilon_t\} \text{ strict white noise,}$$

has constant conditional variance, $\text{var}\,(X_t^*|I_{t-1}^*) = \text{var}\,(\varepsilon_t)$, for all possible sets $I_{t-1}^* = \{x_{t-1}^*, x_{t-2}^*, \ldots\}$.

For α nearly equal to 1, the observed squares x_t^2 will contain long sequences of identical values; for most times x_t^2 will equal x_{t-1}^2. This means the squares X_t^2 are highly autocorrelated. As $X_t^2 = V_t^2$, it is easy to prove

$$E[X_t^2] = \tfrac{1}{2}(\sigma_1^2 + \sigma_2^2), \quad E[X_t^4] = \tfrac{1}{2}(\sigma_1^4 + \sigma_2^4) \text{ and}$$
$$E[X_i^2 X_{i+1}^2] = \alpha E[V_t^2 V_{t+1}^2 | V_t = V_{t+1}]$$
$$+ (1 - \alpha)E[V_t^2 V_{t+1}^2 | V_t \neq V_{t+1}]$$
$$= \tfrac{1}{2}\alpha(\sigma_1^4 + \sigma_2^4) + (1 - \alpha)\sigma_1^2\sigma_2^2$$

and hence it can be shown that

$$\rho_{1,X^2} = \text{cov}\,(X_t^2, X_{t+1}^2)/\text{var}\,(X_t^2)$$
$$= \{\tfrac{1}{4}(2\alpha - 1)(\sigma_1^2 - \sigma_2^2)^2\}/\{\tfrac{1}{4}(\sigma_1^2 - \sigma_2^2)^2\}$$
$$= 2\alpha - 1. \qquad (3.2.5)$$

Likewise it can be proved that $\rho_{\tau,X^2} = (2\alpha - 1)^\tau$, $\tau > 0$. These autocorrelations are the same as those of an AR(1) process with autoregressive parameter $2\alpha - 1$. Equation (3.2.5) shows that if the x_t have low sample autocorrelations but the squares x_t^2 have far higher autocorrelations then it is wrong to conclude that the variance is not constant. The correlation among the squares can be caused by changes in conditional variance.

Step variances, continuous distributions

So far the distribution of X_t has been very simple and this has the advantage of ensuring easy results for the autocorrelations of the squares X_t^2. More realistic and interesting results are obtained if, given a conditional variance v_t^2, X_t has the normal distribution $N(0, v_t^2)$.

Hsu (1977, 1979) has tested a single variance change model on US stock returns. Simplifying the model by supposing $E[X_t] = 0$ gives:

$$X_t = \sigma_1 U_t \qquad 1 \leqslant t \leqslant m$$
$$ = \sigma_2 U_t \qquad m + 1 \leqslant t \leqslant n$$

with $\{U_t\}$ a Gaussian, white noise process having $U_t \sim N(0, 1)$. Hsu tested the null hypothesis $\sigma_1 = \sigma_2$ against the alternative $\sigma_1 \neq \sigma_2$, with m unknown, for 161 weekly returns on the Dow Jones Industrial Average from July 1971 to August 1974. Conclusive evidence of an increased variance from mid-March 1973 onwards was reported and attributed to a surge in news about the Watergate incident. Menzefricke (1981) and Hsu (1982) have given Bayesian analyses of the location of the unknown change-point m.

The process $\{X_t\}$ is obviously non-stationary and uncorrelated, supposing $\sigma_1 \neq \sigma_2$. The squared process $\{X_t^2\}$ does not have meaningful autocorrelations. However, sample autocorrelations calculated from squared returns should be positive for low τ as the first m of the X_t^2 have a different expectation to the final $n{-}m$ squares. The autocorrelations $r_{\tau, x^2, n}$ for n squares will have an asymptotic limit if the ratio $f = m/n$ is fixed as $n \rightarrow \infty$. The limit is constant for all positive τ and lengthy algebra shows it is the positive number

$$\pi = (\sigma_1^2 - \sigma_2^2)^2 / \{(\sigma_1^2 - \sigma_2^2)^2 + 2(1 - f)^{-1}\sigma_1^4 + 2f^{-1}\sigma_2^4\}. \qquad (3.2.6)$$

Very approximately, Hsu's estimates are $f = \frac{1}{2}$ and $\sigma_2^2 = 3\sigma_1^2$ and then π is $1/11 \simeq 0.09$.

Markov variances, continuous distributions

The model just described has one change in the variance of X_t and the X_t have conditional normal distributions. Now suppose at the beginning of every day there is a chance $(1 - \alpha)$ of a variance change from one of σ_1^2 or σ_2^2 to the other possible variance, described earlier by equations (3.2.3) and (3.2.4). These variance changes could reflect occasional changes in the amount of news about the goods, between little news and much news or vice versa. Supposing again that the conditional distribution of X_t given its variance is normal with zero mean, X_t is once more the product $V_t U_t$ with $\{U_t\}$ Gaussian, white noise. The process $\{X_t\}$ is stationary and uncorrelated with variance $\frac{1}{2}(\sigma_1^2 + \sigma_2^2)$.

Given specific information about the conditional standard deviations $v_{t-j}, j \geqslant 0$, the random variable X_t has a conditional variance. In particular,

$$\mathrm{var}\,(X_t | v_t) = v_t^2$$

and

$$\text{var } (X_t | v_{t-1}, v_{t-2} \ldots) = \alpha v_{t-1}^2 + (1 - \alpha)(\sigma_1^2 + \sigma_2^2 - v_{t-1}^2) \qquad (3.2.7)$$

for any v_{t-2}, v_{t-3}, etc. (Notation of the form $A|b_1, b_2, \ldots$ occurs in (3.2.7) and refers to the distribution of A given realizations $b_1, b_2, \ldots$ of appropriate random variables.) Unlike the discrete Markov model, it is impossible to describe the variance of X_t conditional upon all past observations $I_{t-1} = \{x_{t-j}, j \geqslant 1\}$. However, the variance given x_{t-1} can be calculated. Let $L(x|\sigma)$ denote the likelihood of an observation x from the normal distribution $N(0, \sigma^2)$ and let λ be the likelihood ratio $L(x_{t-1}|\sigma_1)/L(x_{t-1}|\sigma_2)$. Then it is possible to prove the result

$$\text{var } (X_t | x_{t-1}) = \frac{\lambda [\alpha \sigma_1^2 + (1 - \alpha)\sigma_2^2] + \alpha \sigma_2^2 + (1 - \alpha)\sigma_1^2}{\lambda + 1}$$

and this conditional variance is a function of x_{t-1}, assuming $\alpha \neq \frac{1}{2}$ and $\sigma_1 \neq \sigma_2$.

To find the population autocorrelations of the stochastic process $\{X_t^2\}$ it is convenient to work out $E[X_t^2]$, $E[X_t^2 X_{t+\tau}^2]$ ($\tau > 0$) and $E[X_t^4]$. The first two expectations are unchanged from the discrete Markov model but $E[X_t^4]$ becomes $3(\sigma_1^4 + \sigma_2^4)/2$ as $E[U_t^4]$ is now 3. It can then be demonstrated that

$$\rho_{\tau,X^2} = \frac{(\sigma_1^2 - \sigma_2^2)^2}{(\sigma_1^2 - \sigma_2^2)^2 + 4(\sigma_1^4 + \sigma_2^4)} (2\alpha - 1)^\tau \qquad (3.2.8)$$

$$< (1/5)(2\alpha - 1)^\tau, \qquad \tau > 0.$$

The continuous distribution of the U_t, compared with the earlier discrete distribution, causes smaller autocorrelation between the squared X_t. If α is almost 1, the autocorrelations will decline slowly from some positive number less than 0.2. The function (3.2.8) has an ARMA(1,1) shape, i.e. there are ARMA(1,1) processes having the same autocorrelations as $\{X_t^2\}$.

This model shows that occasional variance changes with conditional normal distributions can explain significant positive autocorrelation between squared returns. The model also shows that variance changes can explain high kurtosis, for

$$k_X = E[X_t^4]/E[X_t^2]^2$$
$$= 3\{1 + (\sigma_1^2 - \sigma_2^2)^2/(\sigma_1^2 + \sigma_2^2)^2\} > 3.$$

The unconditional distribution of X_t is a mixture of two normal distributions and the mixing causes the higher kurtosis.

3.3 A GENERAL VARIANCE MODEL

The return x_t can be calculated at the end of the day t. This number can always be interpreted as being the realization of a random variable X_t. Before day t begins the return x_t cannot be known and so a probability distribution for X_t can be used to describe the possible outcomes x_t. Then, by the end of the day, various people, companies, and governments will collectively have helped to determine a particular outcome x_t, depending mainly on new information and interpretations thereof.

In a similar way, suppose that by the end of day t the market has determined a conditional standard deviation v_t so that, for fixed v_t, x_t is an observation from a distribution having variance v_t^2. New information about the goods traded or other sources of economic and political information could partially determine v_t, as also could the changing preferences of investors for different goods. During day $t - 1$ it is reasonable to assume v_t is not known exactly although good forecasts may be available. Consequently, v_t can be viewed as the realized value of some random variable V_t. Two important questions are then: firstly at what time does the market determine v_t and secondly what sort of information and type of market behaviour determines v_t? Several possible answers will be summarized later.

Models consistent with the preceding discussion of a conditional standard deviation have been proposed by several researchers, including Granger and Morgenstern (1970), Praetz (1972), Clark (1973), Epps and Epps (1976), Ali and Giaccotto (1982), Engle (1982), Tauchen and Pitts (1983), and the author. These models can all be written in the general form:

$$X_t = \mu + V_t U_t \qquad\qquad (3.3.1)$$

with $\{U_t\}$ a standardized process, so $E[U_t] = 0$ and var $(U_t) = 1$ for all t, and $\{V_t\}$ a process of positive random variables usually having var $(X_t|v_t) = v_t^2$; also $E[X_t] = \mu$ for all t. Nearly everyone has assumed the U_t have normal distributions. Most people suppose the processes $\{V_t\}$ and $\{U_t\}$ are stochastically independent but this is not necessary as Engle (1982) has shown. Stochastic independence is sufficient but not necessary to ensure var $(X_t|v_t) = v_t^2$. For many markets it can be appropriate to assume $\mu = 0$ and μ will always be very small compared with the v_t.

Three classes of processes for $\{V_t\}$ will be reviewed. Firstly, occasional changes in variance so that $V_t = V_{t+1}$ with high probability (Section 3.4); secondly, changes in conditional variance caused by economic forces independent of the market (in the sense that $\{V_t\}$ and $\{U_t\}$ are stochastically independent), perhaps with all processes stationary (Section 3.5); and, thirdly, changes in conditional variance caused by past returns so that V_t depends only on $I_{t-1} = \{x_{t-j}, j > 0\}$ (Section 3.6). All these processes for $\{V_t\}$ will initially be described with the simplifying assumption that $\{U_t\}$ is strict white noise (SWN). Later, in Section 3.7, modelling dependence between the U_t will be introduced.

Assuming $\{U_t\}$ to be SWN and making the reasonable assumption that U_{t+i} is independent of the vector $(U_t, V_t, V_{t+1}, \ldots, V_{t+i})$ for all $i > 0$, we obtain the expected result that the X_t are uncorrelated as, for $\tau > 0$,

$$\text{cov}\,(X_t, X_{t+\tau}) = E[V_t V_{t+\tau} U_t U_{t+\tau}] = E[V_t V_{t+\tau} U_t] E[U_{t+\tau}] = 0.$$

Notation

We will often want to describe results for the squared returns after adjusting for the mean μ. These are defined for random variables X_t by

$$S_t = (X_t - \mu)^2 = V_t^2 U_t^2. \tag{3.3.2}$$

When studying observed returns x_t, the mean μ is usually unknown but can be estimated by a sample mean $\bar{x}$. In these circumstances sample adjusted squares are defined by $s_t = (x_t - \bar{x})^2$. Occasionally μ will be assumed known and the definition $s_t = (x_t - \mu)^2$ used, particularly in Section 3.6. Absolute returns will also be analysed, defined by

$$M_t = |X_t - \mu| = V_t |U_t| \tag{3.3.3}$$

for random variables and for observed data by $m_t = |x_t - \bar{x}|$, μ unknown, or $m_t = |x_t - \mu|$, μ known.

We have now defined several stochastic processes in this chapter and there will be more later on. Table 3.1 summarizes the processes considered in Chapter 3.

Table 3.1   Processes considered in Chapter 3

Process	Definition	References and notes
A	An autoregressive process	See Section 3.6
M	$M_t = \lvert X_t - \mu \rvert$	
S	$S_t = (X_t - \mu)^2$	
T	$T_t = U_t - \varepsilon_t$	See Section 3.7
U	$U_t = (X_t - \mu)/V_t$	$E[U_t] = 0$, var $(U_t) = 1$
V	Generates conditional standard deviations	See Sections 3.3 and 3.7
W	Counts intra-day price changes	See Section 3.5
X	Generates returns	$E[X_t] = \mu$
ε	Strict white noise	$E[\varepsilon_t] = 0$, see Section 3.7
η	Strict white noise	$E[\eta_t] = 0$, see Section 3.5

3.4   MODELLING VARIANCE JUMPS

Extraordinary political events occur from time to time. Often the events are unexpected. We have already noted Hsu's evidence that revelations about the involvement of the US president in the Watergate affair increased the variance of US stocks in 1973. Another dramatic event was the Russian invasion of Afghanistan in 1979, causing turmoil in financial markets, especially the gold market.

If variance changes are solely caused by extraordinary events then there will only be a small probability of a variance change during any trading day. Most pairs of consecutive days (t and $t + 1$) will then have equal conditional standard deviations ($v_t = v_{t+1}$). Extraordinary events will usually increase v_t and presumably after a period of time the event will be forgotten and the conditional standard deviation will fall. It seems sensible to regard $\{V_t\}$ as non-stationary as it is difficult to see how the consequences of very unusual events can be accommodated within a stationary model. The market does not cause extraordinary events and hence the variance jumps, so it is very reasonable to assume $\{V_t\}$ and $\{U_t\}$ are stochastically independent. Many events occur when markets are closed so it is fairly accurate to assume the realized value v_t is determined before trading begins on day t.

Variances have often been linked with trading volumes (e.g. Clark, 1973). A jump in variance therefore suggests a jump in trading volume as the number of traders and their average trading frequency changes. An unexpected, important event could cause a wider variety than usual of opinions about a fair price, and thus a higher trading volume.

A time series of returns will contain an unknown number of jumps, if a jump model is appropriate. Hsu (1977, 1979, 1982) only considers one jump, Ali and Giaccotto (1982) suggest up to four jumps within an eleven-year period. Extraordinary events are by definition rare, so only a few jumps are likely in a series. Accurate estimates of v_t can then be found for most times. The autocorrelations $r_{\tau,s}$ of the adjusted squares s_t should be positive; for in a total $\Sigma\ (S_t - \bar{S})(S_{t+\tau} - \bar{S})$ the products $(S_t - \bar{S})(S_{t+\tau} - \bar{S})$ have positive expectation for the vast majority of times that $v_t = v_{t+\tau}$. Equation (3.2.6) suggests the positive autocorrelation will be fairly small.

3.5 MODELLING FREQUENT VARIANCE CHANGES NOT CAUSED BY PRICES

General models

Linking variance changes solely to extraordinary events is probably an unrealistic simplification of the process generating $\{V_t\}$. Many events could cause changes in conditional standard deviations with minor events causing smaller (yet still important) changes. The relative popularities of markets are always changing. So too is the amount of relevant new information each day, whether it be economical or political. Therefore we now consider models for which v_t can be expected to change daily, although on most days the changes $v_t - v_{t-1}$ will probably be small. Two types of model are considered. In this section we assume that the process determining the v_t does not depend on prices so that

$$V_t = f(V_{t-1}, V_{t-2}, V_{t-3}, \ldots, \eta_t) \tag{3.5.1}$$

for some function f and a random innovation η_t independent of all past returns x_{t-j}, $j > 0$. The alternative possibility, that returns do cause the v_t, is introduced in Section 3.6.

The easiest way to explain how market forces can make v_t a function of events occurring on day t is to represent the return X_t as the sum of intra-day price movements:

$$X_t - \mu = \sum_{i=1}^{W_t} \omega_{it}. \tag{3.5.2}$$

In this equation, W_t and every ω_{it} are random variables. Suppose the ω_{it} are independently and identically distributed as $N(0, \sigma_\omega^2)$, and are independent of W_t. Then given an observed number w_t of intra-day price movements the conditional standard deviation is simply $v_t = \sigma_\omega \sqrt{w_t}$. Returns will display non-linear behaviour if the W_t are autocorrelated.

Tauchen and Pitts (1983) describe an economic model for the reactions of individual traders to separate items of information. They assume $\mu = 0$ and identify w_t with the number of relevant information items during day t. Each news item causes a price movement ω_{it} and a trading volume $v_{it} \sim N(\mu_v, \sigma_v^2)$. Conditional upon w_t items of information, $X_t \sim N(\mu, \sigma_\omega^2 w_t)$ and the day's trading volume is $\sim N(\mu_v w_t, \sigma_v^2 w_t)$. These conclusions show the distributions of returns and trading volume can depend on each other in a complicated fashion. Earlier papers, e.g. Clark (1973), restrict the conditional variance of X_t to be a deterministic function of volume, corresponding to $\sigma_v = 0$. Tauchen and Pitts assumed $\{W_t\}$ is strict white noise. This must, however, be inappropriate, as then $\{X_t\}$ would also be strict white noise and we know this is not so.

More generally, we can identify v_t with a level of market activity covering: the amount and importance of new information, trading volume, the number of active traders, interest in the market relative to others and perhaps also seasonal factors. Many of these activity measures can only be assessed at the end of the day's business. Thus, in this type of model, v_t is realized at the end of day t.

As it is supposed that prices do not cause the conditional standard deviations, it is reasonable to assume $\{V_t\}$ and $\{U_t\}$ are stochastically independent. This can be proved true for model (3.5.2) with $\omega_{it} \sim N(0, \sigma_\omega^2)$. Let $V_t = \sigma_\omega \sqrt{W_t}$ and

$$U_t = \frac{X_t - \mu}{V_t} = \frac{1}{\sigma_\omega \sqrt{W_t}} \sum_{i=1}^{W_t} \omega_{it}.$$

Given any realization v_t, w_t is v_t^2/σ_ω^2, so $\sum \omega_{it} \sim N(0, v_t^2)$ and $U_t \sim N(0, 1)$. As the conditional distribution of U_t is the same for all v_t, U_t and V_t are independent. Likewise, the vectors $U = (U_1, U_2, \ldots, U_n)$ and $V = (V_1, V_2, \ldots, V_n)$ are independent for all n, establishing stochastic independence, providing all sets of variables ω_{it} are independent of V; i.e. individual intra-day price changes are stochastically independent of how many price changes there are.

When $\{X_t - \mu\}$ is the product of stochastically independent processes $\{V_t\}$ and $\{U_t\}$ we will call $\{X_t\}$ a *product process*.

Note that in practice only one realized value is observed each trading day, namely x_t, but that two innovations determine x_t. One innovation (η_t in equation (3.5.1)) will cause the level of market activity v_t and the reaction of the price at this level of activity is summarized by an independent innovation U_t. Given a series x_t, $1 \leq t \leq n$, it is impossible to recover the realized values v_t. Nevertheless, it will be shown later that reasonable estimates of v_t can be found.

Stationary models

The process $\{V_t\}$ could be stationary or non-stationary. Strictly stationary processes imply various results which are derived here and checked against empirical evidence in later sections. In due course it will be concluded that some returns series are non-stationary whilst others are satisfactorily modelled by stationary processes.

Results for stationary $\{V_t\}$ and $\{U_t\}$ can be obtained quickly by applying their assumed stochastic independence. It will also be assumed that both V_t and U_t have finite fourth moments. Let k_U denote the kurtosis of the U_t, so $k_U = E[U_t^4]$ as $E[U_t] = 0$ and $E[U_t^2] = 1$, and let δ denote the mean absolute deviation of the U_t so $\delta = E[|U_t|]$. For normal U_t, $k_U = 3$ and $\delta = \sqrt{(2/\pi)} \simeq 0.798$.

The process $\{X_t\}$ is stationary with variance:

$$E[(X_t - \mu)^2] = E[V_t^2 U_t^2] = E[V_t^2]E[U_t^2] = E[V_t^2].$$

This is a constant although, of course, the conditional variances var $(X_t \mid v_t)$ equal the time-dependent quantities v_t^2. The kurtosis of the X_t is given by

$$k_X = \frac{E[(X_t - \mu)^4]}{E[(X_t - \mu)^2]^2} = \frac{E[V_t^4 U_t^4]}{E[V_t^2]^2} = \frac{k_U E[V_t^4]}{E[V_t^2]^2}. \tag{3.5.3}$$

As $E[V_t^4] > E[V_t^2]^2$ for all positive variables V_t having positive variance, $k_X > k_U$. The unconditional distribution of X_t is a mixture of the conditional distributions $\mu + v_t U_t$, mixing over all possible realizations v_t. The result $k_X > k_U$ confirms that mixing distributions having different variances increases the kurtosis.

As $\{U_t\}$ is assumed at present to be white noise, $\{X_t\}$ is also white noise.

However, the adjusted squares $S_t = (X_t - \mu)^2$ can be autocorrelated; $E[S_t] = E[V_t^2]$ and if $\tau > 0$,

$$E[S_t S_{t+\tau}] = E[V_t^2 V_{t+\tau}^2]E[U_t^2 U_{t+\tau}^2] = E[V_t^2 V_{t+\tau}^2],$$

so

$$\text{cov } (S_t, S_{t+\tau}) = E[S_t S_{t+\tau}] - E[S_t]^2 = \text{cov } (V_t^2, V_{t+\tau}^2).$$

Consequently, the autocorrelations $\rho_{\tau,s}$ of $\{S_t\}$ are related to the autocorrelations ρ_{τ,V^2} of $\{V_t^2\}$ by the linear relationship:

$$\rho_{\tau,s} = \rho_{\tau,V^2}[\text{var } (V_t^2)/\text{var } (S_t)]. \tag{3.5.4}$$

The positive autocorrelations r_{τ,x^2} and $r_{\tau,s}$ observed among observed squares x_t^2 and adjusted squares $s_t = (x_t - \bar{x})^2$, in Section 2.10, is consistent with equation (3.5.4) if the process of conditional variances $\{V_t^2\}$ is positively autocorrelated. Let $a_r = E[V_t^r]$. Then var $(V_t^2) = a_4 - a_2^2$, var $(S_t) = E[S_t^2]$ $- E[S_t]^2 = k_U a_4 - a_2^2$ and so (3.5.4) implies

$$0 \leqslant \rho_{\tau,S}/\rho_{\tau,V^2} \leqslant 1/k_U$$

for any distribution of the V_t.

The absolute returns $M_t = |X_t - \mu|$ have mean $E[M_t] = E[V_t|U_t|] = \delta E[V_t]$. Also $E[M_t^2] = E[V_t^2]$ and so it is easy to obtain var (M_t). For $\tau > 0$,

$$E[M_t M_{t+\tau}] = E[V_t V_{t+\tau}]E[|U_t U_{t+\tau}|] = \delta^2 E[V_t V_{t+\tau}],$$
$$\text{cov } (M_t, M_{t+\tau}) = E[M_t M_{t+\tau}] - E[M_t^2] = \delta^2 \text{ cov } (V_t, V_{t+\tau})$$

and consequently the M_t have autocorrelations

$$\rho_{\tau,M} = \delta^2 \rho_{\tau,V}[\text{var } (V_t)/\text{var } (M_t)]. \tag{3.5.5}$$

In terms of $a_r = E[V_t^r]$, var $(V_t) = a_2 - a_1^2$, var $(M_t) = a_2 - \delta^2 a_1^2$ and thus var $(V_t) \leqslant$ var (M_t) giving

$$0 \leqslant \rho_{\tau,M}/\rho_{\tau,V} \leqslant \delta^2.$$

The lognormal, autoregressive model

All the preceding results are as general as are possible. Constructive models for $\{V_t\}$ will have few parameters whilst permitting the mean and variance to be unconstrained and the feasible autocorrelations to cover a range of possible values consistent with the sample autocorrelations of $|x_t|$ and x_t^2. The models to be described have three parameters. It is assumed that $\{U_t\}$ is Gaussian white noise with $U_t \sim N(0, 1)$.

The distribution of V_t cannot have positive probability of a negative value so a normal distribution is inappropriate. Empirical distributions of sample variances have more extreme variances in the right tail than the left tail (consider Table 2.5). A right-skewed, positive-valued, distribution is required. The lognormal family of distributions is the most convenient for obtaining straightforward mathematical results. It has also been found satisfactory, and better than alternatives, for empirical modelling by Clark (1973) and Tauchen and Pitts (1983). There are two parameters and we adopt the notational definition

$$\log (V_t) \sim N(\alpha, \beta^2), \qquad \beta > 0.$$

The density function has already been given by equation (2.8.4) and it is well known that $E[V_t] = \exp (\alpha + \frac{1}{2}\beta^2)$. As $\log (V_t^r) = r \log (V_t)$, all terms $a_r = E[V_t^r]$ can be calculated and are $\exp (r\alpha + \frac{1}{2}r^2\beta^2)$. In particular, $a_4/a_2^2 = \exp (4\beta^2)$ and equation (3.5.2) shows the kurtosis of returns is

$$k_X = 3e^{4\beta^2} \tag{3.5.6}$$

which can be arbitrarily large.

To find the constants in equations (3.5.4) and (3.5.5), the following variances can be derived:

$$\text{var } (V_t) = e^{2\alpha + \beta^2}(e^{\beta^2} - 1), \qquad \text{var } (V_t^2) = e^{4\alpha + 4\beta^2}(e^{4\beta^2} - 1),$$
$$\text{var } (M_t) = e^{2\alpha + \beta^2}(e^{\beta^2} - \delta^2), \qquad \text{var } (S_t) = e^{4\alpha + 4\beta^2}(3e^{4\beta^2} - 1).$$

Consequently, as $\delta^2 = 2/\pi$ for the standardized normal distribution,

$$\rho_{\tau,S}/\rho_{\tau,V^2} = \{e^{4\beta^2} - 1\}/\{3e^{4\beta^2} - 1\} = A(\beta) \tag{3.5.7}$$

and

$$\rho_{\tau,M}/\rho_{\tau,V} = 2\{e^{\beta^2} - 1\}/\{\pi e^{\beta^2} - 2\} = B(\beta) \tag{3.5.8}$$

for any $\tau > 0$. The ratio $A(\beta)$ increases monotonically with β from $A(0) = 0$ to the upper bound $1/3$ as $\beta \to \infty$. Similarly $B(\beta)$ is monotonic and bounded by 0 and $2/\pi$.

The autocorrelation coefficients and plots presented in Section 2.10 show that any sensible stationary model must have $\rho_{\tau,S}$ and $\rho_{\tau,M}$ positive for several lags τ, hence this must apply to $\rho_{\tau,V}$ and ρ_{τ,V^2} also. The simplest possible model having positive autocorrelations at several lags is an AR(1) process for $\log (V_t)$:

$$\log (V_t) - \alpha = \phi \{\log (V_{t-1}) - \alpha\} + \eta_t, \qquad \phi > 0. \tag{3.5.9}$$

The innovation process $\{\eta_t\}$ is zero-mean, Gaussian white noise, stochastically independent of $\{U_t\}$; var $(\eta_t) = \beta^2(1 - \phi^2)$. A value of ϕ near to 1 would mean the conditional standard deviations change gradually.

Granger and Newbold (1976) prove that the autocorrelations of the Gaussian process $\{\log (V_t)\}$ and the non-Gaussian $\{V_t\}$ are related by

$$\rho_{\tau,V} = \{\exp (\beta^2\rho_{\tau,\log V}) - 1\}/\{\exp (\beta^2) - 1\}$$
$$= \{\rho_{\tau,\log V} + \frac{1}{2}\beta^2\rho_{\tau,\log V}^2 + \cdots\}/\{1 + \frac{1}{2}\beta^2 + \cdots\}.$$

To obtain ρ_{τ,V^2}, replace β^2 by $4\beta^2$ in the right-hand side of these equations. As $\rho_{\tau,\log V}$ is ϕ^τ for the AR(1) process, the autocorrelations of the observable processes $\{S_t\}$ and $\{M_t\}$ are

$$\rho_{\tau,S} = A(\beta)\{\exp(4\beta^2\phi^\tau) - 1\}/\{\exp(4\beta^2) - 1\} \qquad (3.5.10)$$

and

$$\rho_{\tau,M} = B(\beta)\{\exp(\beta^2\phi^\tau) - 1\}/\{\exp(\beta^2) - 1\}. \qquad (3.5.11)$$

Each of these autocorrelation functions steadily decrease, beginning from a number less than 1 and declining towards 0 as τ increases. The functions are very similar to the autocorrelations of an ARMA(1,1) process, namely Ca^τ for constants C and a (equation (1.9.13)), with $1 > C > 0$ and $a > 0$. Consequently, the autocorrelation functions given by equations (3.5.10) and (3.5.11) are reasonably consistent with the plots dispayed in Section 2.10.

The lognormal, autoregressive model has four parameters, α, β, ϕ, and μ. These are estimated from the time series of observed returns in Sections 3.8 and 3.9. It is not possible to find the conditional variance given all past observations, i.e. var $(X_t|x_{t-1}, x_{t-2}, \ldots)$, because the component series $\{v_t\}$ and $\{u_t\}$ are not observed. If, somehow, the past v_t can be discovered then

$$\begin{aligned} \text{var } (X_t|v_{t-1}, \ldots) &= \text{var } (X_t|v_{t-1}) = E[V_t^2|v_{t-1}] \\ &= v_{t-1}^{2\phi} \exp\{2(1 - \phi)\alpha + 2\beta^2(1 - \phi^2)\} \qquad (3.5.12) \end{aligned}$$

but in practice this variance cannot be calculated; an estimate of v_{t-1} could always be substituted and used to help estimate quantity (3.5.12).

3.6 MODELLING FREQUENT VARIANCE CHANGES CAUSED BY PAST PRICES

General concepts

In the previous section it was supposed that the process determining the conditional standard deviations does not depend on past returns or prices. Now an extreme alternative to this assumption is considered, namely that conditional standard deviations are a deterministic function of past returns. Thus,

$$V_t = f(X_{t-1}, X_{t-2}, \ldots) \qquad (3.6.1)$$

for some function f; a very simple example is

$$f(X_{t-1}) = \{\alpha_0 + \alpha_1(X_{t-1} - \mu)^2\}^{1/2}$$

with α_0 and α_1 both positive. We assume throughout this section that $U_t = (X_t - \mu)/V_t$ is normal distributed and independent of all U_{t-i} and all

V_{t-i}, $i > 0$. The X_t are then uncorrelated. Also, given past returns $I_{t-1} = \{x_{t-1}, x_{t-2}, \ldots\}$, v_t can be calculated and then $X_t | I_{t-1} \sim N(\mu, v_t^2)$.

This approach to modelling changes in conditional variances is due to Engle (1982). This section is based on his paper and provides further models and mathematical results. Engle's work is directed at general econometric models possessing constant variance yet changing conditional variance. Its intended value for modelling financial time series is unclear (Engle, 1982, p. 989). However, the ideas are certainly important as they offer potential models for changing conditional variances and these models can and will be assessed using observed data.

There are notable differences between models for X_t based upon conditional variances firstly caused by $H_{t-1} = \{X_{t-1}, X_{t-2}, \ldots\}$, as in this section, and secondly caused by $J_t = \{\eta_t, V_{t-1}, V_{t-2}, \ldots\}$, as in Section 3.5. In the first case, only one innovation per unit time determines X_t (namely U_t) but, in the second, two innovations are required (namely U_t and η_t). When it is correct to model variances using H_{t-1}, the realized value v_t can be observed at the end of day $t - 1$. However, if the true process uses J_t then v_t is determined later, at the end of day t, and the realized value cannot be observed. Another comparison is based on the relationship between the processes $\{V_t\}$ and $\{U_t\}$. Variance models based on H_{t-1} do not have stochastic independence between the two processes (a proof follows later), but it has already been argued that stochastic independence is a reasonable assumption when J_t determines the conditional variance.

Models based upon (3.6.1), with $X_t | I_{t-1} \sim N(\mu, v_t^2)$, have the very desirable property that any parameters in the function f can be estimated by maximizing the likelihood of observed data $x_1, x_2, \ldots, x_n$. Denoting the density function of $N(\mu, v_t^2)$ by $g(x | v_t)$, the likelihood of the data is simply the product $g(x_1 | v_1) g(x_2 | v_2) \ldots g(x_n | v_n)$. Maximum likelihood estimates are given in Section 3.10. Their availability is a considerable advantage over the models given in Section 3.5. However, the models presented in this section have very complicated unconditional distributions and it is difficult to establish conditions for stationarity and then to find the moments of the X_t.

By Section 4.4 we will have described enough results to compare the models of this section with those introduced in the previous section: it will then be concluded that the product processes of Section 3.5 are the better models.

Caused by past squared returns

Engle defines a zero-mean, ARCH(p) process, $\{X_t\}$, by

$$X_t = \left\{ \alpha_0 + \sum_{i=1}^{p} \alpha_i X_{t-i}^2 \right\}^{1/2} U_t \tag{3.6.2}$$

there being $p + 1$ non-negative parameters α_i, with $\alpha_0 > 0$ and $\{U_t\}$ Gaussian white noise, with $U_t \sim N(0,1)$. The acronym ARCH refers to autoregressive conditional heteroscedasticity. A logical extension of (3.6.2) is given by replacing X_t by $X_t - \mu$ for all times t, to give an ARCH(p) process having constant mean $E[X_t] = \mu$.

Consider the process when p is 1. Then,

$$X_t - \mu = \{\alpha_0 + \alpha_1(X_{t-1} - \mu)^2\}^{1/2} U_t$$

and

$$\text{var}(X_t \mid x_{t-1}) = \alpha_0 + \alpha_1(x_{t-1} - \mu)^2. \tag{3.6.3}$$

Large deviations of x_{t-1} from the mean μ then cause a large variance for the next day. The process is stationary with finite variance if, and only if, $\alpha_1 < 1$. The unconditional variance is then $\alpha_0/(1 - \alpha_1)$. The fourth moment is finite if $3\alpha_1^2 < 1$ and then the kurtosis is $k_X = 3(1 - \alpha_1^2)/(1 - 3\alpha_1^2)$, which exceeds 3 for all $\alpha_1 > 0$. For the non-trivial case $\alpha_1 > 0$, there will always be some integer j for which $E[X_t^{2(j+k)}]$ is infinite for all integers $k \geqslant 0$ and so these moments do not exist (Engle, 1982, p. 992). The series of squares $S_t = (X_t - \mu)^2$ and realized values $s_t = (x_t - \mu)^2$ satisfy

$$E[S_t \mid s_{t-1}] = \alpha_0 + \alpha_1 s_{t-1},$$

using (3.6.3). Now, a stationary AR(1) process defined by $A_t = \alpha_0 + \alpha_1 A_{t-1} + U_t$ has $E[A_t \mid a_{t-1}] = \alpha_0 + \alpha_1 a_{t-1}$ and autocorrelations α_1^τ (Section 1.9). This suggests $\{S_t\}$ also has autocorrelations α_1^τ, providing the variance of S_t exists, i.e. $3\alpha_1^2 < 1$. This result is proved at the end of the chapter, in Appendix 3(A).

For a general ARCH(p) process, $\{X_t\}$, define an associated AR(p) process by

$$A_t = \sum_{i=1}^{p} \alpha_i A_{t-i} + U_t.$$

The same innovation U_t is used to construct both X_t and A_t. Then, $\{X_t\}$ is stationary if, and only if, $\{A_t\}$ is stationary and then

$$\text{var}(X_t) = \alpha_0/(1 - \{\alpha_1 + \alpha_2 + \cdots + \alpha_p\}),$$

see Engle (1982, Theorem 2). Assuming stationarity, let $\sigma_A^2 = \text{var}(A_t)$. Then it is shown in Appendix 3(A) that if the kurtosis exists it will equal $3/(3 - 2\sigma_A^2)$; it appears the kurtosis exists if $\sigma_A^2 < 1.5$. It is also shown in the appendix that $\{S_t\}$ and $\{A_t\}$ have the same autocorrelations, so $\rho_{\tau,S} = \rho_{\tau,A}$ for all τ, whenever the fourth moment of X_t is finite. This result provides a constructive method for finding the autocorrelations of the squares of a general ARCH process. It is not possible to derive the autocorrelations of $M_t = |X_t - \mu|$.

As $V_t^2 = \text{var}(X_t|X_{t-1}, \ldots)$ depends on $(X_{t-i} - \mu)^2 = V_{t-i}^2 U_{t-i}^2, 1 \leqslant i \leqslant p$, it follows that $\{V_t\}$ and $\{U_t\}$ are not stochastically independent. To prove this, let j be the least positive integer for which $\alpha_j > 0$. Then $E[V_t^2 U_{t-j}^2] - E[V_t^2]E[U_{t-j}^2]$ can be shown to equal $2\alpha_j E[V_t^2] \neq 0$, disproving stochastic independence because V_t and U_{t-j} are not independent random variables.

Caused by past absolute returns

The conditional variances of X_t need not be a simple linear function of past squared returns. Another plausible formulation is

$$X_t - \mu = \left\{ \alpha_0 + \sum_{i=1}^{p} \alpha_i |X_{t-i} - \mu| \right\} U_t \tag{3.6.4}$$

with $\alpha_0 > 0$ and all $\alpha_i \geqslant 0$. The mathematical properties of (3.6.4) are largely unknown. However, writing $M_t = |X_t - \mu|$, $m_t = |x_t - \mu|$ and $\delta = E[|U_t|]$, $E[M_t|m_{t-1}, \ldots, m_{t-p}]$ is $\alpha_0 + \delta \sum \alpha_i m_{t-i}$. This suggests that $\{M_t\}$ and its associated process $A_t = \delta \sum \alpha_i A_{t-i} + U_t$ have the same autocorrelations, when they exist. It is proved that $\rho_{\tau,M} = \rho_{\tau,A}$ in Appendix 3(A). The relevance of a formulation like (3.6.4), compared with (3.6.2), can be determined by calculating their respective likelihoods from observed data.

ARMACH models

An ARCH process $\{X_t\}$ constructed from strict white noise $\{U_t\}$ will always be uncorrelated whilst the derived processes $\{M_t\}$ and $\{S_t\}$ will have non-zero autocorrelations. These theoretical autocorrelations must be similar to observed autocorrelations if the process is to have any chance of being a satisfactory model for financial returns. We have just seen that either the $\rho_{\tau,S}$ or the $\rho_{\tau,M}$ are the autocorrelations of an AR(p) process when $\{X_t\}$ follows (3.6.2) or (3.6.4). The sample coefficients r_{τ,x^2}, $r_{\tau,s}$, and $r_{\tau,|x|}$ described in Section 2.10 are almost always positive and generally decay slowly as τ increases, but all the coefficients are fairly small. An AR(p) process cannot produce this behaviour for low p. However, the auto-correlations of a stationary ARMA(1,1) process

$$A_t - \phi A_{t-1} = U_t - \theta U_{t-1}, \qquad |\phi| < 1, \tag{3.6.5}$$

are $\rho_{\tau,A} = C\phi^\tau$, with $C = (1 - \theta\phi)(\phi - \theta)/\{\phi(1 - 2\theta\phi + \theta^2)\}$.

This follows from equation (1.9.13) with a replaced by ϕ and b by $-\theta$. Whenever $1 > C$, $\phi > 0$, it is possible to find a positive θ such that $\rho_{\tau,A} = C\phi^\tau$ and then $\phi > \theta$. Equation (3.6.5) can be rewritten as an AR(∞) process, cf. equation (1.9.11):

$$A_t = \sum_{i=1}^{\infty} \alpha_i A_{t-i} + U_t, \qquad \alpha_i = (\phi - \theta)\theta^{i-1} \qquad (i \geqslant 1).$$

Hence a plausible class of ARCH processes for returns, based on (3.6.2), is

$$X_t - \mu = \left\{ \alpha_0 + (\phi - \theta) \sum_{i=1}^{\infty} \theta^{i-1} (X_{t-i} - \mu)^2 \right\}^{1/2} U_t \tag{3.6.6}$$

for some ϕ and θ constrained by $1 > \phi > \theta > 0$. The constraint on ϕ ensures $\{X_t\}$ is stationary. It can be shown that X_t has finite kurtosis if $\phi^2 + 2(\theta - \phi)^2 < 1$. The kurtosis then equals $3(1 - \phi^2)/(1 - 3\phi^2 + 4\theta\phi - 2\theta^2)$ and $\rho_{\tau,S}$ exists and equals $C\phi^\tau$. More algebra shows that the conditional variances V_t^2 are a weighted combination of V_{t-1}^2, $(X_{t-1} - \mu)^2$ and $\sigma_X^2 = \text{var}(X_t) = \alpha_0/\{1 - (\alpha_1 + \alpha_2 + \cdots)\}$:

$$V_t^2 = \theta V_{t-1}^2 + (\phi - \theta)(X_{t-1} - \mu)^2 + (1 - \phi)\sigma_X^2. \tag{3.6.7}$$

To find a plausible class of ARCH processes based upon (3.6.4), substitute $\delta\alpha_i = (\phi - \theta)\theta^{i-1}$ so:

$$X_t - \mu = \left\{ \alpha_0 + (\phi - \theta) \sum_{i=1}^{\infty} \theta^{i-1} |X_{t-i} - \mu|/\delta \right\} U_t. \tag{3.6.8}$$

The conditional standard deviation V_t is then a weighted combination of V_{t-1}, $|X_{t-1} - \mu|$ and $\mu_M = E[|X_t - \mu|] = \delta\alpha_0/\{1 - \delta(\alpha_1 + \alpha_2 + \ldots)\}$:

$$V_t = \theta V_{t-1} + (\phi - \theta)|X_{t-1} - \mu|/\delta + (1 - \phi)\mu_M/\delta. \tag{3.6.9}$$

Assuming $\{X_t\}$ is stationary, $\rho_{\tau,M} = C\phi^\tau$.

The models defined by (3.6.6) and (3.6.8) are constructed from an associated ARMA process and so it is natural to then call $\{X_t\}$ an ARMACH model. There are four parameters: the mean μ, a scale parameter (σ_X or μ_M) and the ARMA parameters ϕ and θ.

3.7 MODELLING AUTOCORRELATION AND VARIANCE CHANGES

All the models described in the previous sections of this chapter share two properties. Firstly, the realized conditional standard deviations v_t are not the same for all days t. Secondly, the standardized returns U_t, defined as the returns minus their mean and divided by their conditional standard deviations, form a strict white noise process. The first property causes autocorrelation among the squares $S_t = (X_t - \mu)^2$ and absolute deviations $M_t = |X_t - \mu|$, whilst the second ensures the X_t are uncorrelated.

There can, however, be low yet statistically significant correlation between returns on different days, a conclusion asserted by various researchers and confirmed by tests in Chapter 6. To model any such autocorrelation, the second property must be altered. Recall the general factorization of $X_t - \mu$:

$$X_t - \mu = V_t U_t \tag{3.7.1}$$

with several conditions on $\{U_t\}$ in all the models described so far, including these four: (a) the U_t have independent and identical distributions, (b) $E[U_t] = 0$, (c) var $(U_t) = 1$, and (d) U_t and V_t are independent. Stronger conditions replace (d) in Sections 3.5 and 3.6; by (d') $\{U_t\}$ and $\{V_t\}$ are stochastically independent in the former section and, in the latter section, (d'') $(U_t, U_{t+1}, \ldots, U_{t+i})$ is independent of $(V_t, V_{t-1}, \ldots, V_{t-j})$, for all $i, j \geqslant 0$ and t. To obtain non-zero correlation between X_t and $X_{t+\tau}$ for some positive lag τ, it is obviously necessary to change condition (a). It is convenient to retain the factorization (3.7.1), conditions (b), (c), and, whenever possible, (d).

Condition (a) must be changed to allow $\{U_t\}$ to be autocorrelated, yet $\{U_t\}$ ought not to be very different from a strict white noise process. One possibility is a linear process defined by a linear combination of variables from a zero-mean, strict white noise process $\{\varepsilon_t\}$, thus

$$\text{(a*):} \quad U_t = \sum_{i=0}^{\infty} \theta_i \varepsilon_{t-i} \qquad (3.7.2)$$

for constants θ_i (perhaps all zero for i greater than some integer q), with $\theta_0 = 1$. We should then expect $\theta_1, \theta_2, \ldots$ to be small numbers as we have already seen in Chapter 2 that there is very little, if any, autocorrelation among returns. In (3.7.2), let $T_t = U_t - \varepsilon_t$. Then $\{U_t\}$ is almost strict white noise because $\{U_t\}$ is the sum of the strict white noise process $\{\varepsilon_t\}$ and the autocorrelated process $\{T_t\}$ and the variance of T_t is much less than the variance of ε_t. In fact var (T_t)/var (ε_t) is the small number $\sum \theta_i^2$, summing over positive i.

Note that (a*) implies $X_t = \mu + V_t \varepsilon_t + V_t T_t$. The term $V_t \varepsilon_t$ is unpredictable, whereas the product $V_t T_t$ is the reaction on day t to information first known on previous days $t - i, i > 0$. High market activity, represented by a high realization v_t, will then imply a greater quantity of slowly interpreted information, represented by $v_t T_t$, than occurs during periods of low market activity. This does not appear unreasonable.

More generally than (a*), condition (a) can be replaced by

$$\text{(a**):} \quad \{U_t\} \text{ is almost strict white noise.} \qquad (3.7.3)$$

Statement (a**) means there is a decomposition $U_t = \varepsilon_t + T_t$ with $\{\varepsilon_t\}$ strict white noise and var (T_t)/var (ε_t) a small number for all t.

The revised conditions about $\{U_t\}$ enable modelling of an autocorrelated process $\{X_t\}$, having stochastic conditional standard deviation, without altering the interpretation of v_t. The realization v_t remains a measure of market activity on day t. There are doubtless other ways to model a process characterized by weak autocorrelation and changes in conditional standard deviation. The method outlined in this section appears to be satisfactory.

We retain the relationship $X_t - \mu = V_t U_t$. Given a realization v_t of V_t the conditional variance var $(X_t | v_t)$ will be exactly v_t^2 for some processes and very close to v_t^2 for others. We will always say when var $(X_t | v_t)$ is not exactly v_t^2: this occurs once in this section and also in Section 7.2 and is a consequence of v_t telling us something about the conditional distribution of U_t. Because var $(X_t | v_t)$ is always very close to v_t^2, we continue to call v_t the conditional standard deviation although on occasions it is just a very good approximation to the exact conditional standard deviation.

For stationary processes, the autocorrelations of $\{X_t\}$ and $\{U_t\}$ are not identical although they can be very similar. The results presented in earlier sections about the autocorrelations of $\{S_t\}$ and $\{M_t\}$ are no longer exact when $\{U_t\}$ is autocorrelated but they are excellent approximations. We now consider the consequences of autocorrelated U_t, separately for each of the variance models introduced in Sections 3.5 and 3.6.

Variances not caused by returns

For $\{V_t\}$ defined by a functional relationship $V_t = f(V_{t-1}, V_{t-2}, \ldots, \eta_t)$ and $\{U_t\}$ strict white noise, it was shown in Section 3.5 that it is possible to justify the assumption that $\{V_t\}$ and $\{U_t\}$ are stochastically independent. It is reasonable to retain this assumption when $\{U_t\}$ is almost, but not exactly, strict white noise. Then var $(X_t | v_t)$ is v_t^2.

Suppose both $\{V_t\}$ and $\{U_t\}$ are strictly stationary processes and, as before, all fourth order moments are finite. Applying the assumption of stochastic independence, var $(X_t) = E[V_t^2]$ and

$$E[(X_t - \mu)(X_{t+\tau} - \mu)] = E[V_t V_{t+\tau}]E[U_t U_{t+\tau}].$$

As U_t has unit variance, $E[U_t U_{t+\tau}]$ equals the autocorrelation $\rho_{\tau,U}$ and so

$$\rho_{\tau,X} = \rho_{\tau,U}E[V_t V_{t+\tau}]/E[V_t^2]. \tag{3.7.4}$$

Also

$$E[V_t V_{t+\tau}] = E[V_t]^2 + \rho_{\tau,V} \text{ var } (V_t)$$

for all τ, including $\tau = 0$, and thus it can be deduced from (3.7.4) that

$$\rho_{\tau,V} \leq \rho_{\tau,X}/\rho_{\tau,U} \leq 1. \tag{3.7.5}$$

It follows that $\rho_{\tau,X}$ and $\rho_{\tau,U}$ are very similar whenever the V_t are highly and positively autocorrelated.

In Section 3.5 the autocorrelations $\rho_{\tau,S}$ and $\rho_{\tau,M}$ were shown to be constants times ρ_{τ,V^2} and $\rho_{\tau,V}$ respectively (equations (3.5.4) and (3.5.5)), assuming $\{U_t\}$ was strict white noise. When the U_t are autocorrelated, $E[S_t] = E[V_t^2]$ and

$$E[S_t S_{t+\tau}] = E[V_t^2 V_{t+\tau}^2]E[U_t^2 U_{t+\tau}^2].$$

Let $k = E[U_t^4]$ so that var $(U_t^2) = k - 1$. Then,

$$E[U_t^2 U_{t+\tau}^2] = E[U_t^2]^2 + \text{cov }(U_t^2, U_{t+\tau}^2) = 1 + (k - 1)\rho_{\tau,U^2}.$$

Using these equations it can be deduced that cov $(S_t, S_{t+\tau})$ divided by var (S_t) is

$$\rho_{\tau,S} = \rho_{\tau,V^2}[\text{var }(V_t^2)/\text{var }(S_t)] + c_\tau \rho_{\tau,U^2} \qquad (3.7.6)$$

with $c_\tau = (k - 1)E[V_t^2 V_{t+\tau}^2]/\text{var }(S_t)$. As $0 < E[V_t^2 V_{t+\tau}^2] \leqslant E[V_t^4]$ and var $(S_t) \geqslant (k - 1)E[V_t^4]$ it follows that $0 < c_\tau \leqslant 1$. The upper bound can be attained if every V_t equals the same constant with certainty.

The additional term $c_\tau \rho_{\tau,U^2}$ in equation (3.7.6) is negligible when series of financial returns are modelled. For example, if $\{U_t\}$ is Gaussian then $\rho_{\tau,U^2} = \rho_{\tau,U}^2$ (Granger and Newbold, 1976) which will be very small compared with ρ_{τ,V^2} and $\rho_{\tau,S}$. Empirical estimates will confirm this conclusion.

Using similar methods applied to $\{M_t\}$ it can be shown that

$$\rho_{\tau,M} = \delta^2 \rho_{\tau,V}[\text{var }(V_t)/\text{var }(M_t)] + d_\tau \rho_{\tau,|U|} \qquad (3.7.7)$$

with $0 < d_\tau = (1 - \delta^2)E[V_t V_{t+\tau}]/\text{var }(M_t) \leqslant 1$. The extra term due to autocorrelations among the U_t is again negligible if $\{U_t\}$ is almost strict white noise.

Variances caused by returns

In Section 3.6, $X_t - \mu$ was modelled by the product of a strict white noise variable U_t and a conditional standard deviation determined by past returns $V_t = f(X_{t-1}, X_{t-2}, \ldots)$. The process $\{U_t\}$ can be redefined as almost strict white noise in several ways. Unfortunately, none of them provide a complete set of mathematical results. The most convenient way to allow the X_t and U_t to be autocorrelated is to suppose

$$\sum_{i=0}^{\infty} \phi_i(X_{t-i} - \mu) = V_t \varepsilon_t \quad \text{or} \quad X_t - \mu = \sum_{i=0}^{\infty} \theta_i V_{t-i} \varepsilon_{t-i}$$

for constants ϕ_i, θ_i ($\phi_0 = \theta_0 = 1$), $\{\varepsilon_t\}$ zero-mean strict white noise, and $V_t = f(X_{t-1}, X_{t-2}, \ldots)$ as before. The moving-average representation can be rearranged as

$$X_t - \mu = V_t U_t, \quad U_t = \varepsilon_t + \sum_{i=1}^{\infty} \theta_i \varepsilon_{t-i}(V_{t-i}/V_t). \qquad (3.7.8)$$

Then $\{U_t\}$ is almost strict white noise assuming, as we do, that $\Sigma \ \theta_i^2$ is small, summing over positive i. We retain the assumption that U_t has unit variance and then ε_t has variance slightly less than one. Given a past history

$I_{t-1} = \{x_{t-i}, \text{ all } i > 0\}$, every product inside the summation term of (3.7.8) can be calculated and consequently var $(X_t|I_{t-1}) = \text{var } (X_t|v_t) = v_t^2 \text{ var } (\varepsilon_t)$. This means v_t is now a constant times the conditional standard deviation.

The autocorrelations of $\{X_t\}$ can be found by defining $\varepsilon_t' = \varepsilon_t V_t$ and noting that $\{\varepsilon_t'\}$ is white noise with $X_t - \mu = \Sigma \; \theta_i \varepsilon_{t-i}'$, so that

$$\rho_{\tau,X} = \sum_{i=0}^{\infty} \theta_i \theta_{i+\tau} \Big/ \sum_{i=0}^{\infty} \theta_i^2. \tag{3.7.9}$$

When the function f is sufficiently symmetric in past innovations ε to make $\pi_{t,i} = \varepsilon_t V_t/V_{t+i}$ and $\pi_{t+\tau,j} = \varepsilon_{t+\tau} V_{t+\tau}/V_{t+\tau+j}$ uncorrelated for all $i, j, \tau > 0$, the autocorrelations of $\{U_t\}$ are

$$\rho_{\tau,U} = \sum_{i=0}^{\infty} \theta_i \theta_{i+\tau} E[\varepsilon_{t-i}^2 V_{t-i}^2/(V_t V_{t+\tau})]. \tag{3.7.10}$$

The expectation in (3.7.10) cannot be simplified for realistic functions f. Nevertheless, it is seen that $\rho_{\tau,X}$ and $\rho_{\tau,U}$ will be similar if the V_t are highly and positively autocorrelated.

It is impossible to calculate the autocorrelations of either $\{S_t\}$ or $\{M_t\}$ when the U_t are autocorrelated, even for elementary ARCH specifications. However, these autocorrelations are almost the same as those of the uncorrelated process obtained by setting $\theta_i = 0$ for all $i > 0$. For example, if v_t^2 is a linear function of p terms $(x_{t-i} - \mu)^2$,

$$E[S_t|I_{t-1}] = \left(\alpha_0 + \sum_{i=1}^{p} \alpha_i s_{t-i}\right) E[U_t^2|I_{t-1}].$$

As $\{U_t\}$ is almost strict white noise and var $(U_t) = 1$, it follows that $E[U_t^2|I_{t-1}]$ is always close to 1 and hence the constants θ_i are unimportant in the calculation of the autocorrelations $\rho_{\tau,S}$.

3.8   PARAMETER ESTIMATION FOR VARIANCE MODELS

It will be assumed in the rest of this chapter that all stochastic processes are stationary. Models can then be fitted and their parameters estimated. The stationarity assumption will be assessed primarily in Chapter 4, by comparing forecasts based on stationary models with forecasts expected to do well for non-stationary processes.

A realistic stationary model for the conditional standard deviations $\{V_t\}$ will have at least three parameters, two to specify the mean and variance of V_t and at least one to model the autocorrelations. Parameters can be estimated by matching theoretical and sample moments. Let $\mu_V = E[V_t]$, $\sigma_V^2 = \text{var } (V_t)$ and $\delta = E[|U_t|]$. Then, by making our usual assumption that V_t and U_t are independent,

$$E[M_t] = E[V_t]E[|U_t|] = \mu_V \delta \tag{3.8.1}$$

and $E[S_t] = E[V_t^2]E[U_t^2] = \mu_V^2 + \sigma_V^2.$

From data $\{x_1, x_2, \ldots, x_n\}$, the sample averages

$$\bar{x} = \frac{1}{n} \sum_{t=1}^{n} x_t, \quad \bar{m} = \frac{1}{n} \sum_{t=1}^{n} |x_t - \bar{x}| \quad \text{and} \quad \bar{s} = \frac{1}{n} \sum_{t=1}^{n} (x_t - \bar{x})^2$$

can be calculated and hence the estimates

$$\hat{\mu}_V = \bar{m}/\delta, \quad \hat{\sigma}_V^2 = \bar{s} - (\bar{m}/\delta)^2 \tag{3.8.2}$$

are provided by using $\bar{m}$ and $\bar{s}$ to estimate $E[M_t]$ and $E[S_t]$ respectively. It should be noted that estimates for the process $\{V_t\}$ require the distribution of U_t to be known or assumed. In particular, δ is needed in the equations (3.8.2). Applying our usual assumption that $U_t \sim N(0,1)$, δ is approximately 0.798. The estimates of μ_V and σ_V are given in Table 3.2, for all the forty time series.

Many series have low values for the ratio $\hat{\mu}_V/\hat{\sigma}_V$ showing that V_t does not have a normal distribution. For example, if $\mu_V/\sigma_V = 1.65$ and V_t is normal then 5 per cent of the observations v_t are expected to be negative and this is unacceptable as V_t models a positive quantity. Clearly V_t should have a right-skewed distribution.

To estimate an autocorrelation model for $\{V_t\}$ more assumptions are needed. We consider the product and ARCH processes separately.

3.9   PARAMETER ESTIMATES FOR PRODUCT PROCESSES

Suppose, as in Section 3.5, that $\{X_t\}$ is a product process and $\log (V_t) \sim N(\alpha, \beta^2)$. The parameters α and β cannot be estimated by the method of maximum likelihood because the multivariate density of $X_1, X_2, \ldots, X_n$ cannot be evaluated. Simpler methods are necessary; the methods described are the only ones at present available. As $E[V_t] = \exp(\alpha + \frac{1}{2}\beta^2)$ and $E[V_t^2] = \exp(2\alpha + 2\beta^2)$,

$$\beta^2 = \log \{E[V_t^2]/E[V_t]^2\} = \log \{(\mu_V^2 + \sigma_V^2)/\mu_V^2\}.$$

This suggests estimating β^2 by substituting $\hat{\mu}_V$ and $\hat{\sigma}_V$ for μ_V and σ_V. Then, from (3.8.2),

$$\hat{\beta}^2 = \log \{\delta^2 \bar{s}/\bar{m}^2\}. \tag{3.9.1}$$

Also, $\alpha = \log \{E[V_t]^2/\sqrt{E[V_t^2]}\}$ and again replacing μ_V and σ_V by their estimates gives

$$\hat{\alpha} = \log \{\bar{m}^2/(\delta^2\sqrt{\bar{s}})\}. \tag{3.9.2}$$

The estimates $\hat{\alpha}$ and $\hat{\beta}$ are presented in Table 3.2.

Table 3.2 Parameter estimates for variance models

	$\hat{\mu}_V$	$\hat{\sigma}_V$	$\hat{\alpha}$	$\hat{\beta}$
Spot series				
Allied	0.0167	0.0080	−4.197	0.454
Alcoa	0.0158	0.0076	−4.249	0.457
Am. Can	0.0117	0.0054	−4.539	0.438
AT and T	0.0092	0.0041	−4.778	0.425
Am. Brands	0.0121	0.0058	−4.518	0.454
Anaconda	0.0201	0.0122	−4.064	0.560
Bethlehem	0.0157	0.0067	−4.236	0.407
Chrysler	0.0221	0.0105	−3.917	0.453
Dupont	0.0125	0.0050	−4.456	0.383
Kodak	0.0145	0.0059	−4.309	0.393
G. Electric	0.0141	0.0061	−4.344	0.413
G. Food	0.0139	0.0062	−4.371	0.430
G. Motors	0.0126	0.0059	−4.472	0.445
G. Telephone	0.0159	0.0061	−4.211	0.371
Harvester	0.0150	0.0067	−4.287	0.424
FT 30	0.0128	0.0019	−4.371	0.147
Gold	0.0157	0.0098	−4.320	0.575
Silver	0.0158	0.0104	−4.328	0.599
Copper	0.0158	0.0097	−4.311	0.566
Lead	0.0171	0.0109	−4.239	0.582
Tin	0.0105	0.0073	−4.755	0.629
Zinc	0.0158	0.0129	−4.400	0.713
£/$	0.0050	0.0032	−5.479	0.595
Futures series				
Corn (12)	0.0108	0.0072	−4.706	0.604
Corn (6)	0.0101	0.0068	−4.787	0.614
Corn (3)	0.0101	0.0068	−4.780	0.614
Cocoa (12)	0.0168	0.0087	−4.208	0.490
Cocoa (6)	0.0177	0.0082	−4.132	0.440
Cocoa (3)	0.0183	0.0087	−4.101	0.452
Coffee (12)	0.0170	0.0148	−4.356	0.751
Coffee (6)	0.0163	0.0137	−4.385	0.733
Coffee (3)	0.0165	0.0143	−4.383	0.748
Sugar (12)	0.0197	0.0126	−4.099	0.586
Sugar (6)	0.0192	0.0117	−4.113	0.561
Sugar (3)	0.0195	0.0121	−4.101	0.571
Wool (12)	0.0092	0.0095	−5.049	0.851
£/$ (6)	0.0052	0.0030	−5.398	0.530
DM/$ (6)	0.0054	0.0029	−5.322	0.454
SF/$ (6)	0.0068	0.0027	−5.072	0.390
T-bond	0.0100	0.0016	−4.621	0.160

Any two sample moments can be used to estimate α and β. The selection of $\bar{m}$ and $\bar{s}$ may appear arbitrary but it has the advantages of analytic convenience and avoiding high order moments. An alternative would be to calculate the second and fourth moments, then estimate β using the sample kurtosis and equation (3.5.6). Afterwards, using the estimate of β, α can be estimated by matching theoretical and sample second moments. However, kurtosis estimates are relatively inaccurate so it is preferable to use lower order moments. The recommended estimates $\hat{\alpha}, \hat{\beta}$ are non-linear functions of unbiased estimates $\bar{m}, \bar{s}$ and hence $\hat{\alpha}$ and $\hat{\beta}$ could be biased, although any bias will be small for large samples.

Given $\hat{\alpha}$ and $\hat{\beta}$, the distribution of V_t is estimated to have median value $\exp(\hat{\alpha})$ with 95 per cent of the observed v_t predicted to be between $\exp(\hat{\alpha} - 1.96\hat{\beta})$ and $\exp(\hat{\alpha} + 1.96\hat{\beta})$. For the longest series, the sugar futures returns (12 months used per contract), $\hat{\alpha} = -4.099$, $\hat{\beta} = 0.586$ and the 95 per cent interval is from 0.0053 to 0.0523 with median at 0.0166.

Lognormal AR(1)

The autocorrelations of the process $\{\log(V_t)\}$ will depend on certain parameters. In Section 3.5 it was claimed that the simplest and most appropriate stationary model for the logarithms of the V_t is the AR(1) process, which has autocorrelations ϕ^τ. We will now consider methods for estimating ϕ. At the present time it does not seem helpful or necessary to investigate processes with more parameters than the AR(1). However, the methods illustrated for AR(1) could be applied to higher-order auto-regressive processes, although much more computer time would be required.

A set of sample autocorrelations $r_{\tau,s}, r_{\tau,m}$ for several τ, say lags 1 to K, provides information useful for estimating ϕ. From (3.7.6) and (3.7.7) it can be seen that the autocorrelations of $\{U_t^2\}$ and $\{|U_t|\}$ make negligible contributions to $\rho_{\tau,s}$ and $\rho_{\tau,M}$. It will therefore be assumed that $\{U_t\}$ is strict white noise when estimating ϕ. Then

$$\rho_{\tau,S} = A(\beta)\rho_{\tau,V^2} \quad \text{and} \quad \rho_{\tau,M} = B(\beta)\rho_{\tau,V} \tag{3.9.3}$$

with $A(\beta)$ and $B(\beta)$ defined by (3.5.7) and (3.5.8). All the autocorrelations in (3.9.3) are functions of β and ϕ. This is emphasized by using the notation $\rho_{\tau,V^2} = \rho(\tau, V^2, \beta, \phi)$ and $\rho_{\tau,V} = \rho(\tau, V, \beta, \phi)$.

Three methods for estimating ϕ have been evaluated. All of them seek an accurate match between sample and theoretical autocorrelations. Sample autocorrelations are calculated as

$$r'_{\tau,s} = n/(n - k\tau) \sum_{t=1}^{n-\tau} (s_t - \bar{s})(s_{t+\tau} - \bar{s}) \Big/ \sum_{t=1}^{n} (s_t - \bar{s})^2 \tag{3.9.4}$$

and $r'_{\tau,m}$ is defined similarly, k being either 1 for a spot series or the number of contracts used for a futures series. The factor $n/(n - k\tau)$ is included to reduce bias in the estimates; remember, from Section 2.9, that the numerator summation in (3.9.4) excludes those times t for which time $t + \tau$ refers to a different contract. The discrepancies between sample and theoretical autocorrelations will be measured by statistics based on

$$n \sum_{\tau=1}^{K} [r'_{\tau,s} - \rho_{\tau,S}]^2 \quad \text{and} \quad n \sum_{\tau=1}^{K} [r'_{\tau,m} - \rho_{\tau,M}]^2$$

for some number of lags K. The number of returns n is included in order to simplify comparisons between series, since the expected magnitude of a term like $(r'_{\tau,s} - \rho_{\tau,S})^2$ is the variance of an autocorrelation coefficient and so proportional to $1/n$ when ϕ is estimated perfectly.

The methods are now described. It will be argued from the empirical results that the third method is best.

Method 1
The first method substitutes the estimate $\hat{\beta}$, given by (3.9.1), for β and then chooses ϕ to minimize either

$$F_1(\phi) = n \sum_{\tau=1}^{K} [r'_{\tau,s} - A(\hat{\beta})\rho(\tau, V^2, \hat{\beta}, \phi)]^2$$

or

$$F_2(\phi) = n \sum_{\tau=1}^{K} [r'_{\tau,m} - B(\hat{\beta})\rho(\tau, V, \hat{\beta}, \phi)]^2.$$

The optimizations can be performed by calculating these objective functions for various ϕ. I have calculated F_1 and F_2 for $\phi = 0, 0.01, 0.02, \ldots, 0.5,$ $0.505, 0.51, \ldots, 0.9, 0.901, 0.902, \ldots, 0.995$. In all the calculations K was set at 50.

Method 2
A second method is intended to avoid problems when $\hat{\beta}$ is a poor estimate and so the estimated constants $A(\hat{\beta})$ and $B(\hat{\beta})$ are inappropriate. Both β and ϕ are estimated, by minimizing

$$F_3(\beta, \phi) = n \sum [r'_{\tau,s} - A(\beta)\rho(\tau, V^2, \beta, \phi)]^2$$

or

$$F_4(\beta, \phi) = n \sum [r'_{\tau,m} - B(\beta)\rho(\tau, V, \beta, \phi)]^2.$$

These optimizations were performed using an iterative technique which it is not necessary to describe. It suffices to note that considerable computer time was needed to minimize either F_3 or F_4.

Method 3

The optimizations required by the second method can be simplified by noting the approximations

$$\rho(\tau, V, \beta, \phi) \simeq \rho(\tau, V^2, \beta, \phi) \simeq \phi^\tau$$

discussed earlier in Section 3.5. The approximations are best for small values of β. A third method merely minimizes

$$F_5(A', \phi) = n \sum [r'_{\tau,s} - A'\phi^\tau]^2$$

or

$$F_6(B', \phi) = n \sum [r'_{\tau,m} - B'\phi^\tau]^2.$$

These minimizations are straightforward. For example, the best A' when ϕ equals ϕ_0 is, using calculus, $\sum r'_{\tau,s} \phi_0^\tau / \sum \phi_0^{2\tau}$. The possible values considered for ϕ were identical to those considered for the first method.

   Given the estimates $\hat{A}$ and $\hat{\phi}$ minimizing F_5, another estimate of β, denoted by $\hat{\beta}_s$, is given by solving $A(\hat{\beta}_s) = \hat{A}$; in fact

$$\hat{\beta}_s = 0.5 \{ \log [(1 - \hat{A})/(1 - 3\hat{A})] \}^{1/2}.$$

Likewise, if $\hat{B}$ and $\hat{\phi}$ minimize F_6, an implied estimate $\hat{\beta}_m$ solves $B(\hat{\beta}_m) = \hat{B}$ to give

$$\hat{\beta}_m = \{ \log [2(1 - \hat{B})/(2 - \pi\hat{B})] \}^{1/2} \}. \qquad (3.9.5)$$

Results

The second and third methods give almost identical estimates of ϕ. On average, the absolute difference between the two estimates derived from the same set of sample autocorrelations is less than 0.001. Consequently, no further results are given for the second method.

   When the minimum values of F_1 are compared with the minimum values of F_5 it is found that the minima for the third method are less than those for the first method, often considerably so. The same conclusion holds when the minima of F_2 and F_6 are compared. Of course, the third method minimizes over an additional parameter but the improvement thereby obtained does appear to be significant. The third method is therefore preferred and a further reason for preferring it will be demonstrated in Chapter 4.

   Minimizing either F_5 or F_6 gives an estimate $\hat{\phi}$ of ϕ by using the preferred method. The minimum value of F_6 is less than the corresponding minimum value of F_5 for 37 of the 40 series. Thus the $r_{\tau,m}$ would appear to have smaller standard errors than the $r_{\tau,s}$ even though the $r_{\tau,m}$ are generally larger than the $r_{\tau,s}$. It is therefore best to use the $r_{\tau,m}$ to estimate ϕ by minimizing F_6.

   Table 3.3 summarizes the estimates $\hat{B}$ and $\hat{\phi}$ obtained by minimizing

Table 3.3   Estimates for a product process

	By minimizing F_6			Minimum values of	
	$\hat{B}$	$\hat{\beta}_m$	$\hat{\phi}$	F_6	F_2
Spot series					
Allied	0.113	0.275	0.981	59.5	266.4
Alcoa	0.117	0.281	0.980	85.3	294.4
Am. Can	0.076	0.219	0.977	51.2	227.9
AT and T	0.109	0.268	0.914	86.5	111.3
Am. Brands	0.120	0.285	0.927	84.8	114.7
Anaconda	0.091	0.243	0.958	47.6	167.8
Bethlehem	0.073	0.215	0.961	57.3	128.1
Chrysler	0.086	0.234	0.984	57.0	302.0
Dupont	0.158	0.337	0.984	56.5	79.6
Kodak	0.147	0.322	0.983	78.3	128.7
G. Electric	0.183	0.370	0.989	35.9	59.6
G. Food	0.111	0.272	0.987	77.2	283.0
G. Motors	0.118	0.281	0.987	56.9	294.3
G. Telephone	0.098	0.253	0.991	43.9	185.2
Harvester	0.101	0.257	0.979	68.8	247.8
FT 30	0.125	0.292	0.976	45.1	231.4
Gold	0.280	0.501	0.983	130.3	153.6
Silver	0.322	0.562	0.985	62.5	66.0
Copper	0.212	0.408	0.985	91.2	399.9
Lead	0.264	0.478	0.979	81.2	167.7
Tin	0.305	0.537	0.981	126.1	176.8
Zinc	0.357	0.617	0.989	61.9	125.8
£/$	0.197	0.388	0.987	73.2	323.8
Futures series					
Corn (12)	0.383	0.661	0.994	38.6	166.6
Corn (6)	0.413	0.716	0.993	46.9	349.4
Corn (3)	0.463	0.832	0.995	557.7	2449.9
Cocoa (12)	0.244	0.451	0.984	97.5	111.1
Cocoa (6)	0.204	0.397	0.987	117.4	131.9
Cocoa (3)	0.164	0.345	0.989	265.2	355.5
Coffee (12)	0.278	0.498	0.988	121.2	536.9
Coffee (6)	0.298	0.527	0.988	141.7	402.5
Coffee (3)	0.286	0.510	0.994	325.1	697.4
Sugar (12)	0.318	0.556	0.984	65.6	71.5
Sugar (6)	0.290	0.515	0.986	87.7	120.4
Sugar (3)	0.296	0.523	0.979	102.7	130.6
Wool (12)	0.442	0.775	0.990	64.2	87.5
£/$ (6)	0.166	0.347	0.987	76.1	311.4
DM/$ (6)	0.198	0.390	0.985	74.3	105.3
SF/$ (6)	0.210	0.406	0.989	40.4	43.4
T-bond	0.066	0.203	0.995	58.7	70.5

$F_6(B', \phi)$. The table presents $\hat{B}$, the implied estimate $\hat{\beta}_m$, then $\hat{\phi}$, $F_6(\hat{B}, \hat{\phi})$ and, for comparison, the minimum value of $F_2(\phi)$. It can be seen that the least estimate $\hat{\phi}$ for the 23 spot series is 0.914, whilst for the 17 futures series the least $\hat{\phi}$ is 0.979. The median spot estimate is 0.983, the futures median is 0.988. Thus it is clear that either ϕ is nearly 1 when the model is appropriate or the model is inadequate with the process $\{\log (V_t)\}$ probably non-stationary. We will conclude our discussion of the stationarity or otherwise of the conditional standard deviations in Chapter 4. The estimates for futures series taking three months' data from each contract are inaccurate because there are few terms in the numerator of $r_{\tau,m}$ when τ is near the maximum lag used, namely 50 trading days.

A comparison of the two estimates of β, i.e. $\hat{\beta}$ given by (3.9.1) and $\hat{\beta}_m$ given by (3.9.5), shows that $\hat{\beta}_m$ is usually less than $\hat{\beta}$ and the differences are not negligible. It is possible that at least one of the estimates is biased or the assumed model is inaccurate, for example the distribution of the U_t could be slightly non-normal.

Figure 3.1 shows the actual autocorrelations $r'_{\tau,m}$ and the fitted approximation to the theoretical autocorrelations, i.e. $\hat{B}\hat{\phi}^\tau$, for the longest of the 40 series. These sugar returns have $F_6(\hat{B}, \hat{\phi}) = 65.6$ and the fitted curve appears to fit well. A similar graph was presented in Taylor (1982a) based upon the $r_{\tau,s}$ for a slightly shorter sugar series. The article also considered a more detailed model in which $\alpha = E[\log (V_t)]$ can vary from contract to contract.

3.10 PARAMETER ESTIMATES FOR ARMACH PROCESSES

Initially consider an uncorrelated, finite-order, ARCH process, as defined in Section 3.6, so V_t is a function of $X_{t-i} - \mu$ $(1 \leqslant i \leqslant p)$ and $p + 1$ parameters α_i $(0 \leqslant i \leqslant p)$. Denote by ω the set of parameters $\mu, \alpha_0, \alpha_1, \ldots, \alpha_p$. The likelihood function for n observed returns is

$$L(x_1, x_2, \ldots, x_n | \omega) = f(x_1 | \omega) f(x_2 | I_1, \omega) \ldots f(x_n | I_{n-1}, \omega)$$

with $f(x_t | I_{t-1}, \omega)$ denoting the conditional density of X_t given the previous observations $I_{t-1} = \{x_1, x_2, \ldots, x_{t-1}\}$ and the parameter vector ω. These conditional densities can be described for $t > p$ by finding v_t and then using the appropriate normal density:

$$f(x_t | I_{t-1}, \omega) = f(x_t | v_t) = \{\sqrt{(2\pi)} v_t\}^{-1} \exp [-\tfrac{1}{2}(x_t - \mu)^2 / v_t^2].$$

The v_t depend on ω. The maximum likelihood estimate $\hat{\omega}$, for observations $p + 1$ to n, maximizes

$$L_p(\omega) = \prod_{t=p+1}^{n} f(x_t | I_{t-1}, \omega)$$

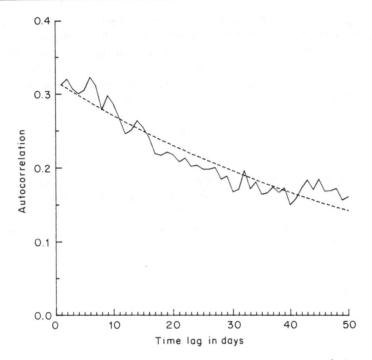

Figure 3.1 Actual (solid curve) and fitted (dashed curve) autocorrelations for the absolute returns when a product process is estimated from the longest sugar futures series

or, equivalently, maximizes

$$\log L_p(\omega) = -\tfrac{1}{2}(n - p) \log (2\pi) - \sum_{t=p+1}^{n} \log (v_t)$$

$$- \tfrac{1}{2} \sum_{t=p+1}^{n} (x_t^2 - \mu)^2 / v_t. \tag{3.10.1}$$

If the process is autocorrelated, equation (3.10.1) provides an acceptable approximation to the likelihood function, so it will be assumed the process is uncorrelated when estimating ω.

At the end of Section 3.6 it was proposed that a suitable ARCH process could be defined by $\alpha_{i+1} = \theta(\alpha_i)$ for all $i > 0$. There are then few parameters in the resulting, infinite-order process, called an ARMACH process. Two possible specifications of an ARMACH process are summarized by equations (3.6.7) and (3.6.9). Both are considered. For either specification we need to estimate μ, a scale parameter ($E[S_t]$ or $E[M_t]$), θ, and a parameter ϕ; recall ϕ now denotes either $\rho_{\tau+1,S}/\rho_{\tau,S}$ or $\rho_{\tau+1,M}/\rho_{\tau,M}$ for all $\tau > 0$.

The following estimation procedure for spot series is recommended as being practical and based on the likelihood function. First, estimate μ by $\bar{x}$ and the scale parameter by $\bar{s}$ or $\bar{m}$ as appropriate. Second, define an estimate $\hat{v}_1$ of v_1, by either $v_1 = \sqrt{\bar{s}}$ or $\hat{v}_1 = \bar{m}/\delta$, depending on the specification chosen. Then, for a particular ϕ and θ, use a recursive equation, (3.6.7) or (3.6.9), to obtain $\hat{v}_t$ ($2 \leqslant t \leqslant n$). This is done by replacing V_t by $\hat{v}_t$, $X_{t-1} - \mu$ by $x_{t-1} - \bar{x}$, σ_X^2 by $\bar{s}$ and μ_M by $\bar{m}$ in the recursive equations. The error $v_t - \hat{v}_t$ will be negligible for large enough t, i.e. the initial error $v_1 - \hat{v}_1$ will no longer be important. Thus the function given by (3.10.1) can be maximized for some integer p, with $\hat{v}_t$ replacing v_t. This optimization provides estimates $\hat{\phi}$ and $\hat{\theta}$, expected to be close to exact maximum likelihood estimates. The choice $p = 20$ has been made for all the calculations.

Futures series require a more complicated procedure. Suppose the series uses returns from k contracts, ending on day T_i for contract i and so beginning on day $T_i + 1$ for contract $i + 1$. For the first contract, v_{21} can be obtained by applying the method for spot series. For subsequent contracts, we need a method for defining $\hat{v}_t$ when $t = T_{i-1} + 1$ and $2 \leqslant i \leqslant k$. Two methods have been tried; each uses 20 returns on contract i from times $T_{i-1} - 19$ to T_{i-1} inclusive. Method A sets $\hat{v}_t$ at time $t = T_{i-1} - 19$ for contract i equal to the value of $\hat{v}_t$ at the identical time for contract $i - 1$. This method then uses (3.6.7) or (3.6.9) as before, with $\bar{s}$ and $\bar{m}$ being the usual averages over all times from 1 to n inclusive. Method B treats each contract separately. Contract i provides averages $\bar{s}_i$ and $\bar{m}_i$ by averaging over times $T_{i-1} - 19$ to T_i inclusive and these averages respectively replace σ_X^2 in (3.6.7) and μ_M in (3.6.9). At time $t = T_{i-1} - 19$ the initial value for contract i is either $\hat{v}_t = \sqrt{s_i}$ or $\bar{m}_i/\delta$, depending on the specification of the ARMACH process. Method A assumes that at any moment in time all contracts have similar conditional standard deviations, whilst method B avoids this assumption. For either method the first return from contract i appearing in (3.10.1) has $t = 21$ when $i = 1$ and $t = T_{i-1} + 1$ when $i \geqslant 2$ with the last return from contract i appearing in (3.10.1) having $t = T_i$.

Results

The ARMACH specification based on (3.6.6) and (3.6.7) has $\rho_{\tau,S} = C\phi^\tau$ whilst the alternative specification, (3.6.8) and (3.6.9), has $\rho_{\tau,M} = C\phi^\tau$ and, in each case, C is a function of ϕ and θ:

$$C = (1 - \theta\phi)(\phi - \theta)/\{\phi(1 - 2\theta\phi + \theta^2)\}. \tag{3.10.2}$$

The log-likelihood, (3.10.1), can be maximized either over $1 > C > 0$,

$1 > \phi > 0$ or over $1 > \phi > \theta > 0$ and the former choice is made here. Given C and ϕ it is possible to obtain θ by rewriting (3.10.2) as

$$\theta^2 - D\theta + 1 = 0, \quad D = \{1 + \phi^2(1 - 2C)\}/\{\phi(1 - C)\}, \quad (3.10.3)$$

and then the relevant solution is $\theta = \{D - \sqrt{(D^2 - 4)}\}/2$, taking the positive square root of $D^2 - 4$.

A search routine was used to seek the numbers $\hat{C}$ and $\hat{\phi}$ maximizing (3.10.1). Estimates accurate to at least two decimal places were sought. When necessary a constraint $\phi \leqslant 0.995$ was applied. Considerable computer time was needed for the optimizations.

Table 3.4 presents estimates $\hat{C}$, $\hat{\phi}$, and $\hat{\theta}$ for the ARMACH specification based on past squared returns. This specification generally has a far higher maximum likelihood than the alternative specification based on absolute returns. The final column of Table 3.4 lists the maximum log-likelihood for the squares specification minus the maximum for the alternative specification. All the futures estimates are for method A, shown in Chapter 4 to be preferable to method B.

Several estimates $\hat{\phi}$ equal the upper limit of 0.995 and many $\hat{C}$ are suspiciously high, as $\hat{C}\hat{\phi}^\tau$ far exceeds the sample autocorrelations $r_{\tau,s}$. Such estimates cast considerable doubt upon the general descriptive value of models based on the ARCH concept.

3.11 SUMMARY

The non-trivial autocorrelation found in series of absolute returns and series of squared returns can be explained by changes in either the variances or conditional variances of the returns. Changes in the level of market activity are probably the cause of the variance changes.

Two contrasting models for returns incorporating changes in conditional variances have been discussed, firstly product processes and secondly ARCH processes. There is sufficient autocorrelation among the absolute and squared returns to estimate the parameters of special versions of these stationary models, i.e. the lognormal, AR(1), product process and the ARMACH processes. Investigations of stationarity and the selection of a best stationary model (when appropriate) require more empirical results and these follow in the next chapter. The parameter estimates show that any successful stationary model must have very high autocorrelation in the series of conditional standard deviations.

Table 3.4   Estimates for ARMACH models

	Based on process S			Difference in log-likelihood
	$\hat{C}$	$\hat{\phi}$	$\hat{\theta}$	
Spot series				
Allied	0.16	0.970	0.894	16.7
Alcoa	0.09	0.995	0.967	30.2
Am. Can	0.08	0.980	0.939	21.2
AT and T	0.20	0.725	0.599	13.8
Am. Brands	0.27	0.790	0.621	21.5
Anaconda	0.10	0.875	0.804	47.5
Bethlehem	0.10	0.940	0.876	27.6
Chrysler	0.08	0.985	0.948	20.1
Dupont	0.21	0.955	0.850	9.1
Kodak	0.16	0.970	0.894	2.0
G. Electric	0.11	0.990	0.950	7.2
G. Food	0.09	0.995	0.969	5.9
G. Motors	0.11	0.975	0.920	7.3
G. Telephone	0.07	0.990	0.961	6.5
Harvester	0.12	0.985	0.936	10.7
FT 30	0.14	0.975	0.910	1.0
Gold	0.33	0.945	0.785	15.8
Silver	0.32	0.985	0.887	9.6
Copper	0.42	0.985	0.862	−0.6
Lead	0.52	0.990	0.863	19.1
Tin	0.73	0.995	0.848	11.6
Zinc	0.62	0.990	0.834	8.5
£/$	0.34	0.970	0.836	53.2
Futures series (Method A)				
Corn (12)	0.57	0.995	0.891	10.9
Corn (6)	0.51	0.995	0.903	16.5
Corn (3)	0.54	0.995	0.897	21.4
Cocoa (12)	0.32	0.985	0.887	13.0
Cocoa (6)	0.28	0.985	0.896	7.7
Cocoa (3)	0.27	0.985	0.899	11.9
Coffee (12)	0.76	0.995	0.837	4.6
Coffee (6)	0.80	0.995	0.819	2.2
Coffee (3)	0.78	0.995	0.828	−7.1
Sugar (12)	0.48	0.990	0.872	22.0
Sugar (6)	0.49	0.985	0.843	7.7
Sugar (3)	0.48	0.985	0.846	10.7
Wool (12)	0.72	0.995	0.852	12.8
£/$ (6)	0.23	0.970	0.871	7.8
DM/$ (6)	0.36	0.985	0.877	2.1
SF/$ (6)	0.38	0.990	0.895	0.7
T-bond	0.11	0.990	0.950	0.3

APPENDIX 3(A)   RESULTS FOR ARCH PROCESSES

Without any loss of generality, assume $\mu = 0$. In this appendix $\{U_t\}$ is standardized, Gaussian, white noise. Firstly, suppose we are interested in the kurtosis and autocorrelation properties of the ARCH specification:

$$X_t = \left\{ \alpha_0 + \sum_{i=1}^{p} \alpha_i X_{t-i}^2 \right\}^{1/2} U_t.$$

Writing $Y_t = X_t/\sqrt{\alpha_0}$, Y_t is $\{1 + \Sigma \alpha_i Y_{t-i}^2\}^{1/2}U_t$. Now X_t and Y_t have the same kurtosis, and the processes $\{X_t^2\}$ and $\{Y_t^2\}$ have identical autocorrelations, always assuming these numbers exist. Therefore we will assume $\alpha_0 = 1$. Let $S_t = X_t^2$, so

$$S_t = \left\{ 1 + \sum_{i=1}^{p} \alpha_i S_{t-i} \right\} U_t^2. \tag{3.A.1}$$

Assuming $E[X_t^4]$ is finite, S_t will have finite variance and mean $\mu_S = 1/(1 - \{\alpha_1 + \cdots + \alpha_p\})$. Equation (3.A.1) can be rearranged to give

$$S_t - \mu_S = U_t^2 \left\{ \sum_{i=1}^{p} \alpha_i (S_{t-i} - \mu_S) \right\} + \mu_S(U_t^2 - 1). \tag{3.A.2}$$

Now U_t^2 is independent of $S_{t-j} - \mu_S$ for all $j > 0$. Thus, when both sides of equation (3.A.2) are multiplied by $S_{t-\tau} - \mu_S$, $\tau > 0$, and expectations are taken,

$$E[(S_t - \mu_S)(S_{t-\tau} - \mu_S)] = \sum_{i=1}^{p} \alpha_i E[(S_{t-i} - \mu_S)(S_{t-\tau} - \mu_S)]. \tag{3.A.3}$$

Dividing all the expectations by var (S_t):

$$\rho_{\tau,S} = \sum_{i=1}^{p} \alpha_i \rho_{\tau-i,S} \qquad \text{for all } \tau > 0. \tag{3.A.4}$$

Equations (3.A.4) are the well known Yule–Walker equations and uniquely determine the $\rho_{\tau,S}$. For the associated zero-mean AR(p) process

$$A_t = \sum_{i=1}^{p} \alpha_i A_{t-i} + U_t, \tag{3.A.5}$$

$$E[A_t A_{t-\tau}] = \sum_{i=1}^{p} \alpha_i E[A_{t-i} A_{t-\tau}]$$

and so

$$\rho_{\tau,A} = \sum_{i=1}^{p} \alpha_i \rho_{\tau-i,A},$$

hence $\rho_{\tau,S} = \rho_{\tau,A}$ for all τ.

To find the kurtosis of the X_t, it is helpful to consider $\sigma_A^2 = \text{var}(A_t)$. Squaring both sides of (3.A.5) and equating the expected values of the two sides:

$$\sigma_A^2 = 1 + \sigma_A^2\left(\sum_{i=1}^{p} \alpha_i^2\right) + 2\sigma_A^2 \sum_{i=1}^{p-1} \sum_{j=i+1}^{p} \alpha_i \alpha_j \rho_{j-i,A}. \tag{3.A.6}$$

Let $\gamma = E[S_t^2]$, so $k_x = E[X_t^4]/E[X_t^2]^2 = \gamma/\mu_S^2$ and $\text{var}(S_t) = \gamma - \mu_S^2$. Then squaring each side of (3.A.1) and taking expected values:

$$\gamma = 3\left\{1 + \gamma\left(\sum_{i=1}^{p} \alpha_i^2\right) + 2\mu_S \sum_{i=1}^{p} \alpha_i + 2\sum_{i<j} \alpha_i \alpha_j E[S_{t-i}S_{t-j}]\right\}. \tag{3.A.7}$$

Now $E[S_{t-i}S_{t-j}] = \text{cov}(S_{t-i}, S_{t-j}) + \mu_S^2 = (\gamma - \mu_S^2)\rho_{j-i,S} + \mu_S^2$. As $\rho_{j-i,S} = \rho_{j-i,A}$, equation (3.A.6) can be used to simplify equation (3.A.7). When this is done, the kurtosis is found to be $k_x = 3/(3 - 2\sigma_A^2)$. Clearly $\sigma_A^2 < 1.5$ is a necessary condition for finite kurtosis. This constraint is a necessary and sufficient condition when $p = 1$ and thus $\sigma_A^2 = 1/(1 - \alpha_1^2)$, see Engle (1982, p. 992). It appears probable that, for any p, $\sigma_A^2 < 1.5$ is a sufficient condition for finite kurtosis but this assertion has yet to be proved.

Secondly, consider the autocorrelation properties of $X_t = \{\alpha_0 + \Sigma \alpha_i|X_{t-i}|\}U_t$. Again we can assume α_0 is 1. Let $M_t = |X_t|$, so

$$M_t = \left(1 + \sum_{i=1}^{p} \alpha_i M_{t-i}\right)|U_t|. \tag{3.A.8}$$

Then M_t has mean $\mu_M = \delta/(1 - \delta\{\alpha_1 + \cdots + \alpha_p\})$ and (3.A.8) can be rewritten as

$$M_t - \mu_M = |U_t|\left\{\sum_{i=1}^{p} \alpha_i(M_{t-i} - \mu_M)\right\} + \mu_M\{\delta^{-1}|U_t| - 1\}$$

and hence for any $\tau > 0$

$$E[(M_t - \mu_M)(M_{t-\tau} - \mu_M)] = \delta \sum_{i=1}^{p} \alpha_i E[(M_{t-i} - \mu_M)(M_{t-\tau} - \mu_M)].$$

These equations imply $\{M_t\}$ has the same Yule–Walker equations and hence autocorrelations as the associated process $A_t = \delta \Sigma \alpha_i A_{t-i} + U_t$.

Chapter 4

Forecasting Standard Deviations

Daily returns are useful information for forecasting the standard deviations of future returns. This chapter compares several forecasts and recommends a convenient forecasting method. The forecasts have many uses, permitting better random walk tests and more accurate option pricing methods.

4.1 INTRODUCTION

Given complete information about present and past returns, denoted $I_t = \{x_{t-j}, j \geq 0\}$, we seek the best predictor of the next day's conditional standard deviation, denoted v_{t+1}. The level of market activity on day $t + 1$ will depend partially on information available before the day begins and, to some degree, I_t will summarize this information. Forecasts of v_{t+1} will be denoted by $\hat{v}_{t+1}$ and, when helpful, regarded as the realized values of random variables $\hat{V}_{t+1}$.

The best predictor of v_{t+1} is sought for four reasons. Firstly, to compare forecasts based upon different variance models and so to acquire evidence about the issue of stationarity and the best model when a stationary one is acceptable. Secondly, to produce a numerical estimate of the volatility of future price-changes by using their estimated standard deviation as a simple risk measure. Thirdly, to provide a day-to-day statistic for rescaling returns to give acceptable data for valid random walk tests (Chapter 5). And, finally, to provide the necessary estimates of future standard deviations for pricing options (Chapter 9).

Option pricing models have several parameters and the most difficult to estimate is the standard deviation. The methods presented in this chapter are very practical.

It is only possible to calculate the actual conditional standard deviations from observed returns if special and, almost certainly, incorrect assumptions are made, for example that an ARCH process generates returns. Thus we cannot calculate forecast errors, $v_{t+1} - \hat{v}_{t+1}$, nor an overall criterion for

summarizing forecast accuracy such as $\Sigma\ (v_{t+1} - \hat{v}_{t+1})^2$. Instead, it is necessary to deduce the relative accuracy of forecasts $\hat{v}_{t+1}$ by considering related
forecasts of an observable series.

Recall that the return x_{t+1} minus its expected value equals $v_{t+1}u_{t+1}$ with
u_{t+1} coming from a distribution having zero mean and unit variance. Also
recall one of the definitions of the absolute return, adjusted for a known
mean μ:

$$m_{t+1} = |x_{t+1} - \mu| = v_{t+1}|u_{t+1}|.$$

A forecast of m_{t+1} tells us something about likely values for v_{t+1}. As the
forecast $\hat{m}_{t+1}$ increases we ought to increase $\hat{v}_{t+1}$, since $|u_{t+1}|$ is best
forecast as a fixed constant because $\{U_t\}$ is exactly or almost strict white
noise. Indeed, sensible forecasts $\hat{m}_{t+1}$ and $\hat{v}_{t+1}$ must be related to each
other, established formally in Section 4.2.

Forecasts $\hat{m}_{t+1}$ based upon the product and ARMACH models are compared with forecasts suitable for non-stationary models in Sections 4.3 and
4.4. These empirical results support the recommendation, made in Section
4.5, that the most appropriate forecast $\hat{v}_{t+1}$ is an exponentially-weighted
moving average of present and past absolute returns.

It is well known that it is difficult to forecast returns by a better forecast
than the past average. Forecasts of m_{t+1} can be significantly better than a
simple average forecast, a consequence of the non-linear structure of the
returns generating process. Forecasts of $s_{t+1} = m_{t+1}^2$ are less successful
and are briefly described in Section 4.4.

When relevant options are traded it is possible to deduce an implied
standard deviation from option prices. The implied value can be used to
forecast the conditional standard deviation. These forecasts have yet to be
compared with the forecasts presented in this chapter.

4.2   KEY THEORETICAL RESULTS

Uncorrelated returns

Initially suppose the standardized random variables $U_t = (X_t - \mu)/V_t$ are
strict white noise and that U_t is independent of V_t and all $X_{t-j}, j > 0$. These
conditions are true for any realistic uncorrelated process $\{X_t\}$, including all
the uncorrelated processes defined in Chapter 3 whether stationary or
non-stationary. As

$$M_{t+1} = V_{t+1}|U_{t+1}|$$

it then follows that

$$E[M_{t+1}|I_t] = E[V_{t+1}|I_t]E[|U_{t+1}|\big||I_t] \qquad (4.2.1)$$
$$= \delta E[V_{t+1}|I_t] \qquad (4.2.2)$$

because the expected value of $|U_{t+1}|$ is its unconditional mean δ whatever the available information I_t. The U_t will be assumed normal so $\delta = 0.798$.

A classical result in statistical forecasting states that optimal forecasts are expected values conditional upon the available information. Thus (4.2.2) suggests the optimal $\hat{M}_{t+1}$ and $\hat{V}_{t+1}$ are related linearly. To confirm this consider mean square errors, denoted MSE and defined by

$$\text{MSE}(\hat{M}_{t+1}) = E[(M_{t+1} - \hat{M}_{t+1})^2] \tag{4.2.3}$$
$$\text{MSE}(\hat{V}_{t+1}) = E[(V_{t+1} - \hat{V}_{t+1})^2]. \tag{4.2.4}$$

Also let $\mu_{M,t+1} = E[M_{t+1}]$ and $\mu_{V,t+1} = E[V_{t+1}]$. These means are not necessarily stationary. They provide simple forecasts having

$$\text{MSE}(\mu_{M,t+1}) = \text{var}(M_{t+1}), \quad \text{MSE}(\mu_{V,t+1}) = \text{var}(V_{t+1}).$$

Now let $\hat{M}_{t+1}$ and $\hat{V}_{t+1}$ be any pair of forecasts satisfying the linear relationship

$$\hat{M}_{t+1} = \delta\hat{V}_{t+1}. \tag{4.2.5}$$

From (4.2.3), then (4.2.5), and the assumption that U_{t+1} is independent of V_{t+1} and I_t:

$$
\begin{aligned}
\text{var}(M_{t+1}) - \text{MSE}(\hat{M}_{t+1}) &= \{E[M_{t+1}^2] - \mu_{M,t+1}^2\} \\
&\quad - \{E[M_{t+1}^2] - 2E[M_{t+1}\hat{M}_{t+1}] + E[\hat{M}_{t+1}^2]\} \\
&= 2\delta E[V_{t+1}|U_{t+1}|\hat{V}_{t+1}] - \delta^2 E[\hat{V}_{t+1}^2] - \mu_{M,t+1}^2 \\
&= \delta^2\{2E[V_{t+1}\hat{V}_{t+1}] - E[\hat{V}_{t+1}^2] - \mu_{V,t+1}^2\} \\
&= \delta^2[\text{var}(V_{t+1}) - \text{MSE}(\hat{V}_{t+1})].
\end{aligned}
$$

Defining the improvements in MSE, upon the forecasts provided by the unconditional means, by

$$\text{IMSE}(\hat{M}_{t+1}) = \text{MSE}(\mu_{M,t+1}) - \text{MSE}(\hat{M}_{t+1})$$

and

$$\text{IMSE}(\hat{V}_{t+1}) = \text{MSE}(\mu_{V,t+1}) - \text{MSE}(\hat{V}_{t+1})$$

it follows that

$$\text{IMSE}(\hat{M}_{t+1}) = \delta^2\text{IMSE}(\hat{V}_{t+1}) \tag{4.2.6}$$

whenever (4.2.5) applies.

An optimal forecast minimizes MSE and maximizes IMSE. Consequently, (4.2.6) proves that optimal forecasts of m_{t+1} and v_{t+1} using the same set of information must be related to each other by (4.2.5). To find the best forecast of v_{t+1} it suffices to obtain the optimal forecast $\hat{m}_{t+1}$ and then define $\hat{v}_{t+1} = \hat{m}_{t+1}/\delta$. Note that it is not necessary to assume the process $\{X_t\}$ is stationary.

Correlated returns

The proof of (4.2.6) fails when the X_t are autocorrelated because then $|U_{t+1}|$ and $\hat{V}_{t+1}$ need not be independent, as assumed in the proof. Nevertheless, a near to optimal forecast of v_{t+1} can be obtained by dividing the best $\hat{m}_{t+1}$ by δ. For example, if $\{X_t\}$ is a product process, so that $\{V_t\}$ and $\{U_t\}$ are stochastically independent, (4.2.1) remains true and so the optimal $\hat{V}_{t+1}$ is

$$\hat{M}_{t+1}/E[|U_{t+1}| \,\big|\, I_t]$$

with $\hat{M}_{t+1} = E[M_{t+1}|I_t]$ being the optimal forecast of M_{t+1}. As $\{U_t\}$ is almost strict white noise, there will be very little autocorrelation among the $|U_t|$ and so the conditional expected value of $|U_{t+1}|$ will be almost exactly δ whatever the information I_t.

Relative mean square errors

It is convenient to discuss mean square errors as a fraction of the overall variance, so relative mean square errors are defined by

$$\text{RMSE}(\hat{M}_{t+1}) = \frac{\text{MSE}(\hat{M}_{t+1})}{\text{var}(M_{t+1})} = \frac{\text{MSE}(\hat{M}_{t+1})}{\text{MSE}(\mu_{M,t+1})} \tag{4.2.7}$$

and

$$\text{RMSE}(\hat{V}_{t+1}) = \frac{\text{MSE}(\hat{V}_{t+1})}{\text{var}(V_{t+1})} = \frac{\text{MSE}(\hat{V}_{t+1})}{\text{MSE}(\mu_{V,t+1})}. \tag{4.2.8}$$

Optimal forecasts give the least possible RMSE with $0 \leqslant \text{RMSE} \leqslant 1$. When the returns process is uncorrelated and $\hat{M}_{t+1} = \delta\hat{V}_{t+1}$ implies (4.2.6), the RMSE values satisfy

$$1 - \text{RMSE}(\hat{V}_{t+1}) = \lambda_{t+1}[1 - \text{RMSE}(\hat{M}_{t+1})] \tag{4.2.9}$$

with $\lambda_{t+1} = \text{var}(M_{t+1})/\{\delta^2 \,\text{var}(V_{t+1})\}$ a constant not depending on forecasts.

Stationary processes

When, furthermore, $\{X_t\}$ is stationary the constant λ_{t+1} is the same number λ for all t. Equation (4.2.9) then shows that the relative accuracy of forecasts $\hat{v}_{t+1}$ can be estimated from the relative, empirical accuracy of forecasts $\hat{m}_{t+1}$ and an estimate of λ. This is done in Section 4.4.

An ARCH process has v_{t+1} equal to a deterministic function of the information in I_t and so it is possible to achieve $\text{RMSE}(\hat{V}_{t+1}) = 0$.

A product process has $\lambda = \rho_{\tau,V}/\rho_{\tau,M}$, this being equation (3.5.5). It is not possible to forecast v_{t+1} perfectly and thus the least value of $\text{RMSE}(\hat{V}_{t+1})$ is positive. Later it will be noted that a typical least value is 0.3 for a plausible product process. At present, just note that estimates of RMSE for forecasts $\hat{V}_{t+1}$ can be used to eliminate either ARCH or product processes from the category of feasible models for returns.

4.3 FORECASTS: METHODOLOGY AND METHODS

Several forecasts of m_{t+1} will be compared for each of the 40 series with the objective of finding a best forecasting method. The best $\hat{m}_{t+1}$ then provide recommended forecasts $\hat{v}_{t+1} = \hat{m}_{t+1}/\delta$ of future standard deviations. All the calculations will use the definition $m_t = |x_t - \bar{x}|$, $\bar{x}$ being the sample mean return calculated over an entire time series.

Accurate forecasting methods are parametric and it is necessary to estimate the parameters found in equations for $\hat{m}_{t+1}$. Misleading results could occur if parameters are estimated from complete time series and then forecasts are evaluated for the same data. It is essential to split each time series into two sections, estimate parameters from the first section and then evaluate forecasts for the remaining data. Parameters will be estimated from observations 1 to n_1 inclusive and forecasts compared for observations $n_1 + 1$ to n. The selection of n_1 must be subjective. Often two parameters need to be estimated but only one number, namely MSE, is estimated from the forecasts. This is the reason for choosing $n_1 = 2n/3$ for spot series. For k futures contracts, n_1 is chosen to put the first $2k/3$ contracts into the parameter optimization set; if $2k/3$ is a fraction then the highest integer less than $2k/3$ is used.

Seven forecasts are compared for spot series. These are now described and followed by a discussion of the comparable forecasts for futures series.

Benchmark forecast

The mean of a process is a simple forecast against which others can be compared. Given I_t, the natural estimate of the mean is

$$\hat{m}_{t+1}^{(1)} = \frac{1}{t} \sum_{s=1}^{t} m_s. \tag{4.3.1}$$

This would be the optimal forecast if the returns process was strict white noise.

Parametric forecasts

On various occasions in Chapter 3 we have noted that the autocorrelations of $\{M_t\}$ can be modelled, exactly or approximately, by $\rho_{\tau,M} = K\phi^\tau$ with

$0 < K < 1, 0 < \phi < 1$. These are the same autocorrelations as those of the ARMA(1,1) process:

$$M_t^* - \mu_M - \phi(M_{t-1}^* - \mu_M) = \varepsilon_t - \theta\varepsilon_{t-1}$$

with $\{\varepsilon_t\}$ uncorrelated, providing θ is chosen to give $K = (1 - \phi\theta)(\phi - \theta)/\{\phi(1 - 2\theta\phi + \theta^2)\}$; see equation (1.9.13) and, in it, replace a by ϕ and b by $-\theta$. To find θ from K and ϕ we must solve

$$\theta^2 - D\theta + 1 = 0, \quad D = \{1 + \phi^2(1 - 2K)\}/\{\phi(1 - K)\}. \tag{4.3.2}$$

Forecasts can be found if $|\theta| < 1$ and consequently the relevant solution is $\theta = \{D - \sqrt{(D^2 - 4)}\}/2$, as $D > 2$ implies the other solution has $\theta > 1$.

The optimal forecast $\hat{M}_{t+1}$ from among the class of linear unbiased forecasts

$$\mu_M + \sum_{i=0}^{\infty} a_i(M_{t-i} - \mu_M)$$

is determined by the autocorrelations $\rho_{\tau,M}$. Thus $\{M_t\}$ and $\{M_t^*\}$ have the same best sequence a_i. From (1.9.15) it follows that the optimal linear forecast of M_{t+1} is

$$\hat{M}_{t+1} = \mu_M + \sum_{i=0}^{\infty} (\phi - \theta)\theta^i(M_{t-i} - \mu_M)$$

$$= \mu_M + (\phi - \theta)(M_t - \mu_M) + \theta(\hat{M}_t - \mu_M). \tag{4.3.3}$$

To produce a forecast $\hat{m}_{t+1}$ it is necessary to replace μ_M, ϕ, and θ by estimates. At time $t > n_1$, μ_M has been estimated by $\hat{m}_{t+1}^{(1)}$ while ϕ, θ have been estimated from observations 1 to n_1. A forecast $\hat{m}_{t+1}$ derived from (4.3.3) depends on the latest observation m_t, the previous forecast $\hat{m}_t$ made at time $t - 1$, and the estimates, thus:

$$\hat{m}_{t+1} = (\hat{\phi} - \hat{\theta})m_t + \hat{\theta}\hat{m}_t + (1 - \hat{\phi})\hat{m}_{t+1}^{(1)}. \tag{4.3.4}$$

Product process forecasts

The product process having lognormal, AR(1) conditional standard deviations has, approximately, $\rho_{\tau,M} = B(\beta)\phi^\tau$ with $\beta^2 = \text{var}(\log(V_t))$ and $B(\beta)$ defined by (3.5.8). Using method 1 of Section 3.9 gives $\hat{\beta}$ from $\bar{m}$ and $\bar{s}$, $\hat{\phi}$ from the $r_{\tau,m}$ and hence a $\hat{\theta}$ by setting $\hat{K} = B(\hat{\beta})$ and solving (4.3.2). These estimates and all the subsequent ones are computed from the first n_1 observations only. The $\hat{\phi}$ and $\hat{\theta}$ given by method 1 define the second forecast $\hat{m}_{t+1}^{(2)}$.

It was claimed in Section 3.9 that method 3, which estimates both B and ϕ directly from the $r_{\tau,m}$, is better than method 1. Estimates $\hat{B}$ and $\hat{\phi}$ give $\hat{\theta}$ by substituting $\hat{B}$ for K and $\hat{\phi}$ for ϕ in (4.3.2). These $\hat{\phi}$ and $\hat{\theta}$ define the third forecast $\hat{m}_{t+1}^{(3)}$. Comparing the accuracies of $\hat{m}_{t+1}^{(2)}$ and $\hat{m}_{t+1}^{(3)}$ provides further evidence about the best way to estimate ϕ for the product process.

ARMACH forecasts

Two special ARCH processes were introduced in Section 3.6. Equation (3.6.9) has V_t a linear function of V_{t-1} and M_{t-1} with $\rho_{\tau,M} = C\phi^{\tau}$. The method used in Section 3.10 provides estimates $\hat{C}$, $\hat{\phi}$, and hence $\hat{\theta}$ and a fourth forecast $\hat{m}_{t+1}^{(4)}$.

The other special process is (3.6.7) with V_t^2 linear in V_{t-1}^2 and M_{t-1}^2. Then $S_t = M_t^2$ has $\rho_{\tau,S} = C\phi^{\tau}$. The parameters C and ϕ can be estimated by the same method of maximum likelihood. This leads to forecasts $\hat{s}_{t+1}$ having (cf. 4.3.4)

$$\hat{s}_{t+1} = (\hat{\phi} - \hat{\theta})s_t + \hat{\theta}\hat{s}_t + (1 - \hat{\phi})\hat{s}_{t+1}^{(1)} \tag{4.3.5}$$

with $\hat{s}_{t+1}^{(1)} = (s_1 + \cdots + s_t)/t$. If this ARCH process is valid then v_{t+1} must be $\sqrt{\hat{s}_{t+1}}$ and thus the fifth forecast of m_{t+1} is $\hat{m}_{t+1}^{(5)} = \delta\sqrt{\hat{s}_{t+1}}$.

EWMA forecasts

The five forecasts described so far all assume a stationary process for returns. This causes the assumed stationary mean μ_M to appear in (4.3.3). Indeed, (4.3.3) can be generalized to show that the best $\hat{m}_{t+N}$, as $N \to \infty$, is μ_M, if I_t is the available information.

It is perfectly reasonable to doubt the assumption of stationarity especially for long series. Estimates of the future mean $E[M_{t+1}]$ calculated from m_s, $s \leq t$, will then be unreliable. A simple and practical way to avoid using μ_M is to set $\phi = 1$ in (4.3.3), giving

$$\hat{M}_{t+1} = \sum_{i=0}^{\infty} (1 - \theta)\theta^i M_{t-i} = (1 - \theta)M_t + \theta\hat{M}_t. \tag{4.3.6}$$

This defines an exponentially-weighted moving average (EWMA). The effect of a change in the mean, sometime in the past, is reduced by assigning most weight to recent observations. An EWMA should forecast well if there are occasional changes in variance such as occur in Hsu's non-stationary models.

From (4.3.6), actual forecasts can be calculated using

$$\hat{m}_{t+1} = (1 - \hat{\theta})m_t + \hat{\theta}\hat{m}_t. \tag{4.3.7}$$

Letting $\gamma = 1 - \hat{\theta}$ and assuming $\mu = 0$,

$$\hat{m}_{t+1} = \gamma|x_t| + (1 - \gamma)\hat{m}_t,$$

an equation used by the author in earlier research to calculate an estimate

$\hat{m}_{t+1}$ of the conditional mean absolute deviation $E[M_{t+1}|I_t]$. Taylor and Kingsman (1979) presented a method for estimating γ based on a likelihood function. Estimates $\hat{\gamma} \approx 0.1$ were obtained for copper and sugar returns. However, the estimation method is too complicated and time consuming to be recommended for further use.

A straightforward way to choose θ or γ is to use (4.3.7) to calculate the $\hat{m}_{t+1}$ as a function of θ and then minimize

$$\sum [m_{t+1} - \hat{m}_{t+1}(\theta)]^2.$$

Using $\hat{m}_{21} = (m_1 + \cdots + m_{20})/20$, the squared forecast errors have been summed over t from 21 to $n_1 - 1$ inclusive. The best θ, to an accuracy of two decimal places, then provides a $\hat{\theta}$ for use in (4.3.7) which is just (4.3.4) with $\hat{\phi} = 1$. This method defines a sixth set of forecasts $\hat{m}_{t+1}^{(6)}$.

The author has used $\gamma = 0.1$ in a number of papers, i.e. $\hat{\theta} = 0.9$, to derive the $\hat{m}_{t+1}$ for a rescaling transformation used to improve random walk tests (e.g. Taylor, 1980, 1982b). To reassess the choice $\gamma = 0.1$ a seventh forecast $\hat{m}_{t+1}^{(7)}$ is defined by $\hat{\theta} = 0.9$ in (4.3.7).

Forecasts 2, 3, 4, 6, and 7 all use the same updating equation (4.3.4), whilst forecast 5 is based on the similar equation (4.3.5). The initial forecasts $\hat{m}_1^{(j)}$ are not important and have been set equal to the average m_t over times 1 to n_1. The later forecasts differ because of the variety of methods used to calculate $\hat{\phi}$ and $\hat{\theta}$. For example, the first US stock series has these estimates:

Forecast	$\hat{\phi}$	$\hat{\theta}$
2	0.840	0.685
3	0.968	0.914
4	0.905	0.819
5	0.915	0.796
6	1	0.960
7	1	0.900

The estimates $\hat{\phi}$ and $\hat{\theta}$ are often similar for these six forecasts. Over many series the differences between estimates can provide a meaningful comparison of the forecasting methods.

Futures forecasts

Futures series can be forecast either as a single series needing minor adjustments when the delivery date of the contract changes (method A) or as a collection of separate contracts, each having its own statistical parameters (method B). The latter situation allows a different mean $E[M_{t+1}]$ for each contract.

As in Section 3.10, suppose $\{x_t\}$ is a series of returns, one per trading day, with returns on contract i from time $t = T_{i-1} + 1$ to $t = T_i$ inclusive. Also suppose there are 20 further returns available on contract i from $t = T_{i-1} - 19$ to $t = T_{i-1}$ inclusive $(i > 1)$. Then an eighth forecast is the estimate of $E[M_{t+1}]$ based on contract i alone:

$$\hat{m}_{t+1}^{(8)} = \sum_{s=T_{i-1}-19}^{t} m_s/(t + 20 - T_{i-1}). \tag{4.3.8}$$

Two major differences between methods A and B are their estimates of μ_M and their initial values of the forecasts for the separate contracts. For $\hat{\mu}_M$, method A follows the procedure for spot series and uses $\hat{m}_{t+1}^{(1)}$, whilst method B uses $\hat{m}_{t+1}^{(8)}$, with a similar replacement of $\hat{s}_{t+1}^{(1)}$ in (4.3.5).

Initial values of $\hat{m}_{t+1}^{(j)}$ at time $t = T_{i-1}$ for contract i and $2 \leqslant j \leqslant 7$ are calculated as follows. Method A sets $\hat{m}_t^{(j)}$ at time $t = T_{i-1} - 19$ for contract i equal to the value of $\hat{m}_t^{(j)}$ at the identical time for contract $i - 1$. Twenty m_t for contract i are then substituted into (4.3.4) or (4.3.5) to give the first forecast $\hat{m}_{t+1}^{(j)}$, $t = T_{i-1}$, for the forecast evaluations. Method B simply averages the twenty m_t for contract i from $t = T_{i-1} - 19$ to T_{i-1} inclusive to give the same forecast $\hat{m}_{t+1}^{(j)}$ for all $j \neq 5$, with a similar average of the s_t for the initial fifth forecast.

The estimates $\hat{\phi}$, $\hat{\theta}$ depend on the method, A or B, for the fourth and fifth forecasts, as described in Section 3.10. The estimate $\hat{\theta}$ depends on the method for the sixth forecast because of the different initial values used when θ is optimized. For the second and third forecasts $\hat{\phi}$, $\hat{\theta}$ do not depend on the method; they are always estimated as in Section 3.9.

Empirical RMSE

Forecasts are compared with actual observations from time $n_1 + 1$ until time n. Their empirical mean square errors are

$$\text{MSE}(\hat{m}, j) = \sum_{t=n_1+1}^{n-1} (m_{t+1} - \hat{m}_{t+1}^{(j)})^2/(n - n_1 - 1). \tag{4.3.9}$$

The natural estimate of $\text{MSE}(\mu_{M,t+1})$ in (4.2.7) is $\text{MSE}(\hat{m}, 1)$ as the first forecast is the estimated value of $\mu_{M,t+1}$ for a stationary process. Therefore empirical relative mean square errors are defined by

$$\text{RMSE}(\hat{m}, j) = \text{MSE}(\hat{m}, j)/\text{MSE}(\hat{m}, 1). \tag{4.3.10}$$

A value of $\text{RMSE}(\hat{m}, j)$ less than 1 will indicate that forecast j should be preferred to the benchmark forecast.

4.4   FORECASTING RESULTS

Absolute returns

The empirical values of the relative mean square errors have been averaged across the 23 spot series and across all the 17 futures series except the short Treasury Bond series. Average values of RMSE(m, j) are as follows.

Forecast j	Model/Method	Spot	Futures method A	Futures method B
2	Product process	0.915	0.774	0.775
3	Product process	0.906	0.766	0.765
4	ARMACH	0.914	0.771	0.803
5	ARMACH	0.906	0.773	0.792
6	EWMA	0.901	0.771	0.771
7	EWMA	0.902	0.767	0.767
8	—	—	—	0.819

All these averages are well below 1 showing that forecasts more accurate than the current mean can be obtained.

Futures series generally have far lower RMSE than spot series. Comparing the averages for methods A and B only reveals an important difference for the ARMACH models with method A preferred. Consequently detailed results are only discussed for method A. The eighth forecast is inferior to the parametric forecasts. This must imply that conditional standard deviations change within the lifetime of a futures contract.

Overall averages for 39 series, using method A for the futures series, are as follows.

Forecast	Model/Method	Average RMSE
2	Product process	0.857
3	Product process	0.848
4	ARMACH	0.855
5	ARMACH	0.851
6	EWMA	0.847
7	EWMA	0.847

The average RMSE are all similar with the EWMA forecasts marginally better than the others. These similar averages are partially caused by the similar estimates $\hat{\phi}$ and $\hat{\theta}$ used to define the different forecasts. To decide which model is appropriate for each series we need further results. These are estimates of RMSE for forecasts of conditional standard deviations and the empirical RMSE for forecasts of absolute returns further into the future than the next day.

Conditional standard deviations

The empirical RMSE of forecasts $\hat{v}_{t+1} = \hat{m}_{t+1}/\delta$ can be estimated under the assumption that the correct model is stationary. From (4.2.9) it can be seen that an appropriate estimate for forecasts $\hat{v}_{t+1}$ based on $\hat{m}_{t+1}$ will be

$$\text{RMSE}(\hat{v}, j) = 1 - \hat{\lambda}[1 - \text{RMSE}(\hat{m}, j)] \qquad (4.4.1)$$

with $\hat{\lambda}$ estimating $\lambda = \text{var}(M_{t+1})/\{\delta^2 \text{var}(V_{t+1})\}$. As

$$\lambda = (E[M_t^2] - E[M_t]^2)/(\delta^2 E[M_t^2] - E[M_t]^2)$$

a convenient estimate of λ is simply

$$\hat{\lambda} = (\bar{s} - \bar{m}^2)/(\delta^2\bar{s} - \bar{m}^2) \qquad (4.4.2)$$

with $\bar{m}$ and $\bar{s}$ the average values of m_t and $s_t = m_t^2$ which have been calculated for complete series.

The 15 estimates of λ for the US stock price series range from 3.1 to 5.4 with 12 of them between 4.0 and 5.0. The range for the 6 metals series is 2.4 to 3.1, for the 16 agricultural futures it is 2.1 to 4.2, and for the 4 currency series, 2.9 to 5.0. The UK share index series gives $\hat{\lambda} = 27.7$ and negative values of $\text{RMSE}(\hat{v}, j)$ indicating an unsatisfactory $\hat{\lambda}$.

Another way to estimate λ assumes the lognormal AR(1) product process is adequate. Then $\lambda = 1/B(\beta)$ and the reciprocal of the estimate $\hat{B}$ found directly from the autocorrelations of the m_t can be used for $\hat{\lambda}$. This method usually gives a higher $\hat{\lambda}$ than (4.4.2).

Any ARCH process has $\text{RMSE}(\hat{V}_{t+1}) = 0$ so the estimates $\text{RMSE}(\hat{v}, j)$ should then be near zero. The product process considered in this chapter has $\text{RMSE}(\hat{V}_{t+1}) = (1 - \phi^2)/(1 - \theta\phi)$; this is correct when the approximation $\rho_{\tau,M} - B\phi^\tau$ is used (the proof is omitted). Using the preferred estimates $\hat{\phi}$ and $\hat{\theta}$ implied by Table 3.3 and averaging $(1 - \hat{\phi}^2)/(1 - \hat{\theta}\hat{\phi})$ over the 39 long series suggests an expected average for $\text{RMSE}(\hat{v}, j)$ of 0.33 for the advocated product process. However, the average values of the estimates $\text{RMSE}(v, j)$ using (4.4.1) and (4.4.2) are approximately one-half for each forecasting method. This appears to rule out ARMACH models for returns and suggests that in a product process $\{V_t\}$ could need more parameters than a lognormal, AR(1) model.

Looking at the estimates of $\text{RMSE}(\hat{v}, j)$ series by series shows they are highly variable and probably far from accurate. Forecast 4, for an ARMACH specification, has an average estimate of 0.49 with 33 estimates greater than 0.25 and 23 estimates exceeding 0.5. Similar figures occur for the alternative ARMACH specification. Thus these models are inadequate and more generally it is concluded that any ARCH model is most unlikely to describe returns adequately. Of the two forecasts based on the product process, namely forecasts 2 and 3, the best is forecast 3. The average of the estimates $\text{RMSE}(\hat{v}, 3)$ is 0.47, 10 estimates are less than 0.3, 7 are between 0.3 and 0.5,

13 are in the range 0.5 to 0.7 and 9 estimates exceed 0.7. Using the alternative way to estimate λ gives a lower average for the estimates RMSE($\hat{v}$, 3) equal to 0.32; however these RMSE estimates could be seriously biased if the autocorrelations of V_t are not close to ϕ^τ for some ϕ.

The forecasts $\hat{v}_{t+1}$ are clearly far from perfect. Nevertheless they are very useful as will be shown in Chapter 5 and subsequently.

Two leading forecasts

The best forecast based on a stationary model for returns is the third forecast. It uses $\hat{\phi}$ and $\hat{\theta}$ estimated directly from the autocorrelations of the absolute returns m_t and will be called the stationary forecast. Forecasts 6 and 7 are suitable for non-stationary variances and their RMSE figures are very similar. For the remainder of this section results are given for the sixth forecast, now called the non-stationary forecast.

Table 4.1 presents RMSE($\hat{m}$, 3) and RMSE($\hat{m}$, 6) for each series. Although the non-stationary forecast has a slightly lower average RMSE it is noticeable that the stationary forecast is better than its rival for most series; forecast 3 outperforms forecast 6 for 25 of the 39 long series. The differences between the RMSE values of the stationary and non-stationary forecasts are usually very small because the forecasts are often similar when ϕ is close to 1 for a stationary model. To gather further insight into the issue of stationarity we consider forecasts further into the future.

More distant forecasts

The stationary forecast was deduced by considering an ARMA(1,1) process. For such processes the optimal predictions for times $t + 1$ and $t + N$, both made at time t, are related by a simple equation. From (1.9.16) it can be deduced that the best forecast of M_{t+N}, made at time t and denoted $\hat{M}_{t,N}$, satisfies

$$\hat{M}_{t,N} - \mu_M = \phi^{N-1}(\hat{M}_{t,1} - \mu_M), \tag{4.4.3}$$

for all $N > 1$ and $\hat{M}_{t,1}$ is just $\hat{M}_{t+1}$. Replacing the parameters ϕ and μ_M by their usual estimates gives the following equation for the stationary forecast, N days hence:

$$\hat{m}_{t,N} - \hat{m}_{t+1}^{(1)} = \hat{\phi}^{N-1}(\hat{m}_{t+1}^{(3)} - \hat{m}_{t+1}^{(1)}). \tag{4.4.4}$$

The non-stationary forecast is the result of setting $\phi = 1$ in the ARMA(1,1) model. This indicates that the appropriate non-stationary forecast N days hence is simply $\hat{m}_{t+1}^{(6)}$ for any N.

For large N the stationary and non-stationary forecasts will often be quite different because of the factor $\hat{\phi}^{N-1}$ in (4.4.4). Defining MSE($\hat{m}$, j, N) and

Table 4.1 Relative mean square errors for forecasts of absolute returns

	Forecasts one day ahead		Forecasts ten days ahead	
	Forecast 3	Forecast 6	Forecast 3	Forecast 6
Spot series				
Allied	0.908	0.910	0.939	0.937
Alcoa	0.914	0.918	0.940	0.941
Am. Can	0.949	0.951	0.963	0.967
AT and T	0.954	0.967	0.993	0.993
Am. Brands	0.966	0.954	0.995	0.976
Anaconda	0.960	0.955	0.998	0.969
Bethlehem	0.954	0.960	0.979	0.977
Chrysler	0.940	0.951	0.964	0.971
Dupont	0.855	0.852	0.889	0.879
Kodak	0.864	0.858	0.912	0.903
G. Electric	0.838	0.777	0.919	0.802
G. Foods	0.909	0.884	0.965	0.900
G. Motors	0.916	0.878	0.982	0.892
G. Telephone	0.930	0.895	0.937	0.906
Harvester	0.931	0.935	0.949	0.951
FT 30	0.941	0.949	0.973	0.996
Gold	0.915	0.930	0.985	1.118
Silver	0.756	0.687	0.910	0.745
Copper	0.851	0.856	0.891	0.908
Lead	0.855	0.884	0.914	0.983
Tin	0.883	0.895	0.999	1.051
Zinc	0.961	0.972	1.036	1.075
£/$	0.883	0.903	1.009	1.058
Futures series				
Corn (12)	0.614	0.605	0.667	0.635
Corn (6)	0.574	0.555	0.659	0.604
Corn (3)	0.565	0.547	0.637	0.585
Cocoa (12)	0.835	0.840	0.910	0.943
Cocoa (6)	0.831	0.837	0.871	0.915
Cocoa (3)	0.907	0.923	0.922	0.950
Coffee (12)	0.878	0.901	0.934	0.984
Coffee (6)	0.744	0.768	0.813	0.864
Coffee (3)	0.728	0.746	0.801	0.851
Sugar (12)	0.764	0.771	0.818	0.835
Sugar (6)	0.746	0.751	0.796	0.814
Sugar (3)	0.750	0.752	0.817	0.833
Wool (12)	0.653	0.651	0.668	0.668
£/$ (6)	0.874	0.873	0.891	0.889
DM/$ (6)	0.866	0.875	0.901	0.927
SF/$ (6)	0.927	0.935	0.945	0.960
T-Bond	0.928	0.850	0.927	0.844

RMSE($\hat{m}$, j, N) in the obvious way, by generalizing (4.3.9) for forecasts N days into the future, we should expected the absolute magnitude of RMSE($\hat{m}$, 3, N) minus RMSE($\hat{m}$, 6, N) to increase as N increases. This is observed for most series. Table 4.1 gives the RMSE values for stationary and non-stationary forecasts when $N = 10$. The average RMSE of the stationary forecasts is now less than that of the non-stationary ones.

Conclusions about stationarity

From Table 4.1 it is clear that stationary models give the best forecasts for the UK share index, the metals excepting silver, and the UK agricultural futures, whilst non-stationary models are indicated for the US stocks, silver, and US corn futures. Currencies, spot or futures, are slightly better forecast by stationary models. Forecasting results for $N = 25$ entirely support all these conclusions.

These forecasting results cannot prove that stationary models are correct. It should be noted that two futures series were proved non-stationary in Section 2.4 whilst the forecasting results suggest using a stationary model. Nevertheless, it is concluded that stationary models can provide a good approximation to the true stochastic process generating financial returns at various markets even when the period studied covers many years.

Another approach

All the results given here are for forecasts of m_{t+N} at some future time $t + N$. It is possible to rework the analysis in terms of forecasts for $s_{t+N} = m_{t+N}^2$ and to use the result that forecasts of s_{t+N} and v_{t+N}^2 ought to be identical. This has been done for $N = 1$ but the improvements in forecast accuracy upon the benchmark forecast are usually less than those reported for the forecasts $\hat{m}_{t+1}^{(j)}$. For example, the average RMSE for $\hat{m}_{t+1}^{(3)}$ is 0.848 compared with an average of 0.905 for the corresponding forecast $\hat{s}_{t+1}^{(3)}$, defined by replacing each letter m by a letter s in (4.3.1) and (4.3.4).

4.5 RECOMMENDED FORECASTS FOR THE NEXT DAY

To predict tomorrow's conditional standard deviation v_{t+1}, we must first choose a method for forecasting m_{t+1}. The results just presented show several methods have almost identical accuracy, when measured by RMSE. Forecasts given by exponentially weighted moving averages (EWMA) are fractionally more accurate than the other forecasts and have two further advantages. Firstly, the EWMA method requires less parameter estimates because ϕ is always 1 and so neither ϕ nor μ_M need to be estimated. Secondly, if for any reason the unconditional variance changes, introducing non-stationarity into the returns process, then the forecasts can reflect the variance change fairly quickly and accurately. These advantages of the non-stationary forecast are particularly relevant for real-time applications. When forecasting more than one day into the future it is less clear which forecast should be used. This is discussed more fully in Chapter 9.

It is recommended that v_{t+1} is predicted using an EWMA forecast for m_{t+1}, determined by a smoothing parameter γ as follows:

$$\hat{v}_{t+1} = \hat{m}_{t+1}/\delta$$

$$= \gamma \sum_{i=0}^{\infty} (1 - \gamma)^i |x_{t-i} - \bar{x}|/\delta$$

$$= (1 - \gamma)\hat{v}_t + \gamma |x_t - \bar{x}|/\delta. \tag{4.5.1}$$

Implementing equation (4.5.1) requires values for δ, γ, and $\bar{x}$. There is no reason to doubt the assumption that returns have conditional normal distributions and thus $\delta \simeq 0.798$. For research studies, $\bar{x}$ can be taken to be the average return during a complete time series and this will be done in Chapters 5, 6, and 7. For real-time applications, it is time consuming to calculate $\bar{x}$ every day from the available returns. Simply setting $\bar{x}$ equal to zero in (4.5.1) makes very little difference to the forecasts $\hat{v}_{t+1}$. This simplification is used in Chapter 8 when assessing trading rules and has appeared in previous publications by the author.

A value γ for a particular series could be found by retrospective optimization as described in Section 4.3. However, the average RMSE figures given in Section 4.4 show that using $\gamma = 0.1$ for all series was as accurate as seeking an optimal γ for each series. The best γ for past data may not be optimal in the future because the RMSE of EWMA forecasts changes relatively little as γ varies between 0.02 and 0.2. This explains why $\gamma = 0.1$ often gave better results than values obtained from optimization over the initial two-thirds of the returns. Back-optimized values of γ have been found for each complete series by minimizing the criterion

$$\sum [m_{t+1} - \hat{m}_{t+1}(\gamma)]^2$$

summing over t from 21 to $n - 1$ inclusive. The best values are recorded in Table 4.2.

Based on these values and the realization that the best past γ is not necessarily the best γ for future forecasts, the values 0.04 for stocks and 0.1 for currencies and commodities are recommended. These values are used in the remainder of this text.

Table 4.2 Best smoothing constants γ (back-optimized)

Spot series	γ	Futures series	γ
Allied	0.05	Corn (12)	0.09
Alcoa	0.05	Corn (6)	0.09
Am. Can	0.03	Corn (3)	0.10
AT and T	0.03	Cocoa (12)	0.10
Am. Brands	0.04	Cocoa (6)	0.09
Anaconda	0.04	Cocoa (3)	0.08
Bethlehem	0.03	Coffee (12)	0.11
Chrysler	0.03	Coffee (6)	0.14
Dupont	0.06	Coffee (3)	0.19
Kodak	0.06	Sugar (12)	0.11
G. Electric	0.06	Sugar (6)	0.10
G. Foods	0.03	Sugar (3)	0.11
G. Motors	0.04	Wool (12)	0.10
G. Telephone	0.03	£/$ (6)	0.07
Harvester	0.04	DM/$ (6)	0.09
FT 30	0.06	SF/$ (6)	0.08
Gold	0.17	T-Bond	0.04
Silver	0.09		
Copper	0.09		
Lead	0.17		
Tin	0.13		
Zinc	0.12		
£/$	0.11		

Table 4.3 Frequency distributions for forecasts of the conditional standard deviation. Percentage frequencies (F) and percentage cumulative frequencies (CF)

Range	Allied		Gold		Sugar (12)		£/$ (6)	
	F	CF	F	CF	F	CF	F	CF
0 to 0.005	0	0	3.7	3.7	1.2	1.2	58.3	58.3
0.006 to 0.010	3.6	3.6	29.8	33.5	20.8	22.0	39.5	97.8
0.011 to 0.015	43.5	47.1	25.6	59.1	25.4	47.4	2.2	100
0.016 to 0.020	35.0	82.1	20.4	79.5	17.9	65.3		
0.021 to 0.025	11.0	93.0	10.4	89.9	11.2	76.5		
0.026 to 0.030	4.7	97.7	3.7	93.5	7.5	84.0		
0.031 to 0.035	1.8	99.5	2.0	95.6	5.8	89.8		
0.036 to 0.040	0.5	100	1.4	97.0	3.5	93.3		
0.041 to 0.045			0.9	97.9	2.5	95.8		
0.046 to 0.050			0.7	98.6	0.9	96.7		
More than 0.050			1.4	100	3.3	100		
Minimum	0.007		0.003		0.003		0.001	
Median	0.015		0.013		0.016		0.004	
Maximum	0.038		0.069		0.084		0.011	

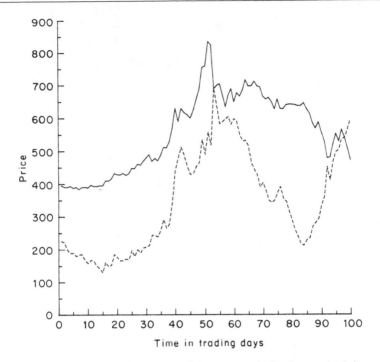

Figure 4.1 Gold prices (solid curve) and forecasts (dashed curve) of the return's conditional standard deviation from November 1979 to March 1980. Dashed curve is 10 000 $\hat{v}_{t+1}$

Examples

Table 4.3 summarizes the recommended forecasts $\hat{v}_{t+1}$ for four series: Allied (the first US stock series), spot gold, sugar futures, and sterling/dollar futures. All four frequency distributions are highly right-skewed. This shows that there are occasional periods of time when the conditional standard deviation far exceeds its usual average value. Prices change by exceptional amounts during these periods.

Figures 4.1 and 4.2 illustrate considerable changes in the forecasts, firstly for gold and secondly for sterling/dollar futures. Both illustrations are exceptional. Figure 4.1 shows 100 gold prices and forecasts centred on 18 January 1980 when the closing price was a record high at $835. The conditional standard deviation remains high after the record price indicating considerable uncertainty about future prices caused, according to popular opinion, by political problems involving Afghanistan. Figure 4.2 shows sterling/dollar prices and forecasts for the June 1976 contract between December 1975 and May 1976. After months of steady trading between $1.97 and $2.01, the price fell in one day from $1.9920 to $1.9425

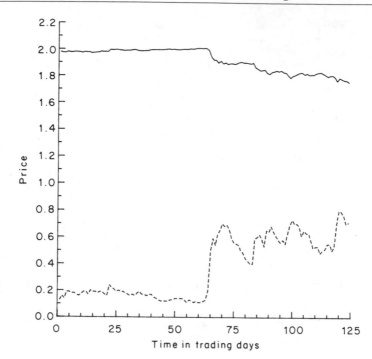

Figure 4.2 Prices of sterling futures (solid curve), in US dollars per pound, and forecasts of the return's conditional standard deviation (dashed curve) from December 1975 to May 1976. Dashed curve is 100 $\hat{v}_{t+1}$

and then continued to fall. The forecast $\hat{v}_{t+1}$ quickly moves from about 0.0013 to more than 0.005. This sudden increase in price volatility is very much a special case for currency futures.

4.6   SUMMARY

Reasonable forecasts of the relevant standard deviation for the next return can be calculated from a weighted average of the absolute values of past returns. It will become clear in Section 5.8 that the forecasts have research applications: they are sufficiently accurate to help define much better estimates of the autocorrelation among daily returns. The forecasts also have practical applications: they provide a very convenient risk measure for traders and require minimal computational effort.

The issue of stationary versus non-stationary models is not important when forecasting the next conditional standard deviation and the cautious strategy of selecting a non-stationary method is recommended. Forecasts ten or more days into the future show that stationary models are acceptable for some series, particularly commodity series. It does appear that stationary models can have important applications, discussed later in Chapter 9 about the pricing of options. When a stationary model is applicable a product process gives a better approximation to the true returns process than does an ARCH process.

Therefore two (or more) innovations are required per unit time if the returns process is to be modelled using independent and identically distributed innovations.

Chapter 5

The Accuracy of Autocorrelation Estimates

The forecasts of the conditional standard deviations derived in Chapter 4 can be used to construct appropriate series for autocorrelation tests of the random walk hypothesis. This chapter shows that the returns series is usually not appropriate but returns divided by their forecast standard deviations define a satisfactory series for random walk tests.

5.1 INTRODUCTION

Suppose n returns x_t are used to calculate some autocorrelation coefficients $r_{\tau,x}$. Let $r_{\tau,x}$ be the realized value of a random variable $R_{\tau,x}$ and recall from Section 1.10 that standard tests based upon the approximation var $(R_{\tau,x}) = 1/n$ are actually joint tests for independence and finite-variance, identical distributions. This joint hypothesis was conclusively rejected in Section 2.10. Of far more practical interest are tests of the hypothesis that returns have constant mean and are uncorrelated, the definition of the *random walk hypothesis* used throughout the remainder of this book. The result var $(R_{\tau,x}) \simeq 1/n$ is not implied by the random walk hypothesis and thus standard tests, based upon an assumed variance $1/n$, can be unreliable. This is demonstrated in Section 5.2 by considering extreme examples of non-linear, uncorrelated processes.

A method for assessing the true variance of an autocorrelation coefficient is described in Sections 5.3 to 5.6 and evaluated for the forty time series in Section 5.7. The true variances are generally far greater than $1/n$. Autocorrelation coefficients should have smaller variances if they are calculated from returns divided by their estimated conditional standard deviations. This rescaling method is described in Section 5.8 and its usefulness for obtaining better autocorrelation estimates is assessed in the rest of the chapter. Random walk tests are presented in Chapter 6.

5.2 EXTREME EXAMPLES

To illustrate the fact that $n[\text{var }(R_{\tau,x})]$ is not always approximately 1 for an uncorrelated process $\{X_t\}$, we consider two examples based on the models introduced in Section 3.2. Firstly, suppose $\{X_t\}$ is constructed from a zero-mean, strict white noise process $\{U_t\}$ by:

$$X_t = \sigma_1 U_t \qquad \text{for } 1 \leqslant t \leqslant m,$$
$$\;\;\;= \sigma_2 U_t \qquad \text{for } m + 1 \leqslant t \leqslant n.$$

Ignoring the sample mean $\bar{X}$, the coefficients are

$$R_{\tau,x} = \sum_{t=1}^{n-\tau} X_t X_{t+\tau} \Big/ \sum_{t=1}^{n} X_t^2. \tag{5.2.1}$$

Keeping σ_1 fixed at a positive number, let $\sigma_2 \to 0$. Then

$$R_{\tau,x} \to \sum_{t=1}^{m-\tau} U_t U_{t+\tau} \Big/ \sum_{t=1}^{m} U_t^2. \tag{5.2.2}$$

These limits are the autocorrelations of $\{U_t\}$ based on m observations. Such autocorrelations have var $(R_{\tau,U}) \simeq 1/m$. Thus $n[\text{var }(R_{\tau,x})] \to n/m$ approximately. The ratio n/m can be arbitrarily high.

  Secondly, suppose $\{X_t\}$ is a stationary and uncorrelated process defined by $X_t = V_t U_t$ with $V_t = \sigma_1$ or σ_2 and $\{V_t\}$ a Markov chain, stochastically independent of zero-mean, Gaussian white noise $\{U_t\}$. Define the transition matrix of the Markov chain by

$$P(V_t = \sigma_i \,|\, V_{t-1} = \sigma_i) = 1 - \lambda_i, \qquad i = 1, 2$$

and assume $0 < \lambda_1, \lambda_2 < 1$. Then if $P(V_1 = \sigma_1)$ is $\lambda_2/(\lambda_1 + \lambda_2) = \pi_1$, say, it will follow that $P(V_t = \sigma_1)$ is π_1 for all t. As $\sigma_2 \to 0$, a result like (5.2.2) can be obtained, except now the numbers of relevant times appearing in the numerator and denominator of $R_{\tau,x}$ are two random variables. It can be proved that

$$n[\text{var }(R_{\tau,x})] > (1 - \lambda_1)^2/\pi_1 \tag{5.2.3}$$

for sufficiently large n and small ratio σ_2/σ_1. The proof is omitted. It follows from a general result proved in Section 5.5. The lower bound in (5.2.3) can be made arbitrarily high; for example, it is more than 8 when $\lambda_1 = 0.09$, $\lambda_2 = 0.01$ and so π_1 is 0.1.

  In both of our extreme examples, several observations x_t are irrelevant when the sample autocorrelations are calculated. The autocorrelations are therefore determined by less than n observations and so the variance of an autocorrelation coefficient becomes more than $1/n$. Much the same situation occurs for autocorrelations calculated directly from financial returns. Because of changes in variance or conditional variance, some observations are less relevant than others when autocorrelations are calculated.

A rather extreme illustration of this point can be given by considering the series of wool returns. Let s_i^2 be the variance for contract i, calculated from n_i returns. There are 13 contracts, $n_1 = 270$ and $n_i = 250$ for $i \geqslant 2$. The denominator of the autocorrelations is $\Sigma (x_t - \bar{x})^2$ and this will approximately equal $\Sigma n_i s_i^2$. It can be verified from Table 2.5 that, for the two years of highest variance, $n_6 s_6^2 + n_7 s_7^2 = 0.37$ but for the other eleven years the total of the products $n_i s_i^2$ is only 0.19. Thus the observations x_t during two years are far more relevant than all the others in determining $\Sigma (x_t - \bar{x})^2$. The same conclusion is valid for $\Sigma (x_t - \bar{x})/(x_{t+\tau} - \bar{x})$ and hence also for $r_{\tau,x}$.

5.3   A SPECIAL NULL HYPOTHESIS

Our objective is to estimate the variance of $R_{\tau,x}$ under the null hypothesis that $\{X_t\}$ is an uncorrelated process. The process $\{X_t\}$ could be non-stationary and it is therefore desirable to make as few assumptions as possible about the generating process. We will assume the X_t have identical means, $E[X_t] = \mu$. Initially we suppose μ is known and then, without loss of generality, μ can be assumed to be zero. In Section 5.7 the equations defining the estimates are revised for the more realistic situation of a constant yet unknown mean.

To obtain estimates, we make the assumption that if $\{X_t\}$ is uncorrelated then the multivariate density of any n random variables is symmetric. Let $f(x_1, x_2, \ldots, x_n)$ denote the multivariate density of the random variables X_t, $1 \leqslant t \leqslant n$, let x denote the vector $(x_1, x_2, \ldots, x_n)$ and define $|x|$ to be the vector $(|x_1|, |x_2|, \ldots, |x_n|)$. Then multivariate symmetry means the likelihood or probability (respectively for continuous or discrete distributions) of x is always the same as that of $|x|$; remember we are assuming $\mu = 0$.

Multivariate symmetry defines the special null hypothesis

$$H_S : f(x) = f(|x|) \text{ for all vectors } x. \tag{5.3.1}$$

When H_S is true, the bivariate density of X_t and $X_{t+\tau}$, denoted $p(x_t, x_{t+\tau})$, has

$$p(x_t, x_{t+\tau}) = p(x_t, -x_{t+\tau}) = p(-x_t, x_{t+\tau}) = p(-x_t, -x_{t+\tau}).$$

Consequently, it can be verified that

$$\int\int x_t x_{t+\tau} p(x_t, x_{t+\tau}) \, dx_t \, dx_{t+\tau} = 0$$

and so H_S implies

$$H_0 : X_t \text{ and } X_{t+\tau} \text{ are uncorrelated whenever } \tau > 0.$$

Obviously H_0 does not imply H_S. However, it is reasonable to assume that any acceptable model satisfying H_0 will also satisfy H_S. As noted previously in Section 3.3, almost all the researchers who have studied realistic uncorrelated processes assume $\{U_t\}$ is Gaussian white noise. It then follows that H_S is true because firstly the U_t are independently distributed and secondly the normal distribution is, of course, symmetric.

5.4 ESTIMATES OF THE VARIANCES OF SAMPLE AUTOCORRELATIONS

As the expected value of every X_t is assumed to be zero, the sample autocorrelations can be defined for n observations by

$$r_{\tau,x} = \sum_{t=1}^{n-\tau} x_t x_{t+\tau} \bigg/ \sum_{t=1}^{n} x_t^2. \tag{5.4.1}$$

There is a negligible difference between this definition and the one adopted earlier when the expected value of X_t is unknown (equation (2.9.1)). The sample autocorrelations are the realizations of the random variables $R_{\tau,x} = \sum X_t X_{t+\tau} / \sum X_t^2$. Let $\alpha_\tau = \text{var}(R_{\tau,x})$. Then we are interested in estimating α_τ using only the n observed returns and the assumption that the multivariate density is symmetric.

The parameters α_τ depend on the multivariate distribution of the X_t, about which we have attempted to assume as little as possible. Given the observations $x_t (1 \leq t \leq n)$ and assuming H_S is true, all that can be deduced about the density function is the following statement: every sequence x_t^*, $1 \leq t \leq n$, for which each x_t^* is either x_t or $-x_t$ has equal likelihood, namely the likelihood of the observed data. There are 2^n such sequences if all the x_t are non-zero: there are less if some zero returns are observed.

Each sequence could have occurred and caused a particular realization of $R_{\tau,x}$. These equiprobable sequences thus provide a discrete conditional distribution for $R_{\tau,x}$. This is the distribution of $R_{\tau,x}$ given that $|X_t| = |x_t|$, $1 \leq t \leq n$. The variance of this conditional distribution is later shown to be

$$a_\tau = \sum_{t=1}^{n-\tau} x_t^2 x_{t+\tau}^2 \bigg/ \left(\sum_{t=1}^{n} x_t^2 \right)^2. \tag{5.4.2}$$

The number a_τ can and will be used to estimate α_τ. This estimate is unbiased when H_S is true, i.e. if a_τ is an observation of $A_\tau = \sum X_t^2 X_{t+\tau}^2 / (\sum X_t^2)^2$ then $E[A_\tau] = \alpha_\tau$. There can be some bias if H_S is false. Its magnitude and the interpretation of a_τ in these circumstances are discussed in Section 5.6.

The a_τ are the only obvious estimates of the parameters α_τ when the only assumption about the X_t is multivariate symmetry. No alternative estimates are known. Other estimates might be obtained if further conditions about the X_t are assumed. However, it is very difficult to select realistic extra conditions. The remainder of this section covers the derivation of a_τ and then shows there is no bias if H_S is true. Readers wishing to avoid further mathematical results should now move on to Section 5.6.

Let $m_t = |x_t|$ and $M_t = |X_t|$ for $1 \leq t \leq n$ and denote by m and M the vectors $(m_1, m_2, \ldots, m_n)$ and $(M_1, M_2, \ldots, M_n)$, respectively. It will be assumed that the X_t have continuous densities so there is zero probability of observing $x_t = 0$; it is straightforward to adapt the following algebra for discrete distributions having $x_t = 0$ as a possible outcome. Assuming continuous densities, discrete random variables π_t can be defined by $X_t = \pi_t M_t$ and the only possible realized values of π_t are 1 and -1. The probability of any feasible realization of $\pi = (\pi_1, \pi_2, \ldots, \pi_n)$ is an n-dimensional integral of the density function of $x = (x_1, x_2, \ldots, x_n)$ over a region $\{x_j > 0, \text{ all } j \in J, x_k < 0, \text{ all } k \notin J \text{ with } 1 \leq k \leq n\}$, for some set J. Assuming H_S is true, all these integrals and probabilities equal the same integral over the region $\{x_j > 0, 1 \leq j \leq n\}$. Consequently, the π_t are independently and identically distributed with $P(\pi_t = 1) = P(\pi_t = -1) = \frac{1}{2}$ when H_S is true. Using this conclusion, var $(R_{\tau,x} | M = m)$ can be calculated.

Writing $R_{\tau,x}$ as $\sum \pi_t \pi_{t+\tau} M_t M_{t+\tau} / \sum M_t^2$,

$$E[R_{\tau,x} | m] = \sum m_t m_{t+\tau} E[\pi_t \pi_{t+\tau}] / \sum m_t^2 = 0$$

because $E[\pi_t \pi_{t+\tau}] = 0$ for all t and all $\tau > 0$. Thus

$$\text{var } (R_{\tau,x} | m) = E[R_{\tau,x}^2 | m] = E\left[\left(\sum \pi_t \pi_{t+\tau} m_t m_{t+\tau}\right)^2\right] / \left(\sum m_t^2\right)^2.$$

As $E[\pi_s \pi_{s+\tau} \pi_t \pi_{t+\tau}] = 0$ for $s \neq t$ and $\tau > 0$, and $E[\pi_t^2 \pi_{t+\tau}^2] = 1$, it follows that when H_S is true:

$$\text{var } (R_{\tau,x} | m) = \sum_{t=1}^{n-\tau} m_t^2 m_{t+\tau}^2 / \left(\sum m_t^2\right)^2.$$

This conditional variance is the estimate a_τ given in equation (5.4.2). Also, if $A_\tau = \sum M_t^2 M_{t+\tau}^2 / (\sum M_t^2)^2$, then for any m:

$$E[A_\tau | m] = E[R_{\tau,x}^2 | m].$$

So, unconditionally, $E[A_\tau] = E[R_{\tau,x}^2] = \text{var } (R_\tau) = \alpha_\tau$ and hence a_τ is an unbiased estimate of α_τ, again assuming H_S is true.

5.5   SOME ASYMPTOTIC RESULTS

The derivation of the estimates a_τ does not require the process $\{X_t\}$ to be stationary and the estimates should be useful for investigations of non-stationary data. It will be assumed in this section that $\{X_t\}$ is stationary and has finite kurtosis. Asymptotic limits can then be derived for the estimates. These limits indicate the probable magnitude of the estimates for various uncorrelated processes and also allow us to assess the size of any bias when the process is not uncorrelated.

Suppose now that $a_{\tau,n}$ denotes the estimate of var $(R_{\tau,X})$ based on n observations, given by equation (5.4.2), and let $b_{\tau,n} = n(a_{\tau,n})$. Then

$$b_{\tau,n} = \left(\frac{1}{n}\sum_{t=1}^{n-\tau} x_t^2 x_{t+\tau}^2\right)\Big/\left(\frac{1}{n}\sum_{t=1}^{n} x_t^2\right)^2$$

and therefore, by the law of large numbers,

$$b_{\tau,n} \rightarrow \beta_\tau = E[X_t^2 X_{t+\tau}^2]/E[X_t^2]^2 \tag{5.5.1}$$

as $n \rightarrow \infty$. A more convenient formula for β_τ can be found by applying the result that cov (X_t^2, X_{t+i}^2) equals $E[X_t^2 X_{t+i}^2] - E[X_t^2]^2$, firstly with $i = \tau$ and secondly with $i = 0$. This gives us the result that β_τ depends on the kurtosis of the X_t, denoted k_X, and the autocorrelations of $S_t = X_t^2$:

$$\beta_\tau = 1 + (k_X - 1)\rho_{\tau,S}. \tag{5.5.2}$$

Clearly, $\beta_\tau = 1$ for any strict white noise process, even if it is not symmetric. Also, when H_S is true,

$$n[\text{var }(R_{\tau,X})] \rightarrow \beta_\tau$$

as $n \rightarrow \infty$, because all the estimates $a_{\tau,n}$ are unbiased. We should expect the $\rho_{\tau,S}$ to be positive for returns and to decline towards zero as τ increases. The β_τ are then always more than one and decline towards one for large τ.

Linear processes

If X_t is a linear combination of the present and past terms from a zero-mean, Gaussian, white noise process $\{\varepsilon_t\}$, then $k_X = 3$ and $\rho_{\tau,S} = \rho_{\tau,X}^2$ (Granger and Newbold, 1976) and hence $\beta_\tau = 1 + 2\rho_\tau^2$. When, however, the ε_t have a non-Gaussian distribution, the results about $\rho_{\tau,S}$ in Section 2.10 show that

$$\beta_\tau = 1 + 2\rho_\tau^2 + (k_X - 3)c_\tau \tag{5.5.3}$$

for certain non-negative c_τ having a small total, i.e. $\Sigma\, c_\tau$ is small summing over positive τ.

Assuming $\{X_t\}$ is not strict white noise, H_S is false and the estimates a_τ can be biased. For example, if $\{X_t\}$ is a linear AR(1) process with autocorrelations ϕ^τ, from Kendall and Stuart (1976, p. 472) we obtain:

$$n[\text{var }(R_{\tau,X})] \rightarrow (1 + \phi^2)(1 - \phi^{2\tau})/(1 - \phi^2) - 2\tau\phi^{2\tau} \neq \beta_\tau.$$

Now if $\phi = 0.1$ the correct asymptotic limit of $n[\text{var }(R_{\tau,X})]$ increases from 0.99 (for $\tau = 1$) to 1.02 for large τ. By comparison, $\beta_1 = 1.02$ and $\beta_\tau = 1$ for large τ when the process is Gaussian. In this example $\Sigma\, c_\tau = \phi^2 = 0.01$ so the term $(k_X - 3)c_\tau$ in equation (5.5.3) will be negligible. We see that the bias in β_τ (and hence estimates a_τ) is very small for a linear, AR(1) process having a sensible, low autoregressive parameter.

Non-linear processes

When $\{X_t\}$ is the product of stochastically independent, stationary processes $\{V_t\}$ and $\{U_t\}$, with our usual conditions on the mean and variance of U_t, equation (5.5.1) shows that

$$\beta_\tau = E[U_t^2 U_{t+\tau}^2]\{E[V_t^2 V_{t+\tau}^2]/E[V_t^2]^2\}. \tag{5.5.4}$$

For strict white noise $\{U_t\}$, the expectation outside the curly brackets is always 1 and the β_τ are determined by the mean, variance, and autocorrelations of $\{V_t^2\}$:

$$\beta_\tau = 1 + \rho_{\tau, V^2}(\text{var }(V_t^2)/E[V_t^2]^2).$$

For the special case when $\{\log(V_t)\}$ is a Gaussian, AR(1) process with variance σ^2 and autocorrelations ϕ^τ, equations (3.5.6), (3.5.7), and (3.5.10) can be substituted into (5.5.2), to show that

$$\beta_\tau = \exp(4\sigma^2\phi^\tau). \tag{5.5.5}$$

Some of the estimates of σ presented in Section 3.9 exceed $\frac{1}{2}$ and generally ϕ is estimated near 1, thus the β_τ could exceed $e = 2.7 \ldots$ for low τ.

When $\{U_t\}$ is not strict white noise, equation (5.5.4) shows that the autocorrelation in the process causes β_τ to be the figure for a comparable uncorrelated process multiplied by $E[U_t^2 U_{t+\tau}^2]$. This multiplicative factor is $1 + (k_U - 1)\rho_{\tau, U^2}$, k_U denoting the kurtosis of the U_t. The factor will be very small. It would be $1 + 2\rho_{\tau, U^2}$ for a Gaussian, linear $\{U_t\}$, then bounded below by 1 and above by 1.02 when $|\rho_{\tau, U}| \leqslant 0.1$.

This multiplicative factor suggests a way to assess the bias in β_τ for a general autocorrelated process $\{X_t\}$. Bias is caused by the autocorrelation in $\{U_t\}$, so let δ_t be the limit of $n[\text{var }(R_{\tau, U})]$ minus the factor $1 + (k_U - 1)\rho_{\tau, U^2}$. Then δ_t is the bias for process $\{U_t\}$ and it will be small; see the preceding sub-section about linear processes. Then the bias

$$n[\text{var }(R_{\tau, X})] - \beta_\tau$$

as $n \to \infty$, will be approximately $\delta_\tau E[V_t^2 V_{t+\tau}^2]/E[V_t^2]^2$ from (5.5.4), i.e. approximately $\delta_\tau\beta_\tau$.

For the uncorrelated ARCH process introduced in Section 3.6 the limit β_τ can only be derived for very special cases because it is difficult to find the kurtosis k_X. For a first-order ARCH process (equation (3.6.3)) with $\rho_{\tau, S} = \phi^\tau$ and $\phi^2 < 1/3$, it is easy to show

$$\beta_\tau = 1 + 2\phi^\tau/(1 - 3\phi^2). \tag{5.5.6}$$

Note that in both of equations (5.5.5) and (5.5.6) changes in conditional variance can cause the β_τ to be arbitrarily large. In each case the β_τ decrease monotonically towards 1 as τ is increased.

5.6 INTERPRETING THE ESTIMATES

Empirical estimates of the variances of autocorrelation coefficients are given in the next section. First, however, we clarify the interpretation of an estimate $b_\tau = n[a_\tau]$ of $n[\text{var} (R_{\tau,x})]$.

Consider the following hypothetical example: 2500 returns yield $r_{1,x} = 0.05$ and $b_1 = 2.25$. Then assuming $R_{1,x}$ has variance $1/n$ we would reject the hypothesis of strict white noise at a 5 per cent significance level, since $r_{1,x}$ is more than $1.96/\sqrt{n} = 0.04$ approximately. However, H_S could well be true with $R_{1,x}$ having variance $2.25/n = 0.03^2$ because $r_{1,x}/0.03$ is only 1.67. Thus we would not be willing to reject H_S nor the hypothesis H_0 of zero autocorrelation using $r_{1,x}$. There might, however, be a series of rescaled returns $\{y_t\}$ defined in a manner that does not introduce spurious autocorrelation. This series could have $r_{1,y} = 0.045$ and an estimate b_1^* of $n[\text{var} (R_{1,y})]$ equal to 1. Then we would be happy to reject H_S and also H_0 at the 5 per cent level whenever the estimate b_1^* is considered reliable. We define satisfactory series $\{y_t\}$ in Section 5.8. If you jumped Section 5.5 you are advised to read the next paragraph and then jump to Section 5.7.

The estimates a_τ have been derived by assuming H_S is true. Researchers often want to test for zero autocorrelation. Thus it is not known, before testing, whether or not H_S is true. How should b_τ be interpreted in these circumstances? The recommended answer has two parts. Firstly, b_τ is either unbiased or has negligible bias and, secondly, if the b_τ are far more than 1 then random walk tests based on the assumption $\text{var} (R_{\tau,x}) \simeq 1/n$ are unreliable.

To motivate this answer, consider some of the asymptotic results recently obtained for stationary processes. When H_S is true, b_τ is an unbiased estimate of $n[\text{var} (R_{\tau,x})]$. If, instead, H_S is false, then b_τ can be biased but the proportional bias, i.e.

$$\{E[B_\tau] - n[\text{var} (R_{\tau,x})]\}/\{n[\text{var} (R_{\tau,x})]\}$$

will always be small for long series (b_τ is the observed value of B_τ). The asymptoptic proportional bias was shown in Section 5.5 to be 3 per cent or less for all τ when $\{X_t\}$ is Gaussian and AR(1), with maximum autocorrelation $\rho_{1,x} = 0.1$. In practice the proportional bias could be higher but it is very unlikely that it could exceed 10 per cent for a sensible model for daily returns. The issue of bias is therefore not very important when estimates b_τ are considered.

Any test of the random walk hypothesis involving autocorrelation coefficients requires the variance of coefficients when the null hypothesis of zero autocorrelation is true. Suppose $X_t = V_t U_t$ and $\{U_t\}$ is almost strict white noise, so, as in Section 3.7, $U_t = T_t + \varepsilon_t$ with $\{\varepsilon_t\}$ strict white noise and $\text{var} (T_t) \ll \text{var} (\varepsilon_t)$. Then equation (5.5.4) shows, for the product of stochastically independent and stationary processes, that the asymptotic estimates β_τ are almost identical for (a) the process $\{X_t\}$ and (b) the uncorrelated process $\{X_t^*\}$ defined by $X_t^* = V_t \varepsilon_t$. Thus, even if H_S is false, we can expect a_τ to be an appropriate estimate of the relevant sample variance when the null hypothesis is true. So, if the b_τ are significantly greater than 1 it is always inappropriate to attempt random walk tests based on the assumption var $(R_{\tau,X}) \simeq 1/n$.

The conclusions in the two previous paragraphs are deduced from results proved for stationary processes. It is possible to satisfy ourselves that these conclusions remain valid if $\{V_t\}$ is not stationary and $\{U_t\}$ is approximately strict white noise.

Estimates b_τ can have high standard errors, discussed further in Section 5.9. Consequently the b_τ should be calculated for several lags τ and a set of estimates considered. Fortunately when this is tried the conclusions are very incisive.

When b_τ is clearly more than 1 the significance level of a test involving $R_{\tau,X}$ will be underestimated. This can be very serious. For example, suppose that $\{X_t\}$ is uncorrelated and $R_{\tau,X} \sim N(0, 2/n)$ but we use a 5 per cent significance level and falsely assume $R_{\tau,X} \sim N(0, 1/n)$. Then the chance of rejecting the random walk hypothesis, using $R_{\tau,X}$ for the test, is

$$P(|Z_1| > 1.96/\sqrt{n}), \qquad \text{with } Z_1 \sim N(0, 2/n),$$

and this probability is

$$P(|Z_2| > 1.96/\sqrt{2}), \qquad \text{with } Z_2 \sim N(0, 1)$$

which equals $P(|Z_2| > 1.386) = 17$ per cent.

5.7   THE ESTIMATES FOR RETURNS

The estimates a_τ of $\alpha_\tau = $ var $(R_{\tau,X})$ derived in Section 5.4 apply the assumption that the means of the X_t are all zero. For a known constant mean μ, all terms x_t in (5.4.2) would be replaced by $x_t - \mu$. To calculate empirical estimates of the autocorrelation variances, all terms x_t are replaced by $x_t - \bar{x}$. The estimate b_τ of $n[$var $(R_{\tau,X})]$ then becomes

$$b_\tau = n \sum_{t=1}^{n-\tau} (x_t - \bar{x})^2 (x_{t+\tau} - \bar{x})^2 \bigg/ \left\{ \sum_{t=1}^{n} (x_t - \bar{x})^2 \right\}^2. \tag{5.7.1}$$

For futures series the numerator summation in (5.7.1) is restricted to those times t for which x_t and $x_{t+\tau}$ are returns from the same contract.

Estimates b_τ are presented in Table 5.1 for lags τ from 1 to 5 days for all 40 series. Many estimates are greater than 2. Several commodity estimates exceed 3. Figures 5.1, 5.2, and 5.3 display the estimates up to lag 30 for the first share series, the gold series, and the longest sugar futures series.

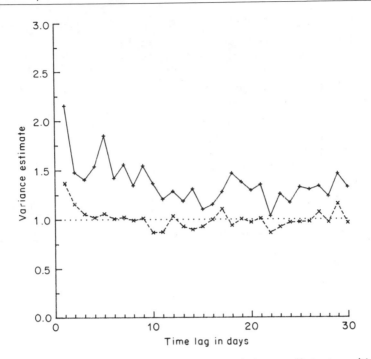

Figure 5.1 Estimates of the variances of autocorrelation coefficients multiplied by the number of observations for the first US stock series. Estimates b_τ for returns ($+$) and b_τ^* for rescaled returns ($\times$)

These estimates tend to decrease as τ increases and so they are fairly consistent with the general asymptotic results of Section 5.5 and the special result (5.5.5).

Stocks generally have lower estimates than currencies or commodities. This is made clear by the following medians and means.

	Median estimate Lag					Mean estimate Lag				
	1	2	3	4	5	1	2	3	4	5
15 US stocks	1.81	1.43	1.43	1.47	1.36	1.79	1.46	1.47	1.43	1.44
4 currency series	2.02	1.62	1.50	1.48	1.59	2.01	1.66	1.55	1.56	1.70
19 commodity series	3.06	3.14	2.83	2.49	2.57	4.13	3.42	3.08	2.85	2.90

The minima of these summary statistics are 1.36 for the stocks, 1.48 for the currencies, and 2.49 for the commodities. Even if the actual variances of coefficients $R_{\tau,x}$ were as low as these minima, divided by n, it would be necessary to change the standard methodology used in random walk tests.

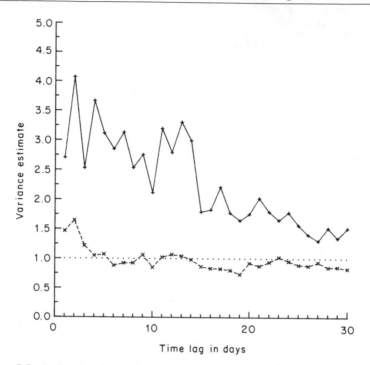

Figure 5.2 Estimates b_τ and b_τ^* for gold returns (+) and rescaled returns (×)

The estimates b_τ prove conclusively that the autocorrelation coefficients of daily returns have variances greater than $1/n$. Therefore random walk tests should not assume the variances of coefficients equal $1/n$. A higher variance is needed when testing for zero autocorrelation in the returns process by examining the sample autocorrelations. Using $1/n$ for the variances is only acceptable when testing for independence and identical distributions, i.e. strict white noise (SWN). However, we saw in Section 2.10 that the SWN hypothesis is false for all series.

5.8 ACCURATE AUTOCORRELATION ESTIMATES

The high variances of conventional autocorrelation coefficients are almost certainly caused by the non-constant conditional variances of the returns. This is shown to be a possible explanation by various equations in Section 5.5, including (5.5.5). To obtain accurate coefficients we need a series possessing a reasonably homogeneous variance. Ideally this would be the series $\{u_t\}$ in which u_t equals $(x_t - \mu)/v_t$. As u_t is the realization of exact or approximate strict white noise $\{U_t\}$, coefficients calculated from the $\{u_t\}$

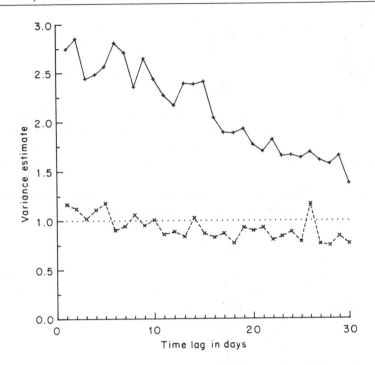

Figure 5.3   Estimates b_τ and b_τ^* for sugar futures returns (+) and rescaled returns (×)

would have orthodox variances, i.e. var $(R_{\tau,U}) \simeq 1/n$. Of course, the realized conditional standard deviations v_t are not observable so u_t cannot be calculated.

Rescaled returns

An approximation to the standardized return $u_t = (x_t - \mu)/v_t$ is given by substituting estimates for μ and v_t. Using $\bar{x}$ for μ and a forecast $\hat{v}_t$ made at time $t - 1$ gives the *rescaled return* defined by

$$y_t = (x_t - \bar{x})/\hat{v}_t \qquad (5.8.1)$$
$$\simeq (x_t - \mu)/\hat{v}_t$$
$$= u_t(v_t/\hat{v}_t).$$

The rescaled return will be similar to the unobservable standardized return whenever $\hat{v}_t$ is a good forecast. Removing $\bar{x}$ from (5.8.1) and the calculation of $\hat{v}_t$, as in the author's previous publications, produces almost identical results.

The forecast $\hat{v}_t$ recommended in Chapter 4 is always used in the calculation of y_t. Initially,

$$\hat{v}_{21} = 1.253 \sum_{t=1}^{20} |x_t - \bar{x}|/20 \tag{5.8.2}$$

and thereafter

$$\hat{v}_t = (1 - \gamma)\hat{v}_{t-1} + 1.253\gamma|x_{t-1} - \bar{x}|. \tag{5.8.3}$$

For stock series $\gamma = 0.04$ and for all other series $\gamma = 0.1$. Futures series need initial forecasts for each contract. For contract i, contributing returns at times $T_{i-1} + 1$ to T_i inclusive to a time series $\{x_t\}$, the twenty returns on contract i from times $T_{i-1} - 19$ to T_{i-1} are used to calculate the initial forecast ($i > 1$).

It is recommended that autocorrelation coefficients are calculated from the series of rescaled returns $\{y_t\}$. These coefficients are

$$r_{\tau,y} = \sum_{t=21}^{n-\tau} (y_t - \bar{y})(y_{t+\tau} - \bar{y}) \Big/ \sum_{t=21}^{n} (y_t - \bar{y})^2. \tag{5.8.4}$$

Times before 21 are left out of (5.8.4) because forecasts $\hat{v}_t$ are not attempted for such times. The coefficients $r_{\tau,y}$ are now shown to have acceptable variances, i.e. if $n^* = n - 20$ then var $(R_{\tau,Y}) \simeq 1/n^*$.

Variance estimates for recommended coefficients

The estimated variances of the coefficients for returns $\{x_t\}$ were obtained by assuming the multivariate symmetry hypothesis H_S. When H_S is true for $\{X_t\}$ it will also be true for the process $\{Y_t\}$ generating the rescaled returns $\{y_t\}$, if we ignore the difference between $\bar{x}$ and μ. This conclusion follows from the definition of $\hat{v}_t$; it is a function of past returns which does not depend on the signs, positive or negative, of $x_{t-i} - \bar{x}, i > 0$. Consequently, the variances of autocorrelation coefficients calculated from rescaled returns can be estimated by the method applied to the returns.

Consider $r_{\tau,y}$ to be the realized value of $R_{\tau,Y}$. Then the estimate b_τ^* of $n^*[\text{var } (R_{\tau,Y})]$ is

$$b_\tau^* = (n - 20) \sum_{t=21}^{n-\tau} (y_t - \bar{y})^2(y_{t+\tau} - \bar{y})^2 \Big/ \left\{ \sum_{t=21}^{n} (y_t - \bar{y})^2 \right\}. \tag{5.8.4}$$

The first twenty returns are needed to obtain the initial $\hat{v}_t$ and hence the summations in (5.8.4) begin at $t = 21$. Table 5.1 presents the estimates b_τ^* at lags 1 to 5 for comparison with the estimates b_τ. All but five of the 200 tabulated estimates b_τ are greater than the corresponding estimate b_τ^*. Therefore $r_{\tau,y}$ is expected to be a more accurate estimate than $r_{\tau,x}$. Figures 5.1, 5.2, and 5.3 compare b_τ and b_τ^* graphically up to lag 30.

Table 5.1   Estimates of n[var (R_τ)] for returns and rescaled returns

	Estimates b_τ from returns x_t Lag					Estimates b_τ^* from rescaled returns y_t Lag				
	1	2	3	4	5	1	2	3	4	5
Spot series										
Allied	2.15	1.48	1.40	1.54	1.85	1.37	1.16	1.05	1.02	1.06
Alcoa	1.92	1.18	1.47	1.51	1.55	1.27	0.94	0.97	0.93	1.07
Am. Can	1.36	1.22	1.28	1.24	1.23	1.17	1.03	1.08	0.97	0.93
AT and T	1.71	1.13	1.36	1.13	0.97	1.33	0.99	1.24	1.08	0.84
Am. Brands	1.91	1.60	1.39	1.26	1.21	1.97	1.48	1.15	1.14	1.03
Anaconda	1.70	1.41	1.43	1.22	1.11	2.09	1.18	1.60	0.86	0.89
Bethlehem	1.47	1.50	1.28	1.15	1.07	1.34	1.14	1.00	0.95	0.88
Chrysler	1.68	1.30	1.33	1.47	1.25	1.23	0.97	1.00	1.14	0.88
Dupont	1.73	1.76	1.50	1.72	1.43	1.33	1.22	1.02	1.14	1.06
Kodak	1.96	1.74	1.96	1.65	2.55	1.11	1.08	1.13	1.05	1.10
G. Electric	1.81	1.89	1.81	1.79	1.91	1.19	1.07	1.02	1.05	1.00
G. Foods	1.88	1.51	1.48	1.52	1.48	1.25	1.02	1.03	1.02	1.10
G. Motors	2.07	1.43	1.59	1.46	1.40	1.27	1.06	1.00	0.97	1.05
G. Telephone	1.61	1.32	1.35	1.48	1.36	1.07	0.95	0.92	1.19	0.96
Harvester	1.82	1.43	1.45	1.29	1.19	1.34	1.02	0.99	1.07	0.97
FT 30	1.38	1.49	1.32	1.32	1.43	0.98	1.11	1.04	1.04	1.05
Gold	2.70	4.07	2.53	3.67	3.11	1.47	1.65	1.22	1.05	1.07
Silver	3.14	4.54	4.45	3.14	4.82	1.14	1.12	0.78	1.20	1.11
Copper	3.06	2.07	1.96	1.82	1.98	1.75	1.05	1.08	0.93	0.94
Lead	4.09	2.60	2.59	2.05	2.03	2.72	2.21	1.32	0.92	1.03
Tin	3.17	3.59	3.64	3.78	3.52	1.27	1.27	0.98	1.25	0.97
Zinc	5.10	4.52	3.81	5.52	4.98	1.61	0.99	1.01	1.03	1.02
£/$	2.11	1.55	1.51	2.05	2.14	3.94	0.42	0.82	0.76	0.43
Futures series										
Corn (12)	3.49	2.69	2.62	2.63	2.38	1.13	1.21	0.96	1.08	0.97
Corn (6)	2.84	3.17	2.87	2.85	2.78	1.14	1.05	1.10	0.97	0.93
Corn (3)	2.85	3.14	2.83	2.77	2.67	0.97	1.05	1.05	0.98	0.99
Cocoa (12)	2.62	2.49	3.16	1.78	2.08	0.95	0.96	1.03	1.16	1.08
Cocoa (6)	2.51	2.36	2.83	1.64	1.85	1.00	0.95	0.95	1.01	0.87
Cocoa (3)	2.36	2.08	2.55	1.65	1.63	1.00	0.91	0.92	1.12	0.84
Coffee (12)	5.77	3.33	2.57	2.01	2.57	2.38	1.25	0.92	0.94	0.86
Coffee (6)	6.92	3.99	3.16	2.31	3.09	2.60	1.15	0.98	1.00	0.85
Coffee (3)	12.55	6.34	3.38	2.65	2.86	2.31	1.11	1.05	1.04	0.81
Sugar (12)	2.74	2.85	2.44	2.49	2.57	1.17	1.12	1.02	1.11	1.18
Sugar (6)	2.61	2.62	2.39	2.33	2.21	1.22	1.07	1.10	1.07	1.11
Sugar ((3)	2.50	2.58	2.27	2.21	2.10	1.27	1.09	1.07	1.03	1.17
Wool (12)	7.43	5.99	6.45	6.82	5.93	1.21	1.45	0.87	1.07	0.97
£/$ (6)	1.89	1.44	1.50	1.23	1.57	1.98	0.83	1.25	0.75	0.84
DM/$ (6)	2.08	1.95	1.71	1.57	1.61	1.34	1.25	1.06	0.93	1.04
SF/$ (6)	1.96	1.69	1.49	1.39	1.46	0.96	1.08	1.03	0.86	1.05
T-bond	1.09	1.27	1.26	1.04	1.08	0.85	1.02	0.96	0.77	0.85

Summary statistics for the b_τ^* are as follows.

	Median estimate Lag					Mean estimate Lag				
	1	2	3	4	5	1	2	3	4	5
15 US stocks	1.27	1.06	1.02	1.05	1.00	1.36	1.09	1.08	1.04	0.99
4 currency series	1.66	0.95	1.05	0.81	0.94	2.06	0.90	1.04	0.83	0.84
19 commodity series	1.22	1.11	1.02	1.04	0.97	1.49	1.19	1.02	1.05	0.99

These statistics are much closer to 1 than the respective statistics for returns. The autocorrelation variances are satisfactory for rescaled returns at lag 2 or higher, for then var $(R_{\tau,Y}) \simeq 1/n^*$, but they are not entirely satisfactory at lag 1.

Exceptional series

Plots of b_τ against τ show the autocorrelation variances exceed $1/n$ for returns, at several lags τ, whichever series is considered. With two exceptions, plots of b_τ^* against τ show the variances are about $1/n$ for rescaled returns although the estimates are often scattered far above and below the line $b_\tau^* = 1$. The exceptional series are the share Anaconda and the spot, sterling/dollar exchange rate. For example, the b_τ^* range from 0.13 to 13.27 for the currency series, considering lags 1 to 50. These meaningless estimates are caused by extreme outliers in the series $\{y_t\}$. Extreme outliers can dominate the estimates because they are squared in the calculations. Clipping outliers more than two standard deviations away from the mean provides satisfactory estimates. Clipping financial time series is discussed by Granger and Orr (1972).

5.9   SIMULATION RESULTS

Neither the estimates b_τ nor the b_τ^* are approximately constant for all τ, suggesting the estimates are not particularly accurate. Accordingly, four processes $\{X_t\}$ have been simulated to provide information about the distributions of the estimates of autocorrelation variances. Two processes are strict white noise, the first is Gaussian and the second has the Student's t distribution with six degrees of freedom. The third process has a step change in variance after half the observations have been simulated; each half is Gaussian, white noise and the second half has variance equal to four times the variance in the first half. The other process is an example of the special product process described in Chapter 3; $X_t = V_t U_t$ with $\{U_t\}$ Gaussian white noise and $\{\log (V_t)\}$ a Gaussian AR(1) process with autocorrelations 0.95^τ and variance 0.25.

Table 5.2   Summary of simulated estimates for series of 1000 returns

	Gaussian noise	t_6 noise	Variance jump	Fluctuating variances
For 100 estimates b_1				
Mean	0.988	1.014	1.323	2.401
Standard deviation	0.057	0.139	0.110	1.690
For 100 estimates b_1^*				
Mean	0.906	0.864	0.915	1.187
Standard deviation	0.067	0.106	0.073	0.152

Reproduced from Taylor (1984) by permission of the Royal Statistical Society.

Each process has been simulated 100 times for series lengths n equal to 500, 1000, or 2000. Table 5.2 summarizes the simulated estimates b_1 and b_1^* for $n = 1000$.

Several conclusions are offered about the random variables B_τ generating the estimates b_τ. Firstly, for Gaussian noise the standard deviation of B_τ is small. Secondly, high kurtosis in the distribution of X_t gives a far higher standard deviation for B_τ than the comparable figure for Gaussian noise. The t_6 distribution has kurtosis equal to 6 and the standard deviation of B_τ is then about twice the Gaussian figure. Thirdly, a step change in variance increases the mean and variance of B_τ but not substantially. Multiplying the variance of normal variables by λ after half the observations gives an asymptotic limit equal to $2(1 + \lambda^2)/(1 + \lambda)^2$ for all the b_τ. The simulations had $\lambda = 4$ and asymptotic limit equal to 1.36. The average b_1 was 1.32, 1.32, and 1.35 for $n = 500$, 1000, and 2000. Fourthly, the B_τ have very high standard deviations when the conditional variance of X_t fluctuates. For the product process and series lengths considered, very approximately $sd(B_1) = 1.0$, $sd(B_{10}) = 0.6$, and $sd(B_{50}) = 0.2$. The distribution of B_1 has high, positive skewness and is highly leptokurtic for the product process. In our example the asymptotic limit of b_1 is $\beta_1 = 2.59$, using (5.5.5). The average value $E[B_1]$ divided by β_1 is approximately 0.85 for $n = 500$ and 0.92 for $n = 2000$.

Simulated estimates b_τ^* for rescaled returns are satisfactorily close to the desired value of 1 needed for standard autocorrelation tests. The estimates b_τ^* have much smaller means and standard deviations than the b_τ for the realistic fluctuating variance process.

5.10   AUTOCORRELATIONS OF RESCALED PROCESSES

Autocorrelation estimates calculated from rescaled returns are less variable than estimates calculated from returns. Rescaling may be thought to create spurious autocorrelation. This section uses theoretical arguments to assert that such anxieties about rescaling are misfounded. Simulations in Section 6.9 confirm this view.

Suppose first that U_t is independent of all U_{t-i} and V_{t-i+1}, $i > 0$, as frequently assumed before, so $\{X_t\}$ is uncorrelated. Also assuming $\bar{X} = \mu$, the random variable Y_t generating rescaled returns is $U_t(V_t/\hat{V}_t)$, $E[Y_t] = 0$ and

$$\text{cov}\,(Y_t,\,Y_{t+\tau}) = E[U_{t+\tau}]E[U_t V_t V_{t+\tau}/(\hat{V}_t \hat{V}_{t+\tau})] = 0$$

for $\tau > 0$, showing $\{Y_t\}$ is then uncorrelated. Now $\bar{X}$ is not μ but their difference will certainly be small for long series. As

$$Y_t = (X_t - \bar{X})/\hat{V}_t = U_t(V_t/\hat{V}_t) - (\bar{X} - \mu)/\hat{V}_t,$$

if this definition is applied to n variables X_t and n forecasts $\hat{V}_t$ to produce n rescaled variables Y_t it can be shown that

$$\text{cov}\,(Y_t,\,Y_{t+\tau}) \simeq -1/n, \qquad 0 < \tau \ll n.$$

As var (Y_t) is very approximately 1, rescaling cannot cause important spurious autocorrelation when the returns process is uncorrelated about a constant mean.

When all processes are stationary and $\{X_t\}$ may be autocorrelated, the following inequalities were obtained as (3.7.5) for product processes:

$$\rho_{\tau,V} \lesssim \rho_{\tau,X}/\rho_{\tau,U} \lesssim 1. \tag{5.10.1}$$

For low τ the estimates in Chapters 3 and 4 show $\rho_{\tau,V} \simeq 1$ whilst, for high τ, $\rho_{\tau,X} \simeq 0$ and so $\rho_{\tau,X} \simeq \rho_{\tau,U}$ for all τ. The autocorrelations of $\{Y_t\}$ cannot be described so easily. Series must be simulated to learn much and this will be done for various autocorrelated processes in Chapters 6 and 7.

5.11   SUMMARY

Autocorrelation coefficients calculated from returns have variances greater than $1/n$. This is a consequence of the changes in returns variance or conditional variance identified in previous chapters. Assuming the autocorrelation variance is $1/n$ when the true variance is greater will make random walk tests unreliable.

Estimates b_τ of n times the autocorrelation variances should be calculated for several lags τ. When the estimates are far more than 1 something must be done to improve random walk tests. Action is necessary for all the returns analysed here. Rescaling the returns produces series whose autocorrelation variances are generally satisfactory.

Chapter 6

Testing the Random Walk Hypothesis

The random walk hypothesis is now tested and rejected for every type of financial asset considered. Naturally the statistical dependence identified is very small and long series and powerful tests are required to prove it exists. Departures from random behaviour are consistent with price-trend models for commodities and currencies but not stocks.

6.1   INTRODUCTION

Several definitions of the random walk hypothesis have been offered, as noted in Section 1.5. The hypothesis that returns have independent and identical distributions (i.i.d.) was rejected comprehensively in Section 2.10. Changes in either variance or conditional variance can suffice to explain the rejection of the i.i.d. hypothesis (Chapter 3). Thus the interesting hypothesis of uncorrelated returns remains untested when the i.i.d. hypothesis is refuted. This is true even if standard autocorrelation tests are applied to returns (Sections 5.6 and 5.7).

A more general null hypothesis can be defined by firstly replacing identical distributions by identical means and secondly replacing independent distributions by uncorrelated distributions, to give

$$H_0: E[X_t] = E[X_{t+\tau}] \quad \text{and} \quad \text{cov}(X_t, X_{t+\tau}) = 0$$
$$\text{for all } t \text{ and all } \tau > 0. \tag{6.1.1}$$

This is our definition of the random walk hypothesis. It has been used before, for example by Granger and Morgenstern (1970). Note that H_0 does not require the process $\{X_t\}$ to be stationary.

Zero autocorrelation is sufficient, at a practical level, to ensure that prices recorded before time t are irrelevant for forecasting prices at times after t. Only the latest price and the assumption of identical means are then needed to find optimal forecasts. Identical means are included in H_0 to ensure the expected value of a sample autocorrelation coefficient is almost zero when the X_t are uncorrelated. Means defined by financial theories need not be constant. Joint tests of such theories and zero autocorrelation are given in Section 6.11 after the results of random walk tests.

Rejection of the random walk hypothesis is not sufficient to refute the efficient market hypothesis. Trading costs can prevent the exploitation of statistical dependence and then the random walk hypothesis is false but the efficient market hypothesis is not. It is easier to test for randomness than for efficiency so it is best to test the random walk hypothesis first. The other hypothesis is investigated in Chapter 8.

Many ways to test the random walk hypothesis have been proposed. Following methodological remarks in Section 6.2 and a review of the distributions of sample autocorrelations in Section 6.3, a variety of tests are described in Section 6.4. Powerful tests are based upon an understanding of plausible alternatives to random behaviour. Consequently, autocorrelations and models consistent with price-trends are discussed in Section 6.5 and used to motivate appropriate test statistics in Section 6.6. The effects of errors in studied prices are noted in Section 6.7. After these preliminaries the results of random walk tests are given in Sections 6.8 and 6.9 and test power is discussed further in Section 6.10.

It is concluded from the tests that returns are slightly autocorrelated. Sections 6.11 and 6.12 show the dependence cannot be explained by changes in interest rates or risk premia, by calendar effects or by market regulations.

6.2 TEST METHODOLOGY

Reliable statistical tests reject a true null hypothesis for a proportion of datasets equal to or less than the significance level. In other words, the significance level is the maximum probability of a Type I error. Correct distributions must be used for sample autocorrelations to give reliable tests of the random walk hypothesis. Otherwise, the significance level will be misleading. In particular the significance level is understated when autocorrelation variances are higher than the results given by large sample theory for a strict white noise process. It was shown in Chapter 5 that this can be a very serious problem. It can be avoided by using rescaled returns.

The choice of significance level is always arbitrary to some degree. A 5 per cent level is used throughout the chapter.

Powerful tests reject a false null hypothesis as frequently as is possible. Such tests minimize the chance of a Type II error for a given significance level. Many popular test procedures are not powerful. For example, the common practice of applying two-tail tests to a number of autocorrelation coefficients, one by one, must give confusing conclusions when some coefficients are significant but several are not. What is needed are specific plausible alternatives to the random walk hypothesis and tests having high power when these alternatives are better models than the random walk. A practical alternative is trends in prices. Models are given in Section 6.5 and tests are derived in Section 6.6.

The rejection region for a test can be either one or both tails of a particular distribution. Deciding to use one tail rather than both can increase test power.

Several random walk test statistics are available so it is tempting to perform several tests. This is understandable yet causes difficulties when the various tests yield different conclusions, as often happens. In principle the most likely alternative hypothesis should be identified, then a powerful test selected and the test conclusion accepted. However, few researchers would be disinterested in the results from other tests. A compromise methodology is followed here. A favoured alternative hypothesis and test are studied, taking other statistics seriously only if their test results are particularly clearcut.

6.3 DISTRIBUTIONS OF SAMPLE AUTOCORRELATIONS

The sample autocorrelation at lag τ, considered as a random variable based on n random variables X_t, is

$$R_\tau = \sum_{t=1}^{n-\tau} (X_t - \bar{X})(X_{t+\tau} - \bar{X}) \bigg/ \sum_{t=1}^{n} (X_t - \bar{X})^2, \quad \bar{X} = \sum_{t=1}^{n} X_t/n.$$

Replacing X_t by the observed return x_t and $\bar{X}$ by $\bar{x}$ gives the observed autocorrelation r_τ. A second subscript is not needed for R_τ and r_τ in this section; all results are for a process $\{X_t\}$.

Information about the distribution of R_τ for true and false null hypotheses is needed to obtain powerful random walk tests. We have already seen asymptotic results, as $n \to \infty$, for strict white noise processes (Section 1.10). These are now extended to include autocorrelated linear processes. It is assumed the X_t have finite variance but not necessarily a normal distribution.

Very low autocorrelation occurs when the random walk hypothesis is false thus test statistics may only just be significant. Relying on asymptotic results can then require justification, so finite sample results are also summarized.

Theoretical conclusions generally assume a linear generating process. Conclusions are given whilst acknowledging that the returns process is not linear. Nevertheless insights from linear conclusions are helpful for tests on a returns process rescaled to make it approximately linear.

Asymptotic limits

The asymptotic distribution of $\sqrt{n}R_\tau$ is $N(0, 1)$ for independent and identically distributed (i.i.d.) X_t, for all $\tau > 0$. Also R_τ and R_ξ are asymptotically independent for $\tau \neq \xi$.

Many tests rely solely on these results. To derive new tests in Section 6.6, results are also needed for autocorrelated processes. For linear $\{X_t\}$, defined in Section 1.10, the asymptotic expected value of R_τ is the population autocorrelation ρ_τ and the asymptotic variance of $\sqrt{n}R_\tau$ equals

$$\omega_{\tau\tau} = \lambda_0 + \lambda_{2\tau} + 2(\lambda_0 \rho_\tau^2 - 2\lambda_\tau \rho_\tau) \tag{6.3.1}$$

with

$$\lambda_i = \sum_{j=-\infty}^{+\infty} \rho_j \rho_{i+j}. \tag{6.3.2}$$

As $n \to \infty$, $\sqrt{n}(R_\tau - \rho_\tau) \to N(0, \omega_{\tau\tau})$. These equations show the variance $\omega_{\tau\tau}$ depends on all the autocorrelations, not simply ρ_τ. The asymptotic covariance between $\sqrt{n}R_\tau$ and $\sqrt{n}R_\xi$ equals

$$\omega_{\tau\xi} = \lambda_{\xi-\tau} + \lambda_{\xi+\tau} + 2(\lambda_0 \rho_\tau \rho_\xi - \lambda_\tau \rho_\xi - \lambda_\xi \rho_\tau). \tag{6.3.3}$$

Also the asymptotic distribution of the vector

$$\sqrt{n}(R_1 - \rho_1, R_2 - \rho_2, \ldots, R_k - \rho_k)$$

is multivariate normal for any k, with means, variances, and covariances as above. All the asymptotic results are proved by Anderson and Walker (1964).

Finite samples

Sample coefficients R_τ always have a bias of order $1/n$. From Moran (1967),

$$E[R_\tau] = -(n - \tau)/\{n(n - 1)\} \tag{6.3.4}$$

for i.i.d. variables. The bias for a general linear process is given by Lomnicki and Zaremba (1957). It can be non-trivial and will be mentioned again in Section 6.7.

Next consider variances and covariances for the R_τ calculated from i.i.d. variables. Application of a method used by Moran (1967, pp. 396–7) proves the conclusion

$$\text{var}(R_\tau) < 1/n \qquad \text{for } \tau > 0 \text{ and } n > \tau. \tag{6.3.5}$$

The alternative definition of sample autocorrelation,

$$R_\tau' = nR_\tau/(n - \tau),$$

has the disadvantage that its variance can be slightly more than $1/n$ (Taylor, 1982b, p. 42). More algebra shows the covariance between coefficients at different lags is of order $1/n^2$ with

$$\text{cov } (R_\tau, R_\xi) < 0 \qquad \text{for } n \geq 2\xi > 2\tau > 0. \tag{6.3.6}$$

These results can increase our confidence in the reliability of asymptotic results. For example, suppose the random walk test statistic is R_1 with rejection of the null hypothesis if $r_1 > 1.645/\sqrt{n}$, a one-tail test. Then (6.3.4) and (6.3.5) show the actual significance level is marginally less than the nominal 5 per cent level when a normal distribution is suitable for R_1. More exact results require computer simulations and examples are presented later in this chapter.

6.4 A SELECTION OF TEST STATISTICS

Autocorrelation, spectral and runs statistics have been used by scores of researchers to investigate the random walk hypothesis. Some articles report only one type of statistic, others all three. Some researchers have simply given the statistics, others have used them for tests. There is no consensus in financial literature about an appropriate set of test statistics. Results will be given for eleven test statistics. Eight of them are now described. They are identical or similar to most published tests. Three further tests are defined later, motivated by the idea of price-trends. It is assumed that autocorrelations r_τ are computed from n observations by a method ensuring that standard asymptotic results (Section 6.3) are applicable when the random walk hypothesis, denoted H_0, is true.

Autocorrelation tests

A popular and simple test uses the first autocorrelation coefficient, rejecting H_0 at the 5 per cent significance level if $\sqrt{n}|r_1| > 1.96$. This test applies the result $\sqrt{n}R_1 \sim N(0, 1)$, approximately, when H_0 is true. The test is logical and powerful if any dependence between returns is expected to be confined to consecutive returns.

When many coefficients r_τ are considered some will probably be significant even if H_0 is true; on average 1 out of 20 would then be significant at the 5 per cent level. Finding a few significant coefficients would not tell us much, unless their lags could be explained theoretically or some overall test statistic is used. The binomial distribution gives the probability of N or more out of k coefficients being significant at, say, the 5 per cent level when H_0 is true. Then H_0 can be rejected if this probability is less than 5 per cent. To obtain a useful test requires numbers k and N_0 for which

$$\alpha(k, N_0) = \sum_{i=N_0}^{k} \frac{k!}{i!(k-i)!} (0.05)^i (0.95)^{k-i} \approx 0.05.$$

One suitable choice is $k = 28$ and $N_0 = 4$, then $\alpha = 0.049$. Define N_r by counting the number of coefficients r_τ having $|r_\tau| > 1.96/\sqrt{n}$, $1 \leq \tau \leq 28$. Then H_0 is rejected at the 5 per cent level if $N_r \geq 4$.

A more natural way to combine k coefficients into a single test statistic is given by

$$Q_k = n \sum_{\tau=1}^{k} r_\tau^2. \tag{6.4.1}$$

When H_0 is true, $n(R_1^2 + \cdots + R_k^2) \sim \chi_k^2$, applying the assumed independence of R_τ and R_ξ, $\tau \neq \xi$. The null hypothesis is rejected for sufficiently high values of Q_k. Results will be given for three tests, using $k = 10, 30$, and 50. The respective tail areas in which H_0 is rejected are $Q_{10} > 18.31$, $Q_{30} > 43.77$, and $Q_{50} > 67.50$. The Q statistic is frequently used in general time series research to test for zero autocorrelation. Note that both N_r and Q_k are not designed to be powerful for a specific alternative to the random walk hypothesis.

Spectral tests

Spectral analysis is an alternative to studying autocorrelations. It is particularly appropriate when cycles in returns are the preferred alternative to random behaviour. A typical cyclical model is

$$X_t = \sum_{j=1}^{J} \alpha_j \cos(\omega_j t - \beta_j) + \varepsilon_t \tag{6.4.2}$$

the α_j, β_j, and ω_j being constants and the ε_t uncorrelated. Cycle j then has frequency ω_j and repeats itself every $2\pi/\omega_j$ time units. The evidence for cycles is not impressive and consequently the discussion of spectral methods will be brief. Granger and Newbold (1977, Ch. 2) describe spectral theory relevant for economic studies and Praetz (1979a) highlights practical problems encountered when testing returns for a flat spectral density. Autocorrelation analysis is much easier than spectral analysis.

The spectral density function for a stationary process can be defined by

$$s(\omega) = \sigma^2/(2\pi)\left[1 + 2\sum_{\tau=1}^{\infty} \rho_\tau \cos(\tau\omega)\right] \qquad 0 \leq \omega \leq 2\pi \tag{6.4.3}$$

with $\sigma^2 = \text{var}(X_t)$. The integral of $s(\omega)$ from 0 to 2π equals σ^2 and $s(\omega) = s(2\pi - \omega)$ so it is only necessary to consider the frequency range 0 to π. There will be peaks in a plot of $s(\omega)$ at the frequencies ω_j for the cyclical model (6.4.2). If, however, the random walk hypothesis is true $s(\omega)$ will be constant for all ω. To test H_0 we need to estimate $s(\omega)$ and then test for a constant spectral density.

Meaningful estimates of $f(\omega) = 2\pi s(\omega)/\sigma^2$ have the general form

$$\hat{f}(\omega) = 1 + 2 \sum_{\tau=1}^{M-1} \lambda_\tau r_\tau \cos (\tau\omega) \tag{6.4.4}$$

with positive and monotonically decreasing λ_τ ensuring consistent estimates. The Parzen weights are used here, defined for fixed M by

$$\begin{aligned} \lambda_\tau &= 1 - 6\tau^2(M - \tau)/M^3 & 0 < \tau \leqslant M/2 \\ &= 2(M - \tau)^3/M^3 & M/2 \leqslant \tau < M. \end{aligned} \tag{6.4.5}$$

Equation (6.4.4) shows spectral estimates are linear functions of the first $M - 1$ autocorrelations. Plots of these r_τ and the estimated spectral density $f(\omega)$, $0 \leqslant \omega \leqslant \pi$, convey the same information. The spectral plot will be more helpful when cycles exist.

Spectral estimates have been calculated using $M = 100$ for spot series and futures series taking a year of returns from each contract. Futures series using less returns per contract must have smaller M, here 40 for six months data per contract and 20 for three months per contract; these series are not very suitable for estimating spectral densities.

Praetz (1979a) shows that $\hat{f}(\omega_1)$ and $\hat{f}(\omega_2)$ are correlated estimates only if $|\omega_1 - \omega_2| \leqslant 3\pi/M$. Consequently tests are here based on $\hat{f}(\omega)$ evaluated for $\omega = 0, 4\pi/M, 8\pi/M, \ldots, \pi$, giving $1 + M/4$ potential test statistics. These statistics can be standardized using the asymptotic theory for sample autocorrelations to give

$$f_j = [\hat{f}(4j\pi/M) - 1]/\sqrt{\left\{ 4 \sum_{\tau=1}^{M-1} [\lambda_\tau \cos (4j\tau\pi/M)]^2/n \right\}} \tag{6.4.6}$$

for $j = 0, 1, \ldots, M/4$. The f_j are effectively independent observations from $N(0, 1)$ for large sample sizes n when H_0 is true.

The most plausible cycle period is one week, when the frequency is $\omega = 2\pi/5$ and the standardized spectral statistic is f_j, $j = M/10$. This test statistic will be denoted f_w to emphasize the period tested. A one-tail test is appropriate.

Some authors, see Praetz (1979a), have counted the significant peaks and troughs in plots of the estimated spectral density. Let N_s count the number of times $|f_j|$ exceeds 1.96 for $0 \leqslant j \leqslant M/4$. Like the number of significant autocorrelations N_r, the test statistic N_s has a binomial distribution when H_0 is true. We reject H_0 if N_s is greater than or equal to a number fixed by M; reject at the 5 per cent level if $N_s \geqslant 4$ ($M = 100$) or $N_s \geqslant 3$ ($M = 40$) or $N_s \geqslant 2$ ($M = 20$) the exact significance levels then being 3.9, 1.5, and 3.3 per cent. Spectral tests will be given for f_w, N_s, and a third statistic motivated later by the idea of price-trends.

The runs test

As returns have a non-normal and perhaps non-stationary distribution, non-parametric tests could be appropriate. The only non-parametric statistic used to date is the total number of runs. A positive run is a sequence of consecutive positive returns, a no-change run is a sequence of zero returns, and a negative run has a similar definition. Let x_t^* be 1, 0, or -1 for positive, zero, or negative x_t respectively. Also let h_t be 0 if $x_t^* = x_{t+1}^*$ and let it be 1 otherwise. Then $h_t = 1$ signifies that x_{t+1} begins a new run and so the total number of runs of all types is

$$H = 1 + \sum_{t=1}^{n-1} h_t. \tag{6.4.7}$$

Suppose there are n_1 positive returns, n_2 zero returns, and n_3 negative returns in a series. Then the mean and variance of the variable $\bar{H}$ generating H, conditional upon n_1, n_2, and n_3, are

$$E[\bar{H}] = n + 1 - \left(\sum n_j^2 / n \right)$$

and

$$\text{var}\,(\bar{H}) = \left\{ \sum n_j^2 \left(\sum n_j^2 + n + n^2 \right) - 2n \sum n_j^3 - n^3 \right\} / (n^3 - n)$$

when a certain null hypothesis H_0^* is true, always summing over $j = 1, 2, 3$ (Mood, 1940). This H_0^* is the hypothesis that the x_t^* are generated by a strict white noise process $\{X_t^*\}$. It is usually assumed that there is no practical difference between H_0 and H_0^*. For large n, $\bar{H}$ is approximately normal so tests can use

$$K = (H - E[\bar{H}])/\sqrt{\text{var}\,(\bar{H})} \tag{6.4.8}$$

rejecting H_0^* (and H_0) at the 5 per cent level if $|K| > 1.96$. Trends would cause fewer runs than expected (so $K < 0$), price reversals would produce more runs ($K > 0$). One-tail tests can be used if either possibility is considered likely.

The runs test is easy to perform and avoids all problems due to variance changes. Its great disadvantage is low test power caused by losing information in the transformation from x_t to x_t^*. To see this, assume x_t^* is always 1 or -1, i.e. suppose there are no zero returns. Then the total runs H are

$$H = 1 + \frac{1}{4} \sum_{t=1}^{n-1} (x_t^* - x_{t+1}^*)^2 = \frac{1}{2}(n + 1) - \sum_{t=1}^{n-1} x_t^* x_{t+1}^*. \tag{6.4.9}$$

As the average of the x_t^* will be approximately zero, their lag one autocorrelation is approximately

$$\sum_{t=1}^{n-1} x_t^* x_{t+1}^* / n$$

because x_t^{*2} is always 1. Thus H is essentially a linear function of a lag one autocorrelation.

However, the first lag autocorrelations of $\{X_t\}$ and $\{X_t^*\}$, denoted ρ_1 and ρ_1^*, generally have $|\rho_1^*| < |\rho_1|$. It is therefore harder to detect dependence using H (or K) than it is using r_1. For example a zero-mean, stationary, Gaussian process $\{X_t\}$ has

$$\rho_1^* = E[X_t^* X_{t+1}^*] = P(X_t^* = X_{t+1}^*) - P(X_t^* \neq X_{t+1}^*)$$
$$= 2P(X_t^* = X_{t+1}^*) - 1 = (2/\pi) \arcsin (\rho_1) \qquad (6.4.10)$$
$$\simeq 0.64\rho_1. \qquad (6.4.11)$$

Equation (6.4.10) is quoted by Granger and Newbold (1977, p. 287), whilst (6.4.11) follows from the fact that ρ_1 must be small. In conclusion, the runs test is essentially a special first lag test having less power than r_1 because it uses less information.

A further problem arises if thin trading causes several no-change runs. These may be responsible for less total runs than expected thereby refuting independence (and H_0^*) but not the random walk hypothesis (H_0).

6.5 THE PRICE-TREND HYPOTHESIS

The idea of trends in prices is a specific alternative to the random walk hypothesis. Trends are a popular alternative to randomness, particularly in market literature.

A price-trend is essentially a general movement of prices in a fixed direction, up or down. Published evidence for trends is sparse compared with publications favouring random behaviour. This may, however, be the consequence of using inappropriate random walk tests. Stevenson and Bear (1970) and Leuthold (1972) offer some evidence for trends although Praetz (1976b) has criticized their methods.

Trends would imply that prices do not adjust fully and instantaneously when new information becomes available. Instead, some new information would have to be incorporated slowly into prices. Trends will occur if information is used imperfectly, for example if enough people are irrational or rational but unable to interpret all information quickly and correctly.

The trend idea is covered thoroughly in this book. Autocorrelations consistent with trends are now defined and appropriate random walk tests are deduced in Section 6.6, then models and forecasts are described in Chapter 7 followed by the profitable results of trading rules in Chapter 8.

Price-trend autocorrelations

Slow interpretation of a particular information item will cause several returns to be partially determined by the same information. The fundamental trend idea is that these several returns are all influenced in the same way, either towards a positive conditional mean or towards a negative conditional mean. Thus trends will cause positive autocorrelations. The impact of that current information which is not fully reflected in the current price, upon future returns, should diminish as time goes on. Thus the autocorrelations should decrease as the lag increases. We know that all autocorrelations must be small. Therefore trends imply:

$$\rho_\tau > 0, \ \rho_\tau > \rho_{\tau+1} \quad \text{and} \quad 1 \gg \rho_\tau, \qquad \text{all } \tau > 0, \tag{6.5.1}$$

i.e. $1 \gg \rho_1 > \rho_2 > \rho_3 > \cdots > 0$.

To progress to a testable alternative to the random walk hypothesis requires parametric autocorrelation functions consistent with the observations summarized by (6.5.1). The simplest such functions define the *price-trend hypothesis*, first investigated in Taylor (1980):

$$H_1 : \rho_\tau = Ap^\tau, \qquad A, p, \tau > 0. \tag{6.5.2}$$

The autocorrelations ρ_τ may refer to either the returns X_t or the standardized returns $U_t = (X_t - \mu)/V_t$. We use the notation H_1 to emphasize an alternative hypothesis to the random walk hypothesis H_0. Once more we are considering the autocorrelations of ARMA(1, 1) processes.

There are two parameters in H_1. Parameter A measures the proportion of information not reflected by prices within one day. Parameter p measures the speed at which imperfectly reflected information is incorporated into prices. As $A \to 0$ or $p \to 0$, information is used perfectly. When price-trend models are credible we will later discover that typical parameter values are $A = 0.03$ and $p = 0.95$. Low values for A are inevitable whilst values for p near to 1 indicate trends lasting for a long time.

An example

Many statistical models are consistent with the price-trend hypothesis and detailed examples will be presented in Section 7.2. One simple example assumes the return X_t is the sum of an autoregressive trend component μ_t and an unpredictable residual e_t:

$$X_t = \mu_t + e_t, \tag{6.5.3}$$
$$\mu_t - \mu = p(\mu_{t-1} - \mu) + \eta_t,$$
$$E[e_t] = E[\eta_t] = E[e_t e_{t+\tau}] = E[\eta_t \eta_{t+\tau}] = E[e_t \eta_s] = 0$$

for all s, t and $\tau > 0$. As

$$\text{cov}(X_t, X_{t+\tau}) = \text{cov}(\mu_t, \mu_{t+\tau}) = p^\tau \text{var}(\mu_t)$$

for all $\tau > 0$, it follows that H_1 is true with $A = \text{var}(\mu_t)/\text{var}(X_t)$.

Price-trend spectral density

From (6.4.3) and (6.5.2), the spectral density function for the price-trend hypothesis is a constant times

$$f(\omega) = 1 + 2A \sum_{\tau=1}^{\infty} p^{\tau} \cos(\tau\omega) \tag{6.5.4}$$

$$= 1 - A + A(1 - p^2)/\{1 - 2p \cos(\omega) + p^2\}.$$

The function $f(\omega)$ decreases monotonically from $f(0) = 1 + 2Ap/(1 - p)$ to $f(\pi) = 1 - 2Ap/(1 + p)$. There will be a single thin peak at $\omega = 0$ if $p \approx 1$.

6.6 TESTS FOR RANDOM WALKS VERSUS PRICE-TRENDS

Powerful tests of the random walk hypothesis H_0 against the price-trend hypothesis H_1 can be constructed using the theoretical distributions of sample autocorrelations. Comprehensive details are given in Taylor (1982b). We will now derive test statistics T^* and f_0 given by equations (6.6.2) and (6.6.3) respectively.

Suppose firstly that k sample autocorrelations are to be used in a test and they are the realized values of the vector $R = (R_1, R_2, \ldots, R_k)$. Assume secondly that the asymptotic results of Section 6.3 are applicable to R, with $E[R] = \rho$. Then $\sqrt{n}(R - \rho)$ has a multivariate normal distribution, $N(0, \Omega_k)$, for some $k \times k$ matrix Ω_k. When H_0 is true, $\rho = (0, 0, \ldots, 0)$ and Ω_k is the $k \times k$ identity matrix I_k. When H_1 is true, $\rho = (Ap, Ap^2, \ldots, Ap^k)$ and $\Omega_k \approx I_k$ if A is small; for typical parameters ($A = 0.036$, $p = 0.97$) the entries $\omega_{\tau\xi}$ in the matrix Ω_k have $1.15 > \omega_{\tau\tau} > 1$ and $0.22 > \omega_{\tau\xi} > 0$ ($\tau \neq \xi$), see Taylor (1982b, pp. 42–3). To motivate practical test statistics it is assumed thirdly that the matrix Ω_k can be replaced by I_k even if H_1 is true.

The alternative hypothesis H_1 has two unspecified parameters. Now consider the best test if these parameters are fixed to give the restricted alternative $H_1^* : \rho_\tau = A^* \phi^\tau$. The optimal test of H_0 against H_1^* using observed autocorrelations $r = (r_1, r_2, \ldots, r_k)$ must use the likelihood-ratio statistic whose logarithm is

$$l = \log\{L(r|H_1^*)/L(r|H_0)\}$$

with $L(r|.)$ denoting the likelihood of the vector r. Applying all the assumptions previously stated,

$$l \approx nA^* \sum_{\tau=1}^{k} \phi^\tau r_\tau + l_0$$

with l_0 a constant independent of r. Thus H_0 should be rejected if

$$T_{k,\phi} = \sum_{\tau=1}^{k} \phi^{\tau} r_{\tau} \tag{6.6.1}$$

exceeds a number determined by the significance level and the number of returns.

The test parameter ϕ should reflect prior opinions about the trend parameter p. Of course k and ϕ must be chosen before calculating the r_{τ}. These choices must be largely subjective, because A and p will be unknown if H_1 is true. One way to choose k and ϕ is to seek values giving high test power whenever A, p, and n fall inside a set S of plausible trend parameter values and series lengths.

In 1979, the set S defined by $0.01 \leq A \leq 0.04$, $0.8 \leq p \leq 0.975$, and $250 \leq n \leq 2000$ was considered appropriate after studying some of the copper and sugar returns but none of the other returns tested here. For this S the best k is 30 and the best ϕ is 0.92. These test parameters have power close to the best obtainable using the k and ϕ optimal for any specific triple (A, p, n) in S, see Taylor (1982b, pp. 44–5). (The power calculations used a 5 per cent significance level and the correct matrix Ω_k; this matrix was not assumed to be I_k when H_1 is true.) The set S is still considered appropriate and therefore it is still recommended that tests for trends use $k = 30$ and $\phi = 0.92$.

When H_0 is true and standard asymptotic results are assumed, $\Sigma \, \phi^{\tau} R_{\tau}$ has mean zero and variance $\Sigma \, \phi^{2\tau}/n$. Consequently, as $n \rightarrow \infty$, the test statistic

$$T^* = T_{30,0.92} \Big/ \left(\sum_{\tau=1}^{30} 0.92^{2\tau}/n \right)^{1/2}$$

$$= 0.4274\sqrt{n} \sum_{\tau=1}^{30} 0.92^{\tau} r_{\tau} \tag{6.6.2}$$

is an observation from $N(0, 1)$ if H_0 is true. We accept H_0 if $T^* < 1.65$ and accept H_1 if $T^* \geq 1.65$, using a 5 per cent significance level.

The recommended statistic T^* has high power for testing H_0 against H_1 because it uses several coefficients r_{τ} and exploits the price-trend prediction of positive autocorrelation, decreasing as the lag increases. Any similar linear function of several autocorrelations, say $w_1 r_1 + w_2 r_2 + \cdots + w_k r_k$ with monotonically decreasing positive weights w_{τ}, is likely to provide a fairly powerful test statistic. Choosing the w_{τ} proportional to 0.92^{τ} may appear arbitrary. The Parzen weights λ_{τ} used to define spectral estimates (see (6.4.5)) provide an alternative set of weights w_{τ}. The standardized density statistic at zero frequency is the following linear function of $M - 1$ sample autocorrelations:

$$f_0 = \sum_{\tau=1}^{M-1} \lambda_{\tau} r_{\tau} \Big/ \left(\sum_{\tau=1}^{M-1} \lambda_{\tau}^2/n \right)^{1/2}. \tag{6.6.3}$$

This is the only spectral statistic likely to have high power when the alternative hypothesis is price-trends. We reject H_0 at the 5 per cent level if $f_0 \geq 1.65$. The parameter value M has been selected as in Section 6.4.

6.7   CONSEQUENCES OF DATA ERRORS

Price series often contain errors. Checking large returns against another source will find any large errors which can then be corrected. Small errors may remain and sometimes it is impossible to check a series because of insufficient information about dates. The primary consequence of errors is to decrease r_1, because an error in the price z_t causes errors in the two returns x_t and x_{t+1} one being positive and the other negative.

A model for price errors is

$$\log (Z_t) = \log (Z_t^*) + \delta_t$$

with Z_t, Z_t^*, and δ_t generating the analysed price, the true price, and an error respectively with a very high chance that $\delta_t = 0$. Assuming $\{\delta_t\}$ is white noise, stochastically independent of true returns $\{X_t^*\}$, with $\psi = \text{var }(\delta_t)/\text{var }(X_t^*)$, it can be shown that the theoretical autocorrelations ρ_τ of the analysed returns are related to those of the true returns ρ_τ^* by

$$\rho_1 = (\rho_1^* - \psi)/(1 + 2\psi), \quad \rho_\tau = \rho_\tau^*/(1 + 2\psi) \text{ if } \tau \geq 2.$$

Estimating ψ is difficult but it is clear that the major impact of errors occurs at the first lag.

The T^* test is particularly vulnerable to data errors. An obvious remedy when errors are suspected is to ignore r_1 and then T^* should be replaced by

$$U^* = 0.4649\sqrt{n} \sum_{\tau=2}^{30} 0.92^\tau r_\tau. \tag{6.7.1}$$

As with T^*, the asymptotic distribution of U^* is $N(0, 1)$ when the random walk hypothesis is true. Simulations have shown that the test power lost by using U^* instead of T^*, when there are no data errors, is very low if H_1 is true and p is nearly 1. It therefore seemed prudent in previous research to insure against data errors by using U^* for empirical tests. Data errors may be rarer than once feared, according to the test results soon to be presented.

The simulations made it clear that asymptotic theoretical results consistently overestimate the power of T^*. This is due, at least partially, to a downward bias in the sample coefficients. When H_1 is true,

$$E[R_\tau] - \rho_\tau \simeq -[1 + \tau A p^\tau + 2Ap/(1 - p)]/n, \tag{6.7.2}$$

an approximation deduced from Lomnicki and Zaremba (1957, p. 156). For example if $A = 0.02$, $p = 0.95$, and $n = 1000$, then the bias $E[R_\tau] - \rho_\tau$ is about −0.002 and the correct mean of the variable generating T^* is about 0.27 less than the 1.84 predicted by asymptotic theory.

Let $m = 1/(1 − p)$ measure the duration of trends, explained properly in Section 7.2. Figure 6.1, reprinted from Taylor (1980), shows the regions for trend parameters A and m over which T^* and U^* are estimated to have power greater than 0.5, when the significance level is 0.05, the alternative to random behaviour is price-trends and there are 500, 1000, or 2000 returns.

On a given curve, there is estimated to be a 50 per cent probability of falsely accepting the random walk hypothesis when there are in fact trends in the stochastic process; north-east of the curves this probability is less than 50 per cent. These curves are based on simulations, not asymptotic theory. Figure 6.1 illustrates the advantages of long series compared with short series. It is certainly desirable for series to span at least eight years providing at least 2000 daily returns.

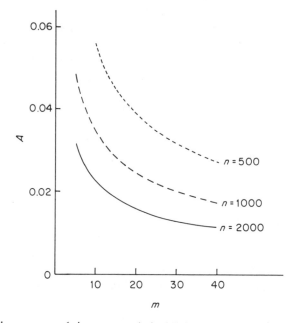

Figure 6.1 The power of the test statistic U^* is approximately 0.5 on the curves when the significance level is 0.05. _Reproduced from Taylor (1980) by permission of the Royal Statistical Society_

6.8 RESULTS OF RANDOM WALK TESTS

The eleven test statistics considered are T^* (equation (6.6.2)), U^* (6.7.1) and f_0 (6.6.3) intended to detect any evidence for trends, N_r and N_s which respectively count the number of significant autocorrelations and spectral estimates, $r_1\sqrt{n}$ which relies on any important autocorrelation to occur at a single day's lag, Q_k (k = 10, 30, 50) summarizing several autocorrelations (6.4.1), f_w the test for a weekly cycle, and K the non-parametric runs statistic (6.4.8). All the autocorrelation and spectral statistics are functions of autocorrelation coefficients r_τ. These coefficients have been calculated from rescaled returns y_t, for the reasons given in Chapter 5, particularly in 5.7 and 5.8. The coefficients are denoted $r_{\tau,y}$ or sometimes simply r_τ.

Readers are reminded that

$$y_t = (x_t - \bar{x})/\hat{v}_t, \tag{6.8.1}$$

$$\hat{v}_t = (1 - \gamma)\hat{v}_{t-1} + 1.253\gamma|x_{t-1} - \bar{x}| \tag{6.8.2}$$

and

$$r_{\tau,y} = \sum_{t=21}^{n-\tau} (y_t - \bar{y})(y_{t+\tau} - \bar{y}) \bigg/ \sum_{t=21}^{n} (y_t - \bar{y})^2. \tag{6.8.3}$$

See Section 5.8 for complete details about these equations including the selection of initial $\hat{v}_t$. In (6.8.2), γ is 0.04 for stock series and 0.1 for the others. As with other autocorrelation estimates, the numerator summation in (6.8.3) for futures series is over those t for which x_t and $x_{t+\tau}$ are returns from the same contract. The number of terms in the denominator of $r_{\tau,y}$ is $n - 20$ and denoted by n^*. Whenever necessary n^* replaces n in the equations defining test statistics.

Table 6.1 presents $r_{1,y}$, the number of $r_{i,y}$ over lags 1 to 30 in each of the six classes introduced in Section 2.9 and, for comparison, the first-lag coefficient $r_{1,x}$ calculated from returns 21 to n inclusive.

Table 6.2 gives the values of the 11 test statistics for all 40 series. Values significant at the 5 per cent level appear in italic. It can be seen that a large number of the statistics are significant. Before calculating the test values, my preferred test statistic was U^*. This statistic is not significant for any of the stock series. Indeed the highest stock value is 0.62, far below the critical value 1.65. However, U^* rejects the random walk hypothesis for every commodity and currency series with the single exception of the wool series. The other trend statistics, T^* and f_0, each reject the random walk hypothesis for every commodity and currency series. Thus there is evidence for trends in commodity and currency prices but not in stock prices.

Looking at the other test statistics for stocks it is seen that $r_{1,y}\sqrt{n^*}$ is significant for all the series, often at a very low significance level. Therefore all the long price series are not random walks: their daily returns are not the output of an uncorrelated process having constant mean. The short Treasury Bond series does not reject the random walk hypothesis but it has insufficient observations to give decisive results.

Table 6.1   Autocorrelations $r_{\tau,y}$ for rescaled returns

	Lag 1		Lags 1–30, frequency by class					
	$r_{1,y}$	$r_{1,x}$	1	2	3	4	5	6
Spot series								
Allied	0.072	0.087	0	0	15	14	1	0
Alcoa	0.187	0.150	0	0	19	10	0	1
Am. Can	0.133	0.143	0	1	17	11	0	1
AT and T	0.098	0.088	0	0	21	8	1	0
Am. Brands	0.095	0.093	0	1	17	11	1	0
Anaconda	0.047	0.056	0	0	16	14	0	0
Bethlehem	0.106	0.107	0	0	20	9	0	1
Chrysler	0.045	0.044	0	1	12	17	0	0
Dupont	0.131	0.114	0	0	14	15	0	1
Kodak	0.054	0.035	0	0	16	13	1	0
G. Electric	0.101	0.099	0	0	14	15	0	1
G. Food	0.113	0.089	0	0	16	13	0	1
G. Motors	0.055	0.049	0	0	17	12	1	0
G. Telephone	0.065	0.051	0	0	19	10	1	0
Harvester	0.079	0.085	0	0	16	13	1	0
FT 30	0.051	0.039	0	1	13	15	1	0
Gold	−0.012	−0.053	0	0	8	19	3	0
Silver	−0.066	−0.080	0	1	11	16	1	1
Copper	−0.017	−0.056	0	0	10	19	1	0
Lead	0.021	−0.020	0	0	6	24	0	0
Tin	0.030	0.021	0	0	11	19	0	0
Zinc	−0.009	−0.074	0	0	8	22	0	0
£/$ spot	0.097	0.038	0	0	3	23	4	0
Futures series								
Corn (12)	−0.016	−0.027	0	0	10	18	2	0
Corn (6)	−0.010	0.005	0	0	10	19	1	0
Corn (3)	0.001	0.013	0	0	9	20	1	0
Cocoa (12)	0.045	0.015	0	0	8	17	5	0
Cocoa (6)	0.071	0.034	0	0	7	18	5	0
Cocoa (3)	0.091	0.070	0	0	8	20	2	0
Coffee (12)	0.104	0.026	0	0	8	17	4	1
Coffee (6)	0.131	0.062	0	0	9	18	2	1
Coffee (3)	0.131	0.063	0	0	8	19	2	1
Sugar (12)	0.063	0.044	0	0	2	26	2	0
Sugar (6)	0.084	0.064	0	0	1	27	2	0
Sugar (3)	0.085	0.064	0	0	3	24	3	0
Wool (12)	0.040	0.075	0	0	12	18	0	0
£/$ (6)	0.073	0.030	0	0	5	23	2	0
DM/$ (6)	0.023	0.007	0	0	10	17	3	0
SF/$ (6)	0.005	0.048	0	0	8	20	2	0
T-bond	−0.051	−0.088	0	3	14	10	3	0

Note: Autocorrelations for rescaled returns are allocated to these six classes: (1) $r < -0.1$, (2) $-0.1 \leqslant r < -0.05$, (3) $-0.05 \leqslant r < 0$, (4) $0 \leqslant r \leqslant 0.05$, (5) $0.05 < r \leqslant 0.1$, (6) $r > 0.1$.

Table 6.2   Values of the random walk test statistics

	T^*	U^*	$\sqrt{n}^*r_1$	N_r	Q_{10}	Q_{30}	Q_{50}	N_s	f_0	f_w	K
Spot series											
Allied	0.73	−0.82	*3.77*	4	*23.55*	*54.20*	*70.50*	6	−0.16	−1.09	*−3.11*
Alcoa	*2.87*	−1.06	*9.77*	3	*102.91*	*124.40*	*145.30*	9	0.25	0.51	*−7.71*
Am. Can	*1.84*	−0.97	*6.94*	2	*58.30*	*85.40*	*99.53*	6	0.31	*1.92*	*−4.79*
AT and T	0.19	*−1.98*	*5.11*	4	*40.89*	*64.56*	*77.21*	4	−0.71	*2.97*	*−4.00*
Am. Brands	−0.74	*−2.92*	*4.94*	3	*44.65*	*63.24*	*76.96*	7	−1.08	*3.07*	−0.52
Anaconda	−0.31	−1.37	*2.43*	1	14.81	23.07	34.78	0	−0.11	0.96	*−4.80*
Bethlehem	−0.26	*−2.65*	*5.54*	2	*45.63*	*61.40*	*88.49*	4	−1.32	−0.01	*−2.72*
Chrysler	−0.03	−1.05	*2.37*	5	*26.78*	*51.05*	*71.43*	2	0.88	−0.16	−1.56
Dupont	*3.22*	0.58	*6.82*	2	*52.04*	*66.15*	*75.90*	6	*1.84*	0.27	*−3.82*
Kodak	−0.42	−1.68	*2.84*	1	*19.91*	37.37	*54.56*	3	0.11	0.22	*−3.79*
G. Electric	1.24	−0.92	*5.30*	2	*38.98*	*59.61*	*70.54*	4	0.25	*1.75*	*−3.65*
G. Food	0.79	−1.67	*5.92*	2	*46.13*	*67.32*	*87.00*	4	−1.09	0.64	*−4.55*
G. Motors	−0.23	−1.47	*2.86*	5	*25.89*	*51.00*	*60.01*	2	−0.38	*4.51*	*−3.99*
G. Telephone	−0.28	−1.76	*3.40*	2	*20.04*	40.36	49.02	2	−1.55	*1.71*	*−3.78*
Harvester	0.89	−0.81	*4.15*	2	*24.67*	42.17	*68.94*	2	−0.29	−0.45	−1.56
FT 30	1.41	0.62	*2.13*	2	*20.31*	39.93	49.04	2	0.16	0.88	−1.85
Gold	*4.73*	*5.36*	−0.51	5	*29.31*	*63.26*	*88.20*	3	*4.87*	−0.83	*4.45*
Silver	*1.94*	*3.04*	*−2.16*	3	*34.03*	*49.30*	*68.64*	6	*2.54*	0.19	*3.57*
Copper	*4.03*	*4.84*	−1.08	5	*37.85*	*53.85*	*71.34*	4	*3.99*	−1.11	1.91
Lead	*3.82*	*3.66*	1.15	3	10.33	36.75	66.84	1	*5.43*	−0.33	1.52
Tin	*2.24*	*1.74*	1.63	1	15.96	29.29	48.47	3	*2.83*	0.98	−0.56
Zinc	*2.12*	*2.52*	−0.51	1	8.41	23.11	*50.22*	2	*3.46*	−0.35	−0.57
£/$	*6.56*	*5.29*	*4.30*	6	*35.28*	*80.60*	*125.69*	3	*9.05*	1.19	*−2.28*
Futures series											
Corn (12)	*1.89*	*2.46*	−0.93	2	15.51	36.34	*61.09*	1	*2.10*	1.16	1.89
Corn (6)	*3.03*	*3.54*	−0.57	3	*22.04*	38.64	*51.78*	3	*3.31*	*2.37*	1.75
Corn (3)	*3.29*	*3.56*	0.04	3	*27.15*	36.07	42.74	3	*2.75*	*2.72*	1.79
Cocoa (12)	*6.65*	*6.24*	*2.34*	9	*41.57*	*83.18*	*92.76*	3	*6.39*	0.89	−0.85
Cocoa (6)	*6.34*	*5.40*	*3.51*	6	*36.25*	*72.99*	*85.16*	1	*6.42*	0.81	−0.60
Cocoa (3)	*6.43*	*5.08*	*4.46*	3	*46.43*	*65.33*	*72.56*	3	*5.99*	0.85	−1.34
Coffee (12)	*6.96*	*5.25*	*5.42*	6	*66.60*	*84.14*	*100.54*	3	*5.05*	−0.30	*−2.91*
Coffee (6)	*6.67*	*4.46*	*6.53*	5	*76.36*	*88.02*	*101.32*	5	*6.42*	0.92	*−2.97*
Coffee (3)	*6.20*	*3.96*	*6.51*	4	*71.27*	*83.92*	*91.85*	5	*6.32*	*2.47*	*−1.89*
Sugar (12)	*7.87*	*6.61*	*4.56*	7	*73.17*	*105.59*	*122.70*	3	*7.76*	*1.69*	*−3.42*
Sugar (6)	*8.97*	*7.29*	*5.76*	7	*85.01*	*109.70*	*132.63*	2	*8.66*	1.28	*−4.59*
Sugar (3)	*9.26*	*7.57*	*5.86*	8	*92.94*	*114.51*	*121.00*	3	*8.71*	*1.76*	*−4.41*
Wool (12)	*2.26*	1.49	*2.27*	4	*19.96*	42.31	64.64	3	*2.05*	−0.50	*−3.99*
£/$ (6)	*3.53*	*2.46*	*3.23*	2	16.67	32.70	41.54	2	*3.38*	*2.03*	−1.08
DM/$ (6)	*4.83*	*4.82*	1.01	3	*29.76*	*56.79*	64.08	1	*4.88*	1.40	1.13
SF/$ (6)	*3.01*	*3.19*	0.21	3	13.24	42.17	53.28	1	*3.01*	0.63	0.81
T-bond	−0.02	0.46	−1.14	0	11.39	23.72	38.44	1	−0.29	0.15	*2.30*
Critical point(s)	1.65	1.65	±1.96	4	18.31	43.77	67.50	4[a]	1.65	1.65	±1.96

Notes

[a] 4 for spots and futures (12), 3 for futures (6), 2 for futures (3).

Values significant at the 5 per cent level appear in italic

Table 6.3   **Frequency of random walk rejections by test statistics**

16 stock series		15 commodity and currency series	
Statistic	*Frequency*	*Statistic*	*Frequency*
r_1	16	T^*	15
Q_{10}	15	f_0	15
K	12	U^*	14
Q_{30}	11	Q_{10}	10
Q_{50}	11	Q_{30}	8
N_s	9	Q_{50}	7
f_w	6	r_1	7
N_r	4	N_r	7
T^*	3	K	6
f_0	1	N_s	4
U^*	0	f_w	2

Note: Frequency records the number of series whose test values are significant at the 5 per cent level.

Returns from different series on the same day can be correlated. For example, there is low correlation for any pair of US stocks and any pair from lead, tin, and zinc, with very high correlation for any two futures series defined for the same commodity. This is not particularly serious for the stocks or metals. Test results for any two corn series are highly dependent and likewise for cocoa, coffee, and sugar. The correlation between test statistics is described further in Appendix 6(A).

Many researchers have claimed the random walk hypothesis is false so our rejection of the hypothesis is not particularly surprising. Using the trend statistics makes the conclusion of non-random behaviour clearer for several series. Working with long series allows the rejection of random behaviour for every series. It is interesting to note which statistics reject the null hypothesis most often. Stock series and the other series are discussed separately as their stochastic processes are clearly different.

Stocks

Table 6.3 shows the number of times the random walk hypothesis is rejected, by test statistic, for the 16 stock series. Only $r_1\sqrt{n^*}$ rejects for every series. The high scores for the Q_k statistics are entirely due to the dominant contribution of $n^*r_1^2$ to the total $n^*(r_1^2 + \cdots + r_k^2)$; a modified statistic $n^*(r_2^2 + \cdots + r_k^2)$ rejects for very few series. The runs statistic K has a high score because it is essentially a first-lag coefficient too (Section 6.4). Only six series show significant evidence for the weekly cycle caused by lower than average returns on Mondays (Section 2.5). The scores for all the

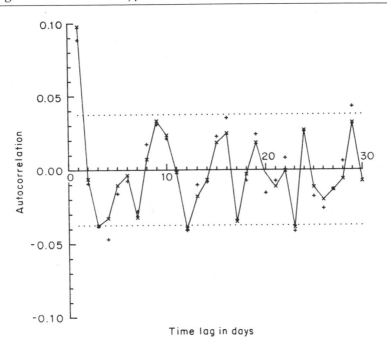

Figure 6.2 Autocorrelation coefficients for the stock American Telephone and Telegraph, shown for returns (+) and rescaled returns (×). Dotted lines indicate $\pm 1.96/\sqrt{n^*}$

trend statistics are very low. Reducing γ in (6.8.2) from 0.04 to 0.02 changes the score for $r_1\sqrt{n^*}$ to 15 (the index series does not reject the null hypothesis), whilst for $\gamma = 0.08$ the score is still the maximum possible.

The autocorrelations of US stock returns have two interesting features. Firstly, there is significant positive autocorrelation at lag 1, also noted by Perry (1982) for more and longer series. It is unlikely that a trading rule could exploit the small autocorrelation. Secondly, the majority of coefficients at higher lags are negative, shown previously by Fama (1965). For rescaled returns, 67 per cent of the coefficients are negative at lags 2 to 10 inclusive, 54 per cent are negative over lags 11 to 30. For lags 2 to 10, 24 of the 135 coefficients are less than $-1.96/\sqrt{n^*}$; 6 of these 24 occur at lag 2.

The coefficients $r_{\tau,y}$ and the spectral estimates $\hat{f}(\omega)$ for AT and T are plotted on Figures 6.2 and 6.3 respectively. This stock has the median first coefficient (0.098) for the 15 series. Coefficients $r_{\tau,x}$, calculated from returns, are also shown on Figure 6.2. It is clear that the greatest autocorrelation occurs at lag 1 and only at lag 1 are the coefficients highly significant (the dotted lines on Figure 6.2 indicate $1.96/\sqrt{n^*}$ and $-1.96/\sqrt{n^*}$). The greatest spectral density corresponds to a five-day cycle. This series is one of the six stock series having f_w significant at the 5 per cent level.

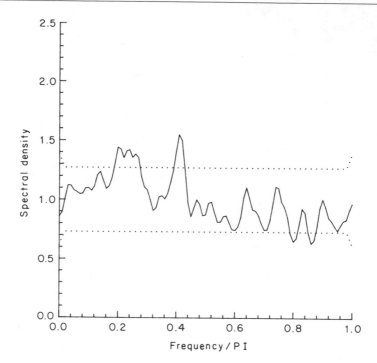

Figure 6.3 Estimated spectral density for American Telephone and Telegraph stock calculated from rescaled returns. Graph shows $\hat{f}(\omega)$ plotted against ω/π. Estimates above the upper dotted line or below the lower line are significant at the 5 per cent level

Commodities and currencies

It has already been noted that test results for any pair of futures series for the same commodity are similar. Therefore only one series per commodity is considered when counting the number of times each statistic rejects the random walk hypothesis. The series taking six-month blocks for prices from each contract have been chosen for corn, cocoa, coffee, and sugar. This block size avoids any thin trading more than six months before delivery. It also provides less biased coefficients than series using three-month blocks; bias occurs because there are less than $n^* - \tau$ products in the numerator of $r_{\tau,y}$ for futures series.

Fifteen series are now discussed, covering metals (six spot series), farm products (five futures series) and currencies (one spot and three futures series). Table 6.3 lists the number of times the random walk hypothesis is rejected, by test statistic, for the 15 commodity and currency series. The trend statistics outscore all the other statistics. Both T^* and f_0 reject for all 15 series, U^* rejects for 14 and the next statistic only rejects 10 times. The first-lag statistic and its non-parametric alternative, the runs statistic, only

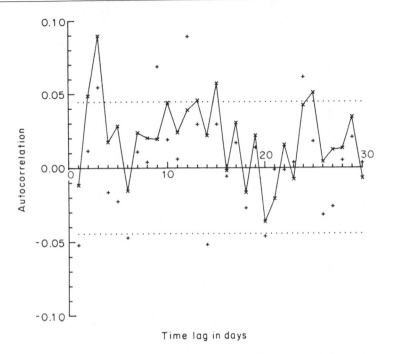

Figure 6.4 Autocorrelation coefficients for gold returns (+) and rescaled returns (×)

score 7 and 6 respectively. There is minimal evidence for weekly (or any other) cycles; f_w scores 2. Other values of γ in (6.8.2) give similar results. For $\gamma = 0.05$, T^* and U^* both score 14, for $\gamma = 0.2$, T^* scores 15 and U^* scores 13.

Clearly trend statistics are best for tests on commodity and currency series whilst first lag statistics are best for stock series. Different models are obviously needed for the two types of series. Models having positive autocorrelation at several lags are indicated for commodities and currencies. About 81 per cent of the coefficients at lags 1 to 10 are positive for the 15 series, 77 per cent positive over lags 11 to 20 and 63 per cent positive over lags 21 to 30. This preponderance of positive coefficients suggests that trend models, with p near to unity, will be close to the unknown process generating the observed series.

Figures 6.4, 6.5, and 6.6 show the autocorrelations $r_{\tau,y}$ for gold, sugar, and £/$ futures; the $r_{\tau,x}$ are also plotted. The first twenty sugar coefficients $r_{\tau,y}$ are all positive. Every statistically significant $r_{\tau,y}$ on these figures is positive. Notice that the $r_{\tau,x}$ and $r_{\tau,y}$ can be quite different relative to the scale used. Also notice the higher variance of the $r_{\tau,x}$, especially on Figure 6.4. Figures 6.7, 6.8, and 6.9 display the spectral estimates $\hat{f}(\omega)$ for the same three series. Each figure shows a sharp peak at zero frequency.

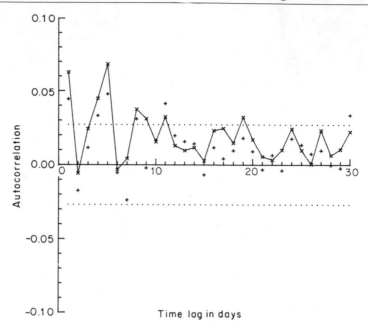

Figure 6.5   Autocorrelation coefficients for sugar futures returns (+) and rescaled
returns (×)

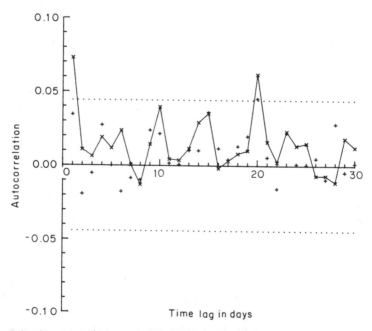

Figure 6.6   Autocorrelation coefficients for sterling futures returns (+) and
rescaled returns (×)

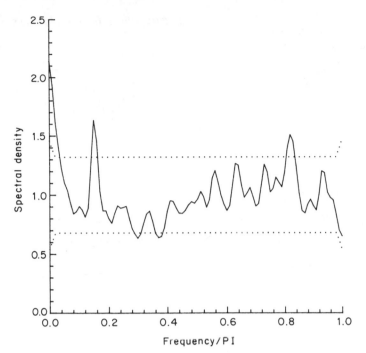

Figure 6.7   Estimated spectral density for gold calculated from rescaled returns

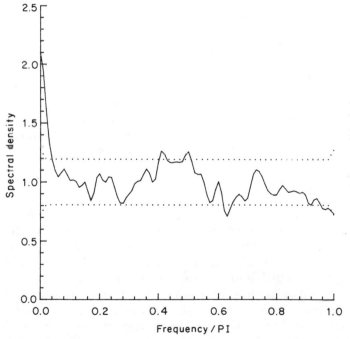

Figure 6.8   Estimated spectral density for sugar futures calculated from rescaled returns

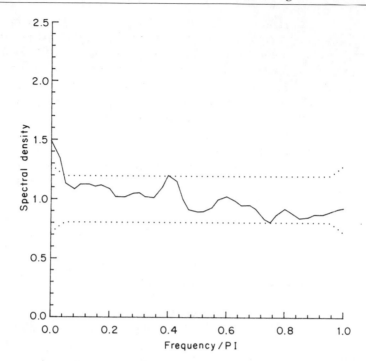

Figure 6.9   Estimated spectral density for sterling futures calculated from rescaled returns

Table 6.2 can be used to see if dependence between futures returns is greatest when the contract still has several trading months remaining, perhaps due to thin trading. The test results show that dependence is not notably greater for series using twelve-month blocks than it is for series using six-month blocks. The same conclusion holds when six- and three-month blocks are compared. Autocorrelation among futures returns is not caused by thin trading several months before the delivery date.

About the rest of this chapter

The results of random walk tests applied to rescaled returns show that stock, commodity, and currency prices are not random walks. Thus we have established that daily returns are not uncorrelated observations from distributions having identical means. The next section discusses results from applying tests to the returns instead of the recommended rescaled returns. These results also show that prices are not random walks. The ease with which the random walk hypothesis is rejected is partly due to using long series and partly due to choosing an appropriate test statistic. This is demonstrated in Section 6.10.

Expected returns need not be constant even when prices perfectly reflect relevant information. A more general null hypothesis is investigated in Section 6.11 based upon returns having expected values determined by some appropriate equilibrium theory. Tests of the more general hypothesis will be shown to give very similar results to random walk tests. It then follows that some relevant information is reflected in prices during the days following its first impact upon the market.

Sections 6.11 and 6.12 show that the apparent inefficient use of information extends beyond calendar effects and is not caused by market rules restricting prices nor by dealers buying and selling at different prices. Figures given in Section 6.13 suggest the inefficiencies occurred throughout the full period of the long time series.

6.9 SOME TEST RESULTS FOR RETURNS

It was shown in Chapter 5 that tests based upon the autocorrelation coefficients of returns will be unreliable because the variances of the coefficients exceed $1/n$ when the random walk hypothesis is true. Now let T_x^* and T_y^* respectively denote T^* when coefficients $r_{\tau,x}$ and $r_{\tau,y}$ are used. A very surprising conclusion is revealed when the tests are evaluated using the coefficients $r_{\tau,x}$: for each of the 40 series T_x^* is less than T_y^*, often by a considerable amount. Table 6.4 shows the values of T_x^*, T_y^*, and $T_y^* - T_x^*$. The number of random walk rejections, at the 5 per cent level for T_x^*, is only 6 out of 15 for the commodity and currency series. A majority of series and lags have $r_{\tau,y} > r_{\tau,x}$; see Table 6.1 for first-lag coefficients. The rejections count for $r_{1,x} \sqrt{n}$ is 14 out of 16 for the stocks series.

Considering random variables $R_{\tau,X}$ and $R_{\tau,Y}$, it appears true that $E[R_{\tau,X}] < E[R_{\tau,Y}]$ and this explains the observed conclusion $T_x^* < T_y^*$. The observation $T_x^* < T_y^*$ for all series is itself evidence against the random walk hypothesis. Random walks have been simulated to confirm this deduction. One set of 40 series, each containing 2020 returns, was created by simulating Gaussian white noise. The mean difference $r_{1,y} - r_{1,x}$ was 0.0002 and the mean for $T_y^* - T_x^*$ was 0.06 with $T_x^* > T_y^*$ for 13 series. Two values of T_x^* and three values of T_y^* were significant at the 5 per cent level. Another set of 40 series had fluctuating conditional variances with $X_t = V_t U_t$; $\{\log (V_t)\}$ was Gaussian with variance 0.25 and autocorrelations 0.985^{τ} and $\{U_t\}$ was Gaussian white noise. Again there were 2020 simulated returns in each series. The mean for $r_{1,y} - r_{1,x}$ was -0.0055, the average of $T_y^* - T_x^*$ was -0.13 and 21 series had $T_x^* > T_y^*$. It can safely be concluded that real price series are not random walks. Two values of T_y^* and six values of T_x^* exceeded 1.65 in the second set of simulations. Of course, the standard deviation of T_x^* is more than one for these simulations; the estimated value was 1.37. The $r_{\tau,y}$ were calculated using $\gamma = 0.1$ in all the simulations.

Table 6.4   Trend statistics for returns and rescaled returns

	T_x^*	T_y^*	$T_y^* - T_x^*$
Spot series			
Allied	−0.06	0.73	0.79
Alcoa	1.72	2.87	1.15
Am. Can	0.87	1.84	0.97
AT and T	−0.17	0.19	0.36
Am. Brands	−1.89	−0.74	1.15
Anaconda	−1.30	−0.31	1.00
Bethlehem	−0.62	−0.26	0.36
Chrysler	−0.64	−0.03	0.60
Dupont	2.23	3.22	0.99
Kodak	−1.03	−0.42	0.61
G. Electric	0.15	1.24	1.08
G. Food	0.41	0.79	0.38
G. Motors	−0.86	−0.23	0.63
G. Telephone	−0.45	−0.28	0.17
Harvester	0.22	0.89	0.67
FT 30	0.84	1.41	0.57
Gold	0.58	4.73	4.14
Silver	0.19	1.94	1.75
Copper	1.38	4.03	2.65
Lead	−0.74	3.82	4.57
Tin	−0.32	2.24	2.57
Zinc	−0.87	2.12	2.99
£/$	0.91	6.56	5.65
Futures series			
Corn (12)	1.67	1.89	0.22
Corn (6)	2.96	3.03	0.07
Corn (3)	2.78	3.29	0.51
Cocoa (12)	3.22	6.65	3.44
Cocoa (6)	2.94	6.34	3.40
Cocoa (3)	4.03	6.43	2.40
Coffee (12)	2.17	6.96	4.80
Coffee (6)	2.85	6.67	3.82
Coffee (3)	2.01	6.20	4.18
Sugar (12)	4.58	7.87	3.29
Sugar (6)	5.62	8.97	3.35
Sugar (3)	5.49	9.26	3.77
Wool (12)	1.12	2.26	1.14
£/$ (6)	1.38	3.53	2.15
DM/$ (6)	1.83	4.83	3.00
SF/$ (6)	2.72	3.01	0.30
T-bond	0.13	0.46	0.33

A fairly satisfactory explanation of the positive differences $T_y^* - T_x^*$ will be provided in Chapter 7. Institutional factors cannot suffice as the positive differences occur for a diverse set of markets. The rescaling transformation from x_t to y_t must play some part in an explanation; the positive differences increase as γ increases for all the stocks but only half the other series. The most likely explanation is that the non-random component of returns is relatively large when the conditional standard deviation is relatively small. This idea will be explored for trend models in Sections 7.3 and 7.4, and there shown to provide a possible explanation for the commodity and currency series.

6.10 POWER COMPARISONS

The evidence for the claim that none of the series is a random walk is very strong. Table 6.3 shows the relative power of the test statistics if the claim is accepted. Clearly choosing an appropriate test increases power. Test power will increase as the number of observations increases. These properties of test power are now illustrated by numerical examples.

Firstly, following Taylor (1982b, pp. 55–6), consider test power when the price-trend hypothesis (H_1) is true. The trend statistics ought then to have higher power than other statistics, just as the converse would hold for other types of non-randomness, for example a first-order moving average. Quantification of the power gained when H_1 is true can help to show if the observation that T^* rejects the random walk hypothesis more frequently than r_1, etc., can be used to support trend models as an explanation of price behaviour.

Returns were simulated for the following model consistent with $H_1 : X_t = \mu_t + e_t$, the trend μ_t is either μ_{t-1} with probability p or a new independent value with chance $1 - p$, var $(\mu_t) = A$ var (e_t) and the e_t are strict white noise. Series of 1500 returns were simulated with $A = 0.034$ and $p = 0.944$. The model was twice replicated 1000 times with the e_t first normal distributed and second distributed as Student's t with six degrees of freedom. The trends μ_t had normal distributions. Independent realizations of identical distributions were used, so the rescaling transformation was neither required nor used.

Tests on weekly and monthly data are often reported. To compare their power with tests performed on daily data, returns over one week and four weeks were computed in the obvious way and then the first lag coefficients $r_{1,W}$ and $r_{1,M}$ were calculated. For trend models, the theoretical autocorrelations $\rho_{\tau,k}$ of returns aggregated over k days are related to the daily first-lag autocorrelation ρ_1 and $m = 1/(1 - p)$ thus:

$$\rho_{\tau,k} = \mathrm{cor}\left(\sum_{i=1}^{k} X_{t+i}, \sum_{j=1}^{k} X_{t+k\tau+j}\right)$$

$$= \rho_1[m(1 - p^k)]^2 p^{(\tau-1)k}/[k + 2m\rho_1\{k - m(1 - p^k)\}].$$

For the simulations, $\rho_1 = 0.032$, $\rho_{1,5} = 0.115$, $\rho_{1,20} = 0.169$ and the expected values of the test statistics $\sqrt{n}r_1$, $\sqrt{(n/5)}r_{1,W}$, and $\sqrt{(n/20)}r_{1,M}$ are approximately 1.24, 1.99, and 1.46.

Table 6.5 lists the estimated powers of the various tests for a 5 per cent significance level, when $A = 0.034$, $p = 0.944$, and $n = 1500$. The powers for the two distributions are very similar. The trend statistics T^*, U^*, and f_0 are far more powerful than their competitors for the realistic values of A, p, and n. Thus the higher scores of the trend statistics in Table 6.3 for commodity and currency series are indeed evidence that price-trend models are appropriate for such series. As expected, the best first-lag coefficient for detecting trend behaviour uses weekly returns.

Secondly, consider test power as a function of the number of returns. The test statistic $r_{1,y}\sqrt{n^*}$ has been calculated for the first $n^* = 250$, 500, 1000, and 2000 rescaled returns in each of the US stock series. Four of the fifteen test values are significant at the 5 per cent level when $n^* = 250$, increasing to six significant when $n^* = 500$, eight significant when $n^* = 1000$ and fourteen significant when $n^* = 2000$. The share index series

Table 6.5 **Estimated powers for 1500 observations from a trend model**

Statistic	Percentage rejections of the random walk hypothesis	
	Normal residuals	Student residuals
T^*	87	86
U^*	84	85
f_0	78	77
$r_{1,W}$	57	61
Q_{10}	46	47
Q_{30}	38	39
$r_{1,M}$	35	34
r_1	33	34
Q_{50}	31	32
K	26	36
N_S	7	8
f_W	3	4

Notes: Trend parameters $A = 0.034$, $p = 0.944$. Significance level 5 per cent.
Reprinted with permission from the *Journal of Financial and Quantitative Analysis* (Taylor, 1982b).

gives a significant result for $n^* \geq 500$. Likewise the test statistic T_y^* has been calculated for subsets of the commodity and currency series. Contracts covering one, two, four, or eight years were used for the futures series. For the 15 series discussed in Section 6.8, only one value of T_y^* is significant when $n^* \simeq 250$, five are significant when $n^* \simeq 500$ and nine are significant when $n^* \simeq 1000$. The statistics are significant for every series having more than 2000 observations.

These results show that it is highly desirable to study series containing at least 2000 returns. A study of several shorter series, say 1000 returns in each, will probably give some significant and some non-significant test values. It would then be difficult to state clear conclusions.

6.11 TESTING EQUILIBRIUM MODELS

So far the null hypothesis has been defined to include the joint assumptions that returns are uncorrelated and have a constant mean. When this hypothesis is true the conditional expected returns, $E[X_t | I_{t-1}]$, will in practice depend neither on the time t nor upon the observed past returns I_{t-1}. Random walk tests implicitly assume a model of market equilibrium for which the equilibrium expected return is constant. Such a model is an approximation to realistic theories of equilibrium expectations. The approximation is usually considered satisfactory when testing the hypothesis that prices perfectly reflect available information (Fama, 1976, Ch. 5, especially pp. 149–51).

Let I_{t-1}^* be a set representing information used at time $t - 1$ to establish equilibrium expectations for the next day. The set I_{t-1}^* need not contain I_{t-1}. Also let μ_t denote the *equilibrium expected return*, namely $E[X_t | I_{t-1}^*]$, and define the *excess return* to be $e_t = X_t - \mu_t$. Then excess returns will be uncorrelated if a market uses information perfectly but returns would then appear to be slightly autocorrelated if the μ_t change with time. It is now shown that any such autocorrelation among returns is very small and can usually be ignored.

In certain equilibrium models μ_t and $E[X_t | I_{t-1}]$ are always non-negative. The price process $\{Z_t\}$ is then a *submartingale* since $E[Z_t | z_{t-1}, z_{t-2}, \ldots] \geq z_{t-1}$.

Stocks

The standard equilibrium model for stock returns is the capital asset pricing model (CAPM) attributed to Sharpe (1964) and Lintner (1965) and explained by Fama (1976) and Brealey and Myers (1984) among others. The model relates the equilibrium expected return for a particular stock to the same quantity for the whole market:

$$\mu_t = E[X_t \,|\, I^*_{t-1}] = r_{ft} + \beta_t \{E[X_{mt} \,|\, I^*_{t-1}] - r_{ft}\}.$$

In this equation, X_{mt} is the market return, β_t measures the stock's risk and r_{ft} is the risk-free rate of interest; the model has been stated for convenience in nominal terms. Let r_{pt} be the term in curly brackets, called the *risk premium*. The beta-coefficient β_t can change with time and its weighted average over all stocks is unity. To simplify the discussion suppose $\beta_t = 1$ for all t. This is not a serious simplification for the following argument. Then the return X_t conditional upon $I^*_{t-1} = \{r_{ft}, r_{pt}, \beta_t\}$ is

$$X_t \,|\, I^*_{t-1} = \mu_t + e_t = r_{ft} + r_{pt} + e_t. \tag{6.11.1}$$

It is a matter of simple observation that interest rates r_{ft} change with time. Financial theory requires r_{pt} to be positive but does not assume the risk premium is constant, although measuring changes in the premium is very difficult (Merton, 1980). If we are willing to model the equilibrium expected returns by a stationary process, then perfect market efficiency implies

$$\text{cov} \, (e_t, e_{t+\tau}) = 0, \qquad \tau > 0,$$

and

$$\text{cov} \, (X_t, X_{t+\tau}) = \text{cov} \, (\mu_t, \mu_{t+\tau}).$$

Hence the autocorrelations of a stationary returns process for a perfect efficient market are

$$\rho_{\tau,X} = \text{cov} \, (\mu_t, \mu_{t+\tau})/\text{var} \, (X_t).$$

In these circumstances an upper bound ρ^* for the autocorrelations is given by

$$|\rho_{\tau,X}| \leqslant \text{var} \, (\mu_t)/\text{var} \, (X_t) = \rho^*. \tag{6.11.2}$$

Given μ_t, the equivalent expected return in annual terms is $\exp \, (250\mu_t + 125\sigma^2) - 1$ assuming $e_t \sim N(0, \sigma^2)$ and 250 trading days in a year. Over a period of ten years it would be likely that the range for annual expected returns was less than 20 per cent, especially for returns before 1980. The corresponding range for μ_t, say μ' to μ'', will then be constrained by $250(\mu'' - \mu') \leqslant \log \, (1.2)$. A reasonable bound for var (μ_t) is given by the variance of a uniform distribution over the interval μ' to μ'', namely $(\mu'' - \mu')^2/12$. A typical stock has returns variances $(0.015)^2$ (Section 2.4). Thus one estimate of the upper bound in (6.11.2) is

$$\hat{\rho} = [\log \, (1.2)/250]^2/[12(0.015)^2] = 0.0002. \tag{6.11.3}$$

If we follow Merton (1980) and postulate a relationship $r_{pt} = a_j v_t^j$ for some j, v_t being the conditional standard deviation of e_t, then ρ^* can be calculated exactly from the distribution of V_t if r_{ft} is assumed constant. I have considered log $(V_t) \sim N(-4.4, 0.45^2)$, cf. Section 3.9, and assumed r_{pt}

corresponds to a 10 per cent annual premium, approximately, when v_t equals the median value of its distribution. Then $r_{pt} = 0.025v_t$ gives $\rho^* = 0.0001$ whilst $r_{pt} = 1.6v_t^2$ gives $\rho^* = 0.0007$.

Clearly if stationary processes are assumed it is impossible for day-to-day changes in the equilibrium expected return to be the cause of important autocorrelation among stock returns. The variation in μ_t is trivial compared with the variation in excess returns e_t. Other equilibrium models, such as the arbitrage pricing theory investigated by Roll and Ross (1980), will give the same conclusion. Returns on market indices compared with returns on individual stocks have similar risk premia but smaller variances and hence ρ^* is higher.

Simulation results

Computer simulations confirm that changes in equilibrium expected returns have little effect upon the sample autocorrelations of returns and rescaled returns. Three sets of 40 random walks have been simulated and statistics such as $r_{1,x}$, $r_{1,y}$, T_x^*, and T_y^* calculated. Returns in each series have had hypothetical equilibrium terms μ_t added to them and then the statistics have been recalculated. Notation like $\Delta r_{1,x}$ will represent the statistic $r_{1,x}$ for a series $\{\mu_t + e_t\}$ minus the statistic for the series $\{e_t\}$. Differences $\Delta r_{1,x}$, ΔT_x^* etc., measure the effect of the time-dependent expected returns.

All the simulated series have 2020 returns with 2000 used in all tests. The simulated processes have average returns variances equal to 0.015^2. The first set of random series are Gaussian white noise. Set two contains series whose variance multiplies by four after half the observations, each half being Gaussian white noise. The third set is an appropriate product process with parameter values based on Tables 3.2 and 3.3. Separate random numbers were used for each series.

Firstly, a long trend in equilibrium expected returns was investigated, defined by $\mu_t = a_0 t$ with a_0 chosen to make the expected annual return increase from 0 to 20 per cent over eight years. Table 6.6 lists the average values of $\Delta r_{1,x}$, $\Delta r_{1,y}$, ΔT_x^*, ΔT_y^*, and $\Delta(T_y^* - T_x^*)$ and also gives the standard deviations in brackets, separately for each set of 40 series; standard errors for the means are estimated by the standard deviations divided by $\sqrt{40}$. All rescaled returns were obtained using $\gamma = 0.1$. Secondly, the risk premium was set proportional to the conditional standard deviation of returns. Assuming a constant risk-free rate, $\mu_t = rf + a_1 v_t$ for some number a_1. Following the argument given after equation (6.11.13), a_1 was chosen to be 0.025. Table 6.6 summarizes the results for the second and third sets of series. As the first set has constant v_t and hence constant μ_t, no new results are then obtained. Thirdly, the equilibrium expected returns were assumed to be a constant (rf) plus $a_2 v_t^2$, with $a_2 = 1.6$; again see Table 6.6 for a summary of the results.

Table 6.6 Summary of simulation results for various expected returns models

Model[a] for μ_t	Set[b]	$\Delta r_{1,x}$	$\Delta r_{1,y}$	ΔT_x^*	ΔT_y^*	$\Delta(T_y^* - T_x^*)$
$a_0 t$	1	0.0004[c](0.0006[d])	0.0004(0.0006)	0.07(0.12)	0.08(0.12)	0.01(0.03)
	2	0.0002(0.0005)	0.0002(0.0006)	0.05(0.11)	0.06(0.13)	0.01(0.05)
	3	0.0004(0.0005)	0.0007(0.0007)	0.09(0.11)	0.13(0.15)	0.04(0.11)
$rf + a_1 v_t$	2	0.0001(0.0002)	0.0001(0.0003)	0.02(0.05)	0.03(0.07)	0.01(0.03)
	3	0.0004(0.0007)	0.0005(0.0007)	0.07(0.13)	0.09(0.12)	0.02(0.08)
$rf + a_2 v_t^2$	2	0.0003(0.0004)	0.0004(0.0006)	0.06(0.09)	0.08(0.13)	0.02(0.05)
	3	0.0016(0.0036)	0.0011(0.0015)	0.28(0.70)	0.21(0.28)	−0.08(0.48)
Day effects	1	−0.0031(0.0028)	−0.0029(0.0027)	0.01(0.09)	0.00(0.09)	−0.01(0.04)
	2	0.0003(0.0040)	−0.0003(0.0034)	0.01(0.10)	−0.04(0.10)	−0.05(0.09)
	3	−0.0028(0.0022)	−0.0045(0.0033)	0.07(0.11)	−0.03(0.12)	−0.10(0.10)
Month effects	1	0.0009(0.0009)	0.0007(0.0012)	0.10(0.15)	0.10(0.16)	0.00(0.06)
	2	0.0012(0.0015)	0.0019(0.0019)	0.14(0.19)	0.28(0.23)	0.15(0.14)
	3	0.0005(0.0009)	0.0020(0.0018)	0.04(0.11)	0.25(0.23)	0.21(0.23)

[a] Defined in Section 6.11.
[b] Conditional variances are constant for Set 1, have a step change for Set 2, and follow an autoregressive, lognormal process for Set 3.
[c] Sample mean for a sample of size 40.
[d] Sample standard deviations are bracketed.

The results from these simulations show that changes in μ_t indeed induce negligible autocorrelation for almost all series. When μ_t depends on v_t^2 and high values occur for v_t there can be more substantial induced autocorrelation. For the third set one series had $\Delta r_{1,x} = 0.0199$, $\Delta r_{1,y} = 0.0073$, $\Delta T_x^* = 4.17$, and $\Delta T_y^* = 1.47$, the next largest differences were far smaller at 0.0093, 0.0036, 1.38, and 0.51, whilst four of the T_y^* with changing μ_t were significant compared with two significant values for constant μ_t.

Further simulations have incorporated the calendar effects described in Section 2.5. These time-dependent expected returns represent market imperfections rather than equilibrium expectations, in the absence of a satisfactory equilibrium theory. Firstly, μ_t for Mondays minus μ_t on any other day was defined to be -0.0023 and the standard deviation of e_t was multiplied by 1.2 on Mondays, whilst keeping the overall average variance at $(0.015)^2$. These simulations provide the fourth group of results in Table 6.6. Secondly, μ_t in January minus μ_t in any other month was defined to be 0.0018. This gives the fifth group of results in Table 6.6. The table shows that calendar effects induce more measured autocorrelation than can be attributed to a plausible equilibrium model. As predicted theoretically, it is seen that adding US calendar effects to an uncorrelated series makes the first-lag coefficient negative (positive) on average when only weekly (monthly) effects are considered. Combining the effects gives an expected negative first-lag autocorrelation.

The final column of Table 6.6 shows that none of the models for expected returns can explain the large positive differences $T_y^* - T_x^*$ observed for the 40 real series. Monthly effects could explain some but only a small fraction of the positive differences.

Tests

Let H_{0e} denote the null hypothesis that there is zero autocorrelation among excess returns for a particular model of market equilibrium and/or calendar effects. Tests of H_{0e} can be constructed by using an estimate $\hat{\rho}$ of the upper bound ρ^* appropriate to the null hypothesis and then altering standard random walk tests. For example, the test based on $r_{1,y}$ would reject H_{0e} at the 5 per cent level if

$$|r_{1,y} \sqrt{n^*}| > 1.96 + \hat{\rho}\sqrt{n^*}.$$

The adjustment added to 1.96 is only 0.02 if $n^* = 2500$ and $\hat{\rho} = 0.0004$. This would be reasonable if calendar effects are ignored. Even if $\hat{\rho}$ was as high as 0.004 the statistic $r_{1,y}\sqrt{n^*}$ would reject H_{0e} for all the stock series.

Similarly a test based on T_y^* rejects H_{0e} if

$$T_y^* > 1.65 + 0.4274\hat{\rho}\sqrt{n^*} \sum_{\tau=1}^{30} 0.92^\tau = 1.65 + 4.51\hat{\rho}\sqrt{n^*}.$$

The term added to 1.65 would usually be small although the required adjustment to T_y^* is greater than that to $r_{1,y}\sqrt{n^*}$.

Other equilibrium models

At a theoretical level and assuming perfect markets, it is plausible to assume futures have zero equilibrium expected returns (Section 2.3). Returns from holding commodity inventories ought to depend on at least interest rates and perhaps also risk premia and convenience yields. Tests of H_{0e} for spot commodity returns thus require a relevant estimate of ρ^*. As the variances of such returns are greater than for stocks, one possibility is to use the stocks estimate ignoring calendar effects, i.e. 0.0004. Then H_{0e} is rejected for all six metal series using an adjusted T_y^* and for all six excepting tin using an adjusted U_y^*. Another possibility is to be very cautious and allow for unknown calendar effects too. There are at present no results linking metal returns to the calendar but choosing $\rho^* = 0.003$ looks safe from Table 6.6. Then three of the six series would reject H_{0e} using an adjusted T_y^* and five still reject using an adjusted U_y^*.

Equilibrium expected returns from spot currencies will depend on interest rates. Suppose for example the relevant one-day rates are $I_{\$,t}$ and $I_{£,t}$ for deposits in the US and the UK from time $t - 1$ to t and let z_t be the number of dollars sold for one pound on day t. Adopting our usual definition of the return x_t from holding an investment, i.e. the change in price logarithms, the equilibrium expected return will be approximately $I_{£,t} - I_{\$,t}$. The approximation is almost perfect if spot traders are risk-neutral or there is no risk premium. The interest rate differential is continually changing. Its range over a decade is likely to be much less than the 20 per cent assumed to derive the upper bound (6.11.3) for stocks. However, the returns variance for stocks has been about six times as large as for currencies. A satisfactory upper bound for most currencies will be six times the figure in (6.11.3), i.e. 0.0012. An adjusted T_y^* or U_y^* will then comfortably reject H_{0e} at the 5 per cent level for the spot £/$ series.

Conclusion

Subtracting equilibrium expectations and calendar effects from returns has little effect upon tests for randomness. The weak dependence between returns claimed earlier is not caused by the variables considered in this section.

6.12   INSTITUTIONAL EFFECTS

Many futures exchanges limit the amount prices can change from day to day. Dealers at spot and futures markets quote separate bid and ask prices. These institutional features prevent markets determining one price reflecting all relevant information. We now consider the consequences for random walk tests.

Limit rules

Various US futures contracts cannot be traded at prices differing by more than a certain amount from the previous day's close or settlement price. The IMM rules governing sterling futures for the period studied in this text, 1974 to 1982, prohibited trading at a price $0.05 above or below the previous day's settlement with two exceptions: wider limits are defined after consecutive limit days and there is no limit in the weeks just before delivery. Only 10 of the 1991 sterling settlement prices are constrained by the limit rules and no consecutive limit days are observed. Roll (1984) describes limit rules for orange juice futures and finds limit moves are relatively common. One or both of two contracts moved the limit on slightly over 10 per cent of the trading days in his sample.

   UK futures have less exacting rules. Cocoa trading, for example, stops for half-an-hour after the price moves more than a fixed amount from the previous close but after the break prices are no longer restricted. Sugar trading is similar and coffee prices are never limited. Thus UK futures prices at the close are very rarely restricted.

   Limit restrictions will cause positive autocorrelation among returns when information is used perfectly. When a market closes limit-up, subsequent prices must include the upward movement prevented on the limit day. A high positive return on the limit day will be followed by one or more returns having higher than average (conditional) expected values. Similar dependence occurs for limit-down days.

   Simulations can give approximate values for the autocorrelation induced by limit rules. The results can only be approximate because it is impractical to simulate intra-day price changes. A simulated random walk defines a series of perfect market prices $\{z_t^*\}$. This series defines market limited prices $\{z_t\}$, for some limit parameter θ, by:

$$
\begin{aligned}
z_t &= z_t^* && \text{if } (1 + \theta)z_{t-1} \geqslant z_t^* \geqslant (1 - \theta)z_{t-1}, \\
&= (1 + \theta)z_{t-1} && \text{if } z_t^* > (1 + \theta)z_{t-1} \\
&= (1 - \theta)z_{t-1} && \text{if } z_t^* < (1 - \theta)z_{t-1}.
\end{aligned}
\tag{6.12.1}
$$

Keeping θ constant for all t is convenient and unlikely to affect the conclusions. Clearly intra-day price movements are ignored: for example if $\theta = 0.04$, $z_0^* = 100$, and z^* falls all morning to 95 but closes at $z_1^* = 105$,

Table 6.7   Summary of simulation results for a simple limit rule

θ/σ	Percentage limit days	Average values of			
		$\Delta r_{1,x}$	$\Delta r_{1,y}$	ΔT_x^*	ΔT_y^*
Set 1					
1.5	14.6	0.10	0.09	2.10	1.83
2	4.9	0.04	0.03	0.66	0.56
2.5	1.3	0.01	0.01	0.17	0.13
3	0.3	0.00	0.00	0.03	0.03
Set 2					
1.5	10.6	0.14	0.07	4.59	1.82
2	5.2	0.09	0.03	2.59	0.86
2.5	2.7	0.06	0.02	1.57	0.44
3	1.5	0.04	0.01	0.99	0.24

Notes: Conditional variances are constant for Set 1 and follow an autoregressive, lognormal process for Set 2. Percentage limit days refers to days when the market limited price is not the perfect market price.

then it is seen that $z_1 = 104$ whereas the correct market limited price is 96.

Zero risk premia were assumed in the simulations. Then, if simulated random returns x_t^* come from a stationary process having variance σ^2, the autocorrelation induced by limit moves depends on the ratio θ/σ. Two sets of forty series $\{z_t^*\}$ have been simulated. As in Section 6.11 each series gives 2020 returns. The first set has Gaussian white noise returns. The other set has substantial fluctuations in conditional standard deviations V_t, the returns being uncorrelated with log (V_t) having standard deviation 0.6 and autocorrelations 0.985 [r].

Table 6.7 summarizes the induced autocorrelation as a function of θ/σ. Notation like $\Delta r_{1,x}$ refers to $r_{1,x}$ for market limited returns minus $r_{1,x}$ for perfect market returns. Appropriate ratios θ/σ have been between 1.5 and 2 for orange juice and more than 3 for currencies. From Table 6.7 it is suggested that limit moves need to be considered carefully if more than 2 per cent of the prices are restricted by limit regulations.

It is clear, as should be expected, that limit rules induce far more autocorrelation among returns than among rescaled returns when conditional variances fluctuate. Therefore the significant autocorrelation claimed for the futures investigated in this book cannot be caused by limit rules because their returns are less autocorrelated than their rescaled returns. It appears that limit rules do not affect the random walk tests for the markets studied here. However, as shown by Roll (1984), limit rules at other markets need to be investigated in more depth.

Bid–ask spreads

Brokers and dealers quote different buying and selling prices. The differences are very small for a high volume asset. For most futures the bid–ask range is less than 0.1 per cent of an average price on most days. The range for stocks is generally higher in percentage terms. In Section 2.1 it was recommended that the average of the bid and ask prices is used to define a closing price. If, however, only one of bid and ask is available to a researcher then some spurious autocorrelation may occur. This is now claimed to be negligible.

Firstly, suppose the analysed price z_t is either a bid or ask price but it is not known which it is. Let z_t^* be another way to measure the closing price, perhaps the bid and ask average or perhaps some equilibrium price. Then let δ_t be defined by $z_t = (1 + \delta_t)z_t^*$. It is appropriate to assume the δ_t are uncorrelated with zero mean. The theoretical autocorrelations of returns x_t calculated from the z_t will be lower than those for returns x_t^* derived from the z_t^*. In particular, for stationary processes and uncorrelated X_t^*, the spurious autocorrelation is approximately

$$\rho_{1,x} \simeq -\text{var}\,(\delta_t)/\text{var}\,(X_t), \qquad \rho_{\tau,x} = 0 \text{ for } \tau > 1.$$

Considering futures, when $|\delta_t| \leqslant 0.001$ and var $(X_t) \geqslant (0.002)^2$, the first-lag autocorrelation is between 0 and -0.0007.

Secondly, suppose z_t is always the selling price so that every δ_t is positive. Making reasonable assumptions about the δ_t any spurious autocorrelation will be zero or negative. These assumptions, for a stationary process $\{\delta_t\}$ having autocorrelations ρ_τ, are $\rho_{\tau-1} - \rho_\tau \geqslant \rho_\tau - \rho_{\tau+1} \geqslant 0$ for all positive τ; a satisfactory example is the autocorrelations ϕ^τ, $\phi > 0$.

Bid–ask spreads are most unlikely to cause spurious positive autocorrelation. Therefore such spreads cannot explain the significant positive values of the random walk test statistics.

6.13   RESULTS FOR SUBDIVIDED SERIES

The results presented in this chapter show that some information is not reflected correctly by prices as fast as it could be. There have been considerable advances in communications technology in recent years so we might expect the amount of dependence between returns to decline as time progresses. This possibility is now investigated by comparing test statistics for the two halves of each series.

Dependence between stock returns was detected using the first autocorrelation coefficient, $r_{1,y}$, calculated from rescaled returns. This coefficient has also been calculated from each half of the fifteen stock series, in every case using 1365 rescaled returns. All thirty coefficients are positive.

Twelve are significant at the 5 per cent level for the first half (1966 to mid-1971) and fourteen are significant for the second half (mid-1971 to 1976). For nine of the fifteen series the coefficient for the later period exceeds that for the earlier period. There is no evidence that the dependence decreased after 1971. Coefficients $r_{1,x}$ calculated from returns provide identical conclusions, all thirty again being positive.

A rank correlation test ranks the values of r_1 to see if stocks with high dependence in the first period have higher than average dependence in the second period. The correlation between the ranks of $r_{1,x}$ in the two periods is 0.850 and for the ranked $r_{1,y}$ it is 0.543. Both rank correlations are significant at the 5 per cent level (one-tail test). It thus appears that certain stocks consistently have higher than average autocorrelation. Alcoa had the highest r_1 for both halves whether calculated from returns or rescaled returns.

Dependence among commodity and currency returns was demonstrated using the trend statistic T_y^*. This statistic has also been evaluated for each half of the appropriate series. For the six metal, five agricultural, and four currency series discussed in Section 6.8 it is found that 13 out of 15 have T_y^* significant at the 5 per cent level for the first half with 11 significant for the second half. All the metal test values are higher in the first half than the second. There is not a clear pattern for the agricultural futures and the currency series. Coffee and sugar statistics are slightly higher for their first halves, corn and cocoa give very similar values for both halves, and the currency series split evenly between higher values in the first and second halves. It is noted that T^* for half a series is, with one exception, always greater for rescaled returns than for returns.

6.14 CONCLUSIONS

Prices did not follow random walks at the markets considered. Daily returns calculated from prices were not generated by some uncorrelated process having a constant mean. These conclusions have been established for many actively traded stocks, commodities, and currencies so it is likely that they apply to almost any financial asset.

More generally prices do not reflect information fully and instantaneously and thus markets are not perfectly efficient. This conclusion follows from Section 6.11 and the inefficiencies extend beyond calendar effects and institutional constraints. Of course the statistical dependence identified by random walk tests is very small and therefore prices reflect most information accurately and fairly quickly. Nevertheless it appears some information is not used as well as it could be.

Daily returns from US stocks on consecutive days are positively correlated, also noted by Perry (1982) and others. The first-lag autocorrelation coefficient is small and usually in the range 0.05 to 0.15. There is no evidence for longer term trends but, instead, there may be a tendency towards negative dependence at time lags of more than one day. The logical ARMA model for US stock returns is a first-order moving average, MA(1), although this cannot represent any dependence at lags beyond a single day. Forecasts derived from MA(1) models could be an input to a trading rule for stocks. However, any ordinary citizen using such a rule is certain to incur trading costs far greater than any gross profits (cf. Fama and Blume, 1966). This concludes our discussion of US stocks: the markets are efficient according to any practical definition (e.g. Jensen, 1978) but prices do not always correctly reflect relevant information on the day it becomes available.

Contrasting results are obtained for commodities and currencies. The statistical dependence among daily returns occurs at several lags, therefore some information takes several days to be fully reflected by prices. An explanation based upon price-trends is consistent with the sample auto-correlations, a majority of them being positive. Appropriate theoretical autocorrelations are those of a mixed autoregressive, moving-average process, ARMA(1, 1). Price-trend models are described further in Chapter 7 and suitable forecasts of future returns are assessed. These forecasts can be used to help construct trading rules which may provide futures traders with consistent net excess profits. Some trading results are presented in Chapter 8.

Two methodological conclusions are emphasized. Firstly, random walk tests must use rejection criteria which are valid for the null hypothesis considered. Hence, following the arguments given in Chapter 5, the parametric tests have been evaluated using rescaled returns. Results are similar when returns are used but their correct interpretation is unclear. For some reason rescaled returns display more dependence than returns. A number of elementary explanations have been explored unsuccessfully. Further efforts follow in Chapter 7 and are more successful.

Secondly, some test statistics are substantially more powerful than their competitors for the detection of certain autocorrelation structures. It is recommended that r_1 is used for random walk tests on stock data and a trend statistic is used for commodities and currencies. The statistic T^* involves subjectively chosen constants and if this is unacceptable the zero-frequency statistic f_0 can be used to test for the trend alternative. Other test statistics give poor results for the series tested here. In particular the runs test cannot be considered satisfactory because it uses relatively little information, see Section 6.4.

Interesting results can be obtained from 1000 rescaled returns if a powerful test statistic is chosen, however longer series should be used if possible. Large returns should be checked against a secondary source if one is available and then the tests will be more reliable, see Section 6.7.

6.15 SUMMARY

The random walk hypothesis is false for every long series tested. Stock prices can take a day longer than necessary to reflect information correctly. It is believed this informational inefficiency cannot be exploited. Commodity and currency prices have reflected relevant information slower and the efficiency of their markets will be investigated in Chapter 8.

APPENDIX 6(A)   CORRELATION BETWEEN TEST VALUES FOR TWO RELATED SERIES

Suppose $\{Y_{1,t}\}$ and $\{Y_{2,t}\}$ are stationary, cross-correlated processes, their interdependence being entirely contemporaneous so that

$$\text{cor } (Y_{1,s}, Y_{2,t}) = \lambda \qquad \text{if } s = t,$$
$$= 0 \qquad \text{otherwise,}$$

for some $\lambda \neq 0$. Without loss of generality it is assumed each process has mean zero and variance one. There will be some correlation between $R_{1,\tau}$ and $R_{2,\tau}$, defined here by

$$R_{i,\tau} = \sum_{t=1}^{n-\tau} Y_{i,t} Y_{i,t+\tau} \Big/ \sum_{t=1}^{n} Y_{i,t}^2, \qquad i = 1, 2.$$

Define A_n, B_n, and C_n by

$$A_n = \frac{1}{n} \sum_{t=1}^{n-\tau} \sum_{t=1}^{n-\tau} Y_{1,s} Y_{1,s+\tau} Y_{2,t} Y_{2,t+\tau},$$

$$B_n = \frac{1}{n} \sum_{t=1}^{n} Y_{1,t}^2 \quad \text{and} \quad C_n = \frac{1}{n} \sum_{t=1}^{n} Y_{2,t}^2,$$

so that $n R_{1,\tau} R_{2,\tau}$ equals $A_n / (B_n C_n)$.

Assuming each process is strict white noise, as n increases:

$$E[A_n] \rightarrow E[Y_{1,t} Y_{1,t+\tau} Y_{2,t} Y_{2,t+\tau}] = \lambda^2,$$
$$B_n \rightarrow 1 \quad \text{and} \quad C_n \rightarrow 1,$$

hence

$$n E[R_{1,\tau} R_{2,\tau}] \rightarrow \lambda^2$$

and

$$\text{cor } (R_{1,\tau}, R_{2,\tau}) \to \lambda^2 \text{ also.} \tag{6.A.1}$$

A similar argument shows there is no asymptotic correlation between $R_{1,\tau}$ and $R_{2,\xi}$ whenever $\tau \neq \xi$. It then follows that for any constants a_τ the linear combinations L_1 and L_2 defined by

$$L_i = \sum_{\tau > 0} a_\tau R_{i,\tau}$$

have correlation λ^2 too. The trend statistics T^*, U^*, and f_0 provide relevant examples.

The result (6.A.1) should be a good approximation if the processes are uncorrelated rather than strict white noise. Estimates of λ are low for either returns or rescaled returns from different assets. Typical estimates are between 0.25 and 0.5 for pairs of metals.

Chapter 7

Forecasting Trends in Prices

Detailed models for trends in prices are now conjectured and used to forecast returns. Slight improvements upon random walk forecasts are shown theoretically and empirically. Further theoretical results show that trend models imply traders might be able to use the forecasts advantageously.

7.1   INTRODUCTION

If there are trends in commodity and currency returns it will be difficult to predict them. No forecast of the next return can be substantially more accurate than a forecast based upon a random walk model. We have to settle for very slight improvements in forecast accuracy at best and perhaps none at all.

Price-trend models offer the best chance to find improvements upon random walk forecasts. Specifications of trend models must to some degree be pragmatic, conjectural, and simplistic. Two specifications are described in Section 7.2 and assessed by considering the empirical accuracy of the forecasts they suggest. Model parameters are estimated in Section 7.3 and used to show why rescaled returns can be more autocorrelated than returns in Section 7.4. Theoretical and empirical forecasting results are presented in Sections 7.5 and 7.6 respectively. Having shown that price-trend forecasts can out-perform random walk forecasts, some theoretical calculations are given in Section 7.7 showing that the forecasts would be valuable if the models are specified perfectly.

7.2   PRICE-TREND MODELS

Trends will only occur if some information is reflected in several consecutive returns. We assume each item of information is reflected either quickly or slowly. Only quickly reflected information is fully incorporated into prices on the same day as it first becomes known by market agents.

Assuming returns X_t have stationary mean μ, we can write

$$X_t = \mu + (\mu_t - \mu) + e_t \tag{7.2.1}$$

with e_t being the response to quickly reflected information and $\mu_t - \mu$ the response to slowly reflected information. By definition the e_t have zero mean and are uncorrelated whilst the μ_t have mean μ and are auto-correlated. Also μ_s and e_t are uncorrelated, but not necessarily independent, for all s and t. Thus var (X_t) = var (μ_t) + var (e_t) and, for stationary processes, A = var (μ_t)/var (X_t) is a measure of the proportion of slowly reflected information.

The trend idea requires slowly reflected information to influence several returns in the same way. Suppose a particular news item is first available on day t and, when it is properly understood by everyone, changes the price logarithm by ω_t. If the news is slowly reflected it contributes to $\mu_{t+\tau} - \mu$ for several $\tau \geq 0$, otherwise it contributes to e_t. Supposing a slow interpretation, the trend idea suggests a contribution $\alpha_\tau \omega_t$ to $\mu_{t+\tau} - \mu$ with the α_τ non-negative and summing to one. These α_τ might be random variables but will be supposed to be deterministic to simplify the discussion. As time goes on, more and more people properly understand the information, therefore monotonically decreasing α_τ are appropriate. The simplest model for the α_τ then supposes $\alpha_{\tau+1}/\alpha_\tau = p$ for all $\tau > 0$ with $1 > p > 0$. Then $\alpha_\tau = (1 - p)p^\tau$ and the response $\alpha_0 \omega_t$ on the first day is a fraction $1 - p$ of the total response. Let $m = 1/(1 - p)$. Then the total response is equal to m times the first day's response and m will be called the mean trend duration.

Applying all the preceding assumptions and, furthermore, assuming stationarity, $\{\mu_t\}$ is an AR(1) process having autocorrelations p^τ:

$$\mu_t - \mu = p(\mu_{t-1} - \mu) + \zeta_t. \tag{7.2.2}$$

The residual ζ_t represents the effect of all the slowly reflected news first available on day t. There might be no such news and then ζ_t is zero or there might be several items with $\zeta_t = \alpha_0 \Sigma \omega_{it}$, using an obvious notation. Assuming $\{e_t\}$ is stationary it then follows that the returns have auto-correlations

$$\rho_{\tau,X} = Ap^\tau, \tag{7.2.3}$$

as in the price-trend hypothesis, equation (6.5.2). Other trend processes have the same autocorrelations (Taylor, 1980, Section 2).

So far we have sketched a model for the trend component $\{\mu_t\}$ but more details are needed to specify a complete model for returns $\{X_t\}$. In particular, the consequences of changing conditional variances need to be specified. Two possibilities will be described and compared throughout this chapter.

A non-linear trend model

Conditional standard deviations V_t were linked with the general level of market activity in Chapter 3. This market level will be related to the quantity of recent information and other variables. As the amount of new information per unit time increases, the amount reflected slowly may also increase. Assuming the proportion reflected slowly is constant across time leads to a product process, as in Taylor (1980). This is defined by (7.2.1) and

$$\mu_t - \mu = V_t T_t, \quad e_t = V_t \varepsilon_t. \tag{7.2.4}$$

Then defining U_t to be $T_t + \varepsilon_t$ we obtain the product process representation $X_t = \mu + V_t U_t$. The processes $\{V_t\}$, $\{T_t\}$, and $\{\varepsilon_t\}$ are assumed to be stochastically independent, $\{\varepsilon_t\}$ is zero-mean strict white noise, $E[T_t] = 0$, var $(\varepsilon_t) = 1 - A$ and var $(T_t) = $ var $(\mu_t)/$var $(X_t) = A$. This model will be called a *non-linear trend model* because the process $\{\mu_t\}$ is non-linear.

Now consider stationary models with the standardized trend component $\{T_t\}$ having autocorrelations p^τ. Then the standardized returns process $\{U_t\}$ has autocorrelations

$$\rho_{\tau,U} = Ap^\tau \tag{7.2.5}$$

and, applying (3.7.4), the returns $\{X_t\}$ have

$$\rho_{\tau,X} = Ap^\tau \{E[V_t V_{t+\tau}]/E[V_t^2]\}. \tag{7.2.6}$$

The term in curly brackets is less than one (see (3.7.5)). Typically it decreases from 0.99 at lag 1 to 0.84 at lag 50 (Taylor, 1982a, p. 216). Note $\{\mu_t\}$ is now not AR(1) and therefore $\rho_{\tau,X}$ is not Ap^τ. When $\{T_t\}$ is stationary and (7.2.5) applies but $\{V_t\}$ and hence $\{X_t\}$ are not necessarily stationary, conditional autocorrelations can be defined by

$$\mathrm{cor}\ (X_t, X_{t+\tau} | v_t, v_{t+\tau}) = \mathrm{cor}\ (U_t, U_{t+\tau}) = Ap^\tau. \tag{7.2.7}$$

To define a complete model for the simulations presented later it will be supposed that $\{\log (V_t)\}$ and $\{T_t\}$ are Gaussian (hence linear) AR(1) processes with autocorrelations ϕ^τ and p^τ respectively and that the ε_t have normal distributions.

Another way to model a constant proportion of slowly reflected information retains the equation $e_t = V_t \varepsilon_t$ but models μ_t using the AR(1) equation (7.2.2) with $\zeta_t = V_t \xi_t$ for strict white noise ξ_t. This has some appeal because it is a logical development of the ideas used to define (7.2.2). Unfortunately it does not permit $\{X_t\}$ to be a product process.

A linear trend model

Suppose now that as the amount of new information per unit time changes the amount reflected slowly remains constant. This suggests retaining

(7.2.1) and $e_t = V_t^* \varepsilon_t$ but now the processes $\{\mu_t\}$, $\{V_t^*\}$, and $\{\varepsilon_t\}$ are stochastically independent. When v_t^* is relatively high there will be more noise in the returns but no increase in the size of trends and thus there is less dependence among returns. Less autocorrelation should then be observed when the variance of returns is relatively high.

Assuming all processes are stationary let $A = \text{var}(\mu_t)/\text{var}(X_t)$ once more and let the variance of the zero-mean, strict white noise process $\{\varepsilon_t\}$ be $1 - A$. Also let $\sigma^2 = \text{var}(X_t)$. Then given a realization v_t^* of V_t^* the conditional variance of X_t is $A\sigma^2 + (1 - A)v_t^{*2}$.

We consider models having autoregressive trends with i.i.d. residuals so $\{\mu_t\}$ is linear and AR(1) with autocorrelations p^τ. Then

$$X_t = \mu_t + e_t, \quad e_t = V_t^* \varepsilon_t$$

and

$$\mu_t - \mu = p(\mu_{t-1} - \mu) + \zeta_t \tag{7.2.8}$$

and these equations define a *linear trend model*. The returns then have autocorrelations

$$\rho_{\tau,X} = Ap^\tau. \tag{7.2.9}$$

The correct definition of the standardized return is now

$$U_t = (X_t - \mu)/V_t$$

with

$$V_t = \alpha V_t^* \tag{7.2.10}$$

and

$$\alpha = \sqrt{(1 - A + A\{E[V_t^{*2}]E[V_t^{*-2}]\})}. \tag{7.2.11}$$

These equations ensure that the U_t have mean zero and variance one. Furthermore, as U_t equals $(\varepsilon_t/\alpha) + (\mu_t - \mu)/V_t$ the process $\{U_t\}$ is almost strict white noise. Although V_t and U_t are not independent, every pair V_s and U_t are uncorrelated. Given a realized value v_t, the conditional variance of X_t is $A\sigma^2 + (1 - A)v_t^2/\alpha$ and will be approximately v_t^2 since A must be small and hence $\alpha \simeq 1$. It can easily be shown that the standardized returns have autocorrelations

$$\rho_{\tau,U} = Ap^\tau\{E[V_t^2]E[V_t^{-1}V_{t+\tau}^{-1}]/\alpha\}.$$

The term in curly brackets can be far more than one. If $\{\log(V_t)\}$ is Gaussian and highly autocorrelated, with variance β^2, then

$$\rho_{\tau,U} \simeq Ap^\tau e^{4\beta^2}. \tag{7.2.12}$$

As estimates $\hat\beta$ are often about 0.5 the ratio $\rho_{\tau,U}/\rho_{\tau,X}$ could exceed 2.7.

The comparison of (7.2.9) with (7.2.12) shows rescaled returns will display more autocorrelation than returns for a linear trend model. Such models might therefore be able to explain the empirical observation $T_y^* > T_x^*$, explored further in Section 7.4.

A complete model for simulations is defined by supposing $\{\log (V_t)\}$ and $\{\mu_t\}$ are Gaussian, AR(1) processes with autocorrelations ϕ^τ and p^τ and that the ε_t have normal distributions. Approximation (7.2.12) is then very good for low A and high ϕ, the exact result being

$$\rho_{\tau,U} = Ap^\tau e^{(3+\phi^\tau)\beta^2}/(1 - A + Ae^{4\beta^2}).$$

7.3   ESTIMATING THE TREND PARAMETERS

Methods

Estimates of the two trend parameters, A and p, are needed to obtain optimal linear forecasts. An ARMA(1, 1) process has autocorrelations Ap^τ if its parameters are defined appropriately. These parameters, p and q, are convenient for finding the optimal linear forecasts for trend models. If $\{\xi_t\}$ is white noise and $\{P_t\}$ is defined by $P_t - pP_{t-1} = \xi_t - q\xi_{t-1}$ then its autocorrelations are Ap^τ with $A = (p - q)(1 - pq)/\{p(1 - 2pq + q^2)\}$, see equation (1.9.13). Given A and p, q is the solution of

$$q^2 - q\{1 + (1 - 2A)p^2\}/\{(1 - A)p\} + 1 = 0 \qquad (7.3.1)$$

and $q < 1$.

The parameters p and q (and hence A) could be estimated by maximizing the likelihood of the data if the returns process was linear. This maximization is impossible for practical non-linear processes. Thus estimates have been obtained by matching theoretical and observed autocorrelations as in Section 3.9. We consider the following functions, defined for K auto-correlations:

$$F_1(A, p) = n \sum_{\tau=1}^{K} (r'_{\tau,x} - Ap^\tau)^2 \qquad (7.3.2)$$

and

$$F_2(A, p) = (n - 20) \sum_{\tau=1}^{K} (r'_{\tau,y} - Ap^\tau)^2. \qquad (7.3.3)$$

Autocorrelations $r_{\tau,x}$ and $r_{\tau,y}$ are defined by (2.9.1) and (6.8.3) respectively with n the number of returns used to calculate $r_{\tau,x}$; $r'_{\tau,x}$ is $r_{\tau,x}$ multiplied by $n/(n - k\tau)$ to reduce bias and $r'_{\tau,y}$ has a similar definition with k being either 1 for a spot series or the number of contracts for a future series. I have used $K = 50$ for spot series and $K = 20, 30$, or 50 for futures series based on 3, 6, or 12 months data per contract.

When trend sizes depend on market volatility (a non-linear trend model) both $r'_{\tau,x}$ and $r'_{\tau,y}$ are approximately unbiased estimates of $\rho_{\tau,U} = Ap^{\tau}$. However, $r'_{\tau,y}$ has smaller variance and so the numbers $\hat{A}$ and $\hat{p}$ minimizing F_2 are appropriate estimates. If, on the other hand, trends are independent of volatility (a linear trend model) then $r'_{\tau,y}$ is a highly biased estimate of $\rho_{\tau,x} = Ap^{\tau}$ whilst $r'_{\tau,x}$ is unbiased although often inaccurate. It is probably best in these circumstances to seek the numbers $\hat{A}$ and $\hat{p}$ minimizing F_1.

To minimize either F_1 or F_2 mean trend durations $m = 1/(1 - p) = 2, 3, 4, \ldots, 40$ days are considered and for a given m the best unconstrained A can be obtained using calculus. For a fixed m and hence p the function F_1 is minimized by

$$A^*_{1,m} = \sum_{\tau=1}^{K} p^{\tau} r'_{\tau,x} \Big/ \sum_{\tau=1}^{K} p^{2\tau}. \qquad (7.3.4)$$

Likewise, we obtain $A^*_{2,m}$. Sometimes $A^*_{i,m}$ is negative so it is necessary to consider:

$$\hat{A}_{i,m} = A^*_{i,m} \text{ if } A^*_{i,m} > 0,$$
$$= 0 \text{ otherwise.}$$

Let $S_{i,m} = F_i(\hat{A}_{i,m}, 1 - 1/m)$ for $i = 1, 2$, and $m = 2, \ldots, 40$. Minimizing $S_{i,m}$ over m gives the estimates $\hat{A}_i$ and $\hat{p}_i$ minimizing F_i, and hence $\hat{m}_i$ and also $\hat{q}_i$ by appropriate substitutions in (7.3.1). A constraint on $\hat{p}$, here $\hat{p} \leqslant 0.975$ ($\hat{m} \leqslant 40$), appears to be necessary as $S_{i,m}$ can continue decreasing by very small amounts as m increases.

Futures

Table 7.1 presents estimates for the futures series. The estimates $\hat{A}_i$, $\hat{m}_i$, $\hat{p}_i$, and $\hat{q}_i$ are given, also $F_i(\hat{A}_i, \hat{p}_i)$ and the comparable function value for a random walk model, i.e. $F_i(0, 0)$. It can be seen that the majority of the estimates of m exceed 10 trading days. Thus, if the statistical methods used here are reliable, it takes over a fortnight for some information to be fully reflected by prices. These methods were first published in 1980 and no serious objections to them are known.

The estimates of A are, of course, very small. More than half of the estimates $\hat{A}_1$ are more than 0.02 and a majority of the $\hat{A}_2$ exceed 0.04. The estimated proportion of the returns variance attributable to trends is thus 10 to 100 times as large as the proportion explainable by the assorted equilibrium models discussed in Section 6.11.

For most of the series $A^*_{i,m}$ decreases monotonically as m increases. Only corn series have any negative $A^*_{i,m}$ and then only for $m \leqslant 4$. Six of the estimates $\hat{m}_i$ in Table 7.1 are 40 days because of the previously mentioned constraint.

Table 7.1 Estimates of price-trend parameters for futures series

	Function optimized	$\hat{A}$	$\hat{m}$	$\hat{p}$	$\hat{q}$	$F(\hat{A}, \hat{p})$	$F(0, 0)$
Series							
Corn (12)	F_1	0.0092	40	0.975	0.967	181.7	186.5
	F_2	0.0109	33	0.970	0.961	72.7	78.4
Corn (6)	F_1	0.0213	14	0.929	0.911	99.2	109.0
	F_2	0.0164	40	0.975	0.962	33.8	47.9
Corn (3)	F_1	0.0195	27	0.963	0.947	104.3	117.6
	F_2	0.0213	40	0.975	0.959	46.9	27.5
Cocoa (12)	F_1	0.0225	18	0.944	0.926	112.6	124.0
	F_2	0.0485	17	0.941	0.906	56.9	105.4
Cocoa (6)	F_1	0.0203	29	0.965	0.949	88.8	100.9
	F_2	0.0493	18	0.944	0.909	41.8	88.9
Cocoa (3)	F_1	0.0330	19	0.947	0.922	51.8	72.4
	F_2	0.0636	12	0.917	0.870	24.2	74.0
Coffee (12)	F_1	0.0191	11	0.909	0.893	84.5	89.2
	F_2	0.0770	8	0.875	0.819	60.6	113.0
Coffee (6)	F_1	0.0276	11	0.909	0.887	86.2	95.2
	F_2	0.0982	6	0.833	0.763	44.6	98.6
Coffee (3)	F_1	0.0171	40	0.975	0.962	102.3	111.3
	F_2	0.0798	8	0.875	0.817	38.8	89.8
Sugar (12)	F_1	0.0229	18	0.944	0.926	76.4	99.4
	F_2	0.0367	22	0.955	0.927	66.3	138.5
Sugar (6)	F_1	0.0335	15	0.933	0.907	54.4	89.9
	F_2	0.0521	16	0.938	0.899	34.3	125.3
Sugar (3)	F_1	0.0322	16	0.938	0.912	48.0	81.3
	F_2	0.0601	14	0.929	0.885	33.5	135.6
Wool (12)	F_1	0.0974	2	0.500	0.453	254.2	264.5
	F_2	0.0436	3	0.667	0.639	72.8	77.8
£/$ (6)	F_1	0.0120	40	0.975	0.965	20.9	25.1
	F_2	0.0244	34	0.971	0.952	24.6	40.5
DM/$ (6)	F_1	0.0189	12	0.917	0.901	39.7	43.4
	F_2	0.0480	13	0.923	0.887	45.3	71.2
SF/$ (6)	F_1	0.0234	17	0.941	0.922	46.7	54.9
	F_2	0.0206	40	0.975	0.959	45.2	57.7

Figure 7.1 shows plots of $S_{i,m}$ against m for the longest sugar series. The minimum value of $S_{2,m}$ is only 66.3 which is close to the 50 expected when the $r'_{\tau,y}$ have variance $1/(n-20)$. The least value of $S_{1,m}$ is higher (often much higher for other series) because the $r'_{\tau,x}$ have variances greater than $1/n$. Figure 7.2 shows plots of $\hat{A}_{i,m}$ against m for the same series.

Comparing the estimates $\hat{A}_1$ with the estimates $\hat{A}_2$ it is clear that for most series $\hat{A}_2$ is much larger than $\hat{A}_1$. When m is the average of $\hat{m}_1$ and $\hat{m}_2$, the ratio $\hat{A}_{2,m}/\hat{A}_{1,m}$ is approximately 1 for corn, 1.7 for sugar, 2 for cocoa and the currencies, and 2.5 for coffee. It appears from these figures that a linear

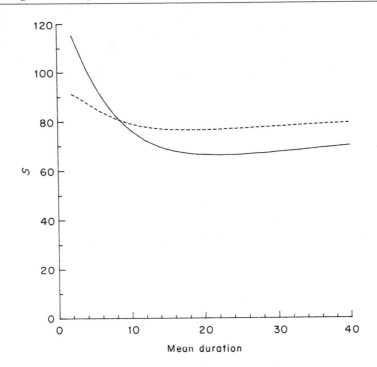

Figure 7.1 Plots of $S_{i,m}$ against the mean trend duration m for sugar futures returns ($i = 1$, dashed curve) and rescaled returns ($i = 2$, solid curve)

trend model is a better model than a non-linear trend model but something 'in between' may be even better.

The median $\hat{m}_1$ and the median $\hat{m}_2$ are both about 17 days with the median values of $\hat{A}_{1,17}$ and $\hat{A}_{2,17}$ being 0.022 and 0.044 respectively. A typical futures standard deviation is $\sigma_X = 0.02$. Then, using the median $\hat{A}_{1,17}$, the trend component has standard deviation equal to $\sigma_\mu = 0.02\sqrt{0.022} = 0.0030$. Furthermore, suppose the trend μ_t equals its standard deviation σ_μ. The expected return over day t is then 0.3 per cent and the partially interpreted information is eventually expected to change the price by about 17 times 0.3 or 5 per cent.

Spots

Table 7.2 presents estimates for the six metals series and the spot currency series. All the estimates $\hat{A}_1$ are virtually zero and the estimates $\hat{A}_2$ for the metals are smaller than for the futures. The negligible $\hat{A}_1$ are probably the result of negative first-lag coefficients $r_{1,x}$ (Table 2.9), indicating a reversal effect which obscures any price-trend behaviour.

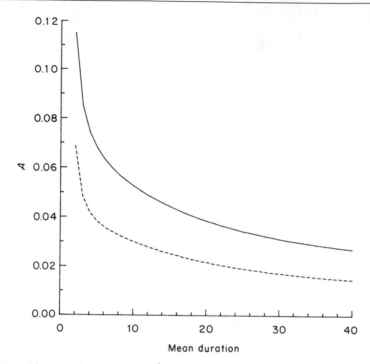

Figure 7.2 Plots of the estimates $\hat{A}_{i,m}$ against m for sugar futures returns ($i = 1$, dashed curve) and rescaled returns ($i = 2$, solid curve)

Table 7.2   Estimates of price-trend parameters for spot series

	Function optimized	$\hat{A}$	$\hat{m}$	$\hat{p}$	$\hat{q}$	$F(\hat{A}, \hat{p})$	$F(0, 0)$
Series							
Gold	F_1	0.0053	20	0.950	0.945	93.1	93.6
	F_2	0.0377	19	0.947	0.919	66.1	90.1
Silver	F_1	0.0047	40	0.975	0.971	173.3	173.8
	F_2	0.0190	40	0.975	0.961	64.2	71.1
Copper	F_1	0.0080	31	0.968	0.961	109.1	112.8
	F_2	0.0220	20	0.950	0.932	54.3	72.0
Lead	F_1	0.0014	40	0.975	0.974	64.2	64.3
	F_2	0.0233	40	0.975	0.958	39.2	68.0
Tin	F_1	0.0017	40	0.975	0.973	85.6	85.7
	F_2	0.0123	40	0.975	0.965	41.1	49.2
Zinc	F_1	0.0028	40	0.975	0.972	149.3	149.7
	F_2	0.0148	40	0.975	0.963	39.6	51.3
£/$	F_1	0.0093	40	0.975	0.967	80.0	83.1
	F_2	0.0460	40	0.975	0.946	54.5	128.6

Accuracy

The estimates $\hat{A}$, $\hat{p}$, and $\hat{q}$ are far from accurate. Their standard errors are considerable. Results for maximum likelihood estimates of p and q are given by Box and Jenkins (1976) for linear processes but cannot be applied to our estimates. The standard error (s.e.) of $\hat{A}_i$ presumably exceeds that of $A^*_{i,m}$ when $m = \hat{m}_i$. Thus if the autocorrelations have variances $1/n$ we expect from (7.3.4) that

$$\text{s.e.}(\hat{A}) \geqslant \{(1 - \hat{p}^2)/(n\hat{p}^2\}^{1/2}. \tag{7.3.5}$$

For example, $n = 2000$ and $\hat{p} = 0.95$ gives s.e.$(\hat{A})$ equal to at least 0.007. More information about accuracy is desirable and is now obtained using simulations.

7.4   SOME RESULTS FROM SIMULATIONS

Both types of trend model have been simulated in order to obtain insights into the accuracy of the parameter estimates and also to find out if the models can explain the empirical observation $T^*_y > T^*_x$ noted in Section 6.9. Sets of forty series were constructed by using the models described in Section 7.2. Returns having a linear trend component (based upon equations (7.2.8)) were used for sets 1 and 2 with a non-linear component used for sets 3 and 4 (based on (7.2.4)). All simulations had $p = 0.95$, so $m = 20$, and lognormal terms V_t with $\beta = 0.5$ and $\phi = 0.985$. Set 1 had $A = 0.02$ and then the theoretical first lag autocorrelation is 0.019 for returns and 0.050 for standardized returns; set 2 had $A = 0.01$; set 3 had $A = 0.04$ giving a first-lag theoretical autocorrelation of 0.038 for both returns and rescaled returns; set 4 had $A = 0.02$ and different random number sequences were used for each set. All the autocorrelation coefficients were calculated from 2000 observations, as in Section 6.11.

Estimates

Table 7.3 summarizes the estimates $\hat{A}_i$ and $\hat{p}_i$ obtained by minimizing $F_i (i = 1, 2)$ and it also summarizes the coefficients $r_{1,x}$ and $r_{1,y}$. It can be seen that the estimates $\hat{p}_i$ are considerably biased. All the averages of forty estimates $\hat{p}_i$ are less than 0.9 whereas p is 0.95. This downwards bias causes estimates $\hat{A}_i$ to have an upwards bias. For models containing linear trend components, $\hat{p}_2$ has less bias than $\hat{p}_1$ and, as expected, the averages of estimates $\hat{A}_2$ and coefficients $r_{1,y}$ are more than the averages of $\hat{A}_1$ and $r_{1,x}$. For non-linear trend components the $r_{1,y}$ have less bias and smaller standard deviations than the $r_{1,x}$ and the estimates $\hat{A}_2$ and $\hat{p}_2$ are preferred.

Table 7.3   Summary of simulation estimates for two price-trend models

	Linear trend component		Non-linear trend component	
	1	2	3	4
Simulation parameters				
A	0.02	0.01	0.04	0.02
p	0.95	0.95	0.95	0.95
β	0.5	0.5	0.5	0.5
φ	0.985	0.985	0.985	0.985
Coefficients lag 1				
Series x, mean	0.0111	−0.0038	0.0274	0.0076
Series y, mean	0.0364	0.0190	0.0366	0.0177
Series x, st. dev.	0.0357	0.0312	0.0409	0.0481
Series y, st. dev.	0.0236	0.0232	0.0209	0.0292
Mean $\hat{p}_1$	0.816	0.573	0.895	0.716
Estimates $\hat{m}_1$				
Number = 1	1	9	0	5
Number ≤ 4	11	23	3	17
Number ≤ 10	23	27	14	24
Number ≤ 20	29	30	32	28
Number < 40	36	34	37	34
Mean $\hat{p}_2$	0.897	0.810	0.892	0.737
Estimates $\hat{m}_2$				
Number = 1	0	1	0	4
Number ≤ 4	3	12	6	19
Number ≤ 10	18	23	17	24
Number ≤ 20	32	29	30	30
Number < 40	36	37	37	32
Estimates $\hat{A}_1$				
Mean	0.0388	0.0227	0.0453	0.0409
Standard deviation	0.0334	0.0301	0.0328	0.0487
Estimates $\hat{A}_2$				
Mean	0.0483	0.0387	0.0465	0.0400
Standard deviation	0.0254	0.0339	0.0277	0.0422

All the autocorrelation coefficients appear to be downwards biased. For these coefficients $n = 2000$ and the estimated bias over lags 1 to 30 is $-12/n$ for sets 1, 3 and $-6/n$ for sets 2, 4.

It is clear from Table 7.3 that estimates $\hat{A}_i$ and $\hat{p}_i$ are inaccurate even when there are 2000 observations. A confidence region might be defined by all numbers A_0 and p_0 for which $F_i(A_0, p_0)$ is less than $F_i(\hat{A}_i, \hat{p}_i) + \lambda$ for some λ and $i = 1$ or 2. The simulations show that $\lambda = 6$ will not give a 95 per cent confidence region as was incorrectly claimed in Taylor (1982a, p. 222). To obtain a 95 per cent region, λ must be at least 10.

Table 7.4 Summary of trend test statistics for simulated trend models

Model for μ_t	Set	T_x^*			T_y^*			$T_y^* - T_x^*$		
		Mean	SD	Sig.[a]	Mean	SD	Sig.	Mean	SD	Positive[b]
Linear	1	2.26	1.60	24	4.24	1.84	38	1.98	1.08	38
	2	0.59	1.15	9	2.13	1.15	24	1.54	1.13	38
Not	3	3.90	2.01	34	3.90	1.40	39	0.00	1.52	22
linear	4	1.90	2.05	21	2.01	1.56	25	0.11	1.12	24

[a]Number of statistics significant at the 5 per cent level, i.e. exceeding 1.65.
[b]Number of series having $T_y^* > T_x^*$.

A puzzle solved

As models containing linear trends have more autocorrelation among their rescaled returns y_t than their returns x_t, we expect $T_y^* > T_x^*$ for most simulated series this being the puzzling phenomenon observed for real series in Section 6.9. Table 7.4 presents the average values and standard deviations for T_x^*, T_y^*, and the differences $T_y^* - T_x^*$, for each set of forty simulated series. The table also shows the number of series in each set having $T_y^* > T_x^*$ and the numbers of test statistics significant at the 5 per cent level.

The differences $T_y^* - T_x^*$ for sets 1 and 2 show that a linear trend component can explain why these differences are positive for real series. Thirty-eight of the forty differences are positive for each of sets 1 and 2. The average difference is 2.0 for set 1 compared with 3.1 for the six metals series and 2.5 for the sixteen futures series. The average difference for simulated series will be proportional to $\sqrt{n}$ and the simulated series are shorter than the real ones. Thus the results for set 1 satisfactorily explain the values of differences $T_y^* - T_x^*$ observed for commodity and currency series. Notice that because T_y^* usually exceeds T_x^* the former statistic is more powerful for random walk tests. Table 7.4 shows the extra power can be substantial. The average difference for the stock series is 0.7 and cannot be explained comfortably by a trend model having a very small p.

The results for sets 3 and 4 show that trend models having the same autocorrelation between returns for all levels of market volatility cannot explain the observed positive differences. Satisfactory trend models must have decreasing dependence among returns as the conditional standard deviation of returns increases.

7.5 FORECASTING RETURNS: THEORETICAL RESULTS

It is assumed in this section that observed returns $\{x_t\}$ are generated by a stationary stochastic process $\{X_t\}$ having mean μ, variance σ^2, and autocorrelations Ap^τ. We consider linear forecasts of X_{t+h} made at time t and, for each h, seek the constants $a_{i,h}$ minimizing the mean square error (MSE) which is

$$E\left[\left\{X_{t+h} - \mu - \sum_{i=0}^{\infty} a_{i,h}(X_{t-i} - \mu)\right\}^2\right].$$ (7.5.1)

The best constants $a_{i,h}$ for a given horizon h define the optimal linear forecast and it will be denoted $F_{t,h}$.

We know that realistic processes $\{X_t\}$ are non-linear and it is then probable that some non-linear forecast $F^*_{t,h}$ has a smaller MSE than $F_{t,h}$. It is very difficult to find the best non-linear forecast and it would probably not be much more accurate than $F_{t,h}$. Consequently, we only consider linear forecasts.

As the MSE for a linear forecast is a function of the $a_{i,h}$ and the variance and autocorrelations of the X_t it can be assumed that $\{X_t\}$ is described by the ARMA(1, 1) model

$$X_t - \mu - p(X_{t-1} - \mu) = \xi_t - q\xi_{t-1}$$ (7.5.2)

with $\{\xi_t\}$ zero-mean white noise and q defined by equation (7.3.1). Alternatively, we may argue that there is an infinite-order, moving-average representation $X_t = \mu + \sum b_j \xi_{t-j}$ (Section 1.10) and this can be simplified to obtain (7.5.2).

The next return

Making use of the methods presented in Section 1.9 it can be seen from (1.9.11) that

$$X_{t+1} - \mu = \xi_{t+1} + (p - q) \sum_{i=0}^{\infty} q^i(X_{t-i} - \mu)$$

and therefore the optimal linear forecast is

$$F_{t,1} = \mu + (p - q) \sum_{i=0}^{\infty} q^i(X_{t-i} - \mu)$$ (7.5.3)

$$= \mu + (p - q)(X_t - \mu) + q(F_{t-1,1} - \mu).$$ (7.5.4)

Thus an observed forecast $f_{t,1}$ can be calculated using the latest return x_t, the previous forecast $f_{t-1,1}$, and estimates of μ, p, and q. The coefficients in (7.5.3) have total $(p - q) \sum q^i = (p - q)/(1 - q)$ which can be much less than 1.

Now X_{t+1} equals $F_{t,1} + \xi_{t+1}$ and thus the MSE of $F_{t,1}$ equals the variance of ξ_{t+1}. Also the forecast $F_{t,1}$ and the forecast error ξ_{t+1} are uncorrelated (cf. Granger and Newbold, 1977, pp. 122–3). From (1.9.12) it follows that

$$\text{var } (\xi_{t+1}) = \text{MSE}(F_{t,1}) = (1 - p^2)\sigma^2/(1 - 2pq + q^2) \qquad (7.5.5)$$

and thus

$$\text{var } (F_{t,1}) = (p - q)^2\sigma^2/(1 - 2pq + q^2) = Ap(p - q)\sigma^2/(1 - pq). \qquad (7.5.6)$$

Compared with the random walk forecast for X_{t+1}, which is simply μ and has MSE equal to σ^2, the proportional reduction in MSE obtained by using the optimal linear forecast is

$$W_1 = \frac{\sigma^2 - \text{MSE}(F_{t,1})}{\sigma^2} = \frac{\text{var } (F_{t,1})}{\sigma^2} = \frac{Ap(p - q)}{1 - pq}. \qquad (7.5.7)$$

Supposing $\{X_t\}$ is defined by one of the trend models described in Section 7.2, perfect knowledge of the future trend μ_{t+1} would make possible the maximum, feasible, proportional reduction in MSE, namely A. Thus (7.5.7) shows linear forecasts can only obtain the proportion $p(p - q)/(1 - pq)$ of the maximum reduction.

To illustrate the small magnitudes of the numbers described by these formulae suppose $A = 0.03$ and $p = 0.95$ so that $q = 0.9267$. Then the forecast weights have total $(p - q)/(1 - q) = 0.32$, the percentage reduction in MSE using $F_{t,1}$ is $100Ap(p - q)/(1 - pq) = 0.56$ per cent and this is a proportion $p(p - q)/(1 - pq) = 0.18$ of the best that could be achieved using superior and perfect trend forecasts.

More distant returns

For horizons $h > 1$, equation (1.9.16) shows that the optimal linear forecast $F_{t,h}$ is the following function of μ, p, and $F_{t,1}$:

$$F_{t,h} = \mu + p^{h-1}(F_{t,1} - \mu). \qquad (7.5.8)$$

Sums of future returns

Trading decisions require forecasts of the total return from day t to day $t + h$ inclusive. Let $S_{t,h} = X_{t+1} + X_{t+2} + \cdots + X_{t+h}$ be this total. Straightforward algebra shows that the optimal linear forecast of $S_{t,h}$ is simply

$$G_{t,h} = F_{t,1} + F_{t,2} + \cdots + F_{t,h} = h\mu + (1 - p^h)(F_{t,1} - \mu)/(1 - p). \qquad (7.5.9)$$

This forecast has MSE equal to $E[(S_{t,h} - G_{t,h})^2]$, which is less than the MSE of the random walk forecast $(h\mu)$ which is var $(S_{t,h})$. It follows that the proportional reduction in MSE obtained by using the optimal linear forecast is

$$W_h = \frac{\text{var } (S_{t,h}) - \text{MSE}(G_{t,h})}{\text{var } (S_{t,h})} = \frac{\text{var } (G_{t,h})}{\text{var } (S_{t,h})}. \tag{7.5.10}$$

From (7.5.6) and (7.5.9),

$$\text{var } (G_{t,h}) = \left(\frac{1 - p^h}{1 - p}\right)^2 \frac{Ap(p - q)\sigma^2}{1 - pq} \tag{7.5.11}$$

and it is easy to show that

$$\text{var } (S_{t,h}) = \sigma^2[h + 2Ap\{h - (1 - p^h)/(1 - p)\}/(1 - p)], \tag{7.5.12}$$

and hence W_h can be calculated.

For example, if $A = 0.03$ and $p = 0.95$ then $W_1 = 0.56$ per cent, $W_5 = 2.05$ per cent, $W_{10} = 2.92$ per cent, $W_{20} = 3.25$ per cent, and the maximum W_h is $W_{18} = 3.26$ per cent. For these trend parameters the ratio var $(S_{t,h})/(h\sigma^2)$ is 1.11, 1.23, and 1.41 for $h = 5$, 10, and 20 with limit $1 + 2Ap/(1 - p) = 2.14$ as $h \to \infty$.

7.6   EMPIRICAL FORECASTING RESULTS

We now compare price-trend forecasts with random walk forecasts over a selection of forecast horizons for commodity and currency series. Each series has been split as in Section 4.3. The first two-thirds of a series is used to estimate the parameters appearing in the forecasting equations, then forecasting accuracy is compared on the final third of the series. The notation $f_{t,1}^{(j)}$ will refer to forecast number j of the return x_{t+1} made at time t whilst $g_{t,h}^{(j)}$ describes the corresponding forecast of the total return $x_{t+1} + x_{t+2} + \cdots + x_{t+h}$ over the next h days. Of course $f_{t,1}^{(j)}$ equals $g_{t,1}^{(j)}$.

Benchmark forecasts

Forecasts based upon trend models must be compared with some benchmark forecast. Random walk forecasts when expected returns are zero define our first set of forecasts by

$$g_{t,h}^{(1)} = 0. \tag{7.6.1}$$

These forecasts are logical for futures series when it is believed there is no risk premium. The obvious random walk forecast when expected returns are believed to be non-zero utilizes the latest sample mean. Thus our second set of forecasts are

$$g_{t,h}^{(2)} = h \sum_{s=1}^{t} x_s/t. \tag{7.6.2}$$

Price-trend forecasts

We consider three forecasts derived from price-trend models and estimates of the model parameters. Initially we suppose the expected return is zero, a reasonable assumption when studying futures prices. The parameters p and q have been estimated from returns x_t and rescaled returns y_t using the methods given in Section 7.3 applied to two-thirds of each series, say times $t = 1$ to n_1 inclusive. Estimates $\hat{p}$ and $\hat{q}$ calculated from x_t, $1 \le t \le n_1$, define the third set of forecasts by adapting (7.5.4) and (7.5.9) to give

$$f_{t,1}^{(3)} = (\hat{p} - \hat{q})x_t + \hat{q}f_{t-1,1}^{(3)}$$

and

$$g_{t,1}^{(3)} = (1 - \hat{p}^h)\,f_{t,1}^{(3)}/(1 - \hat{p}). \tag{7.6.3}$$

The fourth set of forecasts, $g_{t,h}^{(4)}$, are defined in a similar way to the third set by using estimates $\hat{p}$ and $\hat{q}$ calculated from y_t, $1 \le t \le n_1$. These estimates are probably biased because the results presented in Section 7.3 show the y_t are more autocorrelated than the x_t. It may therefore be better to recognize that $\hat{p}$ and $\hat{q}$ estimated from various y_t ought to be used to forecast later y_t. Linking forecasts of rescaled returns, returns, and conditional standard deviations by the equation

$$\hat{y}_{t+1} = f_{t,1}/\hat{v}_{t+1} \tag{7.6.4}$$

it then follows (Taylor, 1980, p. 357) that an appropriate forecast of x_{t+1} is defined by

$$f_{t,1}^{(5)} = (\hat{v}_{t+1}/\hat{v}_t)\{(\hat{p} - \hat{q})x_t + \hat{q}f_{t-1,1}^{(5)}\}. \tag{7.6.5}$$

Forecasting all future conditional standard deviations by $\hat{v}_{t+1}$ it can be deduced that

$$g_{t,h}^{(5)} = (1 - \hat{p}^h)\,f_{t,1}^{(5)}/(1 - \hat{p}).$$

Summary statistics

Given forecasts $g_{t,h}^{(j)}$ made for the final third of a series, say for $n_1 < t \le n - h$, empirical mean square errors can be calculated as

$$\text{MSE}(h, j) = \sum_{t=n_1+1}^{n-h} (x_{t+1} + \cdots + x_{t+h} - g_{t,h}^{(j)})^2/(n - n_1 - h). \tag{7.6.6}$$

Percentage reductions in MSE relative to the benchmark forecast k are then defined by

$$PMSE(h, j, k) = 100\{MSE(h, k) - MSE(h, j)\}/MSE(h, k) \qquad (7.6.7)$$

with k chosen to be 1 or 2.

The magnitude of forecast errors depends upon the conditional standard deviation of the returns. Thus the MSE and PMSE statistics tell us more about forecasting accuracy when the conditional standard deviation is high than about accuracy averaged over all variance possibilities. It is therefore relevant to consider scaled forecast errors also, defined as forecast errors divided by an appropriate estimated standard deviation. These scaled errors define the weighted MSE and PMSE by

$$WMSE(h, j) = \frac{1}{n - n_1 - h} \sum_{t=n_1+1}^{n-h} \left(\frac{x_{t+1} + \cdots + x_{t+h} - g_{t,h}^{(j)}}{\hat{v}_{t+1}} \right)^2$$

$$(7.6.8)$$

and

$$PWMSE(h, j, k) = 100\{WMSE(h, k) - WMSE(h, j)\}/WMSE(h, k)$$
$$(7.6.9)$$

with $\hat{v}_{t+1}$ essentially defined as before, in fact (4.5.1) or (5.8.3) with $\bar{x}$ set equal to zero. It should be noted that the WMSE criterion for $h = 1$ can be written in terms of forecasts $\hat{y}_{t+1}^{(j)}$ of $y_{t+1} = x_{t+1}/\hat{v}_{t+1}$ as

$$\sum (y_{t+1} - \hat{y}_{t+1}^{(j)})^2/(n - n_1 - 1).$$

Thus WMSE measures forecasting accuracy applied to rescaled returns.

Futures

Results are tabulated for eight futures series. Series using twelve months data per contract were selected for corn, cocoa, coffee, and sugar, to minimize the number of initial values required for the forecasting equations. The other four series are for wool, sterling, deutschmarks, and Swiss francs. When a contract contributed returns from time $t_1 + 20$ until time t_2 to a series, with further returns on this contract available from t_1 to $t_1 + 19$, then I set $f_{t,1}^{(j)} = 0$ for $t = t_1 - 1$ and all j and the value of $\hat{v}_t$, for $t = t_1$, was set at 1.253 times the average of $|x_t|$ over times t_1 to $t_1 + 19$. Forecasts $f_{t,1}^{(j)}$ were then calculated for times t_1 to $t_2 - h$ and included in the calculation of MSE etc. for times $t_1 + 19$ to $t_2 - h$ inclusive. (For $h > 1$ no forecasts were made from $t_2 - h + 1$ to $t_2 - 1$; (7.6.6) and (7.6.8) were revised appropriately.)

Comparing the two benchmark forecasts showed it is better to assume a zero expected return than to predict returns using past average values. Consequently k is 1 when percentage reductions in MSE relative to a benchmark forecast are calculated. Table 7.5 presents these percentage reductions, $PMSE(h, j, 1)$ and $PWMSE(h, j, 1)$, for $h = 1, 5, 20$ and $j = 3, 4,$

Table 7.5 **Percentage reductions in mean square error**

Forecast	$PWMSE(h, j, 1)$ [a]			$PMSE(h, j, 1)$ [b]		
	$j = 3$	4	5	$j = 3$	4	5
$h = 1$						
Corn (12)	0.08	0.09	0.12	0.12	0.14	0.15
Cocoa (12)	0.50	0.99	0.98	0.45	0.78	0.74
Coffee (12)	0.30	0.22	−0.26	−0.25	−1.37	−3.71
Sugar (12)	0.29	0.25	0.10	−0.22	−0.39	−0.69
Wool (12)	0.04	−0.24	−0.44	0.28	−0.67	−1.08
£ (6)	0.28	0.32	0.32	0.13	0.02	−0.07
DM (6)	0.64	0.97	1.04	0.14	0.08	−0.04
SF (6)	−1.07	0.33	0.19	−1.81	−0.19	−0.48
$h = 5$						
Corn (12)	0.49	0.61	0.83	0.89	1.12	1.26
Cocoa (12)	1.90	3.96	4.05	2.23	4.53	4.88
Coffee (12)	0.76	0.32	−1.07	−0.24	−1.78	−9.20
Sugar (12)	2.12	2.12	1.35	−0.51	−1.35	−3.18
Wool (12)	−0.05	−1.14	−2.07	−0.69	−2.70	−4.41
£ (6)	0.72	0.65	0.64	0.32	−0.29	−0.95
DM (6)	1.64	2.49	2.93	0.57	0.54	0.57
SF (6)	0.38	1.25	0.62	−0.53	−0.43	−1.54
$h = 20$						
Corn (12)	0.58	0.63	1.26	0.49	0.29	1.33
Cocoa (12)	0.96	1.50	1.38	2.13	4.42	5.23
Coffee (12)	0.65	0.46	0.06	−4.06	−5.43	−14.22
Sugar (12)	4.16	4.54	3.17	1.39	−0.51	−4.32
Wool (12)	−0.28	−5.30	−8.27	−0.24	−6.18	−12.06
£ (6)	0.86	−0.01	0.42	2.81	1.99	2.67
DM (6)	1.73	2.63	2.84	1.25	1.84	1.39
SF (6)	0.81	3.24	0.67	0.87	1.69	−2.56

[a]Weighted MSE reduction, defined by equation (7.6.9).
[b]Unweighted MSE reduction, defined by (7.6.7).
[c]Number of forecasts evaluated for $h = 1$ were: corn 1248, cocoa 1005, coffee 1006, sugar 1781, wool 1250, £, DM, SF all 754.

5. The following average percentage reductions in MSE are obtained by the three price-trend forecasts.

	Average PMSE			*Average PWMSE*		
	$j = 3$	4	5	$j = 3$	4	5
$h = 1$	−0.14	−0.20	−0.59	0.18	0.28	0.26
5	0.25	−0.04	−1.58	0.99	1.28	0.91
20	0.58	−0.22	−2.82	1.21	0.96	0.18

Every PWMSE average is greater than the corresponding PMSE average. This shows that it is harder to achieve any reduction in MSE when the conditional variance of returns is relatively high. This conclusion is in line with the deduction in Section 7.3 that a linear trend model is better than the non-linear trend model there considered. It would appear that as the variance of returns decreases the magnitude of trends does not and thus forecasting the trend component becomes easier.

Looking at the PWMSE averages it is seen that all are positive although all are, of course, very small. This strongly suggests that it is possible to find forecasts marginally better than random walk forecasts, especially when the variance of returns is not substantial. The third and fourth forecasts have comparable accuracy and are better than the fifth set. The average reductions in MSE are, as predicted, greater for $h > 1$ than for $h = 1$.

The best results were obtained for the cocoa, sugar, and deutschmark series using the PWMSE criterion. It is difficult to imagine how the more successful series could have been identified before assessing the forecasts. Certainly the reductions in MSE expected after studying the first two-thirds of the series were a poor guide to future forecasting accuracy. For example, the anticipated PWMSE figures for sugar were 1.15 per cent for $h = 1$, 4.26 per cent ($h = 5$), and 7.10 per cent ($h = 20$), for $\hat{p}$ and $\hat{q}$ from rescaled returns, but the actual PWMSE were only 0.25, 2.12, and 4.54 per cent for the fourth forecast.

The PMSE averages are mainly negative and confirm the extra difficulty forecasting returns when their variance is high. The coffee and wool results are particularly uninspiring and the poor Swiss franc result for $h = 1$ is due to a high estimate $\hat{A}$ with $\hat{p} = 0.5$.

Spots

Results are given for the spot currency series and six spot metal series (gold, silver, copper, lead, tin, and zinc). Their returns ought to have positive means and indeed the latest sample mean is a marginally better predictor than an assumed zero mean. Thus k is 2 in calculations of PMSE and PWMSE. Also the price forecasts are marginally improved by replacing μ by the latest mean $f_{t,1}^{(1)}$ in equations (7.5.4) and (7.5.9). With these modifications the average percentage reductions in MSE for price-trend forecasts are as follows.

	Average PMSE			*Average PWMSE*		
	$j = 3$	4	5	$j = 3$	4	5
$h = 1$	−0.13	−0.50	−1.00	0.15	0.28	0.02
5	−0.13	−1.56	−3.62	0.73	1.03	0.30
20	0.45	−1.80	−6.14	0.91	1.28	−0.16

The spot averages confirm the conclusions deduced from the futures averages. It is possible to achieve slight reductions in MSE but only when the variance of returns is relatively low. Again the third and fourth forecasts are superior to the fifth set. All but one PWMSE spot average is positive and they are similar to the futures averages. On the other hand, all but one PMSE spot average is negative and they are more negative than the futures averages. The best results occurred for the fourth forecast with $h = 20$, particularly for silver (3.1 per cent reduction in WMSE), lead (4.3 per cent), and tin (2.0 per cent).

7.7 FURTHER FORECASTING THEORY

It appears that price-trend forecasts can be slightly more accurate than random walk forecasts, but are they of practical value? Some theoretical results are now given showing that price-trend forecasts are potentially valuable on some days, to be followed in Chapter 8 by the profitable results of appropriate trading rules. We continue to assume that returns are generated by a stationary process, having mean μ, variance σ_X^2 and auto-correlations Ap^τ.

The correlation between the forecast $F_{t,1}$ and tomorrow's unobservable trend component μ_{t+1} will be denoted by λ. Using the properties of $F_{t,1}$ given in Section 7.5,

$$\text{var}(F_{t,1}) = \text{cov}(F_{t,1}, X_{t+1}) = \text{cov}(F_{t,1}, \mu_{t+1})$$

and thus

$$\lambda = \sqrt{\{\text{var}(F_{t,1})/\text{var}(\mu_{t+1})\}} \tag{7.7.1}$$
$$= \sqrt{\{p(p - q)/(1 - pq)\}} \tag{7.7.2}$$

making use of (7.5.6). For the typical values $A = 0.03$, $p = 0.95$, and $q = 0.9267$ the correlation λ is 0.43. Note from (7.7.1) that the standard deviations of $F_{t,1}$, μ_{t+1}, and X_{t+1} are related by

$$\sigma_F = \lambda \sigma_\mu = \lambda \sigma_X \sqrt{A}. \tag{7.7.3}$$

Expected changes in prices

The optimal linear forecasts are unbiased. Therefore if the forecast $f_{t,1}$ is k standard deviations from its mean μ the expected return over day $t + 1$ is $\mu + k\sigma_F$ and the expected return over h days, i.e. the expected change in the price logarithm, is

$$h\mu + k\sigma_F(1 - p^h)/(1 - p).$$

This differs from the random walk prediction $h\mu$ by

$$k\lambda\sigma_X\sqrt{A}(1 - p^h)/(1 - p), \tag{7.7.4}$$

applying (7.7.3). Now an investor can wait until k is relatively large, say $k = 2$. Then the expected additional returns when $A = 0.03, p = 0.95$, and $\sigma_X = 0.02$ are 2.4 per cent for $h = 10$, and 3.8 per cent for $h = 20$, increasing to 6.0 per cent for very large h. Such figures suggest that a decision-taker who need not act upon every forecast may be able to use selected forecasts advantageously.

Forecasting the direction of the trend

It can be important to forecast the direction (up or down) of any trend correctly. We estimate the probability of correctly forecasting the direction by assuming μ_{t+1} and $F_{t,1}$ have a bivariate normal distribution. Then

$$\mu_{t+1} \mid f_{t,1} \sim N(f_{t,1}, (1 - \lambda^2)\sigma_\mu^2).$$

Thus, if firstly $\mu = 0$ and secondly the forecast $f_{t,1}$ is a positive number $k\sigma_F$, the estimated probability that the trend is positive becomes

$$P(N(k\lambda\sigma_\mu, (1 - \lambda^2)\sigma_\mu^2) > 0) = \Omega(k\lambda/\sqrt{(1 - \lambda^2)}) \qquad (7.7.5)$$

with $\Omega(.)$ the cumulative distribution function of the standard normal distribution. When λ is 0.43 the estimated probability of correctly forecasting the trend's direction is 0.68 and 0.83 for forecasts σ_F and $2\sigma_F$ respectively. These figures suggest that on many days the direction of the trend can be predicted correctly.

Forecasting prices

Suppose $g_{t,h}$ is the optimal linear forecast of $\log (z_{t+h}/z_t) = x_{t+1} + \cdots + x_{t+h}$. Then a simple forecast of z_{t+h} is $z_t \exp (g_{t,h})$. This forecast will be biased. An unbiased forecast can be obtained if it is assumed that the conditional distribution of $S_{t,h} = \log (Z_{t+h}/Z_t)$ given z_t and $I_t = \{x_t, x_{t-1}, \ldots\}$ is normal. It then follows that the best forecast of z_{t+h} is

$$E[Z_{t+h} \mid I_t, z_t] = z_t E[\exp (S_{t,h} \mid I_t)]$$
$$= z_t \exp (g_{t,h} + \tfrac{1}{2}[\text{var} (S_{t,h}) - \text{var} (G_{t,h})] \qquad (7.7.5)$$

which can be evaluated using (7.5.11) and (7.5.12).

7.8 SUMMARY

Price-trend forecasts can provide very small reductions in mean square forecast error. Such reductions appear to vary inversely with the appropriate conditional variance of returns. This can be explained by the magnitudes of trends being determined independently of the conditional variances of the random component of returns.

Two ways to estimate the trend parameters have been suggested. Although different estimates arise for the same series the forecasting accuracies achieved are similar on average. Non-linear forecasts might be better than the optimal linear forecasts discussed, especially if the weights given to past observations vary inversely with both the conditional variances and the time lag.

Chapter 8

Evidence Against the Efficiency of Futures Markets

Price-trend models are now used to construct trading rules. These rules are compared with the best investment strategies when investors believe the efficient market hypothesis is true. The trading results are shown to give better results for all six futures series considered and therefore the corresponding markets are unlikely to be efficient.

8.1   INTRODUCTION

A market will be said to use information efficiently if there is no way to use the information to increase expected wealth by frequent trading. This definition is discussed in Section 8.2. We continue to consider only the information provided by the present and past prices. An efficient market implies all trading rules are worthless, i.e. price information cannot indicate the best times to buy or sell.

Many professional traders disbelieve market efficiency. Advertised success stories rarely present a complete and honest description of trading results, for reasons left to the reader's imagination. The academic community on the other hand generally favours the efficient market paradigm. This is commendable for share markets but much less is known about the efficiency of futures markets. We should expect academic publications to be biased towards market efficiency. As Granger (1979, p. 104) remarks: 'If such a [foolproof] strategy were found, it would hardly be made public, even by an academic'. However, not all academics have sufficient capital to run a successful trading system!

Potentially profitable trading rules are presented in Section 8.7 but better rules exist. Trading rules having a good chance of making the efficiency of futures markets appear dubious are discussed. In this respect, the rules are highly successful. The combination of expected return and risk is deliberately not optimized and other important improvements are known to be possible.

Profitable trading results are given for cocoa, coffee, sugar, sterling, deutschmark, and Swiss franc futures in Section 8.9. The other available futures prices (for corn and wool) are relatively out of date. Concentrating on the six selected series may be considered a biased decision based upon hindsight. This is denied. These series would have appeared to be promising ones for trading rule research if only the first half of every series available had been subjected to random walk tests and the estimation of price-trend parameters. Trading rules rarely do well on share prices, see Fama and Blume (1966) and Ball (1978).

Trading rule research is fraught with methodological problems. Several are apparent in earlier studies of futures markets (Section 8.3) and studying futures introduces problems measuring returns and risks (Section 8.4). Section 8.5 summarizes trading conditions for ordinary investors and Section 8.7 lists realistic assumptions for assessing the performance of trading rules.

Theoretical and empirical evidence against efficient pricing is described. Little is known about the amount of autocorrelation required to refute the efficient market hypothesis. Efficiency is likely if any non-zero autocorrelations are small and confined to low lags. It is possible for markets to be inefficient, however, if small autocorrelations occur at several lags. Theoretical arguments are given in Section 8.6.

Each futures series is divided into two parts for a realistic assessment of practical trading rules. The first part (calibration contracts) is used to select two trend parameters and two trading constants, a process aided by simulating a price-trend model (Section 8.8). The second part (test contracts) is only used to assess the results of hypothetical yet realistic trading. Average net returns are shown in Section 8.9 to exceed the comparable averages from efficient market strategies for all six series. The implications of these results are discussed in Section 8.10. Figure 8.1 summarizes the methodology used to investigate market efficiency. Note the important role of price models.

8.2   THE EFFICIENT MARKET HYPOTHESIS

We adopt a practical definition of the efficient market hypothesis. The hypothesis is said to be true if the risk-adjusted return, net of all costs, from the best trading rule is not more than the comparable figure when assets are traded infrequently. This is essentially the definition given by Jensen (1978). It assumes trading rules buy and sell the same goods fairly often, typically more than once a year. In comparison, goods should be traded at efficient markets as little as possible to minimize costs. Note that investors may never want to trade assets like futures when they believe the markets are efficient.

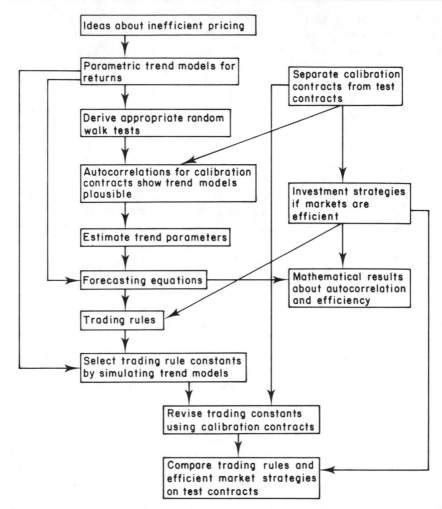

Figure 8.1   A summary of methodology. *Reproduced (with revisions) from Taylor (1983) by permission of Basil Blackwell, Oxford*

Trading rules generate more business for brokers than efficient market strategies and therefore have higher transaction costs. Thus rejection of the random walk hypothesis does not necessarily imply rejection of the efficient market hypothesis. In addition to transaction costs there are costs due to differing bid and ask prices, the acquisition of information, the interpretation of information and perhaps taxes. It costs almost nothing to obtain daily closing prices. Developing trading systems is, however, time consuming and requires specialist skills. The associated costs are impossible to measure and will be ignored: only the inventor of a trading system can decide if the development costs are less than any net profits. Daily interpretation of information requires time too. Very little time is needed to operate the rules described in this chapter. Similarly, negligible computer resources are required.

Risk must be considered when trading results are assessed. Ideally, risk should be discussed in a portfolio context. Thus alternative investments such as shares must not be forgotten when futures trading is contemplated. Fortunately it is fairly easy to take account of such alternatives because returns from futures are almost uncorrelated with share returns (Dusak, 1973; Bodie and Rosansky, 1980).

Our definition of the efficient market hypothesis has the advantage of being practical at the cost of being person dependent. Resources, opportunities, and attitudes towards risk vary between people. In particular, ordinary investors face higher trading costs than market members.

8.3 PROBLEMS RAISED BY PREVIOUS STUDIES

Few investigations into the performance of trading rules upon futures prices have been published and almost none after 1976. This is surprising as work by Stevenson and Bear (1970, 1976), Leuthold (1972, 1976), and Martell and Philippatos (1974) suggests some US markets are inefficient. These studies do not prove inefficiencies. Their evidence, however, does raise interesting possibilities deserving further research. The articles cited, and others, also draw attention to several important methodological issues.

Filter rules

The trading rule assessed in most research articles is the filter rule of Alexander (1961) or some variation thereof. It depends on a single parameter g. If futures are bought, called a long position, then they are held until the price falls g per cent from a peak; i.e. for a purchase on day i sell on the first day $j > i$ for which the price z_j is g per cent or more below the maximum price between days i and $j - 1$ inclusive. After cancelling the long position, futures are sold short on day j and the short position held until the price rises g per cent from a trough; i.e. go long again on the first day $k > j$ for which z_k is g per cent or more above the minimum price between days j and $k - 1$ inclusive. The range $0.5 \leqslant g \leqslant 25$ has been considered.

Filter rules are intended to let profits accumulate when there is a distinct trend, changing from long to short and vice versa when the trend appears to have changed direction. An initial position can be taken as soon as the price has moved g per cent from its initial level. The rule can be assessed on a series of daily closing prices, though real trades may not be possible or practical at exactly the close. Fama and Blume (1966) discuss filter rules in more detail.

Stevenson and Bear (1970) evaluated $1\frac{1}{2}$, 3, and 5 per cent filters on daily corn and soybeans futures prices between 1957 and 1968. The 5 per cent filter rule (their rule 2A) was more profitable than a buy and hold strategy after deducting commission costs. Buy and hold is a series of long positions, futures being bought on the first day a contract is considered and sold on the corresponding final day. Annual rates of return for the filter rule and the competing buy and hold strategy were not given. Impressive dollar profits were published yet cannot be interpreted easily.

Leuthold (1972) evaluated six filter sizes for daily live beef futures prices from 1965 to 1970. Profits occurred for five filter sizes after deducting commission costs. These profits were not compared with buy and hold as Leuthold believed this strategy was not the appropriate benchmark. The 3 per cent filter gave the largest profit. However, profits were highly sensitive to the filter size, being negative for the 5 per cent filter and positive again for the 10 per cent filter. High rates of return on a margin investment were given. They are difficult to interpret.

Bird (1985) has evaluated filter rules for cash and forward transactions at the London Metal Exchange. These forward contracts are similar to futures. Risk-adjusted profits may have been possible before July 1977 but not in later years.

Other applications of filters to futures offer less of a challenge to the efficient market hypothesis. Martell and Philippatos (1974) claim adaptive rules are successful but give insufficient details. Praetz (1975), for Sydney wool futures from 1966 to 1972, found no evidence that filter rules were superior to buy and hold.

Published results, particularly those of Stevenson, Bear, and Leuthold, cannot refute market efficiency for commodity futures because an adequate methodology has yet to be established. Three problems are emphasized.

Benchmarks

It is far from obvious what the returns from a filter rule should be compared with (Leuthold, 1972; Cargill and Rausser, 1975). The issue of risk premia is relevant. Risk-free assets, such as government securities or bank deposits, are appropriate for comparisons if it is believed there is never a risk premium. On the other hand, buy and hold must be assessed if a positive premium is believed to exist. Recall from Section 2.3 that the empirical evidence is indecisive but perhaps favours the view that there are premia for agricultural futures. Another complication is a bias in filter rules when there is a positive premium, caused by taking short positions against the premium (Praetz, 1976a). This bias makes it harder to identify any market inefficiencies.

Significance

Very little can be said about the distribution of filter returns when the null hypothesis of an efficient market is true. Thus the results of Stevenson, Bear, and Leuthold cannot be used to refute the efficient market hypothesis (Praetz, 1976b). For tests of the less general random walk hypothesis, Praetz (1979b) and Bird (1985) have derived test statistics based upon filter decisions. They assumed normal and identically distributed returns. It is unclear how much these strong conditions can be relaxed. Furthermore, we must appreciate that the distribution of a filter result is not the same for the two hypotheses, random walk and efficient market. Filter results are functions of sums of certain returns X_t (Praetz, 1979b) and the variances of these sums depend on the autocorrelations of the X_t, which do not have to be zero for an efficient market.

Optimization

Any trading result obtained by a retrospective optimization of the filter size g must be evaluated cautiously (Praetz, 1976b). Most published studies contain a dubious optimization. Traders could not guess the best filter size in advance and it is unlikely an optimized filter will be optimal in the future. The correct procedure is, of course, to split the prices. Then choose g using the first part and evaluate this g upon the remaining prices. This procedure requires many years of daily prices.

8.4   PROBLEMS MEASURING RISK AND RETURN

Recall that our preferred definition of an efficient market refers to risk-adjusted net returns. Ideally this definition should be applied to trading results.

Returns

Returns from share investments can be measured easily. This is not so for commodity futures because of margin trading. A position can be taken in a futures market by depositing 10 per cent or less of the position's value with a broker. It is possible to define the return from a trade by identifying the margin deposit with the amount invested (Leuthold, 1972). The investment is then highly risky. However, losses may well exceed the (initial) deposit so definitions involving margin payments are surely inappropriate.

It is arguable that a better approach is to consider some sum to be invested in a futures fund, then to calculate the fund's return after deducting commission costs and including interest earned on money not required by brokers. Perhaps interest can also be earned on the margin deposits. Trading amounts would have to be chosen to make the chance of losing more than the entire fund negligible.

Risk

Once we have a way to calculate the return from a trading strategy it is necessary to consider adjustments for risk. Returns can often be improved by taking greater risks but any higher returns thereby obtained do not refute market efficiency. Risk-adjusted returns are desirable. These can be found for share investments by using a model that prices risk, e.g. the capital asset pricing model mentioned in Section 6.11. The expected reward for accepting a share's undiversifiable risk is then proportional to the covariance between share return and the return on the market portfolio made up of all shares. Applying this idea to filter results may appear tricky but a satisfactory solution is given by Ball (1978) for studies involving several shares.

Commodity futures again pose problems. Empirical estimates of correlations between returns from US futures and US shares indices are very close to zero (Dusak, 1973; Bodie and Rosansky, 1980). Perhaps the market portfolio should be defined to include more than shares. Futures should not be included, as in Carter *et al.* (1983), because the aggregate position in futures is always zero (Black, 1976). Instead, privately owned agricultural and mineral resources may be relevant. Another approach is to consider consumption risk in a pricing model (Breeden, 1980).

Accepting zero covariance between returns from futures and diversified share portfolios has important consequences. Investors need not be rewarded for risks borne by buying futures, as such risks can be diversified away (Black, 1976). Then the expected return from futures is zero and, theoretically, no risk adjustments are needed for trading results.

However, if reality and theory differ futures may still be expected to pay a risk premium. It would then be an excellent idea to augment share portfolios by including futures. Bodie and Rosansky (1980) have argued that combining commodity futures with a diversified share portfolio would have decreased the standard deviation of annual returns from 19 to 13 per cent without any reduction in the expected return. Trading rules should be compared with buy and hold in these circumstances. Risk measurement is now difficult as zero covariance and a positive risk premium are contradictory in the usual asset pricing framework. When the measurement of risk reappears in Section 8.6 an intuitive solution will be proposed.

Necessary assumptions

To conclude the comments on problems faced when researching trading rules, note that assumptions must be made about prices. Usually it is assumed trades can be transacted at published closing prices. This presupposes a highly liquid market. It also supposes each trading decision has no effect on subsequent prices. In particular the quantity traded must be relatively small and other traders do not react to the trading rule's recommendations.

8.5 TRADING CONDITIONS

Throughout this chapter we consider futures trading from the standpoint of an ordinary investor. The investor can only trade by giving instructions to a broker. Brokers charge commission for opening and closing a futures position (a 'round trip'). They also require a margin deposit when a trade is opened. This deposit is intended to ensure that the investor can pay for any losses. Further margin deposits may be demanded if the price moves against the investor. UK brokers do not pay interest on margin deposits. US investors are more fortunate. They may be able to deposit Treasury bills and later keep the interest paid on the bills.

Commission rates are either fixed by the market's clearing house or competitively by brokers. Rates change from time-to-time. Suppose a trade is opened at a price z_t for T units thus involving goods worth $Q = Tz_t$ when the trade begins. Then we will assume a single payment of cQ is made at time t to a broker covering all trading costs. We make the simplifying assumption that c is the same constant for all times considered. We include commission and additional costs due to different bid and ask prices in the total cost cQ. An appropriate value of c for cocoa, coffee, and sugar futures traded in London is between 0.5 and 1.0 per cent. Currency futures traded at Chicago have far lower dealing costs; c was about 0.2 per cent for the years studied here.

Margin requirements depend on the broker and the investor's credit-worthiness. It will be assumed that dQ is deposited with a broker when a trade is opened, for some constant d. Conservative values for d are 10 per cent for the London agriculturals and 3 per cent for the Chicago currencies.

When the price moves against the investor, the effective deposit becomes the sum of all margin deposits minus the current loss on the futures. If this balance falls below eQ it will be assumed, from Section 8.7 onwards, that the balance is restored to dQ by making a further margin deposit. Again e is some positive constant and $e < d$.

Futures are defined by standard contracts. Thus T, the number of units traded, is in practice some multiple of a basic lot size. Recent lot sizes are

10 tonnes of cocoa, 5 tonnes of coffee, 50 tonnes of sugar, 25 000 pounds sterling, 125 000 deutschmarks and 125 000 Swiss francs. The value Q of one lot recently ranged from £5000 to £20 000 for the agricultural goods and from $25 000 to $60 000 for the currencies.

An astute UK investor need not pay tax on gains from futures trading. I assume the same situation applies in the US and therefore tax will not be mentioned again.

8.6   THEORETICAL ANALYSIS

Sufficiently large and long-lived trends in prices will make a market inefficient. Either returns or rescaled returns have autocorrelation Ap^{τ} at lag τ days when a price-trend model applies. It is of interest to know how large A and p must be to create inefficiencies. Theoretical answers can be given although several assumptions must be made. Practical answers are less definite and are offered in later sections.

An investor's optimal strategy when a futures market is efficient could be do nothing (i.e. forget this market) or buy and hold futures. Even when there is no risk premium it could be optimal to buy and hold (we see why later). Consequently, a market will be called inefficient in this section if an investor can adopt a trading strategy outperforming bank deposits when that is the preferred benchmark *and* can adopt another strategy outperforming buy and hold should that be the preference. The strategies and their profit potential were first described in Taylor (1983).

Trading strategies

Trades will be initiated for certain values of the standardized forecast k, defined for a stationary returns process by

$$k = (f_{t,1} - \mu)/\sigma_F. \tag{8.6.1}$$

Here σ_F is the standard deviation of the variable generating the optimal linear forecast $(f_{t,1})$ of the next return (x_{t+1}) with μ the unconditional average return.

Firstly, suppose the preferred benchmark is a risk-free investment, say depositing cash in an interest-bearing bank account. Strategy 1 is intended to earn a high return when a substantial upward trend is predicted:

(1a) Invest at a risk-free rate on day 0,
(1b) Buy on day $t > 0$ if k exceeds some number k_0,
(1c) Sell on day $t + N$ and revert to a risk-free investment.

The trader chooses k_0 and N. It is not necessary to say how much is bought and sold. Strategy 1 is clearly risky. Nevertheless if strategy 1 makes more on average than a comparable risk-free investment then the strategy can be viewed as an asset whose inclusion in a diversified portfolio will improve the investor's combination of expected return and risk.

Secondly, assume the benchmark is buy and hold. Strategy 2 abandons the long position when a substantial down-trend is predicted:

(2a) Buy T units of futures on day 0,
(2b) Sell on day $t > 0$ if k is less than some number $-k_0$ and invest all cash returned by the broker at the risk-free rate for N days,
(2c) Buy the same quantity of goods again on day $t + N$.

I assert that strategy 2 is less risky than buying and holding T units of futures. The reason is that strategy 2 has an open position in futures less often than buy and hold. Thus strategy 2 will be clearly superior to buy and hold when the strategy has the higher expected return, for it also has the lower risk.

Assumptions

Several assumptions must be made to obtain exact results. These are as follows:

(i) There are a few wealthy well-informed investors. Such people know all the parameters of the process generating prices, so they know the trend parameters A and p. They can trade without altering the path prices take. They also have sufficient wealth to engage in maximal share market diversification thus ensuring the risks of strategies 1 and 2 can be ignored.

(ii) The returns process is Gaussian. Thus all sets of returns have multivariate normal distributions. Returns have mean μ and variance σ^2.

(iii) Departures from a benchmark strategy always last N days, N being fixed in advance of any trading.

(iv) Trading costs equal to cQ are paid when a position worth Q is opened.

(v) Only one margin deposit per trade is required: an amount dQ is held by a broker who pays no interest upon it.

(vi) One interest rate applies to all risk-free lending and borrowing, whatever the duration of the deposit or loan. Simple interest is calculated at the rate r per trading day and paid when the future ceases to trade.

(vii) Each futures contract is traded for one year.

(viii) Money can be transferred instantaneously between the investor's bank account and broker.

It must be noted that (i) is too optimistic because parameter estimates are always inaccurate. However (iii) works against the investor as forecasts after departing from the benchmark strategy are ignored. Also (ii) represents a considerable simplification.

Conditions for trading profits

Firstly, we compare a risk-free investment of capital C on day 0 with strategy 1. Buying futures worth Q on day t at the price z_t when $k > k_0$ leaves $C - (c + d)Q$ in the risk-free account. At time t the selling price on day $t + N$ is uncertain and described by the random variable Z_{t+N}. The wealth obtained from strategy 1 on day $t + N$ is the random variable

$$W_1 = Ctr + \{C - (c + d)Q\}(1 + Nr) + dQ + Q(Z_{t+N} - z_t)/z_t.$$
$$(8.6.2)$$

Forming expectations at time t using the standardized forecast k, the expected wealth at time $t + N$ exceeds that from risk-free investment if

$$E[W_1 | k] > C(1 + tr + Nr),$$

which simplifies to

$$E[(Z_{t+N} - z_t)/z_t | k] > c + Nr(c + d). \tag{8.6.3}$$

This inequality states that strategy 1 is better than a risk-free investment if the expected proportional price change exceeds the trading costs and the interest forfeited on the deposit and trading costs.

Secondly, beginning with capital C on day 0, compare buying and holding futures worth Q with strategy 2. Let day t be the first after day 0 on which $k < -k_0$. Then strategy 2 sells on day t and buys the same quantity back at time $t + N$ to give wealth

$$W_2 = \{C - (c + d)Q\}\{1 + (t + N)r\}$$
$$+ [dQ + Q(z_t - z_0)/z_0][1 + Nr] - cQZ_{t+N}/z_0 \tag{8.6.4}$$

after completing transactions at time $t + N$. At the same time buy and hold gives wealth

$$W_{BH} = \{C - (c + d)Q\}\{1 + (t + N)r\} + dQ + Q(Z_{t+N} - z_0)/z_0.$$
$$(8.6.5)$$

Again taking expectations at time t, strategy 2 is better than buy and hold up to time $t + N$ if

$$E[W_2 | k] > E[W_{BH} | k]. \tag{8.6.6}$$

Sufficient conditions are, from Taylor (1983), $z_t > z_0$ and

$$(1 + Ndr)/(1 + c) > E[Z_{t+N}/z_t | k]. \tag{8.6.7}$$

When (8.6.7) and hence (8.6.6) are true it is possible that strategy 2 expects to have less money earning interest at time $t + N$ than buy and hold. To ensure this does not happen it suffices to add the further conditions $z_t/z_0 > (1 - d)/(1 - d - c)$ and

$$1 > E[Z_{t+N}/z_t | k]. \tag{8.6.8}$$

Suppose k_0 has been chosen. Then I will say a market is theoretically inefficient if (8.6.3) is true for $k = k_0$ and some N and, furthermore, (8.6.7) and (8.6.8) are true for $k = -k_0$ and some other value of N. It is necessary to choose k_0. This number controls the frequency of departures from the benchmark strategy. I have let $k_0 = 1.65$ so departures begin on up to 5 per cent of days.

To assess (8.6.3), (8.6.7), and (8.6.8) for given parameters A, p, μ, and σ we can use equations (7.3.1), (7.5.9), (7.5.11), (7.5.12), (7.7.2), (7.7.3), and (7.7.5). It is advisable to include a constraint on N in any evaluation program, say $N \leq 100$.

Inefficient regions

Results depend on the market parameters c, d, and r and the mean μ and variance σ^2 of returns. Commodities and currencies are discussed separately. Firstly, consider examples based upon London agricultural futures and, following Taylor (1983), the parameter values

$$c = 0.01, \quad d = 0.2, \quad r = 0.12/250, \quad \mu = 0.0005, \quad \sigma = 0.022.$$
$$\tag{8.6.9}$$

These figures are compatible with Table 2.4, the discussion in Section 8.5, and interest rates in 1982, with a high d chosen to try and ensure assuming only one margin deposit is reasonable. The risk-free rate is 12 per cent per annum. The expected annual growth in prices is $E[Z_{250}/Z_0] - 1$. This is $\exp(250\mu + 125\sigma^2) - 1 = 20$ per cent for a random walk and is more when there are trends. Consequently buy and hold is the harder benchmark to beat.

North-east of the curve L_1L_2 on Figure 8.2 a market is theoretically inefficient. The total autocorrelation over all positive lags does not change much on the boundary curve between theoretically efficient and inefficient markets. Denote this total by

$$Y = \sum_{\tau=1}^{\infty} \rho_\tau = \sum_{\tau=1}^{\infty} Ap^\tau = Ap/(1 - p). \tag{8.6.10}$$

Then a market is theoretically inefficient for the parameters (8.6.9) if

$$Y > 0.42 \quad \text{and} \quad 0.975 > p > 0.5. \tag{8.6.11}$$

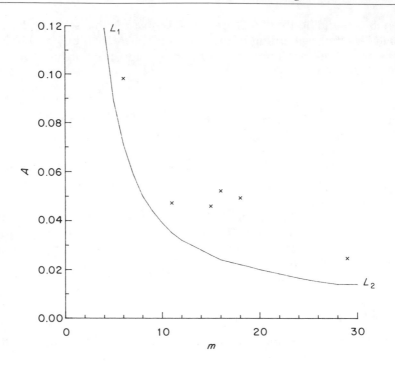

Figure 8.2 A boundary between efficient and inefficient markets (L_1L_2) when there is a risk premium. *Reproduced (with revisions) from Taylor (1983) by permission of Basil Blackwell, Oxford*

Halving d or r moves the boundary a negligible distance. Doubling the trading cost c to 2 per cent increases the dependence required to exploit inefficiencies to $Y > 0.62$ whenever $p > 0.8$.

Of course, it may be argued that there is no risk premium for these markets. Reducing μ to zero makes exploiting inefficiencies easier. A sufficient condition is then $Y > 0.24$ whenever $p > 0.8$. The harder benchmark to beat remains buy and hold because the distribution of the year-end price is skewed: for a random walk $E[Z_{250}/Z_0] = \exp(125\sigma^2) = 1.062$ and thus (8.6.3) shows it is easy to improve on a risk-free investment. Letting $\mu = -\frac{1}{2}\sigma^2$ ensures $E[Z_{250}/Z_0] = 1$ for a random walk and the risk-free benchmark is crucial. Theoretical efficiencies then occur if $Y > 0.18$ and $p > 0.8$.

Secondly, consider examples based upon IMM futures and, following Taylor (1983) again, the parameter values

$$c = 0.002, \quad d = 0.1, \quad r = 0.16/250, \quad \mu = 0, \quad \sigma = 0.006.$$

$$(8.6.12)$$

The low standard deviation σ causes the risk-free benchmark to be favoured to buy and hold. A market is theoretically inefficient for the above parameter values if

$$Y > 0.17 \quad \text{and} \quad p > 0.8. \tag{8.6.13}$$

Reducing r will reduce the autocorrelation consistent with an efficient market. Paying interest on margin deposits essentially makes d zero. Then $Y > 0.15$ and $p > 0.8$ ensures theoretical inefficiencies. Doubling c to 0.4 per cent increases the autocorrelation required for profitable trades to $Y > 0.31$ whenever $p > 0.8$. Finally, very similar results are obtained if $\mu = -\frac{1}{2}\sigma^2$.

Some implications

The estimates of A and p presented in Chapter 7 can be used to discuss the theoretical efficiency of futures markets. Care is needed because a linear process is assumed for returns in this section but a non-linear process in Chapter 7. The linear process is intended to be an approximation to the true non-linear process operating between times t and $t + N$ inclusive. The autocorrelations of the true process are Ap^τ for the non-linear trend models of Section 7.2 but Ap^τ multiplied by a constant (determined by the conditional variance) for the alternative linear-trend models. It can be argued that suitable values of A when assessing the theoretical efficiency of real markets are $\hat{A}_0 = \hat{A}_1 \exp(\beta^2)$ and $\hat{A}_2$ for the values of σ^2 discussed here; values of $\hat{A}_1$ and $\hat{A}_2$ appear in Table 7.1 and the β values are taken from Table 3.3. Using these estimates and appropriate estimates of p we obtain the following estimates of the total autocorrelation Y.

Estimates of Y

	Estimate of A	
Series	$\hat{A}_0$	$\hat{A}_2$
Cocoa (6)	0.69	0.84
Coffee (6)	0.47	0.49
Sugar (6)	0.64	0.78
£/$ (6)	0.62	0.80
DM/$ (6)	0.26	0.58
SF/$ (6)	0.44	0.80

All these estimates imply a theoretically inefficient market according to the criteria (8.6.11) and (8.6.13). Thus very small autocorrelation at several lags can make markets inefficient. The six estimates of the coordinates (A, p) for the agricultural futures are indicated by crosses on Figure 8.2.

Now consider typical results when the trading strategies deviate from the benchmark strategies. For cocoa and sugar we suppose the mean trend duration m is 16 days (so $p = 15/16$) and A is either 0.036 (from $\hat{A}_0$) or 0.05 (from $\hat{A}_2$). Consider $A = 0.05$. The largest difference between the two sides of inequality (8.6.7) occurs for $k = -1.65$ when $N = 24$. Assume $z_t = z_0$. Then selling futures at $1000 and buying again 24 days later at $974 (on average) makes $26 per unit, to which add $2 interest on the returned deposit then deduct $10 trading costs for a net profit of $18. Thus wealth is increased by $18 for every $1000 of futures sold, i.e. 1.8 per cent of the value of the goods sold. This is 19 per cent per annum assuming 250 trading days per year. Opting instead for $N = 11$ will make $13 per $1000 or 29 per cent per annum. These figures appear in column 2 of Table 8.1. Results for the lower value of A appear in column 1.

Similar results for hypothetical currency trades are given in the third and fourth columns of Table 8.1. The hypothetical gains are smaller than for the agricultural goods.

Table 8.1   Summary of hypothetical trading results

	1 Cocoa[a]	2 Cocoa	3 £[b]	4 £
Estimate for A	0.036[c]	0.050[d]	0.022[c]	0.036[d]
Estimate for m	16	16	20	20
N maximizing profit/trade	21	24	33[e]	43[e]
Open trade at	1000[f]	1000[f]	1000[g]	1000[g]
Close trade on average at	983	974	1010	1017
Favourable price move	17	26	10	17
Extra interest	2[h]	2		
Interest lost			2[i]	3
Trading costs	10[j]	10	2	2
Total gain ($)	9[k]	18[k]	6	12
Total gain (%)	0.9	1.8	0.6	1.2
Gain in annual terms	10%	19%	5%	7%
N maximizing gain/day	13	11	15	12
Gain in annual terms	14%	29%	6%	11%

[a]And sugar. [b]And DM/$, SF/$. [c]From $\hat{A}_0$. [d]From $\hat{A}_2$. [e]Negligible additional benefits from higher N. [f]Sell. [g]Buy. [h]$1000Ndr$. [i]$1000N(c + d)r$. [j]Maximum expected value. [k]Assumes $z_t = z_0$.

8.7   REALISTIC STRATEGIES AND ASSUMPTIONS

The theoretical results show that it may be possible to exploit slight dependence between returns when a price-trend model is appropriate. Strategies and assumptions are now made as realistic as possible. All the price series are then subdivided. Only the first part of a series is used to select trading parameters so that realistic trading results can be obtained for the second part of a series. These results will show that several markets were probably inefficient during the years studied. The following three sections are based upon an earlier publication (Taylor, 1983, pp. 184–93) updated to include a further year of prices.

Strategies

Trading decisions depend on a standardized forecast calculated by assuming a non-linear trend model:

$$k = f_{t,1}^{(5)}/\hat{\sigma}_F, \tag{8.7.1}$$
$$\hat{\sigma}_F = \hat{v}_{t+1}\{Ap(p - q)/(1 - pq)\}^{1/2}. \tag{8.7.2}$$

The forecast $f_{t,1}^{(5)}$ is defined by (7.6.5). The estimate $\hat{\sigma}_F$ of the forecast's standard deviation has been derived from (7.7.2) and (7.7.3) with $\hat{v}_{t+1}$ an estimate of the next return's standard deviation (equation (5.8.3) with $\bar{x}$ ignored, $\gamma = 0.1$ and 1.253 replaced by 1.333). Whenever necessary, A, p, and q in (8.7.2) are replaced by estimates. There are of course other ways to define a standardized forecast.

Strategies now have two parameters. One controls the commencement of trades (k_1) and the other their conclusion (k_2). Each day begins with a market position: none, long or short. Then k is calculated and the position is reconsidered.

Strategy I is an alternative to buy and hold intended to save money when a substantial downtrend is predicted:

(Ia) Buy on the first occasion that k is more than k_1.
(Ib) When a long position is held:
do nothing if $k \geq k_2$,
sell and take no market position if $k < k_2$.
(Ic) When no position is held:
do nothing if $k \leq k_1$,
buy if $k > k_1$.

We might consider $k_1 = 0$ and $k_2 = -2$. Buy and hold is evaluated by setting $k_1 = -1000$ and $k_2 = -1001$.

Strategy II is an alternative to risk-free investments. It aims to profit from substantial trends in either direction:

(IIa) When no position is held start a trade if $k > k_1$ (buy) or $k < -k_1$ (sell).
(IIb) When a long position is held:
do nothing if $k \geq k_2$,
sell and take no market position if $k < k_2$.

(IIc) When a short position is held:
do nothing if $k \leqslant -k_2$,
buy and take no market position if $k > -k_2$.

We might consider $k_1 = 2$ and $k_2 = 0$.

For both strategies trades have never been started during the final 15 days considered for a contract. If necessary, trades have been concluded on the final day of the month preceding the contract's delivery month.

Assumptions

The list given for the theoretical analysis is revised to make the results realistic. The following assumptions reflect various constraints encountered by investors.

(i) Some investors think they know the stochastic process generating prices. They possess imperfect estimates of the trend parameters from which they can calculate k. They can trade without altering the path prices take.

(ii) Instructions to brokers are made after reading yesterday's closing price in today's newspapers. Decisions then have to be evaluated at the next closing price, in effect one day late. For example, at 9 a.m. the investor has some market position, then reads the price at 4 p.m. on the previous day, then calculates k, then has any changes in market position made later at 4 p.m. Assuming such a long delay is pessimistic but does avoid assuming investors act upon information instantaneously.

(iii) All quantities traded are chosen to make the value of the goods bought or sold at the beginning of a trade, denoted Q, equal to the capital available for investment, denoted C. Keeping Q constant, irrespective of the current price and resources, ensures that the trading strategy is less risky than buy and hold.

Fixing Q at a number different to C merely selects a different combination of expected final capital and risk. For example, doubling Q will double all cash flows and therefore double (a) the difference between expected final capital and the wealth from risk-free investments and (b) the standard deviation of the final capital. Note that the number of lots traded will not be an integer. (Bankruptcy could occur in highly unfortunate circumstances but never has in the calculations performed.)

(iv) Trading costs equal to cQ are paid when a trade worth Q is begun.

(v) An initial margin deposit dQ is sent to a broker. Should the investor's balance fall below eQ then the balance is restored to dQ by sending another deposit. Brokers do not pay interest.

(vi) Every agricultural or simulated futures contract is traded for one year, every currency contract for six months.

(vii) All money not held by the investor's broker is kept in a bank account. It earns simple interest at some rate r per trading day which is credited to the account at the end of each trading period, see (vi).

(viii) If a trade ends on day t the broker returns deposits plus any trading gains minus any trading losses on day $t + D_1$.

(ix) The bank permits immediate withdrawals but then deducts the interest earned on the amount withdrawn during the preceding D_2 days.

All subsequent calculations use $D_1 = 3$ and $D_2 = 5$, the figures applicable to UK investors in 1982. The trading constants for the London agricultural futures have been set at

$$c = 0.01, \quad d = 0.1, \quad \text{and} \quad e = 0.05$$

for comparison with

$$c = 0.002, \quad d = 0.04, \quad \text{and} \quad e = 0.02$$

for the Chicago currency futures. Thus further margin deposits are required if half of the original deposit is lost.

UK interest rates were set at 10 per cent per annum for simulated prices and the first part of the real price series, increasing to 14 per cent for the second part. US rates were taken to be 12 per cent before 1979 and 16 per cent thereafter.

Notes on objectives

The parameters of the trading strategies are chosen to maximize the expected value of an investor's capital at the end of one year, subject to the constraint described by assumption (iii). The derived strategies are not expected to be mean/variance optimal or to maximize expected utility, although the strategies may well be close to optimal. Another objective is to make the efficient market hypothesis appear dubious when it is false. Hopefully the strategies are as good as alternatives concerning this objective.

8.8   TRADING SIMULATED CONTRACTS

To operate the trading rules we need values for A, p, k_1, and k_2. The first part of each futures series, called the calibration contracts, is used to estimate A and p. Then k_1 and k_2 are selected by optimizing trading results upon simulated contracts and the calibration contracts. Simulation is employed to avoid relying on the relatively short historical record defined by the calibration contracts. Only when A, p, k_1, and k_2 are all chosen do we consider trading results for the remaining contracts. These will be called the test contracts.

Every simulated contract has 310 prices generated by a product process: the non-linear trend model of Section 7.2. Simulated returns X_t are defined by $\mu + V_t U_t$ with $\{\log(V_t)\}$ Gaussian (mean α, variance β^2, autocorrelations ϕ^τ) and $\{U_t\}$ also Gaussian (mean 0, variance 1, autocorrelations Ap^τ). The first 60 prices are only used to obtain initial values and then trading is simulated for one year.

Commodities

The calibration contracts are those used to test the random walk hypothesis in Taylor (1980). Buy and hold was highly successful for these contracts and thus defines the commodities benchmark strategy.

Sugar contracts from 1961 to 1973 are compatible with the simulation parameters $\mu = 0.0003$, $\alpha = -4.25$, $\beta = 0.56$, $\phi = 0.98$, $A = 0.04$, and $p = 0.95$. Four hundred contracts have been simulated. The hypothetical investor began each year with £10 000 and ended it with a final capital dependent on k_1 and k_2. Risk-free investments return 10 per cent per annum in the simulations, buy and hold averaged 26.3 per cent and the best version of strategy I averaged 31.7 per cent.

Table 8.2 shows the averages and standard deviations of the annual changes in capital for buy and hold and strategy I when the hypothetical investor correctly estimates A and p, and uses $k_1 = 0$ and $k_2 = 1$. The averages show buy and hold obtaining a 16.3 per cent risk premium and trading adding a further 5.4 per cent to capital. Since the annual standard deviations are very approximately twice the figure for individual stocks the high premium is realistic. The standard deviations are very high and this is why so many contracts need to be simulated. Standard errors for the

Table 8.2 Summary of annual percentage changes in capital for simulated prices

	Benchmark strategy				Trading strategy	
	Mean (%)	St. dev. (%)	k_1	k_2	Mean (%)	St. dev. (%)
Parameters based upon						
Cocoa	58.9	61.6	0	−1.8	60.0	59.9
Coffee	43.5	75.9	0	−1.4	49.7	72.5
Sugar	26.3	62.0	0	−1.0	31.7	58.3
Currencies	12.0	0	0.8	−0.3	16.2	10.2

Reproduced from Taylor (1983, p. 188) by permission of Basil Blackwell, Oxford.

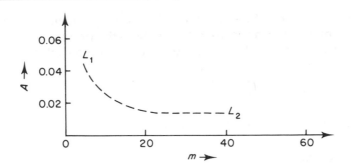

Figure 8.3 Boundary between efficient and inefficient markets for simulated returns. *Reproduced from Taylor (1983) by permission of Basil Blackwell, Oxford*

averages are the standard deviations divided by 20, i.e. about 3 per cent. It can be seen that strategy I is less risky than buy and hold, using the standard deviation as a risk measure.

Even supposing trend models generate prices, investors would have to take decisions using imperfect estimates of A and p. This is not too important. Sugar prices simulated using different values for A and p to those assumed by an investor permit trading profits for a considerable range of trend parameters. North-east of the curve L_1L_2 on Figure 8.3 trading gives better results than buy and hold if an investor selects $A = 0.04$, $p = 0.95$, $k_1 = 0$, and $k_2 = -1$.

Further simulated prices have been obtained using the cocoa and coffee calibration contracts from 1971 to 1976. For cocoa, $\mu = 0.0014$, $\alpha = -4.18$, $\beta = 0.45$, $\phi = 0.987$, $A = 0.044$, and $p = 0.933$ gave an estimated trading gain of 1.1 per cent per annum. For coffee, $\mu = 0.0011$, $\alpha = -4.39$, $\beta = 0.83$, $\phi = 0.9$, $A = 0.12$, and $p = 0.833$ provided an estimated gain of 6.2 per cent. Table 8.2 summarizes the optimal results for 400 simulated contracts.

Currencies

The first calibration contract for each currency is the June 1974 and the last one is the December 1978. Ending with the December 1978 contract was, inevitably, an arbitrary decision. There are no good reasons for a buy and hold benchmark. Thus risk-free investment defines the currencies benchmark strategy.

All appropriate confidence regions for the currency trend parameters are large and encompass similar values. Consequently, common parameters are used for all three currencies. Four hundred contracts have been simulated using $\mu = 0$, $\alpha = -5.34$, $\beta = 0.46$, $\phi = 0.92$, $A = 0.028$, and $p = 0.95$. Table 8.2 summarizes the results for the best trading constants,

$k_1 = 0.8$ and $k_2 = -0.3$. Strategy II then increases the average final capital to 4.2 per cent more than the interest rate. Both the premium from trading and the annual standard deviation are far less than equivalent figures for stocks.

8.9 TRADING RESULTS FOR FUTURES

Calibration contracts

All trading results for the calibration contracts will be favourably biased, because A and p have been estimated from their returns. The following estimates are based on calibration returns and used for both calibration and test contracts.

	$\hat{A}$	$\hat{p}$
Cocoa	0.0440	0.933
Coffee	0.1220	0.833
Sugar	0.0395	0.952
Currencies	0.0280	0.950

Various values of k_1 and k_2 near to the optima estimated by simulation have been considered and final choices for the test contracts have been made by considering trading results from simulated and calibration contracts. It would not be a good idea to rely on the calibration results alone, for the averages for a few years can vary haphazardly when small changes are made to k_1 and k_2.

Sugar results from 1961 to 1973 were much better for $k_1 = 0.4$ and $k_2 = -1.0$ (trading gains 8 per cent per annum) than for $k_1 = 0$ and $k_2 = -1.0$ (trading gains nothing), although both k_1 were equally successful for simulated prices. Consequently, the final choice was $k_1 = 0.4$. Buy and hold was very profitable for cocoa and coffee trading from 1971 to 1976 so it is not surprising that strategy I gave uninspiring results. The cautious choice $k_2 = -1.6$ was made. Currency trades were consistently more profitable than risk-free investments and the results could not be improved by small changes to the trading constants chosen previously.

Table 8.3 summarizes the final selections for k_1 and k_2 and the consequent average annual trading gains, if it had somehow been possible to select A, p, k_1, and k_2 before seeing the calibration prices. The buy and hold results are obtained by supposing $k_1 = -1000$ and $k_2 = -1001$. Trading gains are defined as the change in capital using a trading strategy minus the change in capital using the appropriate benchmark strategy.

Table 8.3   **Average annual percentage changes in capital**

	Benchmark strategy	Trading strategy		Trading gains
	Average (%)	k_1	k_2	Average (%)	Average (%)

	Benchmark strategy Average (%)	k_1	k_2	Trading strategy Average (%)	Trading gains Average (%)
Calibration contracts					
Cocoa	61.5	0	−1.6	61.6	0.1
Coffee	52.3	0	−1.6	49.3	−3.0
Sugar	26.2	0.4	−1.0	34.3	8.1
Sterling	12.0	0.8	−0.3	17.6	5.6
Deutschmark	12.0	0.8	−0.3	20.0	8.0
Swiss franc	12.0	0.8	−0.3	21.6	9.6
Test contracts					
Cocoa	19.5	0	−1.6	21.8	2.3
Coffee	10.5	0	−1.6	12.1	1.6
Sugar	64.4	0.4	−1.0	91.5	27.1
Sterling	16.0	0.8	−0.3	23.4	7.4
Deutschmark	16.0	0.8	−0.3	22.8	6.8
Swiss franc	16.0	0.8	−0.3	22.8	6.8

Reproduced (with revisions) from Taylor (1983, p. 190) by permission of Basil Blackwell, Oxford.

Test contracts

The second part of Table 8.3 shows the average annual changes in capital for the test contracts. Comparing averages for the trading strategies with corresponding averages for the benchmark strategies gives the final column of the table. All of these average annual trading gains are positive, ranging from 1.6 to 27.1 per cent. These average gains are our major evidence for discussing the validity of the efficient market hypothesis. They certainly suggest some important inefficiencies have occurred in past years.

Table 8.4 lists the annual percentage changes in capital for the eighteen agricultural contracts. Changes are given for buy and hold and strategy I along with the number of days futures were owned. The final column gives the number of round trips (one buy and one sell order) for strategy I. The assumed efficient market policy, long in futures all year and earning 14 per cent interest per annum on money not needed for margin deposits, was slightly successful for cocoa, slightly unsuccessful for coffee. Strategy I gave results better by 2 per cent per annum on average for both these commodities. Trading results are similar to buy and hold results because k_2 was extremely low.

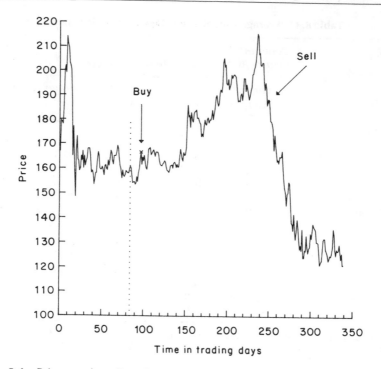

Figure 8.4   Prices and trading decisions (Strategy I) for the December 1976 sugar
futures contract from December 1975 to November 1976

The price of the December 1974 sugar contract soared from £90 in
December 1973 to £560 at the end of November 1974. Buy and hold then
recorded a massive profit matched almost exactly by the trading strategy.
Prices declined during the following four years when the trading strategy
owned futures less than half of the time thereby avoiding buy and hold's
losses. Buy and hold has a high average return for sugar but strategy I is
even better, by an impressive 27 per cent per annum. It appears that the
sugar futures market was inefficient. The conclusions for cocoa and coffee
futures are less clear.

Figure 8.4 shows the trading decisions for one of the more successful
sugar contracts (December 1976). Trades are considered from December
1975 to November 1976. Prices before this period are shown to the left of
the dotted line and were only used to obtain initial values for the forecasts.
Buy and hold would have lost money, buying at £160.2/tonne and selling at
£121.2. Strategy I, however, would have made money by buying at £166.5
and selling 152 trading days later at £187.7, after the upward trend had
ended. No further positions would have been taken.

Table 8.4   **Annual percentage changes in capital for London futures**

	Buy and hold with interest		Strategy I		
	Change (%)	Days owned	Change (%)	Days owned	Round trips
Cocoa					
1977	121.8	252	121.8	252	1
1978	1.9	251	−0.5	192	3
1979	−17.6	252	−18.0	196	4
1980	−28.1	250	−21.6	190	3
1981	19.5	251	27.1	186	3
Average	19.5		21.8		
Coffee					
1977	−2.5	252	3.6	209	4
1978	17.7	251	9.4	227	3
1979	52.2	252	59.8	229	3
1980	−31.3	252	−33.2	198	5
1981	16.6	250	20.8	217	4
Average	10.5		12.1		
Sugar					
1974	535.5	250	537.0	249	1
1975	−57.4	252	13.5	79	2
1976	−13.6	254	25.8	152	1
1977	−20.8	252	5.7	62	1
1978	−13.2	252	12.8	84	2
1979	47.5	250	32.7	165	4
1980	63.2	270	100.2	187	2
1981	−26.4	251	4.4	106	2
Average	64.4		91.5		
Overall average (18 contracts)	37.0		50.1		

Results before 1981 reproduced from Taylor (1983, p. 191) by permission of Basil Blackwell, Oxford.

Table 8.5 presents the percentage changes in capital over six months for trades in each of the eighteen currency contracts. Changes are given for risk-free investment at 16 per cent per annum and for strategy II. Trading gains during 1979 and 1980 are, on average, negligible which caused me to conclude earlier that the results are consistent with efficient pricing (Taylor, 1983, 1985). However, all six 1981 contracts record important trading gains. These gains should certainly be viewed as raising considerable doubts about the efficiency of the currency futures markets. IMM limit rules would have had no adverse consequences. The gains would be higher if the margin deposits could earn interest.

Table 8.5   Semi-annual changes in capital for Chicago futures

	Risk-free investment	Strategy II		
	Change (%)	Change (%)	Days owned	Round trips
Sterling				
June 1979	8.0	9.4	77	2
Dec. 1979	8.0	13.1	89	2
June 1980	8.0	12.1	117	3
Dec. 1980	8.0	7.2	100	3
June 1981	8.0	15.2	90	3
Dec. 1981	8.0	13.1	96	5
Average	8.0	11.7		
Deutschmark				
June 1979	8.0	7.1	86	3
Dec. 1979	8.0	5.1	77	3
June 1980	8.0	9.2	92	2
Dec. 1980	8.0	11.5	86	3
June 1981	8.0	23.7	105	2
Dec. 1981	8.0	11.6	101	3
Average	8.0	11.4		
Swiss franc				
June 1979	8.0	3.3	93	4
Dec. 1979	8.0	4.9	79	3
June 1980	8.0	12.5	89	2
Dec. 1980	8.0	5.0	75	4
June 1981	8.0	22.0	103	2
Dec. 1981	8.0	20.7	98	3
Average	8.0	11.4		
Overall average (18 contracts)	8.0	11.5		

Figure 8.5 shows the trades made for the most successful contract (deutschmark, June 1981). Prices before December 1980, shown to the left of the dotted line, were only used to obtain initial values. Futures would have been sold at 0.5306 $/DM and the trade closed 69 trading days later at 0.4877, then another short position started at 0.4741 and closed out at 0.4303, at the end of May 1981, 36 days later.

The trading gains for the test contracts are surprisingly good compared with the gains expected after analysing the simulated and calibration contracts. Average increases in annual capital are shown in the table opposite. The averages in the final row are the arithmetic means of the six

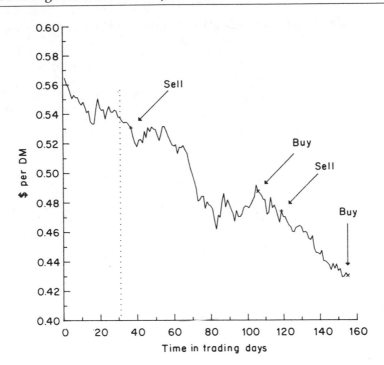

Figure 8.5   Prices and trading decisions (Strategy II) for the June 1981 deutschmark contract from December 1980 to May 1981

	Expected increase		Actual increase
	Simulated contracts (%)	Calibration contracts (%)	Test contracts (%)
Cocoa	0.7	0.1	2.3
Coffee	5.9	−3.0	1.6
Sugar	5.5	8.1	27.1
Sterling	4.2	5.6	7.4
Deutschmark	4.2	8.0	6.8
Swiss franc	4.2	9.6	6.8
Average	4.1	4.7	8.7

(Reproduced, with revisions, from Taylor (1983) by permission of Basil Blackwell, Oxford.)

Table 8.6 Annual profits for a £100 000 trading fund invested in cocoa, coffee, and sugar futures

Year	Buy and hold				Strategy I			
	Gross (£)	Costs (£)	Interest (£)	Net (£)	Gross (£)	Costs (£)	Interest (£)	Net (£)
1977	22 513	−1 000	11 357	32 860	33 410	−2 273	12 597	43 734
1978	−6 407	−1 000	9 573	2 166	−1 757	−2 363	11 380	7 260
1979	17 070	−1 000	11 310	27 380	16 463	−3 630	11 980	24 813
1980	−8 797	−1 000	11 060	1 263	5 640	−3 260	12 747	15 127
1981	−5 633	−1 000	9 873	3 240	8 050	−2 643	12 013	17 420
Average	3 749	−1 000	10 635	13 384	12 361	−2 834	12 143	21 670

Note: Risk-free interest rate 14 per cent p.a.

figures in the columns. Even after excluding the sugar results the average actual increase exceeds the average expected. Thus there is very strong evidence that the general pattern of dependence persists for many years allowing successful trading rules.

These futures markets are surely inefficient. No tests of this claim are presented since none are known.

Portfolio results

Consider a commodity trading fund beginning each year with £100 000 to invest. Suppose one-third of the fund is used to trade each of cocoa, coffee, and sugar. Then for our assumed interest rate a buy and hold policy would have returned 13.4 per cent per annum on average, risk-free investment 14.0 per cent, and strategy I 21.7 per cent on average. Table 8.6 presents profits earned by a hypothetical fund in each of five years. Gross profits are profits from taking positions in futures when trading costs are ignored, net profits are gross profits minus trading costs plus bank interest. Comparing strategy I with buy and hold, the strategy makes an extra £8612 gross, earns £1508 more interest and pays an extra £1834 for commission etc. to give an extra £8286 net, all figures being annual averages for a £100 000 fund.

Likewise consider a $100 000 currency trading fund, invested equally in the three currencies investigated. Then strategy II would have returned 23.0 per cent per annum on average, 7 per cent above the assumed 16 per cent interest rate. Even allowing for a higher rate on long-term cash deposits a fund would have returned attractive profits. Table 8.7 gives details for each of three years. Compared with risk-free investment,

Table 8.7   Annual profits for a $100 000 trading fund invested in currency futures

Year	Risk-free investment	Strategy II			
	Net ($)	Gross ($)	Costs ($)	Interest ($)	Net ($)
1979	16 000	313	−1 163	15 190	14 340
1980	16 000	5 173	−1 137	15 130	19 166
1981	16 000	20 930	−1 150	15 697	35 477
Average	16 000	8 805	−1 150	15 339	22 994

strategy II makes $8805 gross by trading, earns $661 less interest and has trading costs $1105 to give an extra $6994 net, these figures being annual averages for a $100 000 fund with interest only paid once a year.

8.10   TOWARDS CONCLUSIONS

There is ample evidence in the previous section against the efficiency of futures markets. Trading rules constructed from price-trend models are successful when applied to the test contracts of all six futures series. The rules could have been used to obtain trading profits in excess of efficient market predictions in years subsequent to those used for their development. Less sophisticated trend-seeking rules might also have been able to earn excess profits.

Although the efficient market hypothesis has not been proved false, it is far more likely to have been false than true for the markets and years investigated. The hypothesis cannot be tested until someone describes the statistical evidence sufficient to reject it. This task may never be accomplished.

It is obviously difficult to estimate the value of the trading strategies described. After analysing prices in 1981 and earlier years, an expected annual return 4 to 7 per cent above the expected return from either buy and hold or risk-free investment appears possible when the value of futures positions equals the capital invested. Better trading rules exist, offering higher expected returns for the same level of risk. Trading results from 1982 onwards have yet to be calculated.

Measuring the risk of the trading rules is problematic. Some investors and fund managers are likely to consider the risk acceptable, especially if they can combine trading with holding a diversified share portfolio.

Trading rule research is not easy. There are no formal hypothesis tests. Further complications arise because the issue of risk premia is crucial when the efficient market policy is defined for comparisons with trading variants.

Furthermore, many years of prices are required to give any chance of clear conclusions.

Very little autocorrelation is needed to make a market inefficient providing it occurs at several lags. It appears markets can be inefficient when all autocorrelations (excepting lag 0) are between 0 and 0.03. An important statistic for assessing efficiency is the total of the autocorrelations, summing over all positive lags. For price-trend models a total above 0.3 might be sufficient for inefficiencies, whilst 0.6 almost certainly indicates an inefficient market. The latter total is achieved if the trend component accounts for 3 per cent of the variance of returns and the mean trend duration is 20 days. Low totals suffice because trading costs are relatively small.

8.11 SUMMARY

Enterprising investors courageous enough to deviate from efficient market investment principles would have been rewarded by positive net excess returns if they had followed trend-seeking trading rules. Trading any of cocoa, coffee, sugar, sterling, deutschmark, and Swiss franc futures would have been profitable, even after making realistic assumptions about trading costs and the availability of information. Average net excess returns range from 2 to 27 per cent per annum and the consistent gains are unlikely to be the result of remarkably good luck.

Theoretical analysis, by mathematical and simulation methods, show very little autocorrelation can cause markets to be inefficient. The empirical results for practical trading rules strongly support this conclusion. Therefore the efficient market hypothesis is probably false for several futures markets. Price-trend models play a central role in arriving at this conclusion.

Chapter 9

Valuing Options

The value of an option depends on several variables including the variances of future returns. This chapter shows how the variance models developed in Chapter 3 and the price-trend models of Chapter 7 have important implications for option traders.

9.1 INTRODUCTION

An American call option is a contract giving its owner the right to buy a fixed amount of a specified security at a fixed price at any time on or before a given date. The security, often termed the underlying security, could be a stock, commodity, or currency, and perhaps a futures contract. Once bought an option can usually be sold to someone else before the given date, termed the expiration date. Choosing to enforce the contractual rights is referred to as exercising the option and the fixed price is termed the exercise price. Options which can only be exercised on the expiration date are said to be European but are relatively rare, whilst an option to sell is called a put option. We only consider call options. An excellent book on options has recently been published by Cox and Rubinstein (1985). Another informative text is Bookstaber (1981).

The value of an option depends on obvious variables like the exercise price and the expiration date. It also depends on the stochastic process governing the price of the underlying security. This short chapter is theoretical and discusses consequences of the processes described in this book for option traders.

The next section summarizes the value of a call option when the price logarithm changes continuously and at random with the daily returns normal and identically distributed. It is based on results by Black and Scholes (1973) and Merton (1973). The Black–Scholes formula uses the standard deviation of returns and estimates of this statistic are discussed in Section 9.3. More appropriate stochastic processes are considered in

Sections 9.4 and 9.5, in the first case having changes in conditional variances and, in the second, trends in prices. It is shown that option values are sensitive to the specification of the process generating returns.

9.2 BLACK–SCHOLES OPTION PRICING FORMULAE

Consider a call option on one share of a stock which pays no dividends before the option's expiration date. American and European calls have identical values when there are no dividends since it is then sub-optimal to exercise a call before the expiration date. Let t denote the present time and $t + T$ the expiration time with T measured in trading days. Also let $S = z_t$ be the stock's present price and let K be the exercise price. Thus the value of the option on day $t + T$ is $z_{t+T} - K$ if this is a positive number, otherwise the value is zero. Suppose there is a constant rate of interest r such that \$1 invested now is certain to be worth \$exp(rT) after T trading days.

Black and Scholes (1973) assumed the price logarithm followed a continuous-time Wiener process: daily returns then have independent and identical normal distributions. They demonstrated that the value C of a call option depends on K, S, T, r and the standard deviation σ of daily returns. Their formula used the cumulative distribution function of the standardized normal distribution,

$$\Phi(x) = (2\pi)^{-1/2} \int_{-\infty}^{x} e^{-1/2 u^2} \, du,$$

to give the fair call price

$$C = S\Phi(d) - K e^{-rT}\Phi(d - \sigma\sqrt{T}) \tag{9.2.1}$$

with

$$d = \{\log (S/K) + (r + \tfrac{1}{2}\sigma^2)T\}/(\sigma\sqrt{T}). \tag{9.2.2}$$

These formulae follow from the arbitrage properties of a risk-free hedged position containing one share of stock balanced by selling short $1/\Phi(d)$ calls. As time progresses d changes and thus the hedge should, theoretically, be continuously revised. There will be no risk if this can be done, for changes in the value of stock will equal changes in the value of the options plus interest on the equity invested in the hedge.

Equation (9.2.1) is the solution of a second-order differential equation implied by risk-free hedges. An alternative derivation is helpful for motivating results later on. Every hedge and thus every call price is independent of investors' risk preferences. Call prices can therefore be obtained by assuming stocks and options are traded in a risk-neutral world. Then the call value at time t is the discounted expected value at time $t + T$:

$$C = e^{-rT} \int_K^\infty (z - K) f(z) \, dz \qquad (9.2.3)$$

with $f(z)$ the density function of the price Z_{t+T} when daily returns are distributed as $N(r - \frac{1}{2}\sigma^2, \sigma^2)$ to ensure $E[Z_{t+T}] = z_t \exp(rT)$. To show (9.2.1) and (9.2.3) are equivalent we need the following results for the density $f(z)$ of a variable whose logarithm is distributed as $N(\mu_1, \sigma_1^2)$:

$$\int_K^\infty f(z) \, dz = \Phi\{(\mu_1 - \log K)/\sigma_1\} \qquad (9.2.4)$$

and

$$\int_K^\infty zf(z) \, dz = e^{\mu_1 + 1/2\sigma_1^2} \Phi\{\mu_1 + \sigma_1^2 - \log K)/\sigma_1\}. \qquad (9.2.5)$$

To obtain (9.2.1), let $\mu_1 = \log(S) + (r - \frac{1}{2}\sigma^2)T$ and let $\sigma_1 = \sigma\sqrt{T}$.

Black (1976) has shown how to value a call option on a futures contract. Assuming zero equity is invested in futures, $E[Z_{t+T}]$ is z_t in a risk-neutral world. Changing μ_1 to $\log(S) - \frac{1}{2}T\sigma^2$ gives, for European calls,

$$C = e^{-rT}[S\Phi(d) - K\Phi(d - \sigma\sqrt{T})] \qquad (9.2.6)$$

with

$$d = \{\log(S/K) + \frac{1}{2}\sigma^2 T\}/(\sigma\sqrt{T}). \qquad (9.2.7)$$

All these formulae ignore transaction costs and taxes. The stock formula assumes stocks cannot be traded on margin. Generally it is also assumed that the price generating process operates over exactly the same periods that interest can be earned. For exact results when this assumption is replaced by something more realistic see French (1984).

9.3 EVALUATING STANDARD FORMULAE

We know that daily returns over long periods of time are not independent observations from the same normal distribution. However, it may be considered acceptable to make these assumptions for the remaining life of an option which will usually be less than six months and perhaps only a few days. The Black–Scholes formula then gives fair prices which need not be identical to market prices. To calculate C we want σ but must instead substitute some estimate $\hat{\sigma}$ into an option pricing formula. Only the standard deviation needs to be estimated.

Some authors advise estimating σ by the standard deviation of twenty or more recent returns. This appears logical yet the forecast $\hat{v}_{t+1}$ investigated in Chapter 4 may be a better estimate. The forecast attaches greater importance to the most recent returns and the weighting scheme can be optimized by considering forecasting accuracy. High and low prices have considerable potential to improve the accuracy of standard deviation estimates, see Parkinson (1980) and Garman and Klass (1980) for theoretical results and Beckers (1983) for some empirical evidence. More research into highs and lows is necessary and it should be possible to use them to produce an estimate defined like $\hat{v}_{t+1}$ yet having far greater accuracy. Standard deviations of different securities will be interrelated and will probably change together, thus a better $\hat{\sigma}$ may be obtained by studying several securities.

There are many ways to estimate σ and some combination of estimates may well be preferable to simpler estimates. The forecasting methodology described in Chapter 4 offers a convenient way to compare the accuracy of standard deviation estimates and combinations thereof.

Of course, options traders may be able to use information other than past returns to estimate σ. Indeed, options markets could be efficient. There will nearly always be some σ which makes the market price equal to the Black–Scholes price and this σ is called the implied standard deviation. Relevant empirical work includes Latane and Rendleman (1976), Chiras and Manaster (1978), and Beckers (1981b). A suitable combination of the implied standard deviation and estimates from past returns will probably provide the best estimate of σ.

9.4   CALL VALUES WHEN CONDITIONAL VARIANCES CHANGE

Assuming daily returns are created by a strict white noise process is not very appealing. We have seen this assumption is a serious over-simplification for long series (Section 2.10) and this is also true within the lifetime of a futures contract (Section 4.4). Fischer Black, among others, has suggested variances regress over time towards some value (Cox and Rubinstein, 1985, p. 280). The lognormal, AR(1), product process introduced in Section 3.5 has this property: the conditional variance tomorrow is expected to be closer to a median value than today's conditional variance. It was concluded in Section 4.5 that this type of stationary process was acceptable for modelling some but not all series of returns. We discuss call values firstly for a stationary process and later remove this assumption. The returns are assumed to have conditional normal distributions and to be uncorrelated, t is the present time and the call expires at time $t + T$.

Formulae for a stationary process

Suppose the conditional standard deviations $V_t, V_{t+1}, \ldots, V_{t+T}$ are generated by the Gaussian process

$$\log (V_{t+h}) - \alpha = \phi\{\log (V_{t+h-1}) - \alpha\} + \eta_t \tag{9.4.1}$$

for $1 \leqslant h \leqslant T$ with $0 < \phi < 1$. Also the unconditional distribution of $\log (V_{t+h})$ is $N(\alpha, \beta^2)$, the unconditional variance of V_{t+h} is

$$\sigma_V^2 = \exp (2\alpha + 2\beta^2)$$

and the η_t are independently distributed as $N(0, \beta^2[1 - \phi^2])$. Given a realization v_t of V_t suppose the return X_t has distribution $N(\mu, v_t^2)$ for some constant μ. To obtain a continuous-time stochastic process, say $\{Z(s), s \text{ real}\}$, we could assume the price logarithm follows a Wiener process during each trading day with

$$\log \{Z(t + h + c + d)/Z(t + h + c)\} \sim N(\mu d, v_{t+h}^2 d),$$

given an observable realization v_{t+h} and any c, d having $0 \leqslant c < c + d \leqslant 1$.

We now revise the purely theoretical arguments used to obtain the Black–Scholes value of a call option. Theoretically, perfect investors could quickly calculate v_{t+h} from the continuous price record and thus could create risk-free hedges at all times. These hedges will not depend on risk preferences and therefore fair call prices can be obtained by assuming a risk-neutral world. Thus equation (9.2.3) is again appropriate and we need the density function of the price Z_{t+T} on the option's expiration date.

At time t we know the current price z_t and will assume v_t is also known. Given this information,

$$\log (Z_{t+I}) = \log (z_t) + \sum_{h=1}^{T} X_{t+h}$$

has conditional mean $\mu_1 = \log (z_t) + T\mu$ and conditional variance

$$\sigma_1^2 = \sum_{h=1}^{T} E[V_{t+h}^2 | v_t] \qquad (9.4.2)$$

because the returns X_{t+h} are uncorrelated and $E[X_{t+h}^2 | v_t] = E[V_{t+h}^2 | v_t]$. To evaluate (9.4.2) we apply the AR(1) definition, (9.4.1), to give

$$\log (V_{t+h} | v_t) \sim N(\alpha + \phi^h[\log (v_t) - \alpha], \beta^2[1 - \phi^{2h}])$$

and hence

$$E[V_{t+h}^2 | v_t] = \exp \{2\alpha + 2\phi^h[\log (v_t) - \alpha] + 2\beta^2[1 - \phi^{2h}]\}.$$
$$(9.4.3)$$

It is then possible to calculate σ_1^2.

To find the value of μ in a risk-neutral world it is necessary to assume the total $X_{t+1} + \cdots + X_{t+T}$ has a normal distribution for any given v_t. This is not true for $T > 1$ but should permit an excellent approximation to correct call values. Making the assumption, μ is $r - \frac{1}{2}\sigma_1^2/T$ for stocks in a risk-neutral world and note this μ depends on v_t. Applying the normal assumption a second time it can be deduced that a call value for a product process can be

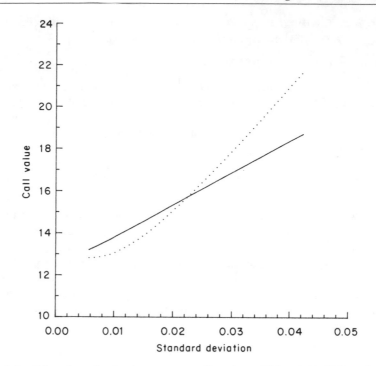

Figure 9.1   Fair values for in-the-money call options ($K/S = 0.9$). Values from the product process formula (solid curve) and the Black–Scholes formula (dotted curve) plotted against the present standard deviation

obtained by the following modification of the Black–Scholes formula, (9.2.1), (9.2.2):

$$\text{replace } \sigma\sqrt{T} \text{ by } \sigma_1 = \left\{ \sum_{h=1}^{T} E[V_{t+h}^2 | v_t] \right\}^{1/2}. \tag{9.4.4}$$

To make the replacement use (9.4.3) and, in practice, v_t, α, β, and ϕ will have to be replaced by estimates. The same revision is applicable to stocks and futures.

Examples

Comparisons between the product process and Black–Scholes formulae are given for stock options four months from expiration ($T = 84$ trading days) with a 10 per cent annual risk-free interest rate ($R = \log [1.1]/252$). For the product process I have supposed $\phi = 0.985$, $\beta = 0.5$, and an overall volatility sd(X_t) $= \sigma_X = \sigma_V = 0.02$, hence $\alpha = -4.16$, in line with the esti-

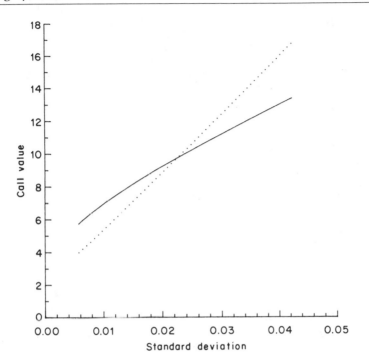

Figure 9.2 Fair values for at-the-money call options ($K = S$) calculated from the product process formula (solid curve) and Black–Scholes formula (dotted curve)

mates presented in Tables 3.2 and 3.3. A present stock price of $100 ($=S$) is considered and options with exercise prices $90, $100, or $110 ($=K$).

Figures 9.1, 9.2, and 9.3 illustrate call values for the three exercise prices. The solid curves represent CPP(v_t), the call value according to the product process formula when the latest conditional standard deviation is v_t. The dotted curves show CBS(σ), the Black–Scholes value when all standard deviations are σ. All curves are plotted for the approximate 95 per cent range for V_t: $\exp(\alpha - 2\beta) \leqslant v_t \leqslant \exp(\alpha + 2\beta)$.

The product process formula provides a higher value than the Black–Scholes formula for low current standard deviations v_t, i.e. CPP(v_t) then exceeds CBS(v_t), and vice versa for high v_t. This is to be expected. If v_t is lower than the median level $\exp(\alpha)$ than v_{t+h} is expected to increase as h increases and the anticipated additional future volatility makes the call more valuable. The percentage difference between CPP(v_t) and CBS(v_t) is particularly large for low v_t and the out-of-the-money option ($K = 110$, Figure 9.3). It is also large, but to a lesser degree, when v_t is high for the same option.

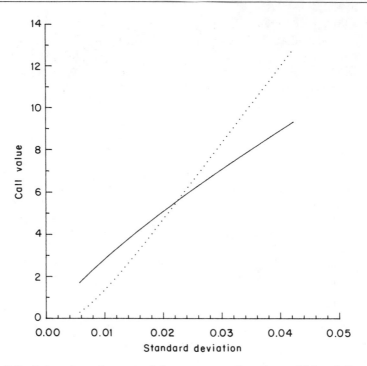

Figure 9.3   Fair values for out-of-the-money call options ($K/S = 1.1$) calculated from the product process formula (solid curve) and Black–Scholes formula (dotted curve)

Table 9.1   **Fair call option values for Gaussian white noise and various product processes**

Conditional standard deviation v_t	K	Black–Scholes	Product process $\phi = 0.98, 0.985, 0.99, 0.995$				$\sigma_\eta = 0.01, 0.03, 0.05$		
0.0094	90	13.01	13.91	13.72	13.49	13.24	13.01	13.05	13.13
	100	5.19	7.14	6.81	6.38	5.83	5.20	5.31	5.56
	110	1.20	3.01	2.69	2.28	1.78	1.22	1.31	1.53
0.0156	90	14.20	14.74	14.65	14.52	14.31	14.02	14.14	14.42
	100	7.30	8.41	8.28	8.08	7.78	7.33	7.52	7.94
	110	3.17	4.26	4.13	3.94	3.63	3.19	3.38	3.79
0.0257	90	16.61	16.06	16.38	16.53	16.64	16.90	17.48	
	100	10.87	10.18	10.37	10.57	10.77	10.91	11.23	11.93
	110	6.74	6.04	6.23	6.44	6.64	6.78	7.11	7.83

Notes: Present stock price $S = 100$, option life $T = 84$ trading days, annual interest rate 10 per cent, unconditional standard deviation 0.02 for the product process.

Table 9.1 illustrates the call prices for four values of ϕ. These are 0.98, 0.985, 0.99, and 0.995 and the table gives figures for log $(v_t) = \alpha - \beta, \alpha$ and $\alpha + \beta$. It can again be seen that the greatest percentage differences between CPP(v_t) and CBS(v_t) occur for low v_t and a high ratio K/S. These differences increase as ϕ decreases.

Non-stationary processes

Conditional variances may not regress towards a median value. Instead of supposing ϕ is just less than 1 it may be more logical to consider the non-stationary case $\phi = 1$ for some series. All the previous results still apply except now

$$E[V_{t+h}^2 | v_t] = v_t^2 \exp(2h\sigma_\eta^2) \tag{9.4.5}$$

with σ_η the standard deviation of the residual terms in the random walk process

$$\log(V_{t+h}) = \log(V_{t+h-1}) + \eta_{t+h}. \tag{9.4.6}$$

The returns process is now non-stationary:

$$\text{var}(X_{t+1})/\text{var}(X_t) = \exp(2\sigma_\eta^2) \neq 1,$$

assuming $\sigma_\eta > 0$ and var (X_t) is finite.

The Black–Scholes formula will always underestimate the true call value when (9.4.6) applies, indeed CPP(v_t) − CBS(v_t) is a positive monotonic function of σ_η for all exercise prices. It is not easy to suggest sensible values of σ_η but it is unlikely that a value above 0.05 will be appropriate. The right-hand columns of Table 9.1 show CPP(v_t) with other variables (excluding ϕ) as for the other columns of the table. Again the percentage differences are greatest for the option out-of-the-money $(K = 110)$ although the differences for $\phi = 1$ are generally less than for $\phi < 1$.

Conclusions

The stochastic behaviour of the volatility of the underlying security is very important when valuing an option. Ignoring possible future changes in volatility can give a seriously incorrect call value. So, unfortunately, can using a stationary model when a non-stationary one is appropriate, and vice versa. Further research into volatilities is clearly desirable.

9.5 PRICE TRENDS AND CALL VALUES

The evidence in Chapters 6 to 8 strongly suggests there have been trends in the prices of commodity and currency futures. Informed investors will probably consider both an underlying security and its options to be mispriced when they believe there are trends in the security's prices. Naturally, trends can only continue to exist if enough traders use information inefficiently.

Price-trends do not exist in the theoretical models used to derive option pricing formulae. It is thus difficult to assess the value of an option to an investor having superior information about the price process. Trends apparently have no consequences for the arbitrage arguments used to price options. For example, when prices follow a binomial process, so each transaction changes the price from some S to either uS or dS (u and d known), then superior information about the probabilities of each possible change is irrelevant when pricing a call by arbitrage (Cox and Rubinstein, 1985, pp. 171–8). Risk-adjusted profits from superior knowledge could presumably be obtained from a position in the security, or its options, or certain combinations thereof, but not necessarily by arbitrage. It is now argued that trading options may then be more profitable than trading the security, assumed to be a futures contract.

A formula for trend models

Someone who believes there are trends in prices will not believe returns are uncorrelated and thus will not believe the variance of the total return $\Sigma X_{t+h} = X_{t+1} + \cdots + X_{t+T}$ is the sum of the variances of individual returns X_{t+h}. The person may want to assess options using a variance for ΣX_{t+h} based upon a trend model since option values depend on such variances. A formula for assessing call options when there are trends is discussed soon. A linear Gaussian process is assumed to keep the equations simple. It is possible, but complicated, to incorporate changing conditional variances into the formula by adapting the methods used in Section 9.4. For simplicity again, the formula ignores any information summarized by the observed forecast $f_{t,1}$ of x_{t+1}. Such information might more naturally be used to consider trading futures. In contrast, superior information about the variance of ΣX_{t+h} should be used to trade options.

Variances are represented in the Black–Scholes formula for stocks and Black's adaptation for futures by the product $\sigma \sqrt{T}$, which is intended to equal the standard deviation of ΣX_{t+h}. Better informed traders may want to include unhedged calls in their portfolios when the true standard deviation exceeds the value believed by other traders, say $\sigma \sqrt{T}$. To help select

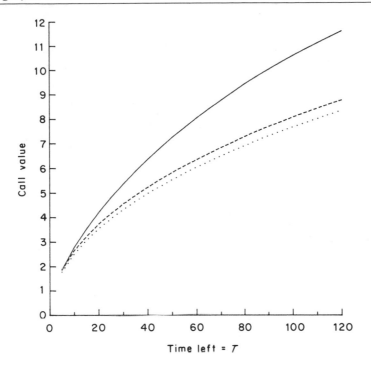

Figure 9.4 Values for an at-the-money call option $(K = S)$ calculated from a formula that assumes trends (solid curve) and from Black's formula for futures (dotted and dashed curves)

profitable calls it is suggested that calls are assessed by replacing $\sigma\sqrt{T}$ with the correct standard deviation for $\Sigma\, X_{t+h}$ in a price-trend model whose daily returns have variance σ^2 and autocorrelations Ap^τ. From (7.5.12), this price-trend formula for assessing call options is given by the following modification of the pricing formulae given in Section 9.2:

$$\text{replace } \sigma\sqrt{T} \text{ by } \sigma_1 = \sigma[T + 2Ap\{T - (1 - p^T)/(1 - p)\}/(1 - p)]^{1/2}. \tag{9.5.1}$$

It is emphasized that this change does not provide a pricing formula based on risk-free hedges. Instead, the price-trend formula might help to identify underpriced calls. Buying such calls should increase the risk-adjusted return expected from a sufficiently diversified portfolio.

Examples

As in the previous comparisons it is supposed that the present price S is $100, the exercise price K is $90, $100, or $110 and the annual interest rate is

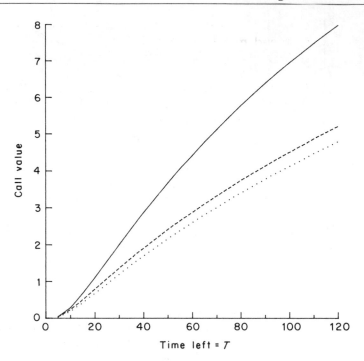

Figure 9.5   Values for an out-of-the-money call option ($K/S = 1.1$) calculated from a trend formula (solid curve) and Black's formula (dotted and dashed curves)

Table 9.2   Call values when there are trends in prices

Standard deviation σ	T	$K = 90$		$K = 100$		$K = 110$	
		CB[a]	CPT[b]	CB	CPT	CB	CPT
0.01	20	9.94	9.97	1.77	2.10	0.03	0.08
	40	9.97	10.19	2.48	3.18	0.19	0.49
	80	10.18	10.90	3.46	4.72	0.67	1.54
	120	10.44	11.57	4.17	5.83	1.16	2.49
0.02	20	10.42	10.77	3.54	4.20	0.68	1.11
	40	11.19	12.20	4.97	6.36	1.70	2.88
	80	12.52	14.62	6.91	9.42	3.41	5.78
	120	13.59	16.46	8.34	11.62	4.79	8.00
0.03	20	11.48	12.21	5.31	6.30	1.96	2.80
	40	13.06	14.81	7.44	9.53	3.85	5.84
	80	15.43	18.78	10.35	14.08	6.70	10.43
	120	17.22	21.68	12.47	17.35	8.86	13.82

[a]Call value using Black's formula.
[b]Value when the formula is adapted for price-trends.

10 per cent. Initially the standard deviation σ is assumed to be 0.02. The parameters of the trend model are $A = 0.03$ and $p = 0.95$ for all the comparisons. These values are similar to many of the estimates obtained in Chapter 7.

Figures 9.4 and 9.5 show call values for futures when K is \$100 and \$110. The solid curves represent CPT(T), the call value when the price-trend formula is used and T trading days remain until the option expires. Dotted curves indicate CB(T), the value given by Black's formula. Both CPT(T) and CB(T) assume perfect estimates of σ. Estimates will actually depend on the time between prices in a sample. A perfect estimate of the variance over one week, $\sigma_5^2 = \text{var}(\log [Z_{t+5}/Z_t])$, will lead to a different option value using Black's formula if $\sigma\sqrt{T}$ is replaced by $\sigma_5\sqrt{(T/5)}$. The corresponding call values are shown by the intermediate, dashed curves.

It is apparent that call options priced by the standard formulae might be considered bargains by investors convinced there is a trend component in returns. Table 9.2 lists values for Black's formula and the trend formula, for $\sigma = 0.01, 0.02,$ and 0.03. Once more the percentage differences are greatest for the out-of-the-money option. For $K = 1.1S$, $\sigma = 0.02$, and $120 \geqslant T \geqslant 25$, the trend formula gives values 65 to 70 per cent above the standard value; the percentage increase when $\sigma = 0.01$ declines with T to 114 per cent when $T = 120$, whilst for $\sigma = 0.03$ it grows with T over the range $100 \geqslant T \geqslant 25$ from 46 to 56 per cent.

9.6 SUMMARY

A very important determinant of option values is the variance of the total return over the remaining life of the option. Estimates of this variance should reflect the fact that (conditional) variances will not have been constant in the past nor can they be expected to be constant until the option's expiration date. It is quite possible that model-based estimates of variance are better than market estimates and there could then be economic gains from option trading. Empirical research into this possibility should yield interesting results.

_____*Chapter* 10___

Concluding Remarks

It has been shown that describing the statistical behaviour of financial prices accurately is a formidable task. This concluding chapter summarizes important features of the price generating process, highlights major implications for buyers and sellers of financial assets, and notes interesting questions for further research.

10.1 PRICE BEHAVIOUR

The stochastic process generating daily returns and hence daily prices is not like the processes commonly described in statistical texts and taught to students. Linear processes cannot be used to model returns. In particular returns are not independent observations from some fixed distribution. Neither can returns be modelled by a linear combination of the present and past terms from such a process, as shown at the end of Chapter 2. Returns must instead be modelled by some non-linear stochastic process. Additionally, it may be necessary to consider non-stationary processes. Relatively little is known about relevant non-linear processes which makes the modelling of returns a challenging activity.

Non-linear behaviour is almost certainly a consequence of changes in the variances of returns caused by variations in the general level of market activity. This level depends upon the preferences of investors and other traders and upon the quantity and importance of relevant information about the asset being traded. Progress has been made in Chapters 3 and 4 towards finding practical models for the variances of returns conditional upon appropriate information sets.

Prices may look like random walks but they are not. Daily returns are not uncorrelated observations sharing a common mean, neither are they uncorrelated with means fixed by economic theories of equilibrium. These conclusions were obtained in Chapter 6 by using appropriate statistical tests. Considerable care is required as many popular tests are unreliable when the process is non-linear and lack test power when there are trends in prices. Rejection of the random walk hypothesis indicates that some information is not reflected accurately by prices on the day it first becomes known. The delay is minimal for stocks but appears to be important for currencies and commodities. Thus accurate models for the returns from many financial assets must be non-linear and possess non-zero auto-correlations at some or all positive lags.

Prices reflect most information efficiently. Some markets, particularly for futures, do not appear to be sufficiently efficient to prevent successful trading using rules based upon statistical models. There is a strong case for trends in prices as a credible alternative to random behaviour for certain currencies and commodities. The realistic assessments of trading rules in Chapter 8 indicate profitable results were possible during years subsequent to the data used to define the rules.

10.2 ADVICE TO TRADERS

Private and corporate investors, businessmen, primary producers, anyone involved in international trade and the brokers and analysts who advise these people can all benefit from a deeper understanding of price behaviour. Many traders are rightly concerned about the risks associated with uncertain changes in prices. These risks can frequently be summarized by the variances of future returns, perhaps directly or by their relationship with relevant covariances in a portfolio context. Variances change and within a few weeks or even days they can increase dramatically and likewise the risks faced by traders. The forecasts of future standard deviations investigated in Chapter 4 can provide up-to-date indications of risk, which might be used to avoid unacceptable risks perhaps by hedging. These forecasts can be improved (see Section 10.3) and the methodology given here allows readers to develop their own improvements.

There will always be some traders who are best called speculators, having neither need of the goods they trade nor intention to possess them for long. In so far that speculators accept risks non-speculators wish to avoid, speculation can be respectable. Informed speculation might even be called investment. Speculators should consider the implications firstly of the trend models, particularly with regard to futures, and secondly of the variance models, particularly with regard to options.

No responsible adviser would claim profits can be made easily by trading financial goods. Markets use information at least reasonably efficiently and large profits can only be obtained by successfully enduring large risks. Nevertheless, the models presented in this text have the potential to modestly increase the returns obtained by sensible speculators. Readers wishing to estimate model parameters from their own price series can use the computer program given in the appendix.

10.3   FURTHER RESEARCH

Our understanding of financial time series is reasonably complete. There are, however, several opportunities for further research. New markets continue to be opened and many people will want to analyse their prices. Research into further series must recognize the non-linear behaviour of returns and must avoid the assumption that returns are independently and identically distributed. It may well be necessary to consider the possibility that prices do not follow a random walk.

Forecasts of future conditional standard deviations can almost certainly be improved. Daily high and low prices should be used to obtain better forecasts and so too should standard deviations implied by option prices whenever available. Seasonal effects, such as a higher standard deviation for returns encompassing weekends, should be considered. The best forecasts can be used for interesting tests of the efficiency of options markets. Comparisons of forecasts derived from stationary and non-stationary models (as in Chapter 4) should be instructive. Better forecasts will be useful when defining rescaled returns for random walk tests.

Modelling any trend component in returns requires some specification of the interdependence (if any) of the trend and the fluctuating variance of returns. This is not straightforward, as shown in Chapter 7. Further research is desirable and an attempt to find unbiased estimates of the trend parameters should be made. Such research has the potential to improve the trading rules discussed in Chapter 8. Naturally more can be done towards investigating the efficiency of futures markets and further research may well be rewarding. Further results about the vexatious issue of whether or not risk premia exist for futures would assist such research.

This book has only discussed models for univariate time series. Multivariate series are defined by several observations made at the same time, for example the daily closing prices of two or more financial assets. Interesting examples are firstly the prices of several stocks, secondly the prices of copper, lead, tin, zinc, and other metals, and thirdly key prices like gold, the national stock index, exchange rates with major trading partners, interest rates, and the price of oil. Each univariate price series defines a series of returns and a set of these series defines a multivariate returns series.

Modelling the interdependence between the returns from different assets would be very interesting. The largest cross-correlation between the returns x_{is} and x_{jt} in series i and j will be contemporaneous if markets are efficient, i.e. when the times s and t are equal. Lead and lag relationships (non-zero correlation for some $i \neq j$ and $s \neq t$) must be considered although any correlations are likely to be small. The cross-correlations between absolute returns are important. They should help to summarize the interdependence of price volatilities for different assets. Standard deviations for some assets may well depend on the same statistic for other assets and lagged relationships are conceivable. Accurate models will probably be multivariate generalizations of the univariate models already described. It would be easiest to begin by supposing all univariate models for returns are uncorrelated and non-linear. Cross-correlations for returns and absolute returns might then indicate a suitable category of multivariate, non-linear models.

10.4 STATIONARY MODELS

All models are necessarily imperfect and can only be approximations to the highly complicated process which produces observed prices. Some models, however, are certainly better than others. Stationary stochastic processes often appear to be acceptable for daily returns. A summary of the best stationary models described earlier concludes our study of financial time series. Recall that the price process $\{Z_t\}$ responsible for generating daily prices indexed by the time variable t is non-stationary, whilst the returns process $\{X_t\}$ may well be considered stationary, it being defined by $X_t = \log (Z_t) - \log (Z_{t-1})$.

Random walks

The logarithms of prices follow a random walk when returns have identical means and are uncorrelated, i.e. when

$$E[X_t] = \mu \quad \text{and} \quad \text{cor} (X_t, X_{t+\tau}) = 0$$

for some constant μ and all times t and all positive lags τ Two Gaussian processes can then be combined to give a stationary and uncorrelated process capable of explaining the major properties of returns. Prices have a tendency to change more often on some days than on others and this is described by the conditional standard deviation V_t. The reaction of the price at this level of market activity is summarized by an independent random variable U_t. An appropriate model is:

$$X_t = \mu + V_t U_t, \tag{10.4.1}$$
$$\log (V_t) - \alpha = \phi \{\log (V_{t-1}) - \alpha\} + \eta_t, \tag{10.4.2}$$

with (a) the U_t have independent normal distributions, all with mean 0 and variance 1, (b) the η_t have independent and identical normal distributions, with mean zero, so $\{\log (V_t)\}$ is a Gaussian, autoregressive process, and (c) the processes $\{U_t\}$ and $\{V_t\}$ are stochastically independent of each other.

This model was studied from Chapter 3 onwards. There are four parameters: the mean return μ and the mean α, standard deviation β and autoregressive parameter ϕ of the process $\{\log (V_t)\}$. The innovation η_t

determines V_t, the measure of market activity on day t. Small seasonal adjustments can be incorporated into the model to make it consistent with the day, weekend, and month effects noted in Section 2.5.

Price trends

The returns from various commodities and currencies display positive dependence. This is consistent with trends in prices. Let μ be the average return, as before, and let $\mu_t - \mu$ summarize the effect of slowly interpreted information upon the return during day t. The proportion of the variation in returns due to trends is denoted by $A = \text{var}\,(\mu_t)/\text{var}\,(X_t)$. Then the best generalization of (10.4.1) and (10.4.2) found so far has autocorrelations

$$\text{cor}\,(X_t,\, X_{t+\tau}) = Ap^\tau, \qquad A,\, p,\, \tau > 0$$

and is defined by

$$X_t = \mu_t + V_t U_t^*, \tag{10.4.3}$$
$$\mu_t - \mu = p(\mu_{t-1} - \mu) + \zeta_t \tag{10.4.4}$$

and $\{V_t\}$ as previously, see (10.4.2), with, furthermore: (i) each of the three processes $\{\zeta_t\}$, $\{\eta_t\}$, and $\{U_t^*\}$ consists of independent and identically distributed normal variables having zero mean, (ii) the three processes are stochastically independent and (iii) their variances are $\text{var}\,(\eta_t) = (1 - \phi^2)\beta^2$, $\text{var}\,(U_t^*) = (1 - A)/\{1 - A + A\,\exp\,(4\beta^2)\}$, and $\text{var}\,(\zeta_t) = A(1 - p^2)\sigma^2$ with

$$\sigma^2 = \text{var}\,(X_t) = \exp\,(2\alpha + 2\beta^2)/\{1 - A + A\,\exp\,(4\beta^2)\}.$$

This is the linear trend model defined in Section 7.2 with minor alterations to the notation. There are six parameters: A and p determine the average magnitude and duration of the trends whilst μ, α, β, and ϕ are defined as in the random walk model.

A Computer Program for Modelling Financial Time Series

This appendix describes a FORTRAN program which calculates many of the statistics and parameter estimates presented in the main text. The program is intended to help readers to model their own series. FORTRAN code is presented after a description of what the program does and the data it requires.

Output produced

The program produces the following information after reading a time series:

(i) *Summary statistics for returns*, their number n, average $\bar{x}$, standard deviation s, variance s^2, test value for zero mean $t = \sqrt{n}\bar{x}/s$, skewness b and kurtosis k (equations (2.3.1)); also the annual compound rate of return G and the estimated simple annual rate of return A (see notes to Table 2.3).

(ii) *Numbers of outliers*, being the numbers of returns more than k standard deviations away from the mean for integers $k \geq 2$ (as in Tables 2.6 and 2.7).

(iii) *The autocorrelations of returns, absolute returns, and squared returns*, for lags between 1 and 30 trading days (equation (2.9.1) for returns and similarly for the transformed series); also the standard error for strict white noise, $1/\sqrt{n}$, and the associated 95 per cent confidence interval, $\pm 1.96/\sqrt{n}$.

(iv) *Parameter estimates for the process generating standard deviations*: estimates $\hat{\mu}_V$ and $\hat{\sigma}_V$ of the mean and standard deviation of the process $\{V_t\}$ (equations (3.8.2)); further estimates given by assuming $\log(V_t)$ has the distribution $N(\alpha, \beta^2)$, namely $\hat{\alpha}$ and $\hat{\beta}$ (equations (3.9.1) and (3.9.2)), an estimate for the median of V_t, $\exp(\hat{\alpha})$, and an estimated 95 per cent interval, from $\exp(\hat{\alpha} - 1.96\hat{\beta})$ to $\exp(\hat{\alpha} + 1.96\hat{\beta})$.

(v) *Estimates for forecasting absolute returns and conditional standard deviations*: $\hat{\phi}$ and $\hat{\theta}$ for the best stationary forecast, given by suppos-

243

ing $\log (V_t)$ has autocorrelations ϕ^τ then obtaining $\hat{B}$ and $\hat{\phi}$ by minimizing the function F_6 (see Section 3.9) and hence getting $\hat{\theta}$ by appropriate substitutions in equation (4.3.2) (these estimates define the third forecast given in Section 4.3); also $\hat{\beta}_m$ given by equation (3.9.5).

(vi) *Estimates of the autocorrelation variances,* multiplied by the number of observations: b_τ for returns (equation (5.7.1)) and b_τ^* for rescaled returns (equation (5.8.4)), for lags 1 to 30.

(vii) *The autocorrelations of rescaled returns,* for lags 1 to 30 (equations in Section 6.8).

(viii) *Random walk test statistics calculated from the autocorrelations of rescaled returns: T^** (equation (6.6.2)), U^* (equation (6.7.1)), $r_1\sqrt{n^*}$, N_r, Q_{10}, Q_{30}, and Q_{50} (see Section 6.4); also the results when T^* and U^* are calculated from the autocorrelations of returns (Section 6.9).

(ix) *Runs analysis,* in particular the runs test statistic K (equation (6.4.8)).

(x) *The estimated spectral density function,* namely $\hat{f}(\omega)$ defined by equations (6.4.4) and (6.4.5) and the standardized statistics f_j equation (6.4.6). These numbers are followed by the random walk test statistics f_0 (equation (6.6.3)), f_w and N_s (Section 6.4).

(xi) *Estimates of the price-trend model parameters* provided by minimizing the functions F_1 and F_2 (equations (7.3.2) and (7.3.3)). The numbers $A_{i,m}$ and $S_{i,m}$ are given, then the estimates $\hat{m}_i$ and $\hat{A}_i$ followed by $\hat{p}_i$ and $\hat{q}_i$ (see Section 7.3).

Computer time required

The program was tested on a VAX 11/780 computer running under the DEC/VAX operating system VMS version V3.5. Compilation and linking took 25 seconds of central processing unit (CPU) time. A further 16 seconds of CPU time were sufficient to execute the program on one of the US stock returns series (2750 observations).

User-defined parameters

Users may have to change some of the statements following the first set of comments and perhaps numbers in the REAL declaration.

The identifier G stores the value of γ used in the calculations of $\hat{v}_t$ (equation (5.8.3)). Replace G = 0.04 by G = 0.1 for commodity and currency series.

For a spot series retain the statement K = 1 as in the program listing. For a series made up from futures contracts, K must equal the number of contracts.

The next two statements define the values of NRFIT and NRM. These values are respectively the number of autocorrelations used firstly to estimate the trend model parameters and secondly the variance model parameters. NRFIT is the integer K in equation (7.3.2), NRM is the integer K in Section 3.9.

The value of NRSP is one more than the number of autocorrelations used in the calculation of the spectral density function. NRSP is the integer M in the definition of the Parzen weights (equation (6.4.5)).

The integer XSIZE equals the size of the arrays X, Y, and SQUARES. Any change to the value given in the program will also require changes in the final line of the REAL declaration. It is likely that XSIZE should be decreased for a futures series, perhaps to 300.

Note that the dimensions of the matrix Z, defined at the end of the REAL declaration, must be at least XSIZE by K.

Optional parameters

Changing the values of NRX and/or NVARR in the fourth DATA statement will change the number of autocorrelations calculated and/or the number of autocorrelation variances estimated.

Input requirements

The user must ensure that the following data is read before the comment "TAKE LOGS":

(i) Prices Z(J, I) with I referring to the contract number and J counting the number of trading days since some starting date. I is always 1 for spot data.

(ii) Integers FIRSTY(I) and LASTY(I) defining the first and last days for which rescaled returns are calculated for inclusion in the autocorrelation calculations; I indicates the contract number.

Two examples will, I trust, make these requirements clear.

First, consider a series of 2000 spot prices, say from 2 January 1978 to 31 December 1985 with the price moving up from 120.5 to 216.7. The following datafile could be read satisfactorily without altering the program.

	22	2000	2000
	20178	120.5	
2000 lines	30178	122.2	
	⋮	⋮	
	311285	216.7	

Here FIRSTY(1) is 22 to allow 20 returns to be used to calculate the initial standard deviation forecast. Prices 21 and 22 are used to obtain the first return appearing in the autocorrelation calculations for random walk tests. The other two numbers in the first line are LASTY(1) and NPRICES, the number of prices to be read.

Second, consider a series defined by 20 futures contracts with prices from February 1976 to December 1985. Suppose these contracts have delivery dates June 1976, December 1976, June 1977, ..., December 1985. A satisfactory data file could commence like this:

		22	90	101	
90 lines		20276		1.675	
		30276		1.673	
		⋮		⋮	
		310576		1.568	First contract
11 lines		10676		1.582	
		⋮		⋮	
		150676		1.591	
		66	191	201	
65 lines		10376		1.612	
		20376		1.608	
		⋮		⋮	
		310576		1.603	
126 lines		10676		1.597	Second contract
		⋮		⋮	
		301176		1.431	
10 lines		11276		1.431	
		⋮		⋮	
		141276		1.415	

There would then be similarly formatted data like the second contract for the remaining 18 contracts.

In this example FIRSTY(1) is again 22 to permit the calculation of essential initial values whilst LASTY(1) is 90 and ensures that the June prices for the June 1976 contract are not used in the calculations. In the first row of the file NPRICES is $90 + 11 = 101$ and equals the number of prices for the June 1976 contract in the file. Note FIRSTY(2) is 66, to make sure the first return from the second contract appearing in the time series uses the prices on 31 May 1976 and 1 June 1976. Twenty returns from the contract before 1 June 1976 are only used to calculate initial values. Also note LASTY(2) is $65 + 126 = 191$ and the second value of NPRICES is $65 + 126 + 10 = 201$. It would be necessary to alter the final statement in the REAL declaration and the statements defining K and XSIZE, perhaps using

$\vdots$

4SQUARES(300), TYPE(3), X(300), Y(300), Z(300, 20)

$\vdots$

K = 20

$\vdots$

XSIZE = 300

About the subroutines

ACF uses the data $X(J1)$, $X(J1 + 1)$, ..., $X(J2)$ stored in an array of size N to calculate the autocorrelations $R(1)$, $R(2)$, ..., $R(NR)$ up to lag NR. M denotes the size of the arrays C and R. Note the observations must have total $X(J1) + X(J1 + 1) + \cdots + X(J2)$ equal to zero (spot data) or total over all contracts equal to zero (futures data). Also see the final sentence in this subsection.

FIT uses autocorrelations $R(I1)$, ..., $R(I2)$ calculated from N observations to find the best trend model estimates MHAT and AHAT constrained by MHAT $\leqslant$ MMAX ($\hat{m}$ and $\hat{A}$ in Chapter 7).

FITV uses appropriate autocorrelations $R(1)$, ..., $R(J1)$ calculated from N observations to find the best estimates BHAT and PHIHAT ($\hat{B}$ and $\hat{\phi}$ in Chapter 3).

MAPARA finds the moving average parameter Q giving autocorrelations AP^{τ} when the autoregressive parameter in an AMRA(1, 1) model is P.

RUNSTEST stores the number of negative runs in $S(1)$, positive runs in $S(2)$ and no-change runs in $S(3)$ for a series of returns $X(N1)$, ..., $X(N2)$. K is the standardized test statistic and E2 is a very small positive number.

SPECTRAL uses autocorrelations $R(1)$, ..., $R(M1 - 2)$ to calculate spectral density estimates $SPEC(1)$, ..., $SPEC(M1)$ corresponding to frequencies $\omega = (j - 1)\pi/(M1 - 1)$ for $j = 1$ to M1. The array SPECD gives the corresponding standardized values when there are N observations. NSIG counts the number of significant estimates for the subset $J = 1, 5, 9, ..., M1$.

VARR is used to estimate the variances of the first NV autocorrelations with XBAR the average of all the observations stored in $X(J1)$, ..., $X(J2)$, averaging over all contracts.

Subroutines ACF, RUNSTEST, and VARR are called once for each futures contract and the results are only meaningful after the whole set of calls has been made.

Fortran program

```
      PROGRAM ABCD
      INTEGER ASIZE,BSIZE,CSIZE,FIRSTX(50),FIRSTY(50),LAST(50),
     1OUTS(20,3),SSIZE,XSIZE
      REAL AEST1(100),AEST2(100),B(30),BSTAR(30),CABS(100),CM(100),
     1CSQD(100),CX(100),CY(100),FIRSTV(50),MBAR,MINDIF,MSUM,N,NY,
     2RABS(100),RM(100),RSQD(100),RX(100),RY(100),
     3SMIN1(100),SMIN2(100),SPEC(101),SPECD(101),SPECSD(101),
     4SQUARES(3000),TYPE(3),X(3000),Y(3000),Z(3000,1)
      DATA ASIZE,BSIZE,CSIZE,SSIZE/100,30,100,101/
      DATA VM,VX,VY,VABS,VSQD,CM,CX,CY,CABS,CSQD/505*0.0/
      DATA RUNS,TYPE,MINDIF,N28,DELTA/4*0.0,0.000001,28,0.798/
      DATA NRX,NVARR,OUTS/30,30,60*0/
      DATA ABSXSUM,XXSUM,MSUM,XSUM,YSUM,X2SUM,X3SUM,X4SUM/8*0.0/
      DATA DENX,DENY,B,BSTAR,TX,TY,UX,UY/66*0.0/
C
C     NUMBERS SPECIFIED BY PROGRAM USER, EXAMPLE FOLLOWS
C        MAX. VALUES FOR NRFIT, NRM AND NRSP ARE 100,100 AND 101
C        DIMENSIONS OF X, Y AND SQUARES MUST EQUAL XSIZE
C        SIZE OF MATRIX Z MUST BE AT LEAST XSIZE BY K
C
      G=0.04
      K=1
      NRFIT=50
      NRM=50
      NRSP=100
      XSIZE=3000
      G1=1.0-G
      NRY=NRSP
      IF(NRY.LT.30)NRY=30
C
C     READ IN PRICES, EXAMPLE FOLLOWS
C
      DO 60 I=1,K
      READ(1,*)FIRSTY(I),LAST(I),NPRICES
      DO 30 J=1,NPRICES
      READ(1,*)IDATE,Z(J,I)
   30 CONTINUE
   60 CONTINUE
C
C     TAKE LOGS
C
      DO 90 I=1,K
      IF(FIRSTY(I).LT.22)FIRSTY(I)=22
      FIRSTX(I)=FIRSTY(I)
      DO 90 J=1,LAST(I)
   90 Z(J,I)=ALOG(Z(J,I))
      FIRSTX(1)=2
C
C     CALCULATE SUMMARY STATISTICS (SECTION 2.3) BEGINNING WITH XBAR
C
      N=0.0
      XSUM=0.0
      DO 100 I=1,K
      N=N+FLOAT(LAST(I)-FIRSTX(I)+1)
  100 XSUM=XSUM+Z(LAST(I),I)-Z(FIRSTX(I)-1,I)
      XBAR=XSUM/N
      N1=N+0.5
      DO 120 I=1,K
      J1=FIRSTY(I)-20
      J2=FIRSTY(I)-1
      VHAT=0.0
      DO 110 J=J1,J2
  110 VHAT=VHAT+0.05*ABS(Z(J,I)-Z(J-1,I)-XBAR)
```

```
      FIRSTV(I)=VHAT
      DO 120 J=FIRSTX(I),LAST(I)
      XJ=Z(J,I)-Z(J-1,I)
      ABSXSUM=ABSXSUM+ABS(XJ)
      XXSUM=XXSUM+XJ*XJ
      XJ=XJ-XBAR
      MSUM=MSUM+ABS(XJ)
      X2SUM=X2SUM+XJ*XJ
      X3SUM=X3SUM+XJ**3
      X4SUM=X4SUM+XJ**4
      IF(J.LT.FIRSTY(I))GOTO 120
      YSUM=YSUM+(XJ/VHAT)
      VHAT=G1*VHAT+G*ABS(XJ)
  120 CONTINUE
      ABSXBAR=ABSXSUM/N
      MBAR=MSUM/N
      SBAR=X2SUM/N
      XXBAR=XXSUM/N
      YBAR=YSUM/(N-20.0)
      XVAR=X2SUM/(N-1)
      XSD=SQRT(XVAR)
      XSKEW=(X3SUM/(N-1))/(XSD**3)
      XKURT=(X4SUM/(N-1))/(XSD**4)
      XTSTAT=XBAR*SQRT(N)/XSD
      WRITE(6,130)N1,XBAR,XSD,XVAR,XTSTAT,XSKEW,XKURT
  130 FORMAT(/1X,'RETURNS',8X,'MEAN',5X,'ST.DEV.',8X,'VAR.',6X,
     1'T-STAT.',7X,'SKEW.',7X,'KURT.',/1X,I6,F13.6,F11.4,F13.6,3F12.2)
      GMRET=100.0*(EXP(252.0*XBAR)-1.0)
      WRITE(6,140)GMRET
  140 FORMAT(/1X,'AVERAGE X IS ABOUT EQUIVALENT TO A',F6.2,
     1'% COMPOUND ANNUAL RETURN')
      AMRET=100.0*(EXP(252.0*XBAR+126.0*XVAR)-1.0)
      WRITE(6,150)AMRET
  150 FORMAT(/1X,'XBAR AND XVAR SUGGEST A',F6.2,
     1'% AVERAGE ANNUAL RETURN')
C
C      SUMMARISE OUTLIERS (SECTION 2.7)
C
      DO 170 I=1,K
      DO 160 J=FIRSTX(I),LAST(I)
      XJ=Z(J,I)-Z(J-1,I)
      STDX=(XJ-XBAR)/XSD
      IF(ABS(STDX).LT.2.0)GOTO 160
      ASTDX=ABS(STDX)
      ISTDX=ASTDX
      IF(ISTDX.GT.20)ISTDX=20
      K2=2
      IF(STDX.LT.0.0)K2=1
      DO 155 K1=2,ISTDX
      OUTS(K1,K2)=OUTS(K1,K2)+1
  155 OUTS(K1,3)=OUTS(K1,3)+1
  160 CONTINUE
  170 CONTINUE
      WRITE(6,180)
  180 FORMAT(//1X,'OUTLIERS EXCEEDING K ST. DEVS.',/2X,'K',4X,
     1'-VE',4X,'+VE',4X,'TOTAL',/1X)
      DO 190 I=2,20
      IF(OUTS(I,3).EQ.0)GOTO 190
      WRITE(6,185)I,(OUTS(I,J),J=1,3)
  185 FORMAT(1X,I2,3I7)
  190 CONTINUE
C
C      CALCULATE AUTOCORRELATIONS OF X, ABS(X) & X*X
C      (SECTIONS 2.9 & 2.10)
C
      DO 220 I=1,K
```

```
            JSTART=FIRSTX(I)
            JEND=LAST(I)
            DO 205 J=JSTART,JEND
  205 X(J)=Z(J,I)-Z(J-1,I)-XBAR
            CALL ACF(X,XSIZE,VX,CX,RX,CSIZE,NRX,JSTART,JEND)
            DO 210 J=JSTART,JEND
  210 X(J)=ABS(X(J)+XBAR)-ABSXBAR
            CALL ACF(X,XSIZE,VABS,CABS,RABS,CSIZE,NRX,JSTART,JEND)
            DO 215 J=JSTART,JEND
  215 X(J)=((X(J)+ABSXBAR)**2)-XXBAR
            CALL ACF(X,XSIZE,VSQD,CSQD,RSQD,CSIZE,NRX,JSTART,JEND)
  220 CONTINUE
            SE=1.0/SQRT(N)
            CIL=-1.96*SE
            CIU=1.96*SE
            WRITE(6,225)N1
            IF(K.GT.1)WRITE(6,226)K
  225 FORMAT(//1X,'AUTOCORRELATION COEFFICIENTS CALCULATED FROM',
      1I6,' OBSERVATIONS')
  226 FORMAT(1X,'AND',I3,' FUTURES')
            WRITE(6,227)
  227 FORMAT(/1X,'LAG',6X,'RETURNS',7X,'ABS. RETURNS',5X,
      1'SQD. RETURNS')
            DO 240 I=1,NRX
            WRITE(6,230)I,RX(I),RABS(I),RSQD(I)
  230 FORMAT(1X,I3,F13.4,F16.4,F17.4)
  240 CONTINUE
            WRITE(6,245)SE,CIL,CIU
  245 FORMAT(/1X,'STANDARD ERROR',F8.4,'   95% CONFIDENCE LIMIT',
      1F8.4,' TO',F8.4,' FOR STRICT W.N.')
C
C
C           ESTIMATE PARAMETERS FOR THE STANDARD DEVIATION PROCESS
C           (SECTION 3.8) AND THE SPECIAL CASE LOGNORMAL AR(1) (SECTION 3.9)
C
            ESTMUV=MBAR/DELTA
            ESTSIGV=SQRT(SBAR-ESTMUV**2)
            ALPHAH=ALOG(MBAR*MBAR/(DELTA*DELTA*SQRT(SBAR)))
            BETAH=SQRT(ALOG(DELTA*DELTA*SBAR/(MBAR*MBAR)))
            VMEDIAN=EXP(ALPHAH)
            VCIL=EXP(ALPHAH-1.96*BETAH)
            VCIU=EXP(ALPHAH+1.96*BETAH)
            WRITE(6,250)DELTA,VMEDIAN,ESTMUV,ESTSIGV,VCIL,VCIU,ALPHAH,
      1BETAH
  250 FORMAT(///1X,'PARAMETER ESTIMATES FOR THE PROCESS V OF CONDITIONAL
      1 STANDARD DEVIATIONS, USING DELTA =',F7.3,//1X,'FOR V, MEDIAN =',
      2F8.4,'   MEAN =',F8.4,'   ST. DEV. =',F8.4,'   95% RANGE FROM',
      3F8.4,' TO',F8.4,/1X,'FOR LOG(V), MEAN (ALPHA) =',F7.3,
      4'   ST. DEV. (BETA) =',F7.3)
            DO 260 I=1,K
            JSTART=FIRSTX(I)
            JEND=LAST(I)
            DO 255 J=JSTART,JEND
  255 X(J)=ABS(Z(J,I)-Z(J-1,I)-XBAR)-MBAR
            CALL ACF(X,XSIZE,VM,CM,RM,CSIZE,NRM,JSTART,JEND)
  260 CONTINUE
            DO 262 I=1,NRM
  262 RM(I)=RM(I)*N/(N-K*I)
            CALL FITV(RM,CSIZE,NRM,N,ESTB,PHIH,FMIN)
            BTEST=2.0-3.141592*ESTB
            IF(BTEST.LT.0.0)WRITE(6,264)
  264 FORMAT(/1X,'ESTIMATED B IS INFEASIBLE')
            IF(BTEST.LT.0.0)BETAMH=0.0
            IF(BTEST.GT.0.0)BETAMH=SQRT(ALOG(2.0*(1.0-ESTB)/BTEST))
            CALL MAPARA(ESTB,PHIH,THETAH)
            WRITE(6,265)FMIN,ESTB,PHIH,THETAH,BETAMH
```

```
  265 FORMAT(/1X,'MINIMUM VALUE OF F6 IS',F6.2,' GIVEN BY B =',
     1F8.4,' AND PHI =',F7.3,/1X,'THESE IMPLY THETA FOR FORECASTING IS
     2',F7.3,' AND ANOTHER BETA ESTIMATE IS',F7.3,//1X,
     3'AUTOCORRELATIONS OF ADJUSTED ABSOLUTE RETURNS M',/1X,'LAG',
     47X,'ACTUAL',7X,'FITTED')
      DO 270 I=1,NRM
      FITTED=ESTB*(PHIH**I)
      WRITE(6,268)I,RM(I),FITTED
  268 FORMAT(1X,I3,2F13.4)
  270 CONTINUE
C
C        ESTIMATE VARIANCES OF AUTOCORRELATIONS (SECTIONS 5.7 & 5.8)
C
      DO 295 I=1,K
      JSTART=FIRSTY(I)
      JX=FIRSTX(I)
      JEND=LAST(I)
      VHAT=FIRSTV(I)
      DO 280 J=JSTART,JEND
      X(J)=Z(J,I)-Z(J-1,I)
      Y(J)=(X(J)-XBAR)/VHAT
  280 VHAT=G1*VHAT+G*ABS(X(J)-XBAR)
      IF(I.GT.1)GOTO 290
      JS1=JSTART-1
      DO 285 J=JX,JS1
  285 X(J)=Z(J,I)-Z(J-1,I)
  290 CALL VARR(X,XBAR,XSIZE,B,BSIZE,DENX,NVARR,JX,JEND,SQUARES)
      CALL VARR(Y,YBAR,XSIZE,BSTAR,BSIZE,DENY,NVARR,JSTART,JEND,SQUARES)
  295 CONTINUE
      X1=N/(DENX*DENX)
      Y1=(N-20.0)/(DENY*DENY)
      DO 300 I=1,NVARR
      B(I)=B(I)*X1
  300 BSTAR(I)=BSTAR(I)*Y1
      WRITE(6,305)G
  305 FORMAT(//1X,'ESTIMATES OF THE VARIANCES OF THE AUTOCORRELATION COE
     1FFICIENTS (* SERIES LENGTH)',/4X,'X-DATA ARE RETURNS',
     2/4X,'Y-DATA ARE RETURNS RESCALED USING GAMMA =',F6.2,
     3//1X,'LAG',4X,'X-DATA',4X,'Y-DATA',/1X)
      DO 320 I=1,NVARR
      WRITE(6,310)I,B(I),BSTAR(I)
  310 FORMAT(1X,I3,2F10.3)
  320 CONTINUE
C
C        CALCULATE AUTOCORRELATIONS OF RESCALED RETURNS AND ASSORTED
C        RANDOM WALK TEST STATISTICS (SECTIONS 6.4, 6.6, 6.7 & 6.9)
C
      DO 340 I=1,K
      JS=FIRSTX(I)
      JSTART=FIRSTY(I)
      JEND=LAST(I)
      VHAT=FIRSTV(I)
      DO 330 J=JS,JEND
      X(J)=Z(J,I)-Z(J-1,I)
      IF(J.LT.JSTART)GOTO 330
      Y(J)=((X(J)-XBAR)/VHAT)-YBAR
      VHAT=G1*VHAT+G*ABS(X(J)-XBAR)
  330 CONTINUE
      CALL ACF(Y,XSIZE,VY,CY,RY,CSIZE,NRY,JSTART,JEND)
      CALL RUNSTEST(X,XSIZE,TYPE,RUNS,ER,SR,RUNT,JS,JEND,MINDIF)
  340 CONTINUE
      NY=N-20.0
      NY1=N1-20
      WRITE(6,225)NY1
      IF(K.GT.1)WRITE(6,226)K
      WRITE(6,350)
```

```
  350 FORMAT(/1X,'LAG',6X,'FOR RESCALED RETURNS')
      DO 370 I=1,30
      WRITE(6,360)I,RY(I)
  360 FORMAT(1X,I3,F13.4)
  370 CONTINUE
      SNX=SQRT(N)
      SNY=SQRT(NY)
      CIUY=1.96/SNY
      NSIGRY=0
      QSUM=0.0
      R1TEST=RY(1)*SNY
      DO 380 I=1,50
      QSUM=QSUM+NY*RY(I)*RY(I)
      IF(I.EQ.10)Q10=QSUM
      IF(I.EQ.30)Q30=QSUM
      IF(I.EQ.50)Q50=QSUM
      IF(I.GT.30)GOTO 380
      TX=TX+(0.92**I)*RX(I)
      TY=TY+(0.92**I)*RY(I)
      IF((I.LE.28).AND.(ABS(RY(I)).GT.CIUY))NSIGRY=NSIGRY+1
  380 CONTINUE
      UX=0.4649*SNX*(TX-0.92*RX(1))
      UY=0.4649*SNY*(TY-0.92*RY(1))
      TX=0.4274*SNX*TX
      TY=0.4274*SNY*TY
      WRITE(6,420)TY,UY,R1TEST,NSIGRY,N28,Q10,Q30,Q50
  420 FORMAT(///1X,'VALUES OF THE AUTOCORRELATION TEST STATISTICS',
     1//3X,'T =',F6.2,',   U =',F6.2,/3X,'R(1) =',F6.2,' SE UNITS',
     2/3X,'NUMBER OF SIGNIFICANT R(TAU) AT THE 5% LEVEL',I4,' OUT OF',
     3I4,/3X,'Q10 =',F7.2,',   Q30 =',F7.2,',   Q50 =',F7.2)
      WRITE(6,430)TX,UX
  430 FORMAT(/1X,'USING RETURNS WOULD GIVE : T =',F6.2,' AND U =',F6.2)
      WRITE(6,440)(TYPE(I),I=1,3),RUNS,ER,SR,RUNT
  440 FORMAT(///1X,'RUNS ANALYSIS',/1X,F7.1,' DOWNS',/1X,F7.1,' UPS',
     1/1X,F7.1,' NO CHANGES',//1X,F7.1,' RUNS OBSERVED',/1X,F7.1,
     2' RUNS EXPECTED',/1X,F7.1,' S.D.',//1X,'RUNS TEST STATISTIC =',
     3F6.2)
      NRSP1=NRSP+1
      CALL SPECTRAL(RY,CSIZE,SPEC,SPECSD,SPECD,SSIZE,NRSP1,NY,NSIGFJ)
      J=NRSP-1
      WRITE(6,460)J,NRSP
  460 FORMAT(///1X,'SPECTRAL DENSITY ESTIMATED FROM FOURIER TRANSFORM OF
     1',/1X,'THE FIRST',I4,' AUTOCORRELATIONS.  PARZEN WINDOW USED.',
     2/1X,'ESTIMATED AT FREQUENCIES PI/',I4,' APART.',//1X,'FREQ/PI',
     32X,'PERIOD',3X,'DENSITY',5X,'SD',5X,'STANDARDISED')
      DO 500 I=1,NRSP1,4
      I1=I-1
      FR=FLOAT(I1)/FLOAT(NRSP)
      IF(I.GT.1)GOTO 480
      WRITE(6,470)FR,SPEC(1),SPECSD(1),SPECD(1)
  470 FORMAT(1X,F6.3,6X,'INF',F9.3,2F10.3)
      GOTO 500
  480 PER=2.0/FR
      WRITE(6,490)FR,PER,SPEC(I),SPECSD(I),SPECD(I)
  490 FORMAT(1X,F6.3,F9.2,F9.3,2F10.3)
  500 CONTINUE
      IW=1+(4*NRSP)/10
      J1=1+NRSP/4
      WRITE(6,520)SPECD(1),SPECD(IW),NSIGFJ,J1
  520 FORMAT(///1X,'SPECTRAL TEST STATISTICS',/3X,'ZERO FREQ.',F8.3,
     1/3X,'WEEK CYCLE',F8.3,/3X,'NUMBER OF SIGNIFICANT F(J) AT THE 5% LE
     2VEL',I4,' OUT OF',I4)
C
C        ESTIMATE TREND MODEL PARAMETERS (SECTION 7.3)
C
      MMAX=40
```

```
      I1=1
      DO 610 I=I1,NRFIT
      RX(I)=N*RX(I)/(N-K*I)
  610 RY(I)=NY*RY(I)/(NY-K*I)
      CALL FIT(RX,CSIZE,I1,NRFIT,AEST1,SMIN1,ASIZE,MMAX,N,MHATX,AHATX)
      CALL FIT(RY,CSIZE,I1,NRFIT,AEST2,SMIN2,ASIZE,MMAX,NY,MHATY,AHATY)
      WRITE(6,620)I1,NRFIT
  620 FORMAT(///1X,'TREND PARAMETERS ESTIMATED FROM AUTOCORRELATIONS',
     1I3,' TO',I3,/1X,'FIRSTLY FROM RETURNS, SECONDLY FROM RESCALED RETU
     2RNS',//4X,'M',5X,'P',10X,'A1',9X,'S1',10X,'A2',9X,'S2')
      DO 640 I=1,MMAX
      P=1.0-1.0/FLOAT(I)
      WRITE(6,630)I,P,AEST1(I),SMIN1(I),AEST2(I),SMIN2(I)
  630 FORMAT(1X,I4,F9.4,2(F11.4,F11.2))
  640 CONTINUE
      PHATX=1.0-1.0/FLOAT(MHATX)
      CALL MAPARA(AHATX,PHATX,QHATX)
      PHATY=1.0-1.0/FLOAT(MHATY)
      CALL MAPARA(AHATY,PHATY,QHATY)
      WRITE(6,650)MHATX,AHATX,PHATX,QHATX,MHATY,AHATY,PHATY,QHATY
  650 FORMAT(/1X,'MINIMISING F1 GIVES : M =',I3,', A =',F7.4,
     1', P =',F7.4,' AND Q =',F7.4,/1X,'MINIMISING F2 GIVES : M =',
     2I3,', A =',F7.4,', P =',F7.4,' AND Q =',F7.4)
      STOP
      END
C
      SUBROUTINE ACF(X,N,V,C,R,M,NR,J1,J2)
      REAL X(N),C(M),R(M)
      DO 100 J=J1,J2
  100 V=V+X(J)*X(J)
      DO 400 I=1,NR
      JEND=J2-I
      IF(JEND.LT.J1)GOTO 300
      K=J1+I-1
      DO 200 J=J1,JEND
      K=K+1
      C(I)=C(I)+X(J)*X(K)
  200 CONTINUE
  300 R(I)=C(I)/V
  400 CONTINUE
      RETURN
      END
C
      SUBROUTINE FIT(R,NR,I1,I2,A,S,NS,MMAX,N,MHAT,AHAT)
      REAL N,R(NR),A(NS),S(NS)
      A(1)=0.0
      S(1)=0.0
      DO 100 I=I1,I2
  100 S(1)=S(1)+N*R(I)*R(I)
      SMIN=S(1)
      MHAT=1
      DO 300 I=2,MMAX
      P=1.0-1.0/FLOAT(I)
      A(I)=0.0
      D=0.0
      DO 200 J=I1,I2
      A(I)=A(I)+R(J)*(P**J)
  200 D=D+P**(J+J)
      A(I)=A(I)/D
      IF(A(I).LT.0.0)A(I)=0.0
      S(I)=S(1)-N*A(I)*A(I)*D
      IF(S(I).GT.SMIN)GOTO 300
      IF(A(I).LT.0.000001)GOTO 300
      SMIN=S(I)
      AHAT=A(I)
      MHAT=I
```

```
  300 CONTINUE
      RETURN
      END
C
      SUBROUTINE FITV(R,NR,J1,N,BHAT,PHIHAT,FMIN)
      REAL N,R(NR),PHI(226)
      DO 10 I=1,51
   10 PHI(I)=0.01*FLOAT(I-1)
      DO 20 I=52,131
   20 PHI(I)=0.5+0.005*FLOAT(I-51)
      DO 30 I=132,226
   30 PHI(I)=0.9+0.001*FLOAT(I-131)
      FMIN=100.0*N
      BESTB=0.0
      DO 200 I=1,226
      IF(I.EQ.1)GOTO 120
      S=0.0
      SP=0.0
      DO 100 J=1,J1
      P=PHI(I)**J
      S=S+R(J)*P
  100 SP=SP+P*P
      BESTB=S/SP
  120 F=0.0
      DO 150 J=1,J1
  150 F=F+N*((R(J)-BESTB*(PHI(I)**J))**2)
      IF(F.GT.FMIN)GOTO 200
      BHAT=BESTB
      FMIN=F
      PHIHAT=PHI(I)
  200 CONTINUE
      RETURN
      END
C
      SUBROUTINE MAPARA(A,P,Q)
      B=(1.0+P*P*(1.0-2.0*A))/(P*(1.0-A))
      Q=0.5*(B-SQRT(B*B-4.0))
      RETURN
      END
C
      SUBROUTINE RUNSTEST(X,N,S,RUNS,ER,SIGR,K,N1,N2,E2)
      REAL K,S(3),T(3),X(N)
      E1=-E2
      RUNS=RUNS+1.0
      DO 200 I=N1,N2
      J=3
      IF(X(I).LT.E1)J=1
      IF(X(I).GT.E2)J=2
      S(J)=S(J)+1.0
      IF(I.EQ.N1)GOTO 100
      IF(J.NE.J1)RUNS=RUNS+1.0
  100 J1=J
  200 CONTINUE
      DO 400 I=1,3
      T(I)=0.0
      DO 300 J=1,3
  300 T(I)=T(I)+S(J)**I
  400 CONTINUE
      ER=T(1)+1.0-T(2)/T(1)
      A=T(2)*(T(2)+(T(1)*(T(1)+1.0)))-2.0*T(1)*T(3)-(T(1)**3)
      SIGR=SQRT(A/((T(1)**3)-T(1)))
      K=(RUNS-ER)/SIGR
      RETURN
      END
```

```
C
      SUBROUTINE SPECTRAL(R,NR,SPEC,SPECSD,SPECD,MS,M1,N,NSIG)
      REAL N,R(NR),SPEC(MS),SPECSD(MS),SPECD(MS),LAMBDA(100)
      M=M1-1
      MM1=M-1
      FM=FLOAT(M)
      DO 100 I=1,M
      A=FLOAT(I)/FM
      LAMBDA(I)=1.0-6.0*A*A+6.0*A*A*A
      IF(A.GT.0.5)LAMBDA(I)=2.0*((1.0-A)**3)
  100 CONTINUE
      NSIG=0
      PI=3.141592
      TWOPI=PI+PI
      DO 400 J=1,M1
      OMEGA=PI*FLOAT(J-1)/FM
      OMK=0.0
      SPEC(J)=1.0
      SPECSD(J)=0.0
      DO 200 K=1,MM1
      OMK=OMK+OMEGA
      IF(OMK.GT.PI)OMK=OMK-TWOPI
      CL=COS(OMK)*LAMBDA(K)
      SPEC(J)=SPEC(J)+2.0*CL*R(K)
      SPECSD(J)=SPECSD(J)+4.0*CL*CL
  200 CONTINUE
      SPECSD(J)=SQRT(SPECSD(J)/N)
      SPECD(J)=(SPEC(J)-1.0)/SPECSD(J)
      J1=J-1
      IF(J1.GT.(4*(J1/4)))GOTO 400
      IF(ABS(SPECD(J)).GT.1.96)NSIG=NSIG+1
  400 CONTINUE
      RETURN
      END
C
      SUBROUTINE VARR(X,XBAR,N,VR,M,D,NV,J1,J2,A)
      REAL X(N),VR(M),A(N)
      DO 100 J=J1,J2
      A(J)=(X(J)-XBAR)**2
  100 D=D+A(J)
      DO 300 I=1,NV
      JEND=J2-I
      IF(JEND.LT.J1)GOTO 300
      K=J1+I-1
      DO 200 J=J1,JEND
      K=K+1
      VR(I)=VR(I)+A(J)*A(K)
  200 CONTINUE
  300 CONTINUE
      RETURN
      END
```

References

Alexander, S. S. (1961) 'Price movements in speculative markets: trends or random walks?', *Industrial Management Review*, **2**, 7–26.

Ali, M. M. and C. Giaccotto (1982) 'The identical distribution hypothesis for stock market prices—location and scale-shift alternatives', *Journal of the American Statistical Association*, **77**, 19–28.

Anderson, T. W. and A. M. Walker (1964) 'On the asymptotic distribution of the autocorrelations of a sample from a linear stochastic process', *Annals of Mathematical Statistics*, **35**, 1296–1303.

Bachelier, L. (1900) 'Theory of speculation', reprinted in P. Cootner (ed.), 1964, *The Random Character of Stock Market Prices*, pp. 17–78 (MIT Press, Cambridge, Massachusetts).

Ball, R. (1978) 'Filter rules: interpretation of market efficiency, experimental problems and Australian evidence', *Accounting Education*, **18**, 1–17, reprinted in Ball *et al*. (1980).

Ball, R., P. Brown, F. J. Finn, and R. R. Officer (eds.) (1980) *Share Markets and Portfolio Theory* (University of Queensland Press, St. Lucia, Queensland).

Banz, R. W. (1981) 'The relationship between return and market value of common stocks', *Journal of Financial Economics*, **9**, 3–18.

Beckers, S. (1981a) 'A note on estimating the parameters of the diffusion-jump model of stock returns', *Journal of Financial and Quantitative Analysis*, **16**, 127–140.

Beckers, S. (1981b) 'Standard deviations implied in option prices as predictors of future stock price variability', *Journal of Banking and Finance*, **5**, 363–382.

Beckers, S. (1983) 'Variances of security price returns based on high, low and closing prices', *Journal of Business*, **56**, 97–112.

Bird, P. J. W. N. (1985) 'The weak form efficiency of the London Metal Exchange', *Applied Economics*, **17**, 571–587.

Black, F. (1976) 'The pricing of commodity contracts', *Journal of Financial Economics*, **3**, 167–179.

Black, F. and M. Scholes (1973) 'The pricing of options and corporate liabilities', *Journal of Political Economy*, **81**, 637–659.

Blattberg, R. C. and N. J. Gonedes (1974) 'A comparison of the stable and Student distributions as statistical models for stock prices', *Journal of Business*, **47**, 244–280.

Bodie, Z. and V. I. Rosansky (1980) 'Risk and return in commodity futures', *Financial Analysts Journal*, May/June 27–39.

Bookstaber, R. M. (1981) *Option Pricing and Strategies in Investing* (Addison-Wesley, Reading, Massachusetts).

256

Box, G. E. P. and G. M. Jenkins (1976) *Time Series Analysis, Forecasting and Control*, revd edn (Holden Day, Oakland, California).

Brealey, R. A. and S. C. Myers (1984) *Principles of Corporate Finance* (McGraw-Hill, New York, 2nd edn).

Breeden, D. (1980) 'Consumption risks in futures markets', *Journal of Finance*, **35**, 503–520.

Brown, S. J. and J. B. Warner (1985) 'Using daily stock returns: the case of event studies', *Journal of Financial Economics*, **14**, 3–31.

Cargill, T. F. and G. C. Rausser (1975) 'Temporal behaviour in commodity futures markets', *Journal of Finance*, **30**, 1043–1053.

Carter, C. A., G. C. Rausser, and A. Schmitz (1983) 'Efficient asset portfolios and the theory of normal backwardation', *Journal of Political Economy*, **91**, 319–331.

Chang, E. C. (1985) 'Returns to speculators and the theory of normal back-wardation', *Journal of Finance*, **40**, 193–207.

Cheng, P. L. (1984) 'Unbiased estimators of long-run expected returns revisited', *Journal of Financial and Quantitative Analysis*, **19**, 375–393.

Chiras, D. and S. Manaster (1978) 'The information content of option prices and a test of market efficiency', *Journal of Financial Economics*, **6**, 213–234.

Clark, P. K. (1973) 'A subordinated stochastic process model with finite variance for speculative prices', *Econometrica*, **41**, 135–155.

Cooper, J. C. B. (1982) 'World stock markets: some random walk tests', *Applied Economics*, **14**, 515–531.

Cornell, W. B. and J. K. Dietrich (1978) 'The efficiency of the market for foreign exchange under floating exchange rates', *Review of Economics and Statistics*, **60**, 111–120.

Cox, J. C. and M. Rubinstein (1985) *Options Markets* (Prentice-Hall, Englewood Cliffs, New Jersey).

Cunningham, S. W. (1973) 'The predictability of British stock market prices', *Applied Statistics*, **22**, 315–331.

Daniels, H. (1966) 'Autocorrelation between first differences of mid-ranges', *Econometrica*, **34**, 215–219.

Dimson, E. and R. A. Brealey (1978) 'The risk premium on U.K. equities', *Investment Analyst*, **52**, 14–18.

Dryden, M. M. (1970a) 'A statistical study of U.K. share prices', *Scottish Journal of Political Economy*, **17**, 369–389.

Dryden, M. M. (1970b) 'Filter tests of U.K. share prices', *Applied Economics*, **1**, 261–275.

Dusak, K. (1973) 'Futures trading and investors returns: an investigation of commodity market risk premiums', *Journal of Political Economy*, **81**, 1387–1406.

Engle, R. F. (1982) 'Autoregressive conditional heteroscedasticity with estimates of the variance of United Kingdom inflation', *Econometrica*, **50**, 987–1007.

Epps, T. W. and M. L. Epps (1976) 'The stochastic dependence of security price changes and transaction volumes: implications for the mixture of distributions hypothesis', *Econometrica*, **44**, 305–322.

Fama, E. F. (1965) 'The behaviour of stock market prices', *Journal of Business*, **38**, 34–105.

Fama, E. F. (1970) 'Efficient capital markets: a review of theory and empirical work', *Journal of Finance*, **25**, 383–417.

Fama, E. F. (1976) *Foundations of Finance* (Basil Blackwell, Oxford).

Fama, E. F. and M. E. Blume (1966) 'Filter tests and stock market trading', *Journal of Business*, **39**, 226–241.

Fama, E. F. and R. Roll (1968) 'Some properties of symmetric stable distributions', *Journal of the American Statistical Association*, **63**, 817–836.

French, D. W. (1984) 'The weekend effect on the distribution of stock prices: implications for option pricing', *Journal of Financial Economics*, **13**, 547–559.

French, K. R. (1980) 'Stock returns and the weekend effect', *Journal of Financial Economics*, **8**, 55–70.

Garman, M. B. and M. J. Klass (1980) 'On the estimation of security price volatilities from historical data', *Journal of Business*, **53**, 67–78.

Geisst, C. R. (1982) *A Guide to the Financial Markets* (Macmillan Press, London).

Giaccotto, C. (1978) Random walk hypothesis of stock market prices reconsidered (PhD dissertation, Lexington, Kentucky).

Gibbons, M. R. and P. J. Hess (1981) 'Day of the week effects and asset returns', *Journal of Business*, **54**, 579–596.

Granger, C. W. J. (ed.) (1979) *Trading in Commodities* (Woodhead-Faulkner, Cambridge, England, 3rd edn).

Granger, C. W. J. and A. P. Andersen (1978) *An Introduction to Bilinear Time Series Models* (Vandenhoeck and Ruprecht, Gottingen).

Granger, C. W. J. and O. Morgenstern (1970) *Predictability of Stock Market Prices* (Heath, Lexington, Massachusetts).

Granger, C. W. J. and P. Newbold (1976) 'Forecasting transformed series', *Journal of the Royal Statistical Society*, **38B**, 189–203.

Granger, C. W. J. and P. Newbold (1977) *Forecasting Economic Time Series* (Academic Press, New York).

Granger, C. W. J. and D. Orr (1972) 'Infinite variance and research strategy in time series analysis', *Journal of the American Statistical Association*, **67**, 275–285.

Greene, M. T. and B. D. Fielitz (1977) 'Long-term dependence in common stock returns', *Journal of Financial Economics*, **4**, 339–349.

Grossman, S. J. and J. E. Stiglitz (1980) 'On the impossibility of informationally efficient markets', *American Economic Review*, **70**, 393–408.

Guimaraes, R. M. C. (1981) National planning of commodity import operations: the case of Portugal's feed grain imports (PhD thesis, Lancaster, UK).

Gultekin, M. and B. Gultekin (1983) 'Stock market seasonality: international evidence', *Journal of Financial Economics*, **12**, 469–481.

Hagerman, R. L. (1978) 'More evidence on the distribution of security returns', *Journal of Finance*, **33**, 1213–1221.

Hsu, D. A. (1977) 'Tests for variance shift at an unknown time point', *Applied Statistics*, **26**, 279–284.

Hsu, D. A. (1979) 'Detecting shifts of parameter in gamma sequences with applications to stock price and air traffic flow analysis', *Journal of the American Statistical Association*, **74**, 31–40.

Hsu, D. A. (1982) 'A Bayesian robust detection of shift in the risk structure of stock market returns', *Journal of the American Statistical Association*, **77**, 29–39.

Ibbotson, R. G., R. A. Sinquefield, and L. B. Siegel (1982) in M. Blume and J. Friedman (eds), *Encyclopedia of Investments* (Warren, Gorham and Lamont, New York).

Jennergren, L. P. (1975) 'Filter tests of Swedish share prices', in E. J. Elton and M. J. Gruber (eds), *International Capital Markets*, pp. 55–67 (North-Holland, Amsterdam).

Jennergren, L. P. and P. E. Korsvold (1974) 'Price formation in the Norwegian and Swedish stock markets—some random walk tests', *Swedish Journal of Economics*, **76**, 171–185.

Jennergren, L. P. and P. Toft-Nielsen (1977) 'An investigation of random walks in the Danish stock market', *Nationalokonimsk Tiddskrift*, **2**, 254-269.

Jensen, M. C. (1978) 'Some anomalous evidence regarding market efficiency', *Journal of Financial Economics*, **6**, 95–101.

Kamara, A. (1984) 'The behavior of futures prices: a review of theory and evidence', *Financial Analysts Journal*, July/August, 68–75.

Keim, D. B. (1983) 'Size-related anomalies and stock market return seasonality: further empirical evidence', *Journal of Financial Economics*, **12**, 12–32.

Keim, D. B. and R. F. Stambaugh (1984) 'A further investigation of the weekend effect in stock returns', *Journal of Finance*, **39**, 819–835.

Kendall, M. G. (1953) 'The analysis of economic time series, Part I: prices', *Journal of the Royal Statistical Society*, **96A**, 11–25.

Kendall, M. G. and A. Stuart (1976) *The Advanced Theory of Statistics* vol. 3 (Charles Griffin, London, 3rd edn).

Kon, S. J. (1984) 'Models of stock returns—a comparison', *Journal of Finance*, **39**, 147–165.

Labys, W. C. and C. W. J. Granger (1970) *Speculation, Hedging and Commodity Price Forecasts* (Heath, Lexington, Massachusetts).

Labys, W. C. and H. C. Thomas (1975) 'Speculation, hedging and commodity price behaviour: an international comparison', *Applied Economics*, **7**, 287–301.

Latane, H. and R. Rendleman (1976) 'Standard deviations of stock price ratios implied in option prices', *Journal of Finance*, **31**, 369–381.

Leuthold, R. M. (1972) 'Random walks and price trends: the live cattle futures markets', *Journal of Finance*, **27**, 879–889.

Leuthold, R. M. (1976) Reply to P. D. Praetz, *Journal of Finance*, **31**, 984–985.

Levich, R. M. (1979) *The International Money Market: an Assessment of Forecasting Techniques and Market Efficiency* (JAI Press, Greenwich, Connecticut).

Lintner, J. (1965) 'The valuation of risk assets and the selection of risky investments in stock portfolios and capital budgets', *Review of Economics and Statistics*, **47**, 13–37.

Lomnicki, Z. A. and S. K. Zaremba (1957) 'On the estimation of autocorrelation in time series', *Annals of Mathematical Statistics*, **28**, 140–158.

MacFarland, J. W., R. P. Pettit, and S. K. Sung (1982) 'The distribution of foreign exchange price changes: trading day effects and risk measurement', *Journal of Finance*, **37**, 693–715.

Mandelbrot, B. (1963) 'The variation of certain speculative prices', *Journal of Business*, **36**, 394–419.

Martell, T. F. and B. P. Helms (1979) 'A reexamination of price changes in the commodity futures markets', in *International Futures Trading Seminar Proceedings Volume V*, pp. 136–159 (Chicago Board of Trade, Chicago).

Martell, T. F. and G. C. Philippatos (1974) 'Adaptation, information and dependence in commodity markets', *Journal of Finance*, **29**, 493–498, discussed 523–524.

Menzefricke, U. (1981) 'A Bayesian analysis of a change in the precision of a sequence of independent normal random variables at an unknown time point', *Applied Statistics*, **30**, 141–146.

Merton, R. C. (1973) 'Theory of rational option pricing', *Bell Journal of Economics and Management Science*, **4**, 141–183.

Merton, R. C. (1980) 'On estimating the expected return on the market', *Journal of Financial Economics*, **8**, 323–361.

Mood, A. M. (1940) 'The distribution theory of runs', *Annals of Mathematical Statistics*, **11**, 367–392.

Moran, P. A. P. (1967) 'Tests for serial correlation with exponentially distributed variates', *Biometrika*, **54**, 395–401.

Niederhoffer, V. and M. F. M. Osborne (1966) 'Market making and reversal of the stock exchange', *Journal of the American Statistical Association*, **61**, 897–916.

Officer, R. R. (1975) 'Seasonality in the Australian capital markets: market efficiency and empirical issues', *Journal of Financial Economics*, **2**, 29–52.

Oldfield, G. S. and R. J. Rogalski (1980) 'A theory of common stock returns over trading and non-trading periods', *Journal of Finance*, **35**, 729–751.

Oldfield, G. S., R. J. Rogalski, and R. A. Jarrow (1977) 'An autoregressive jump process for common stock returns', *Journal of Financial Economics*, **5**, 389–418.

Parkinson, M. (1980) 'The extreme value method for estimating the variance of the rate of return', *Journal of Business*, **53**, 61–65.

Peck, A. E. (ed.) (1977) *Readings in Futures Markets* Volume II (Chicago Board of Trade, Chicago).

Perry, P. R. (1982) 'The time-variance relationship of security returns: implications for the return-generating stochastic process', *Journal of Finance*, **37**, 857–870.

Perry, P. R. (1983) 'More evidence on the nature of the distribution of security returns', *Journal of Financial and Quantitative Analysis*, **18**, 211–221.

Praetz, P. D. (1969) 'Australian share prices and the random walk hypothesis', *Australian Journal of Statistics*, **11**, 123–139.

Praetz, P. D. (1972) 'The distribution of share price changes', *Journal of Business*, **45**, 49–55.

Praetz, P. D. (1973) 'Analysis of Australian share prices', *Australian Economic Papers*, **12**, 70–78.

Praetz, P. D. (1975) 'Testing the efficient markets theory on the Sydney wool futures exchange', *Australian Economic Papers*, **14**, 240–249.

Praetz, P. D. (1976a) 'Rates of return on filter tests', *Journal of Finance*, **31**, 71–75.

Praetz, P. D. (1976b) 'On the methodology of testing for independence in futures prices', *Journal of Finance*, **31**, 977–979.

Praetz, P. D. (1979a) 'Testing for a flat spectrum on efficient market price data', *Journal of Finance*, **34**, 645–658.

Praetz, P. D. (1979b) 'A general test of a filter effect', *Journal of Financial and Quantitative Analysis*, **14**, 385–394.

Rogalski, R. J. (1978) 'The dependence of prices and volume', *Review of Economics and Statistics*, **60**, 268–274.

Rogalski, R. J. (1984) Discussion of paper by Keim and Stambaugh, *Journal of Finance*, **39**, 835–837.

Roll, R. (1984) 'Orange juice and weather', *American Economic Review*, **74**, 861–880.

Roll, R. and S. A. Ross (1980) 'An empirical investigation of the arbitrage pricing theory', *Journal of Finance*, **35**, 1073–1103.

Rosenberg, B. (1970) 'The distribution of the mid-range: a comment', *Econometrica*, **38**, 176–177.

Rozeff, M. S. and W. R. Kinney (1976) 'Capital market seasonality: the case of stock returns', *Journal of Financial Economics*, **3**, 379–402.

Rutledge, D. J. S. (1976) 'A note on the variability of futures prices', *Review of Economics and Statistics*, **58**, 118–120.

Rutledge, D. J. S. (1979) 'Trading volume and price variability: new evidence on the price effects of speculation', in *International Futures Trading Seminar Proceedings Volume V*, pp. 160–186 (Chicago Board of Trade, Chicago).

Scholes, M. and J. Williams (1977) 'Estimating betas from nonsynchronous data', *Journal of Financial Economics*, **5**, 309–327.

Schultz, P. (1985) 'Personal income taxes and the January effect: small firm stock returns before the war revenue act of 1917', *Journal of Finance*, **40**, 333–343.

Schwert, G. S. (1983) 'Size and stock returns, and other empirical regularities', *Journal of Financial Economics*, **12**, 3–12.

Sharpe, W. F. (1964) 'Capital asset prices: a theory of market equilibrium under conditions of risk', *Journal of Finance*, **19**, 425–442.

Sharpe, W. F. (1981) *Investments* (Prentice-Hall, Englewood Cliffs, New Jersey, 2nd edn).

Stevenson, R. A. and R. M. Bear (1970) 'Commodity futures: trends or random walks?', *Journal of Finance*, **25**, 65–81.

Stevenson, R. A. and R. M. Bear (1976) Reply to P. D. Praetz, *Journal of Finance*, **31**, 980–983.

Stonham, P. (1982) *Major Stock Markets of Europe* (Gower, Aldershot).

Tauchen, G. E. and M. Pitts (1983) 'The price variability–volume relationship on speculative markets', *Econometrica*, **51**, 485–505.

Taylor, S. J. (1980) 'Conjectured models for trends in financial prices, tests and forecasts', *Journal of the Royal Statistical Society*, **143A**, 338–362.

Taylor, S. J. (1982a) 'Financial returns modelled by the product of two stochastic processes, a study of daily sugar prices 1961–79', in O. D. Anderson (ed.), *Time Series Analysis: Theory and Practice* 1, pp. 203–226 (North-Holland, Amsterdam).

Taylor, S. J. (1982b) 'Tests of the random walk hypothesis against a price-trend hypothesis', *Journal of Financial and Quantitative Analysis*, **17**, 37–61.

Taylor, S. J. (1983) 'Trading rules for investors in apparently inefficient futures markets', in M. E. Streit (ed.), *Futures Markets—Modelling, Managing and Monitoring Futures Trading*, pp. 165–198 (Basil Blackwell, Oxford).

Taylor, S. J. (1984) 'Estimating the variances of autocorrelations calculated from financial time series', *Applied Statistics*, **33**, 300–308.

Taylor, S. J. (1985) 'The behaviour of futures prices over time', *Applied Economics*, **17**, 713–734.

Taylor, S. J. and B. G. Kingsman (1978) 'Non-stationarity in sugar prices', *Journal of the Operational Research Society*, **29**, 971–980.

Taylor, S. J. and B. G. Kingsman (1979) 'An analysis of the variance and distribution of commodity price-changes', *Australian Journal of Management*, **4**, 135–149.

Teweles, R. J., C. V. Harlow, and H. L. Stone (1974) *The Commodity Futures Game* (McGraw-Hill, New York).

Tinic, S. M. and R. R. West (1984) 'Risk and return: January versus the rest of the year', *Journal of Financial Economics*, **13**, 561–574.

Working, H. (1934) 'A random difference series for use in the analysis of time series', *Journal of the American Statistical Association*, **29**, 11–24.

Working, H. (1960) 'Note on the correlation of first differences of averages in a random chain', *Econometrica*, **28**, 916–918.

Alexander, S. S., 11, 199
Ali, M. M., 28, 38, 68, 70
Andersen, A. P., 52
Anderson, T. W., 25, 136

Bachelier, L., 9
Ball, R., 197, 202
Banz, R. W., 43
Bear, R. M., 12, 141, 200
Beckers, S., 47, 228
Bird, P. J. W. N., 12, 200, 201
Black, F., 15, 36, 202, 226, 227, 228
Blattberg, R. C., 46, 47
Blume, M. E., 11, 171, 197
Bodie, Z., 37, 199, 202
Bookstaber, R. M., 4, 225
Box, G. E. P., 23, 183
Brealey, R. A., 35, 161
Breeden, D., 202
Brown, S. J., 39

Cargill, T. F., 10, 200
Carter, C. A., 202
Chang, E. C., 36, 37
Cheng, P. L., 35
Chiras, D., 228
Clark, P. K., 47, 48, 68, 71, 74
Cooper, J. C. B., 10
Cootner, P., 37
Cornell, W. B., 10, 12
Cox, J. C., 4, 225, 228, 234
Cunningham, S. W., 9

Daniels, H., 28
Dietrich, J. K., 10, 12
Dimson, E., 35
Dryden, M. M., 9, 11

Dusak, K., 10, 36, 37, 199, 202

Engle, R. F., 68, 76, 77, 96
Epps, M. L., 68
Epps, T. W., 68

Fama, E. F., 9, 10, 35, 46, 49, 50, 55, 151, 171, 197
Fielitz, B. D., 49
French, D. W., 227
French, K. R., 39, 41, 42, 59

Garman, M. B., 27, 228
Geisst, C. R., 4
Giaccotto, C., 28, 38, 68, 70
Gibbons, M. R., 41, 49
Gonedes, N. J., 46, 47
Granger, C. W. J., 4, 9, 10, 16, 47, 52, 56, 68, 74, 130, 138, 196
Gray, R. W., 37
Greene, M. T., 49
Grossman, S. J., 11
Guimaraes, R. M. C., 31
Gultekin, B., 43
Gultekin, M., 43

Hagerman, R. L., 46
Harlow, C. V., 4
Helms, B. P., 27
Hess, P. J., 41, 49
Hsu, D. A., 66, 69, 70, 103

Ibbotson, R. G., 35

Jarrow, R. A., 27
Jenkins, G. M., 23, 183
Jennergren, L. P., 10, 11

Jensen, M. C., 10, 171, 197

Kamara, A., 37
Keim, D. B., 41, 43
Kendall, M. G., 9, 121
Kingsman, B. G., 7, 104
Kinney, W. R., 43
Klass, M. J., 27, 228
Kon, S. J., 39, 48
Korsvold, P. E., 10

Labys, W. C., 10, 38
Latane, H., 228
Leuthold, R. M., 12, 141, 200, 201
Levich, R. M., 10, 36
Lintner, J., 161
Lomnicki, Z. A., 136, 145

MacFarland, J. W., 41
Manaster, S., 228
Mandelbrot, B., 46
Martell, T. F., 27, 200
Menzefricke, U., 66
Merton, R. C., 35, 38, 162, 225
Mood, A. M., 140
Moran, P. A. P., 136
Morgenstern, O., 9, 47, 68, 133
Myers, S. C., 35, 161

Newbold, P., 16, 24, 56, 74, 138, 141,
    186
Niederhoffer, V., 27

Officer, R. R., 43, 49
Oldfield, G. S., 27
Orr, D., 130
Osborne, M. F. M., 27

Parkinson, M., 27, 228
Peck, A. E., 37
Perry, P. R., 39, 43, 46, 49, 151
Pettit, R. P., 41
Philippatos, G. C., 200
Pitts, M., 47, 68, 71, 74

Praetz, P. D., 10, 31, 38, 43, 47, 68, 138,
    139, 200, 201

Rausser, G. C., 10, 200, 202
Rendleman, R., 228
Rogalski, R. J., 27, 41, 47
Roll, R., 42, 46, 163, 167, 168
Rosansky, V. I., 37, 199, 202
Rosenberg, B., 28
Ross, S. A., 163
Rozeff, M. S., 43
Rubinstein, M., 4, 225, 228, 234
Rutledge, D. J. S., 40, 47

Schmitz, A., 202
Scholes, M., 15, 49, 226
Schultz, P., 43
Schwert, G. S., 43
Sharpe, W. F., 4, 161
Siegel, L. B., 35
Sinquefield, R. A., 35
Stambaugh, R. F., 41
Stevenson, R. A., 12, 141, 200
Stiglitz, J. E., 11
Stone, H. L., 4
Stonham, P., 4
Sung, S. K., 41

Tauchen, G. E., 47, 68, 71, 74
Taylor, S. J., 68, 90, 142, 175, 198, 210,
    219
Telser, L. G., 37
Teweles, R. J., 4
Thomas, H. C., 38
Tinic, S. M., 43
Toft-Nielsen, P., 10

Walker, A. M., 25, 136
Warner, J. B., 39
West, R. R., 43
Williams, J., 49
Working, H., 9, 28

Zaremba, S. K., 136, 145

Almost strict white noise, 80, 177
Annual returns, commodity futures, 37
  compound rate, 33
  portfolios, 222
  stocks, 35
AR(1) process, 20, 74, 175
Arbitrage pricing theory, 163
ARCH models, 75
  applicability discussed, 107
  theory, 95
ARMACH models, 78
  parameter estimates, 90
ARMA (1,1) process, 21
  as approximation, 75
  autocorrelations, 22
  commodities, 171
  currencies, 171
  optimal linear forecasts, 22, 102, 108,
    186
Asymptotic results, 25, 136
Autocorrelated process, 18
Autocorrelation, calendar effects, 58
  definition, 17
  due to limit rules, 168
  perfect markets, 162
  spurious, 28
Autocorrelation coefficients, 48
  absolute returns, 52
  distributions, 24, 135
  estimated variances, 119, 124, 128
  futures, 50, 152, 170
  metals, 152, 170
  returns, 48
  rescaled returns, 146
  squared returns, 52
  stocks, 49, 50, 151, 170
Autoregressive process, 20, 77
  see also AR(1)

Autoregressive-moving average
    process, 23
  see also ARMA(1,1)

Backshift operator, 20
Benchmark, forecasts, 101, 188
  trading rules, 200, 214, 215
Bid-ask spread, 27
  as trading cost, 203
  autocorrelation consequences, 169
Black–Scholes formula, 226
Brokers, 203, 212
Buy and hold strategy, 200

Calendar effects, 41
  autocorrelation consequences, 58
  January, 43
  Monday, 41
  random walk tests, 150
  simulations, 165
Call option, 225
Capital asset pricing model, 35, 161
Cocoa futures, 31, 217
Coffee futures, 31, 44, 217
Commission costs, 203
Commodity futures, see Cocoa,
    Coffee and Sugar futures
Compound returns, 13
Computer program, 243
Conditional standard deviation, 68
  interpretation, 71, 80
Currency futures, 30, 31
  calendar effects, 41, 42
  limit rules, 167
  Sterling, 114, 154, 219
  standard deviations, 38
  trading example, 221
  trading results, 219

Cycles, 138

Data errors, checks, 28
  consequences, 145
Deutschmark futures, 221
  see also Currency futures
Distributions, 45
  lognormal, 48
  normal, 25
  stable, 46
  Student's *t*, 47
Diversification, 10, 202, 222, 223

Efficient market hypothesis, 10
  conclusions for futures, 223
  conclusions for stocks, 171
  definitions, 10, 197
  semi-strong form, 11
  theoretical analysis, 206
  weak form, 11
Equilibrium expected return, 160
Excess return, 161
Exponentially-weighted moving
    average, 103, 111

Filter rule, 11, 199
  commodity studies, 200
  criticisms, 200
Forecasting ARMA processes, 22, 102,
    108, 186
Forecasting prices, 194
Forecasting returns, empirical results,
    190
  theory, 185, 193
  trading applications, 204, 210
Forecasting standard deviations,
    empirical results, 106, 108
  futures, 104
  recommendations, 110, 128
  theory, 98
Futures markets, 3, 203, 213
  annual returns, 27
  efficiency conclusions, 223
  limit rules, 167
  measuring returns, 201
  trading conditions, 203
  trading results, 217
Futures prices, *see* Cocoa futures,
    Coffee futures, Currency futures,
    and Sugar futures
Futures returns, autocorrelations, 48,
    50, 152

forecasting results, 190
interpretation and definition, 13
trend size and duration, 179
Futures time series, construction, 28,
    30
  contract age and volatility, 40
  contract standard deviations, 38

Gaussian stochastic process, 23, 205
Gold prices, 4, 29, 56, 113, 126, 153

Implied standard deviation, 228
Indices, autocorrelation, 49
  equilibrium results, 163
  Financial Times, 29
Inefficient market defined, 204
Information, efficiently used, 10, 196
  models, 71, 175
  use of, 68, 170, 174, 179
Innovation, 20
Interest rates, 13, 36, 162, 166
International monetary market, 31,
    167, 203
Intra-day, models, 71, 229
  studies, 27
Invertible process, 23, 65

January effect, 43

Kurtosis, 44
  ARCH models, 77
  product processes, 72, 74

Lag, 17
Limit rules, 167, 219
Linear forecasts, optimal, 18, 186
  see also ARMA(1,1) process
Linear stochastic process, 23, 80, 121
  autocorrelation results, 23, 136
  tests, 56
Linear trend model, 176, 242
  evidence in favour of, 185
  simulations, 183
Lognormal, autoregressive model, 73,
    86, 228
  distribution, 48, 74

MA(1) process, 21
  stocks, 171
Margin deposit, 203
Market activity, 71

Mean square error, 18, 186
  definition, 99, 189
  relative, 100
  weighted, 190
Metal prices, 29
  forecasting results, 192
  trend size and duration, 181
Models, 13
  ARCH, 75
  best stationary, 241
  criteria, 14
  product process, 70
  trends, 174
  variances, 67
  see also Price-trend models,
    Stochastic process, *and* Variance
    models
Moving-average process, first order, 21
  infinite order, 24
  see also MA(1)
MSE, *see* Mean square error
Multivariate models, 240
Multivariate normal distribution, 23,
  25, 143, 205
Multivariate symmetry, 118

Non-linear stochastic process,
    example, 65
  implications, 57, 116, 124, 134
  see also Linear stochastic process
Non-linear trend model, 176
  simulations, 183
Non-stationary forecast, 108
Non-stationary process, examples, 66,
  233
  see also Stationary stochastic
    process
Normal distribution, mixtures, 47
  multivariate, 25, 205
  notation, 25
Null hypothesis, 133

Option markets, 4
  definitions, 225
Options, value of, 226
  with trends, 234
  with variance changes, 228
Orange juice futures, 42, 167
Outliers, 44, 130

Parameter estimates, simulations, 183
  trend models, 178
  variance models, 83
Pareto–Levy distribution, 46
Percentage mean square error, 189, 190
Perfect efficient market, 10
  autocorrelation, 162
  tests, 165
Portfolios, 202, 222
Power of tests, 145, 159
Prices, 1
  examples, 4
  futures, 30
  high, low, 27, 228
  sources, 26
  spot, stock, 28
  see also Future prices, Spot prices,
    and Stock prices
Price-trend hypothesis, 141
Price-trend models, 174
  autocorrelations, 141, 159
  biased estimates, 178
  examples, 142, 176
  forecasts, 179
  linear model, 176, 185, 242
  mean trend duration, 175
  non-linear model, 176
  option values, 234
  parameter estimates, 178
  simulations, 159, 183
  spectral density, 143
  test power, 159
  test statistics, 143, 145
  trading rules, 210
  see also Forecasting returns
Process, *see* Stochastic process
Product process, 72
  autocorrelation variances, 112
  including trends, 176
  option valuation, 228
  parameter estimates, 84
  simulations, 130, 157, 214
Profits from trading, 222
Put option, 225

Random walk hypothesis, 8
  definitions, 9, 19, 133
  perfect market variations, 165
  rejected, 147, 157
  test power, 145, 159
  test results, 146, 169
  test statistics, 137, 143, 201

Relative mean square error, 100
  empirical definition, 105, 189
  results, 106, 190
  returns forecasts, 189
  standard deviation forecasts, 107
Rescaled returns, 127
  autocorrelation coefficients, 146
  forecasting, 190
Returns, 12
  annual, 33, 35, 37
  compound, 12
  daily, 12
  excess, 16
  nominal, 13
  portfolio, 22
  real, 13
  rescaled, 127
  simple, 12, 34
  to speculators, 37
Risk, comparisons, 39
  for trading rules, 202, 205, 212
  pricing, 35, 161, 202
Risk premium, futures, 37
  stocks, 35, 162
  trading implications, 200
RMSE, *see* Relative mean square error
Round trip, 203
Runs test, 140
  low power, 140, 171

Sample autocorrelations, 24, 48
  distributions, 135
  see also Autocorrelation coefficients
Settlement prices, 31
Simple returns, 12
  annual, 34
Simulation, calendar effects, 165
  equilibrium effects, 163
  Gaussian process, 130, 157
  limit rules, 167
  product process, 130, 157, 214
  trading rules, 213
  trend models, 145, 159, 183, 214
Skewness, 44
Smoothing constant, 111
Sources of data, 26
Spectral density function, 19, 138
  estimates, 139
  trend models, 143
Spectral tests, 138
Speculation, 36, 239

Split series, *see* Subdivided series
Spot markets, 3
Spot prices, 28
  see also Gold prices, Metal prices,
    Sterling spot price, *and* Stock
    prices
Spurious correlation, 28
Stable distribution, 46
Standard deviations, comparisons, 39
  conditional, 68
  futures, 38, 40, 106
  implied, 228
  option values, 227
  weekend effects, 42
  see also Forecasting standard
    deviations, Variance changes, *and*
    Variance models
Stationary stochastic process, 17
  applicability discussed, 110
  preferred examples, 241
Sterling futures, 114, 154, 219
  see also Currency futures
Sterling spot price, 5, 29
Stochastic independence, 64, 72
Stochastic process, 16
  autocorrelated, 18
  autoregressive, 20
  continuous time, 14, 229
  Gaussian, 23
  linear, 23
  mixed ARMA, 21
  moving-average, 21, 24
  second-order stationary, 17
  strictly stationary, 16
  uncorrelated, 18
  see also Models
Stock prices, 28
  calendar effects, 41, 43
  trading rules, 197
Stock returns, autocorrelations, 49, 151
  MA(1) model, 171
Strategies, *see* Trading rules
Strict white noise, 19
  almost, 80, 177
  test, 52
Strictly stationary process, 16
Student's *t* distribution, 47, 57
  simulations, 130, 159
Subdivided series, forecasting, 101, 188
  random walk tests, 160, 169
  trading rules, 214
Submartingale, 161

Sugar futures, 6, 31, 127, 154, 181
  trading results, 218

Tax, futures trading, 204
  January effect and, 43
Tests, efficient market hypothesis, 201,
    223
  linear hypothesis, 56
  random walk hypothesis, 146, 147
  strict white noise, 52
Thin trading, 27
  index problems, 49
Time series, 16
Time series models, 20, 21, 67, 174
  see also Price-trend models,
    Stochastic process, *and* Variance
    models
Trading conditions, futures, 3, 203, 213
Trading profits, 222
Trading rules, assumptions, 203, 205,
    212
  benchmarks, 200, 214, 215
  costs, 198, 203
  filters, 11, 199
  objectives, 213
  parameters, 216
  portfolio results, 222
  results for futures, 216
  risk, 202, 205, 212
  theoretical analysis, 204
  using trend forecasts, 204, 210
Trading volume, 27, 32

Treasury bills, 35, 36
Treasury bond futures, 32, 147
Trends, 8
  see also Price-trend models

Uncorrelated process, 18

Variance changes, examples, 38
Variance models, 67
  ARCH, 75
  daily changes, 70
  jumps, 66, 69, 117
  lognormal, autoregressive, 73, 86
  parameter estimates, 83
  product process, 70
Variances of sample autocorrelations,
    119
  estimates, 124, 128
  implications for tests, 124
  linear processes, 23, 136
Volatility, *see* Standard deviations,
    and Variance models

Weekend effects, 41, 150
  simulations, 165
Weighted mean square error, 190
White noise, 19
Wiener process, 14, 226
Wool futures, 31, 118

Zero frequency test, 144, 171